WORKSHOP MANUAL
for
TOYOTA COROLLA 1100
and the new
COROLLA 1200

COMPILED AND WRITTEN
BY
PETER R. D. RUSSEK

PUBLISHED BY
INTEREUROPE LIMITED
AUTODATA DIVISION
NICHOLSON HOUSE
MAIDENHEAD, BERKSHIRE
ENGLAND

Type Identification

TWO-DOOR SALOON

KE 10 Series — Corolla 1100
KE 11 Series — Corolla 1200
KE 20 Series — Corolla 1200

FOUR-DOOR SALOON

KE 15 Series — Corolla 1100 Sprinter
KE 17 Series — Corolla 1200 Sprinter
KE 25 Series — Corolla 1200 Coupe

COUPE

ESTATE CAR
KE 16 Series — Corolla 1100
KE 18 Series — Corolla 1200

JACKING POINTS

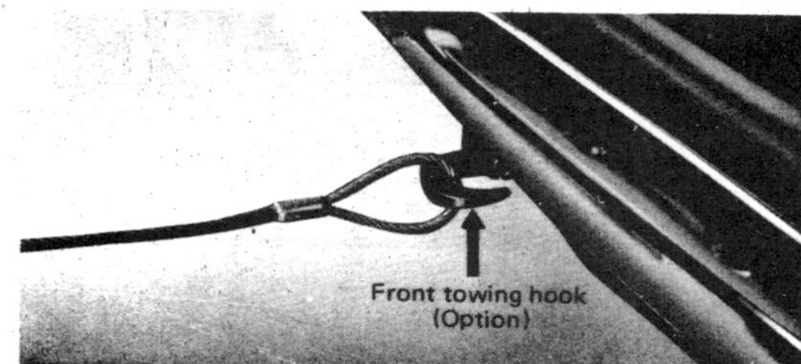

FRONT TOWING POINT

REAR TOWING POINT

INDEX

Introduction

This Workshop Manual was compiled and written with the intention of providing the Toyota Corolla owner and the non-franchised garage with details of all the maintenance and repair operations that they are likely to encounter. Much information from the manufacturer's original service and repair instructions have been condensed and incorporated in the manual in a form which will enable the reader to quickly become familiar with the idiosynchrasies and technicalities peculiar to Toyota Corolla Cars.

The engine described herein is the four-cylinder, in-line, four-stroke K-Engine with the differences for the K-B and K-C engines (1,100 c.c.) and the 3K, 3K-B and 3K-D engines (1,200 c.c.) given as applicable. Changes, incorporated in the new Corolla 1100 after April 1968 and the Corolla 1200 are given at the end of the main sections or are written directly into the text.

In certain cases it will be necessary for the repairer to make use of special tools, and the appropriate numbers and their methods of use are either described in the text or can be taken from illustrations, referred to in the chapter. Sometimes it is possible to use alternative tools (pullers, drifts, etc.) but greatest care must be taken during removal or installation of the part in question when this practice is followed.

Special mention should be made of the fact that a fault finding section is annexed to most of the major sections, thus simplifying the sometimes difficult task of diagnosis. The items listed cover only the most likely causes of trouble, as it is impossible to list every aspect of malfunctioning. This list, however, has been carefully compiled and is used in all our Workshop Manual Publications. The measurement conversions, given in inches have been converted as closely as possible from the original millimetre sizes, however, it is preferable to adhere to the metric dimensions whenever possible. A conversion table is included in the manual.

We have tried to make this Workshop Manual as brief as possible, illustrating rather than detailing the operations, and concentrating not so much on regular maintenance work but more on repair and overhauling operations. This will save valuable time and will also show the reader immediately whether he will be able to carry out the work or not. Experience in producing hundreds of technical publications for the motor car manufacturers has proven that this is the best way for a publication of this nature.

Happy motoring   —   and the fewer times you have to refer to this book the better for you!

Peter R. D. Russek

Fig.A.1. Removal of the front engine mounting nut.

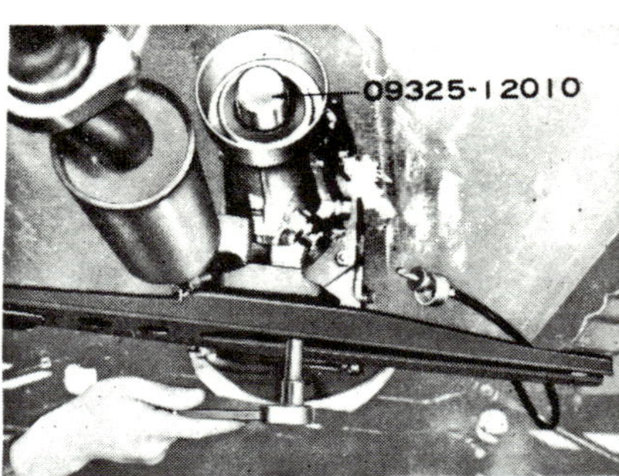

Fig.A.2. Removal of the rear engine mounting bolt.

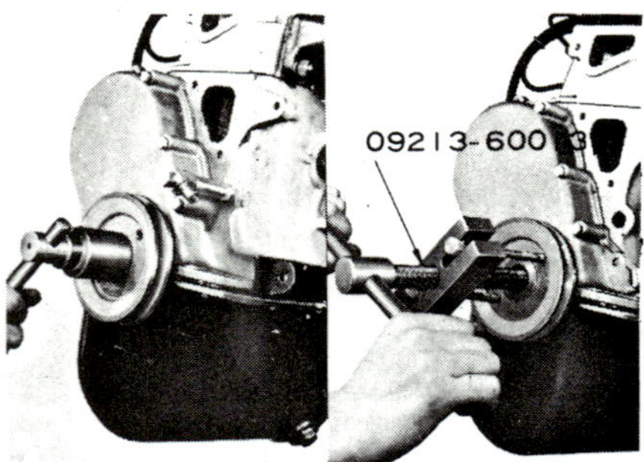

Fig.A.3. Removal of the crankshaft pulley bolt on the left and removal of the pulley by means of the puller on the right.

Fig.A.4. Removal of the spark plug tube.

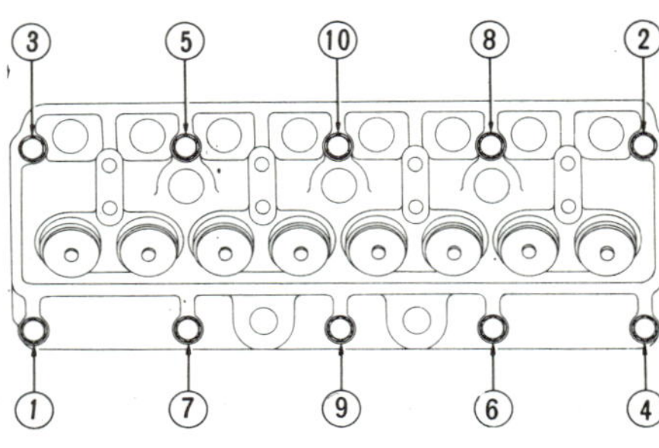

Fig.A.5. Loosening sequence for cylinder head bolts.

Fig.A.6. Removal of piston and connecting rod assembly from the top of the cylinder block.

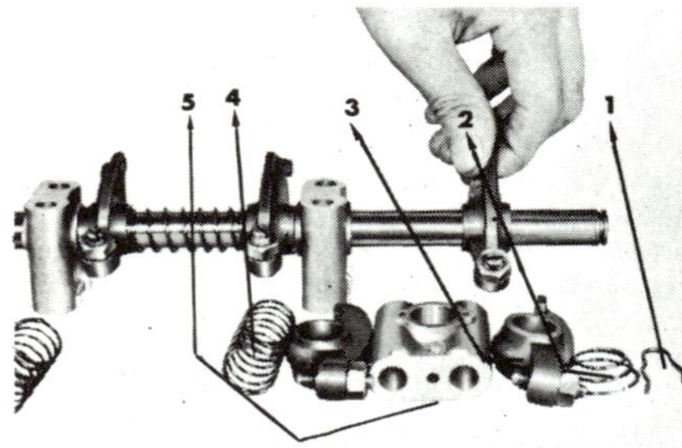

Fig.A.7. The partly dismantled rocker shaft assembly.

1. Spring retainer
2. Conical springs
3. Rocker arms
4. Rocker shaft support
5. Compression springs

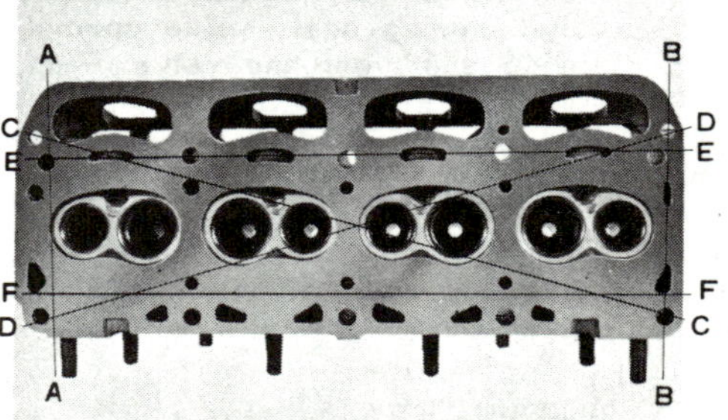

Fig.A.8. Check the cylinder head surface for flatness by placing a straight edge along the lettered lines and inserting a feeler gauge.

Fig.A.9. Measuring the inner diameter of a valve guide.

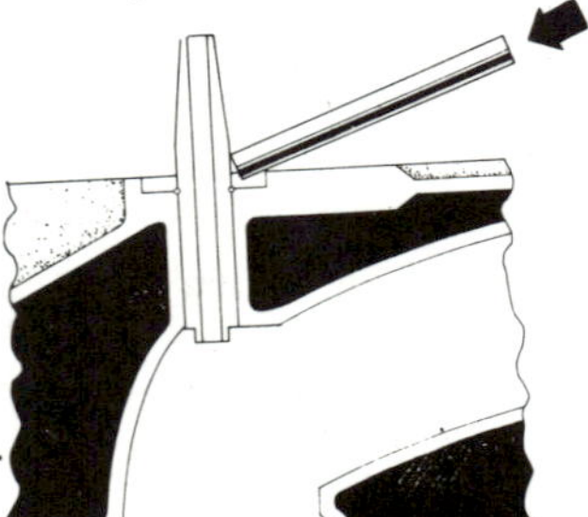

Fig.A.10. When replacing the valve guides, break off the upper part as shown. The arrow represents the hammer.

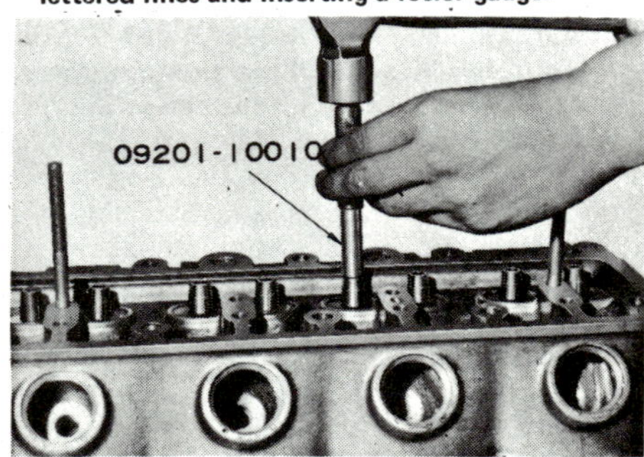

Fig.A.11. Installation of the new valve guide.

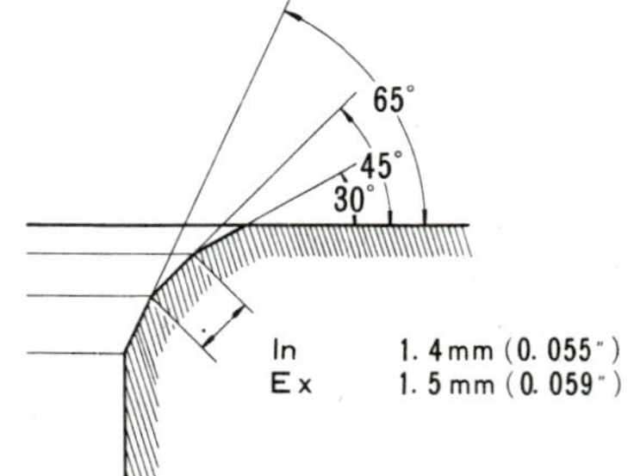

Fig.A.12. Valve seat diagram.

Engine

The K engine fitted to the Toyota Corolla is a four-stroke, four cylinder overhead valve engine with pressure feed lubrication and water cooling. The cylinder head is made of aluminium alloy with wedge shaped combustion chambers. Cylinder block and crankcase are cast integrally, forming a single unit.

The crankshaft is supported in five main bearings. Crankshaft end float is controlled by No.3 main bearing by means of thrust washers, inserted between bearing and crankshaft flange. The pistons are of special light alloy and are fitted with two compression rings and one oil control ring. The piston pin of the piston is offset 1.0 mm towards the camshaft side which contributes to smooth engine operation. The piston pin is secured with circlips at each end.

The camshaft is supported in four bearings. The crankshaft timing sprocket drives the camshaft sprocket through the timing chain.

ENGINE — Removal

Proceed as follows:

Drain the coolant and remove or disconnect the following parts: Starter cable, bonnet, air cleaner, inlet and outlet radiator hoses, R.H. lamp rim, radiator grill, bonnet lock and base, horns, windscreen washer container, radiator, accelerator and choke control cable, water valve, heater control cable, wiring harness connector plugs, front exhaust pipe at the manifold, L.H. front mounting bracket nut. (Fig.A.1).

Disconnect or remove the leads to the water temperature & oil pressure sender units, fuel hose from the water pump, earth cable, R.H. front mounting bracket nut, clutch cable from release lever (retained by "E" clip), coil & reversing lamp leads. Remove the front centre carpet, gear lever boot & cap boot, gear lever using remover 09305-12010.

With the car resting on suitable stands, remove the propeller shaft (insert oil plug 09325-12010 or a spare sliding yoke to prevent oil loss from the gearbox). Disconnect the exhaust pipe bracket and the speedometer drive cable and remove the engine rear mounting insulator bolt. (Fig.A.2.)

Position the jack under the gearbox and remove the engine rear mounting support. Fit a lifting hook to the engine hangers and carefully lift the engine together with the gearbox towards the front and upwards, using a suitable hoist or crane.

ENGINE — Dismantling

Remove the starter motor and the gearbox. Mark the clutch cover and the flywheel suitably with a centre punch and remove the clutch cover together with the driven plate.

Remove the flywheel and the rear end plate and clamp the engine on to a suitable stand. Drain the engine oil.

Remove the alternator and the V-belt, water outlet, thermostat, fan and fan pulley, alternator adjusting link and the water pump.

Remove the crankshaft pulley bolt and withdraw the pulley with the special puller 09213-60013 as shown in Fig.A.3. Remove the water drain plug, disconnect the vacuum and fuel pipes from the carburettor, remove the heat insulator, manifold assembly, engine hanger, gasket, alternator bracket, L.H. engine front mounting bracket, heat insulator, oil dipstick. Disconnect the vacuum line from the distributor and remove the distributor. Remove the spark plugs with the spark plug spanner and remove the spark plug tubes and the gaskets. (Fig.A.4). Disconnect the fuel line and remove the fuel pump, insulator and the gaskets.

Remove the R.H. engine mounting bracket, unscrew the oil filter with the special wrench 09228-22010 (for alternative means see section "Lubrication System" under "Oil Filter — Removal") and unscrew the oil filter bracket from the engine. Remove the rocker cover and the rocker shaft assembly complete with rocker arms and push rods. Ensure that the push rods are kept in the same order as removed, to assist in correct assembly.

Remove the cylinder head bolts, following the sequence in Fig.A.5 and remove the cylinder head together with the gasket. From the right-hand side of the engine remove the push rod covers and the cam followers. The cam followers should be kept in the same order as removed. Now turn the engine over and remove the oil sump, gasket, timing chain cover and gasket and the crankshaft rear oil seal retainer (Fig.A.6), chain tensioner and vibration damper.

The camshaft timing sprocket mounting bolt, timing sprocket and chain, camshaft thrust plate and front end plate can then be removed. The camshaft is pulled out through the front of the cylinder block, being carefully supported to avoid damage to the camshaft bearing. Remove the oil pump.

Loosen the big end bearing cap bolts, lift off the caps and remove the connecting rod/piston assemblies from the top of the cylinder block. Make sure the assemblies are kept in their numbered order. Remove the main bearing cap bolts, lift off the caps together with the lower bearing shells and lift out the crankshaft. The upper bearings can now be removed and should be retained in their numbered order.

Compress the valve springs with a suitable compressor, remove the cotter halves and release the valve spring retainer, valve spring seal, valve spring, spring seat and the valve.

From the rocker shaft remove the retainers (1), conical springs (2), rocker arms (3), springs (5) and support (4). (Fig.A.7).

To remove the pistons from the connecting rods, extract the gudgeon pin circlips from the piston bosses, heat the piston from 70 - 80°C (158 - 176°F) on a hot plate and push out the gudgeon pin. Using a suitable ring expander lift the piston rings from the pistons, keeping them in their correct order of removal.

If the gearbox clutch shaft pilot bearing in the crankshaft requires replacement, remove the old one with bearing puller

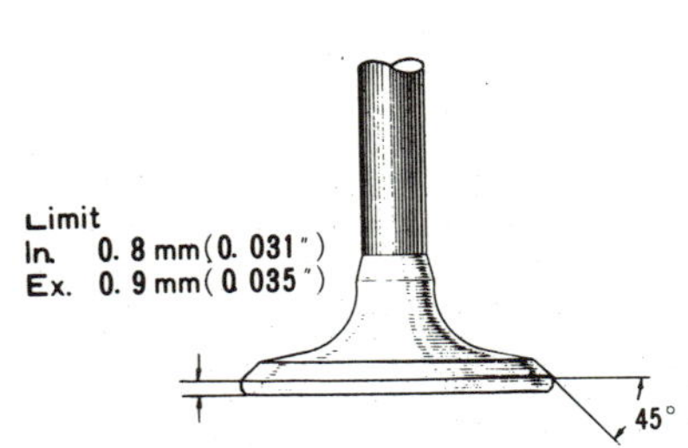

Fig.A.13. Valve seat angle diagram.

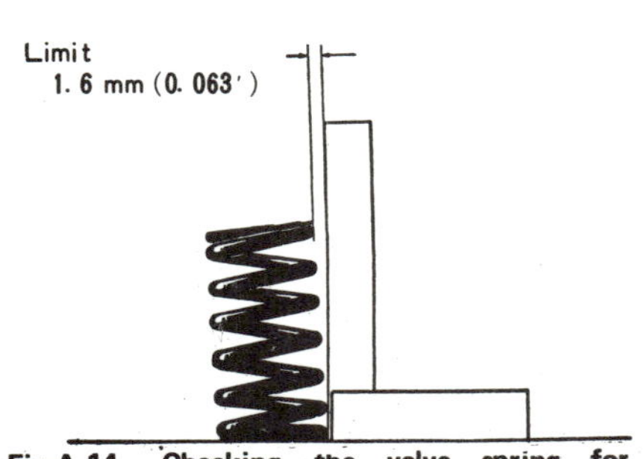

Fig.A.14. Checking the valve spring for squareness by means of a steel square.

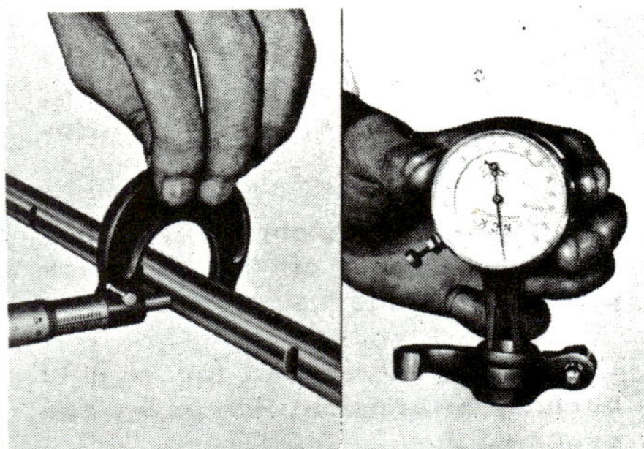

Fig.A.15. Measuring rocker shaft and inner diameter of rocker arm.

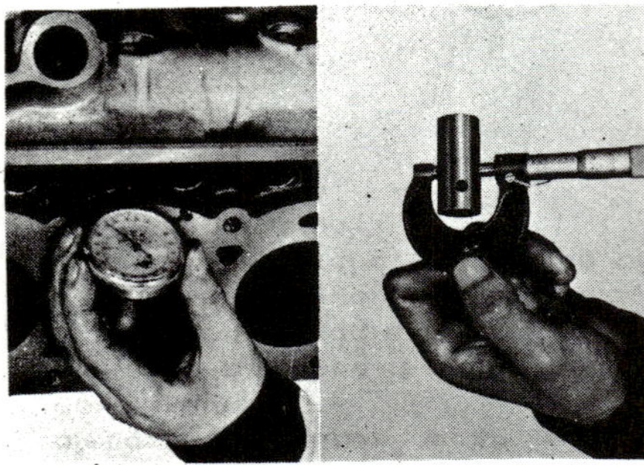

Fig.A.16. Measuring valve tappet and inner diameter of tappet bore.

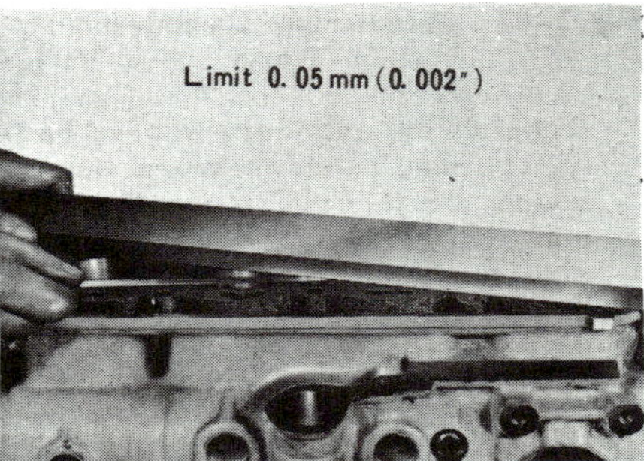

Fig.A.17. Checking the cylinder block face for flatness.

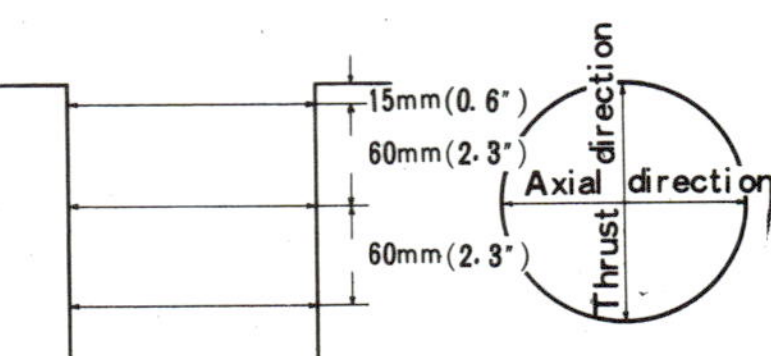

Fig.A.18. The measuring points for the cylinder bore.

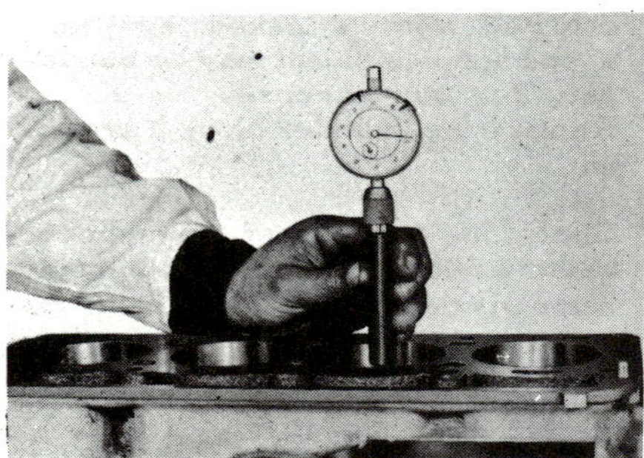

Fig.A.19. Measuring the inner diameter of a cylinder bore.

Fig.A.20. Measuring the piston running clearance by means of a feeler gauge and a spring scale.

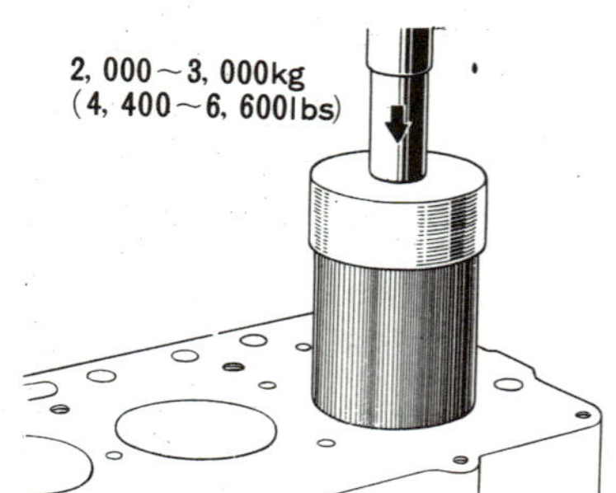

Fig.A.21. Installation of a cylinder liner.

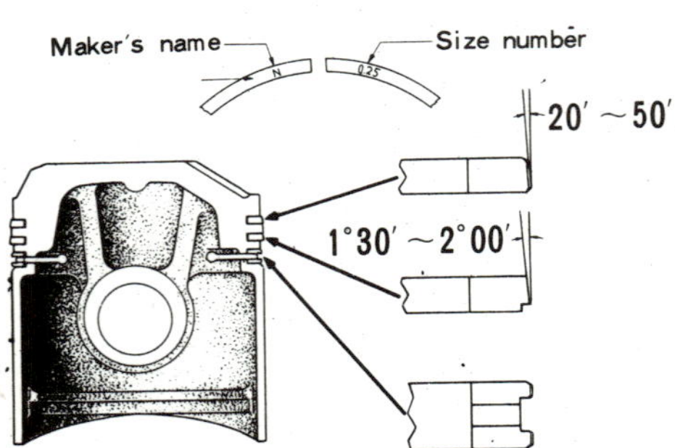

Fig.A.22. Section through the piston rings with installation positions.

Fig.A.23. Measuring the piston ring end gap by means of a feeler gauge.

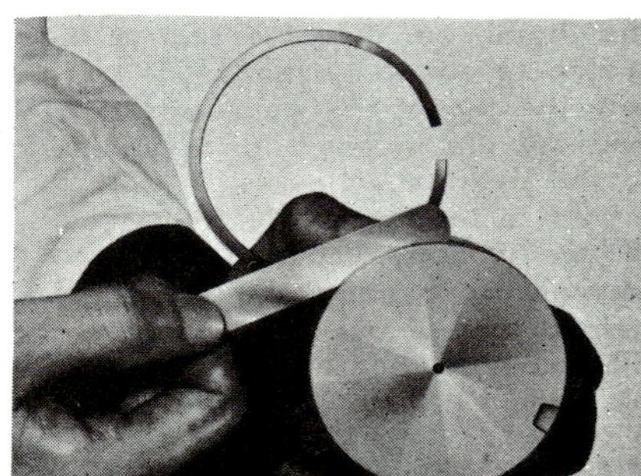

Fig.A.24. Measuring the height clearance of a piston ring in the piston ring groove.

09303-35010.

Remove the timing sprocket from the crankshaft.

ENGINE — Inspection and Overhaul

Thoroughly clean all parts of dirt, oil and water scale before inspection and before attempting to carry out overhaul operations. Blow out all passages with compressed air. Remove all carbon deposits from the top of the pistons, combustion chambers, cylinder head, and valves, but do not remove metal from any of the parts.

Inspect and overhaul the parts as follows:

CYLINDER HEAD

Check the cylinder head for cracks and the joint face for burrs or unevenness and replace if necessary. Apply a water pressure of 5 kg/sq.cm (70 psi.) to the cylinder head passages to check for leaks. The flatness of the head can be checked by means of a straight edge placed across the head, checking the clearance between head and straight edge with a pair of feeler gauges. If the clearance exceeds 0.0015 in. (0.04 mm) regrind the cylinder head surface.

Similarly check the surface of the manifold gasket face and correct if the distortion exceeds 0.004 in. (0.1 mm).

VALVE GUIDE BUSHES

Check the clearance between the valve stem and the valve guide bores which must not exceed 0.004 in. (0.1 mm) for the inlet and 0.005 in. (0.12 mm) for the exhaust valve. The specified clearances are as follows:

Inlet valve: . . . . 0.001 - 0.002 in. (0.035 - 0.065 mm)
Exhaust valve: . . . . 0.002 - 0.003 in. (0.045 - 0.080 mm)

An easy way of checking the clearance is to insert the valve stem into the guide and move it from left to right. If this movement exceeds 0.01 in. (0.25 mm) the guide needs replacing. When fitting new guides, proceed as follows:

Break off the upper part with a brass punch as shown in Fig.A.10 and heat the cylinder head to 80 - 100°C (180 - 212°F). Remove the remainder of the guide with special drift 09210-10010 from the cylinder head. Fit the snap ring to the new valve guide and fit the guide from the top of the cylinder head until the snap ring contacts the cylinder head face, using the same tool as for removal. If the special tool is not available, another suitable drift can be used, which should be stepped at one end so that it can be inserted into the guide. (See Fig.A.11). After installation ream the valve guide to 0.315 - 0.316 in. (8.01 - 8.03 mm).

VALVE SEATS

Check the valve seats for damage or wear. The valve seats are refaced with a valve cutter as follows:

Cut the seat face roughly, using a 30° cutter. Next use the 65° cutter and cut the seat to the approx. size. Finally use the 45° cutter to finish the seat. (Fig.A.12).

When grinding with the 45° cutter leave an allowance for the lapping of the valve seat, in order to obtain a seat width of 0.055 in. (1.4 mm). Cut the bottom with a 35° cutter and the top with a 65° cutter until the correct width is obtained.

After cutting the valve should contact the valve seat exactly in the centre, but to check apply a thin coat of red lead in the seat and insert the valve. Apply a light pressure and check the contact. If the seating is too high, use the 35° cutter, but if too low, use the 65° cutter. Finally grind the valve, until the valve seat has a dull appearance. Carefully remove all grinding compound.

VALVES

Check the valve face for pits, grooves, scores and other damage. Check the stem for distortion and wear. When inspecting the valve heads, check in particular for burrs, cracks and corrosion. If the valve head edge is worn down to 0.031 in (0.8 mm) for the inlet valve and 0.035 in. (0.9 mm) for the exhaust valve (Fig.A.13) replace the valve. If necessary grind the valve on a valve grinding machine, taking off only enough material to remove pits and grooves.

Grooves and scores at the end of the valve stem may be removed and the ends re-chamfered. Do not remove more than 0.02 in. (0.5 mm) of the material. The valve length is as follows:

Inlet valve . . . . .3.94 in. (100.0 mm)
Exhaust valve . . . . .3.95 in. (100.2 mm)

VALVE SPRINGS

Measure the free length of the valve springs and replace if less than specified. Also test the spring pressure. Check the valve springs for distortion by placing a steel square on to a surface plate. Position the valve spring against the square edge and slowly rotate the spring. The clearance between the top of the spring and the edge should not exceed 0.063 in. (1.6 mm). (Fig.A.14).

Valve Spring Specifications

Fitted length . . . . 1.51 in. (38.4 mm)
Free length . . . . 1.76 in. (45.1 mm)
Fitted load . . . . 55.1 lb. (25.0 kg)

VALVE ROCKER SHAFT AND LEVERS

Check the valve rocker levers and the shaft. If necessary replace the bushes of the shaft. The clearance between the shaft and the rocker levers should be 0.0002 to 0.0016 in. (0.006 to 0.042 mm). A wear limit of 0.003 in. (0.08 mm) is acceptable. (Fig.A.15). Minor wear of the rocker arm lever ends can be rectified by means of an oil stone or a valve grinding machine. The springs should be replaced if weak or rusty.

INLET AND EXHAUST MANIFOLD

Check for damage, corrosion or distortion. The manifold face should be flat to 0.008 in. (0.2 mm) when it is checked as described for the cylinder head face.

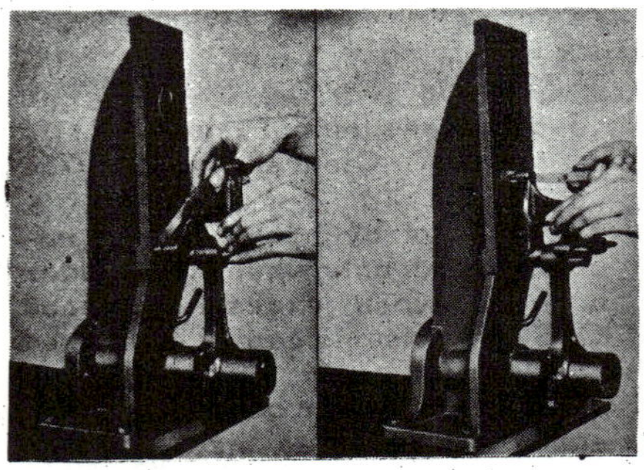

Fig.A.25. Checking a connecting rod for bend or twist by means of an alignment tool.

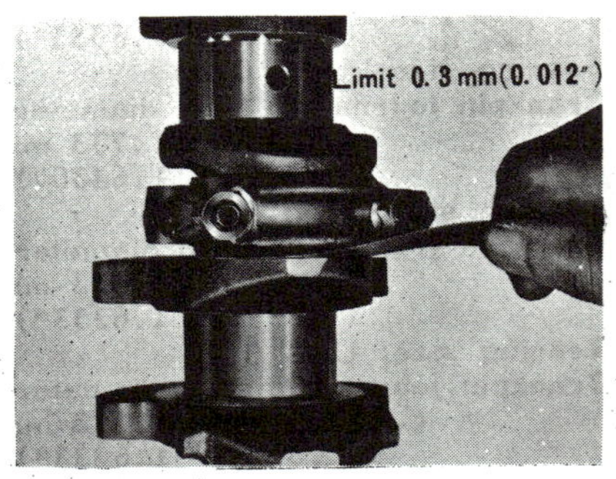

Fig.A.26. Measuring the end float of a connecting rod bearing on the crankpin.

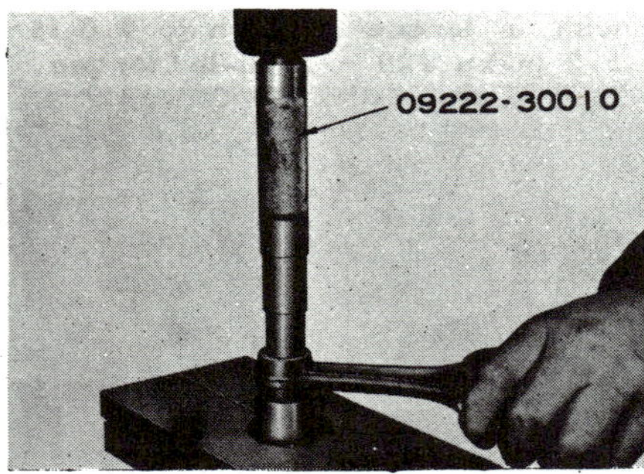

Fig.A.27. Installation of a small end bush.

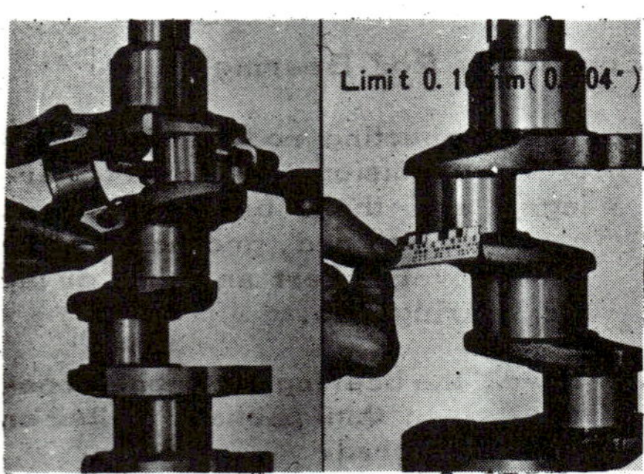

Fig.A.28. Checking the bearing running clearance by means of a "Plastigage" scale.

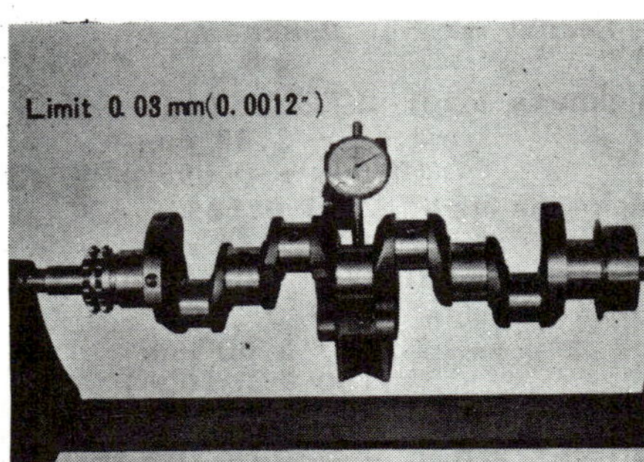

Fig.A.29. Checking the crankshaft for run-out.

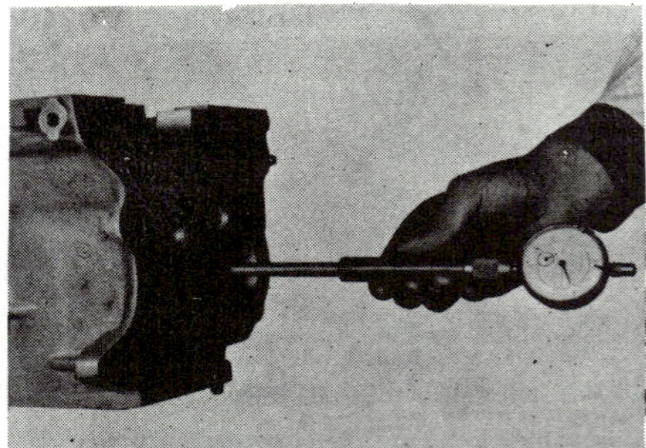

Fig.A.30. Measuring the inner diameter of the camshaft bearing.

Fig.A.31. Measuring the camshaft end float by means of a feeler gauge.

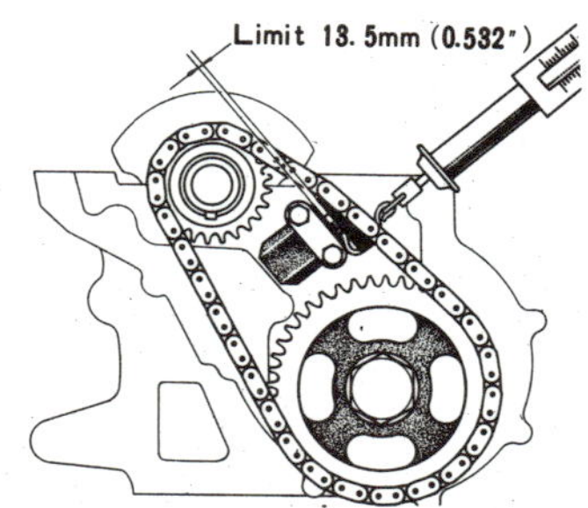

Fig.A.32. Checking the timing chain tension by means of a spring scale.

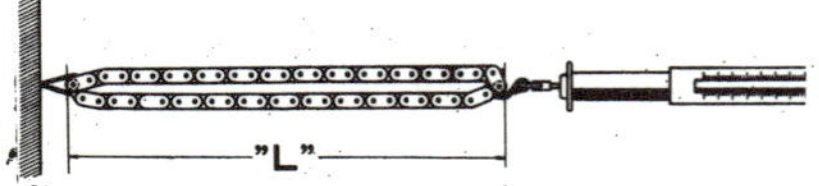

Fig.A.33. Measuring the timing chain length. The dimension "L" should be 10.7 in.

VALVE TAPPETS

Check the tappets for wear and damage and measure the clearance between the tappet outer diameter and the tappet locating bores. (Fig.A.16). If the clearance exceeds 0.004 in. (0.1 mm) fit oversize tappets and ream out the locating bores to obtain a running clearance of 0.0013 - 0.007 in. (0.019 - 0.033 mm).

Valve Tappet Specifications

Standard dia. . . . . . 0.786 - 0.787 in. (19.974 - 19.995 mm)
Tappet bore . . . . 0.787 - 0.788 in. (20.00 - 20.021 mm)

Oversize - 0.002 in. (0.05 mm):
    Diameter . . . . . . 0.788 - 0.790 in. (20.024 - 20.065 mm)
    Tappet bore . . . . . 0.789 - 0.790 in. (20.05 - 20.071 mm)

PUSH RODS

Inspect the push rods for damage and replace if necessary.

CYLINDER BLOCK

By applying a water pressure of 70 psi. (5 kg/sq.cm) to the water ports, check the cylinder block for leaks. If leaking, repair or replace the block. Check the flatness of the cylinder block surface in the same manner as described for the cylinder head and regrind the surface if the deviation is more than 0.002 in. (0.05 mm. (Fig.A.17).

CYLINDER BORE

Check the cylinder bore for ovality by measuring the diameter by means of a dial gauge at the top, bottom and centre. (Fig.A.18 and Fig.A.19). Make sure that the gauge is inserted at right angles and parallel. If necessary rebore the cylinder bores to fit oversize pistons. The correct diameter should be 2.955 to 2.957 in. (75.00 - 75.05 mm). If the bores are worn less than 0.008 in. (0.02 mm) below the given diameter, hone the cylinder walls and fit new pistons with the correct clearances.

The piston size is marked on the package and also in the piston crown. Pistons are available in oversizes from o/s. 0.010 to o/s. 0.040 in. (0.25 to 1.0 mm).

To bore the cylinder, measure the piston skirt at right angles to the gudgeon pin boss, with the gudgeon pin removed, at a temperature of 20°C (68°F).

Check the running clearance of the pistons in the cylinders, which should be between 0.001 - 0.002 in. (0.03 - 0.05 mm). To do this, insert a feeler gauge of 0.001 in. (0.03 mm) thickness and 0.5 - 0.6 in. (12 - 15 mm) wide into the cylinder. Invert the piston and insert into the cylinder so that the gudgeon pin is parallel with the crankshaft axis. With a spring scale attached to the feeler gauge, withdraw the feeler gauge and check the reading, which should be 2.2 - 5.5 lbs. (1.0 - 2.5 kg). (Fig.A.20).

CYLINDER LINERS

If the o/s. 1.00 piston cannot be used, due to the cylinder bores being worn excessively, fit cylinder liners, which are available in three sizes with outer diameters from 3.114 to 3.115 in. (79.091 to 79.126 mm) and bore diameters from 3.111-3.114 in. (79.031 - 79.086 mm). Bore the cylinder block in accordance with the size to be installed. The fitting clearance between the liner and the block should be 0.0015 - 0.0024 in. (0.04 - 0.06 mm).

The fitting pressure should be 4,400 - 6,600 lbs. (2000 - 3000 kg). Press in the liner until the top of the liner is flush with the cylinder block gasket surface. Finally bore out the liners to take standard size pistons. (Fig.A.21).

PISTONS AND GUDGEON PINS

Examine the pistons and the piston ring grooves for wear and replace pistons if necessary. Make sure that the gudgeon pin has the correct fit when inserted at a temperature of 70 - 80°C (158 - 175°F).s,

PISTON RINGS

Install each ring into the cylinder bore and check the piston ring gap with a feeler gauge. (Fig.A.22 and A.23). The ring gap should be 0.006 - 0.014 in. (0.15 - 0.35 mm) for all rings. Check the side clearance of the piston rings in the grooves of the piston. The clearance for the two compression rings should be 0.0012 - 0.0027 in. (0.03 - 0.07 mm) for the upper ring and 0.0008 - 0.002 in. (0.02 - 0.06 mm) for the lower ring. The clearance for the oil control ring should be 0.0006 - 0.002 in. (0.015 - 0.060 mm). (Fig.A.24). Rings are fitted with the marked face uppermost.

CONNECTING RODS

Check the connecting rods for bend and twist, using a conventional connecting rod aligning tool. (Fig.A.25). The max. allowance of bend is 0.002 (0.05 mm) per 4 in. (100 mm) length and for twist the max. allowance is 0.006 in. (0.15 mm) for each 4 in. (100 mm).

Fit the connecting rod to the crankshaft and check the side play of the big end bearings, which should be 0.004 to 0.008 in. (0.11 - 0.214 mm) and should not exceed 0.012 in. (0.3 mm). (Fig.A.26).

If the small end bushes are worn, replace them using the special mandrel 09222-30010 (Fig.A.27) or another suitable drift that will not damage the small end or the bush on re-installation. After installation ream out the bush to obtain a proper fit of the gudgeon pin. The clearance limit is 0.002 in. (0.05 mm).

CONNECTING ROD BIG END BEARINGS

Check the condition of the bearings and clean the crankpin journals. Replace obviously damaged bearing shells. Place a piece of "Plastigage" on the crankpin journal over the full width of the bearing and parallel to the crankshaft axis and fit the big end bearing together with the bearing cap. Tighten the bolts to 29 - 37 lb.ft.(4.0 - 5.2 kgm). Then remove the cap and check the width of the "Plastigage" with the "Plastigage" scale. (Fig.A.28). Read off the widest point in order to get the minimum clearance.

If the clearance exceeds 0.004 in. (0.10 mm), undersize bearings must be fitted. Regrind the crankpin journal to obtain a running

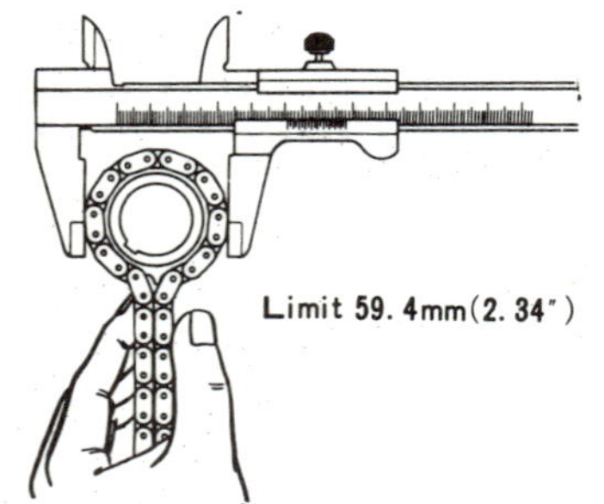

Fig.A.34. Measuring the diameter of the crankshaft sprocket.

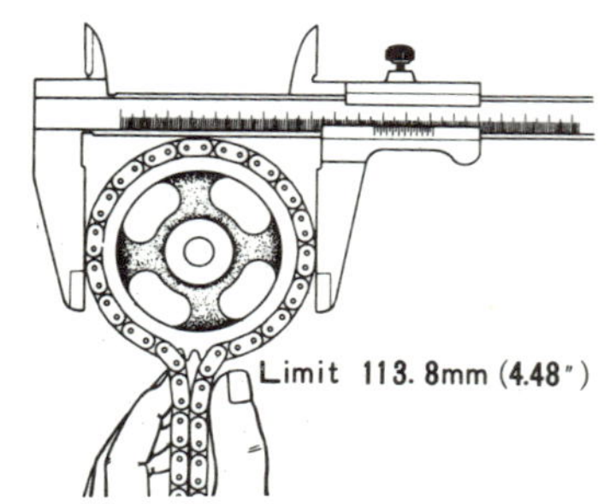

Fig.A.35. Measuring the diameter of the camshaft sprocket.

Fig.A.36. Checking the flywheel face for run-out.

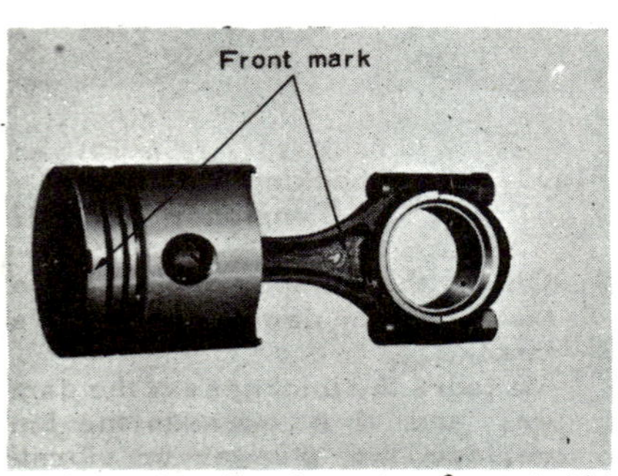

Fig.A.37. Correct assembly of piston and connecting rod.

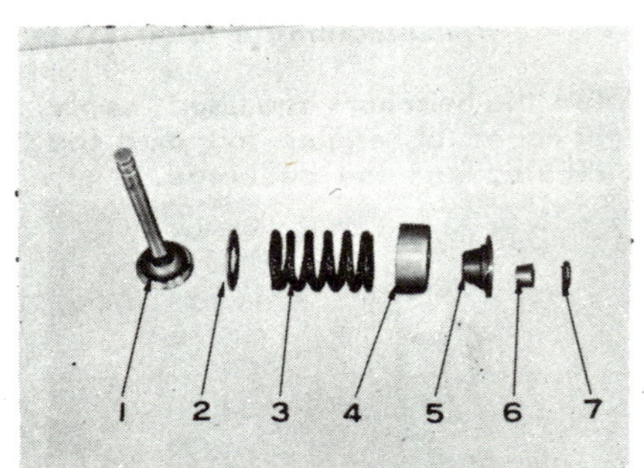

Fig.A.38. Exploded view of a valve.

1. Valve
2. Washer
3. Valve spring
4. Spring seal
5. Valv spring cup
6. Valve cotter
7. 'O' ring

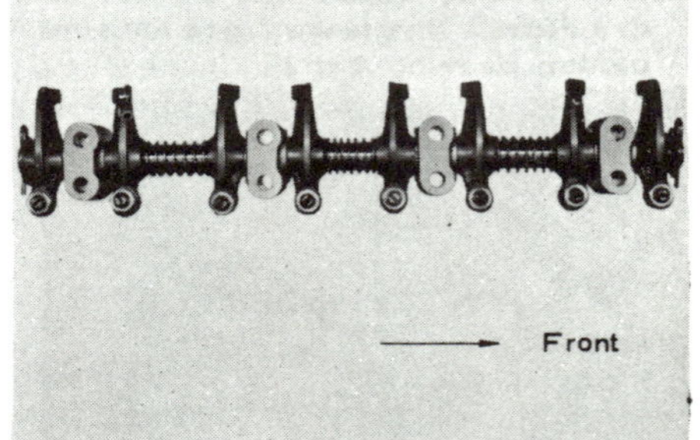

Fig.A.39. Fitting direction for the rocker shaft assembly. Note the position of the two types of rocker arms.

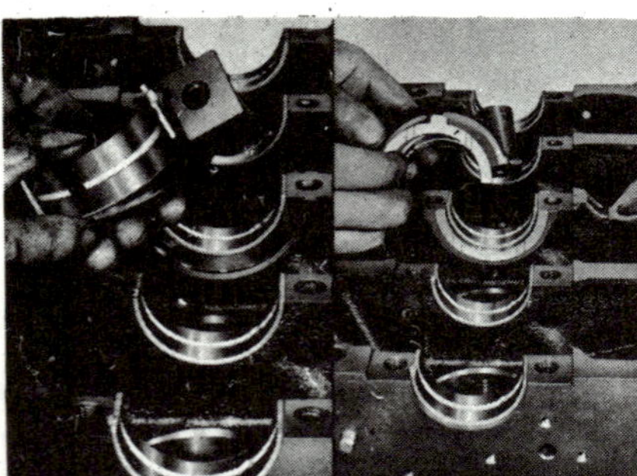

Fig.A.40. Installation of the main bearing shells (left) and of the thrust washer (right).

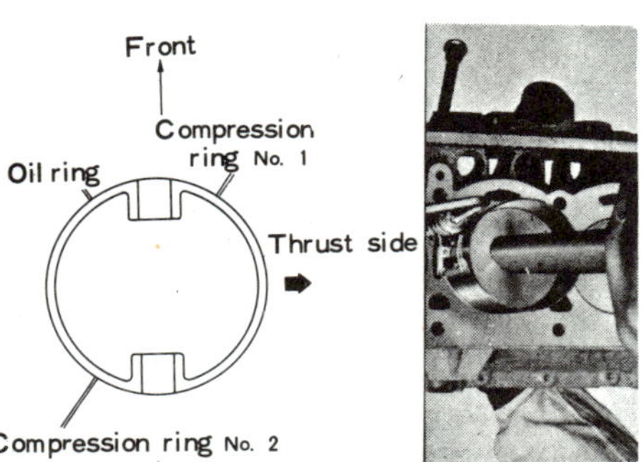

Fig.A.41. The correct spacing of the piston ring gaps (left) and installation of the piston.

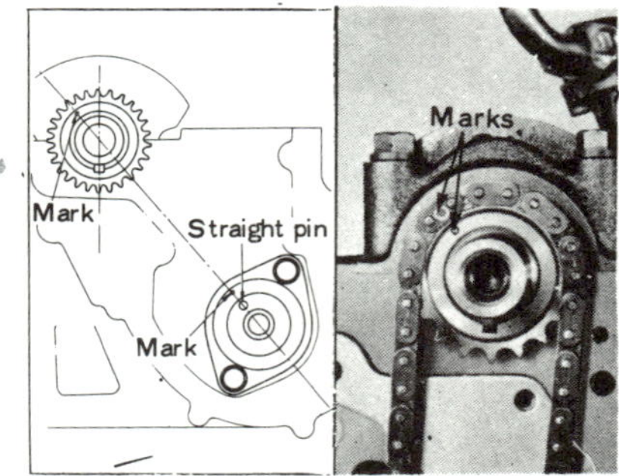

Fig.A.42. The correct arrangement of the timing marks.

clearance of 0.0006 - 0.0016 in. (0.016 - 0.040 mm). Bearings are available in undersizes of 0.25, 0.50, 0.75 mm. There is also an undersize of 0.05 mm which is only recommended when a new crankshaft is fitted and the correct clearance cannot be obtained.

CRANKSHAFT

Check the crankshaft for run-out and replace the crankshaft if the run-out exceeds 0.0012 in. (0.03 mm) (Fig.A.29). Examine the crankpin journals and main bearing journals for ovality, which should not exceed 0.0003 in. (0.008 mm). If necessary regrind the crankshaft. The wear limit for the crankshaft journal diameter is 1.6526 - 1.6535 in. (41.976 - 42.00 mm).

Check the crankshaft end float at the centre bearing. If the end float exceeds 0.012 in. (0.3 mm) replace the thrust bearings. The specified end float should be 0.002 - 0.009 in. (0.04 - 0.222 mm). Thrust bearings are available in two oversizes of 0.005 and 0.010 in. (0.12 and 0.25 mm). Make sure to fit the thrust bearing side with the oil groove to the crankshaft flange.

CRANKSHAFT BEARINGS

Check the crankshaft main bearings in a similar manner as described for the big end bearings, tightening the bearing cap bolts to 39 - 48 lb.ft. (5.4 - 6.6 kgm). The specified running clearance of the bearings is 0.0006 - 0.0015 in. (0.016 - 0.040 mm). If the clearance exceeds 0.004 in. (0.10 mm) replace by fitting undersize bearings. Undersize bearings are available as follows: 0.25, 0.50, 0.75 mm. The u/s. 0.05 mm is only recommended when fitting a new crankshaft and bearings and the correct running clearance cannot be obtained.

CAMSHAFT BEARINGS

Check the bearings for wear or damage and check the bearing running clearance by measuring the difference between the bearing inner diameter and the journal outer diameter. The running clearance is 0.0010 - 0.0025 in. (0.025 - 0.066 mm). If the clearance exceeds 0.004 in. (0.1 mm) replace the bearings as follows:

Remove the expansion plug from the end of the camshaft rear bearing and fit the camshaft bearing remover and replacer 09215-22010. Hold the shaft with suitable spanner to prevent it from turning and tighten the nut at the other end in order to withdraw the bearings, Position the new bearings so that the oil holes are in line with the holes in the bearing location bores and install the bearings with the above mentioned tool. After installation of the undersize bearings ream them to obtain the running clearance of 0.001 - 0.0025 in. (0.0025 - 0.066 mm). Install a new expansion plug with jointing compound.

CAMSHAFT

Check the camshaft for run-out, using a dial gauge and straighten or replace the camshaft when the run-out exceeds 0.0012 in. (0.03 mm). Inspect the cam lobes for scores or wear. Check the camshaft end float and replace the thrust washer when the end float exceeds 0.012 in. (0.3 mm). (Fig.A.31). The correct end float is 0.003 - 0.0051 in. (0.07 - 0.138 mm).

Inspect the camshaft bearing journals for scores and abnormal wear. The ovality should not exceed 0.008 in. (0.02 mm). If necessary regrind the camshaft journals to fit undersize camshaft bearings. Bearings are available in the following undersizes: 0.005 and 0.010 in. (0.125 and 0.25 mm).

CAMSHAFT SPROCKET AND TIMING CHAIN

When the timing chain is pulled by a spring balance with 22 lbs. (10 kg) the clearance between the chain tensioner plunger and the body should not exceed 0.532 in. (13.5 mm). (Fig.A.32). If this is exceeded, proceed as follows:

Check the chain for damage. Measure the length of the chain when pulled with 11 lbs. (5 kg) by means of a spring balance. The length "L" in Fig.A.33 should not exceed 10.7 in. (273 mm).

Measure the diameter of the crankshaft and camshaft sprockets as shown in Fig.A.34 and A.35. Replace the sprocket in question when the diameter is less than 2.34 in. (57.4 mm) in the case of the crankshaft sprocket or 4.48 in. (113.8 mm) in the case of the camshaft sprocket.

CHAIN TENSIONER AND VIBRATION DAMPER

Inspect for wear and damage, smooth operation when oiled. If worn or faulty, replace as a unit. Measure the damper thickness and the tension plunger and replace if less than 0.47 in. (12 mm) for the tension plunger and 0.27 in. (7 mm) for the vibration damper plunger.

FLYWHEEL

Inspect the friction face for the clutch driven plate for wear and damage and replace the flywheel as necessary. Check the flywheel for run-out, using a dial gauge and if necessary again replacing the flywheel when the run-out exceeds 0.008 in. (0.2 mm). If the ring gear is badly worn, remove by heating it to about 150° to 200°C (300 to 390°F) and tap it off the flywheel. Refit in reverse order (Fig.A.36).

CRANKSHAFT OIL SEALS

Replace all oil seals on assembly. Remove oil seals, using puller 09308-10010 and replace the front oil seal with mandrel 09223-22010 and rear oil seal with mandrel 09250-10011.

ENGINE — Assembly

Apply engine oil to the sliding or rotating portions of cylinder walls, pistons, bearings, gears, etc. and renew all gaskets, seals and packings, lockwashers and split pins.

Heat the pistons from 70 - 80°C (158 - 176°F) and assemble pistons, connecting rods, piston pins and securing circlips. Make sure that the front identification on the piston crown and the "T" stamped in the connecting rod are facing the same direction. (Fig.A.37). Fit the piston rings to the pistons, ensuring that the markings of the pistons are uppermost and that the rings are fitted according to their numbers.

Place the valves into the valve guides and fit the parts shown in

Fig.A.43. Installation of timing chain No.2 and location of timing marks.

Fig.A.44. Installation of the chain damper.

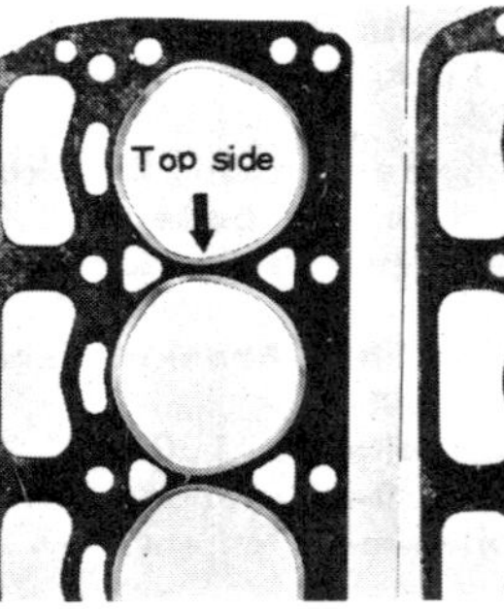

Fig.A.45. The cylinder head gasket must be fitted as shown in the left-hand illustration.

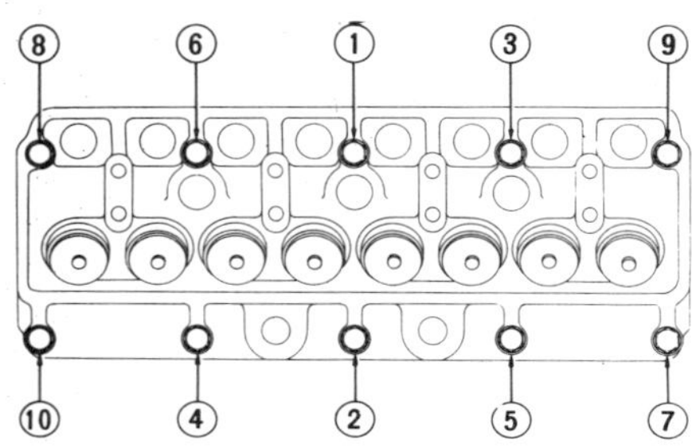

Fig.A.46. The tightening sequence for the cylinder head bolts.

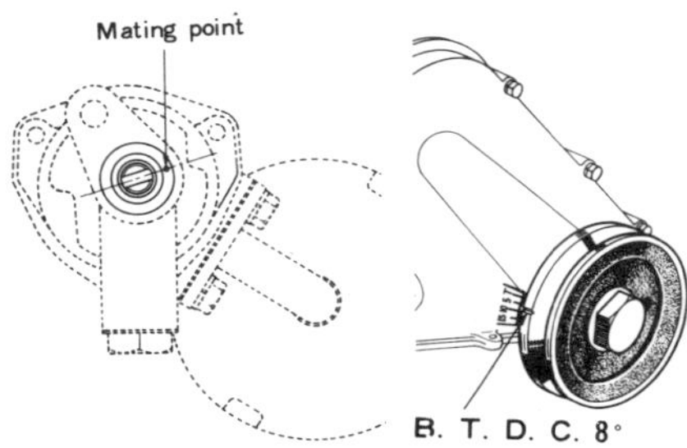

Fig.A.47. The installation position for the distributor and the timing marks on the crankshaft pulley.

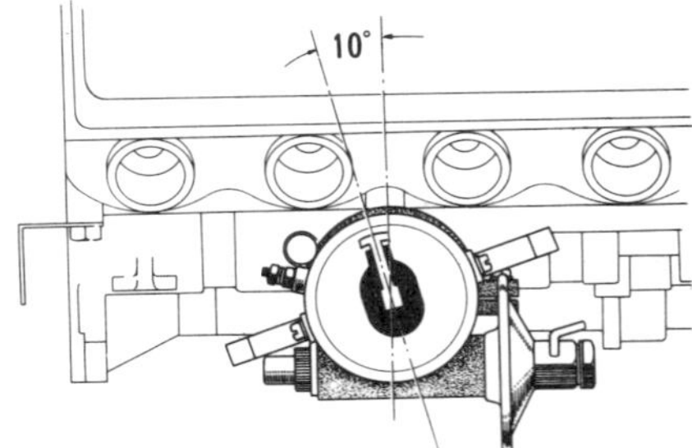

Fig.A.48. The distributor rotor position before installation.

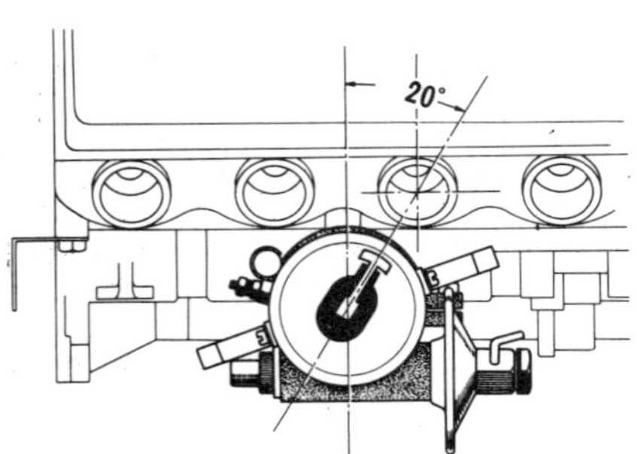

Fig.A.49. The distributor rotor position after installation.

Fig.A.50. Installation of the flywheel.

Fig.A.51. Installation of clutch and driven plate.

Fig.A.38 in the given assembly order. Compress the valve springs with a suitable compressor and fit the collet halves (6) and the 'O' ring (7).

Install the compression springs, rocker levers, rocker supports, tension springs and the lock springs on the rocker shaft. Note that the rocker levers are handed - see Fig.A.39 - also the "F" marking in the rocker supports must face forwards.

Clean the seatings for the upper parts of the main bearing shells and insert them into the crankcase. Apply oil to the bearings and the crankshaft journals and insert the crankshaft carefully into the crankcase. Fit the thrust washers into the cylinder block taking care that the oil grooves face the crankshaft thrust side (Fig.A.40)

Fit the shells to the bearing caps and the thrust washer to the centre cap. Attach the bearing caps to the cylinder block and tighten the bearing cap bolts uniformly to a torque of 39 - 47 lb.ft. (5.4 - 6.6 kgm).

Check that the piston ring gaps are uniformly distributed, apply oil to the pistons and using a piston ring clamp install the pistons in the original cylinders if the same pistons are re-used, from the top of the cylinder block. (Fig.A.41). Carefully guide the connecting rod to avoid damaging the journals. The notch in the piston crown must face forwards.

Fit the big end bearing shells, lubricate with oil and assemble the bearings to the crankpins, tightening the nuts to 29 - 37 lb.ft. (4.0 - 52. kgm). There should be an end float of 0.004 - 0.008 in. (0.11 - 0.214 mm) on each big end bearing.

Fit the oil pump assembly, tightening the bolts to 7 - 11 lb.ft. (1.0 - 1.5 kgm).

Install the front end plate with a new gasket, tightening the retaining bolts to 4 - 6 lb.ft. (0.6 - 0.9 kgm). The same torque applies when fitting the camshaft thrust plate retaining bolts. Align the "O" marking on the camshaft timing sprocket with the camshaft pin (Fig.A.42) and fit the timing chain so that the two marks on it line up with the 'O' mark on the camshaft and crankshaft sprockets (Fig.A.43). Secure the camshaft retaining bolt with 16 - 22 lb.ft. (2.3 - 3.1 kgm).

Install the chain tensioner and vibration damper assemblies (Fig.A.44), the timing cover and the drain tube clamp: All bolts should be tightened to 4 - 6 lb.ft. (0.6 - 0.9 kgm) The same torque is used for the bolts securing the rear oil seal retainer.

Apply sealing compound to the sump gasket and fit the sump, tightening the bolts to 2 - 3 lb.ft. (0.25 - 0.35 kgm). Fit the crankshaft pulley and the securing bolt. The torque for the bolt is 29 - 43 lb.ft. (4.0 - 6.0 kgm). Oil and fit the tappets in their original positions.

Invert the engine and fit a new cylinder head gasket taking care that the top side is uppermost. Fig.A.45 shows the difference between the two sides of the cylinder head gasket. Fit the cylinder head on to the cylinder block, insert the bolts and gradually and evenly tighten the cylinder head bolts in the sequence shown in Fig.A.46 to 36 - 48 lb.ft. (5.4 - 6.6 kgm). Fit the pre-assembled rocker shaft assembly and the push rod, tightening the rocker shaft pedestals to 13 - 16 lb.ft. (1.8 - 2.2 kgm). Adjust the valve rocker clearance as described later on. The correct values are as follows:

Inlet valve . . . . .0.003 in. (0.08 mm)
Exhaust valve . . . . .0.007 in. (0.18 mm)

To fit the distributor, rotate the crankshaft until No.1 piston is at T.D.C. on the compression stroke and align the V-groove in the crankshaft pulley with the corresponding mark on the timing cover for the engine in question (See Engine Tuning Data for setting). Fig.A.47 shows the position of the crankshaft for engines with timing setting of 8° B.T.D.C. Then align the oil pump shaft slot until it is in line with the mating point on the oil pump body. With the octan selector set to the normal position enter the distributor into the cylinder block so that the rotor is in the position shown in Fig.A.48. When fully pushed in, the distributor will rotate slightly and will end up in the position shown in Fig.A.49 if correctly installed. Turn the distributor housing until the contact points begin to open and tighten the clamp screw.

Fit the rocker arm cover, spark plug tubes, gaskets, spark plugs and ignition leads. Fit fuel pump, insulator and two gaskets to the cylinder block, tightening the nuts to 7 - 11 lb.ft. (1.0 - 1.5 kgm).

Install the R.H. engine mounting bracket, tightening the bolts to 14 - 22 lb.ft. (2.0 - 3.0 kgm) and the oil filter bracket with gasket. Torque 7 - 11 lb.ft. (1.0 - 1.5 kgm). Fit the oil filter element and the dipstick. Fit the L.H. mounting bracket and heat insulator. (Same torque as for R.H. bracket).

Fit the alternator bracket, tightening the bolts to 7 - 11 lb.ft. and the manifold assembly and the gasket, tightening the nuts to 14 - 22 lb.ft. (2.0 - 3.0 kgm). With the same torque fit the bolts for the engine hanger.

Install the following in the order given: Carburettor, heat insulator, water outlet housing, thermostat, water outlet pipe and gasket, water pump assembly, gasket and fan belt tensioning link (tightening all bolts to 7 - 11 lb.ft. (1.0 - 1.8 kgm). Fit the by-pass hose and clamp securely. The fan pulley and the fan are tightened with 4 - 6 lb.ft. (0.6 - 0.9 kgm).

Fit the alternator to the mounting bracket, insert the tube and tighten the bolts to 11 - 14 lb.ft. (1.5 - 2.0 kgm). Fit the fan belt and adjust by pushing the alternator away from the engine until a deflection of 0.3 - 0.5 in. (8 - 13 mm) is obtained on the longest run of the belt.

Fit the drain tab (sealing compound on the threads) into the cylinder block. Fit the rear end plate, tightening the bolts to 4 - 5 lb.ft. (0.6 - 0.9 kg). Install the flywheel and insert the mounting bolts with the lock washers. Tighten the bolts to 39 - 46 lb.ft. (5.4 - 6.6 kgm). Bend over the lock washers to secure the bolts in position. (Fig.A.50).

Using clutch guide mandrel 09301-12010 or a spare clutch shaft and assemble the clutch pressure plate with the driven plate to the flywheel. Gradually and evenly tighten the clutch securing bolts to a torque reading of 7 - 11 lb.ft. (1.0 - 1.5 kgm) in a diagonal pattern. (Fig.A.51).

Fit the sump breather tube and hose and connect to the rocker arm cover. Connect the gearbox to the engine and tighten the bolts to 36 - 51 lb.ft. (5.0 - 7.0 kgm). Fit the starter motor, stiffener plate and the clutch operating cable.

ENGINE — Installation

The installation is carried out in reverse order to the removal procedure, but the following points should be noted:

Fill the engine with 5.0 pints of the recommended engine oil (2.85 U.S. qts., 2.7 litres) and with 1 gall. (5 U.S. qts.; 4.7 litres) coolant. Check and adjust the clutch pedal free play to obtain the correct play of 0.6 - 1.2 in. (15 - 30 mm) at the clutch pedal. Start the engine and check for water, oil or fuel leaks. When the engine has reached its operating temperature, adjust the valves as follows:

Valve Clearance - Adjustment

With the engine running at idling speed (600 or 650 rpm. depending on model), insert a feeler gauge between valve stem and rocker lever and check that the clearances are in accordance with the values given below:

Clearance at 80°C (176°F):
K-engine: . . . . 0.008 in. (0.2 mm) — Inlet
0.012 in. (0.3 mm) — Exhaust
K-B engine: . . . . 0.008 in. (0.20 mm) — Inlet
0.014 in. (0.36 mm) — Exhaust

Clearance at 20°C (68°F):
K-engine . . . . 0.003 in. (0.08 mm) — Inlet
0.007 in. (0.18 mm) — Exhaust
K-B engine . . . . 0.004 in. (0.10 mm) — Inlet
0.009 in. (0.23 mm) — Exhaust

To adjust the clearance, slacken off the adjusting screw lock nut and turn the adjusting screw in the appropriate direction until the correct clearance is obtained. Tighten the locknut.

Technical Data

GENERAL SPECIFICATIONS

	K	K-B	K-C	3K	3K-D & 3K-B
Number of cylinders	4	4	4	4	4
Bore	75 mm (2.95 in.)	75 mm (2.95 in.)	75 mm (2.95 in.)	75 mm (2.95 in.)	75 mm (2.95 in.)
Stroke	61 mm (2.40 in.)	61 mm (2.40 in.)	61 mm (2.40 in.)	66 mm (2.598 in.)	66 mm (2.598 in.)
Capacity	1077 c.c.	1077 c.c.	1077 c.c.	1166 c.c.	1166 c.c.
Compression ratio	9:1	10:1	9:1	9.0:1	10:1
Compression pressure	12.0 kg/sq.cm. (170 psi.)	13.0 kg/sq.cm. (185 psi.)	12.0 kg/sq.cm (171 psi.)	12.0 kg/sq.cm. (171 psi.)	13.0 kg/sq.cm. (185 psi.)
Gross horse power (SAE)	60 HP at 6,000 rpm.	73 HP at 6,600 rpm.	60 HP at 6,000 rpm.	73 HP at 6,000 rpm.	79 HP at 6,600 rpm.
Gross max. torque (SAE)	8.5 kgm at 3,800 rpm.	9.0 kgm at 4,600 rpm.	8.5 kgm at 3,800 rpm.	9.5 kgm at 3,800 rpm.	9.6 kgm at 4,200 rpm. *

* The values given applies to the 3K-D engine. The data for the 3K-B engine are as follows: Gross horse power — 83 HP at 6,600 rpm.; Max. torque — 10.4 kgm (75 lb.ft.) at 4,600 rpm.; Compression pressure 13.0 kgm (185 psi.).

CYLINDER HEAD

Max. distortion of cylinder head face:
1100 . . . . .0.001 in. (0.04 mm)
1200 . . . . 0.004 in. (0.1 mm)
Max. distortion of manifold gasket
face . . . . 0.004 in. (0.1 mm)
Valve seat contacting face:
Inlet valve . . . . 0.056 in. (1.4 mm)
Exhaust valve . . . . 0.059 in. (1.5 mm)
Valve seat angle . . . . 45°
Valve seat correction angles . . . . 30°, 45°, 65°

CYLINDER BLOCK

Cylinder bore diameters:
Standard . . . . 75.00 - 75.05 mm (2.952 - 2.955 in.)
Wear limit . . . . 0.008 in. (0.2 mm)
Max. taper . . . . 0.0008 in. (0.02 mm)
Max. out-of-round . . . . 0.0008 in. (0.02 mm)
Crankshaft bearing
diameter . . . . 2.126 - 2.127 in. (54.004-54.028 mm)

Camshaft bearing bore diameter:
No.1 . . . . 1.890 - 1.891 in.(48.00-48.025 mm)
No.2 . . . . .1.870 - 1.871 in.(47.500-47.525 mm)
No.3 . . . . 1.850 - 1.851 in.(47.00-47.025 mm)
No.4 . . . . .1.831 - 1.832 in.(46.500-46.525 mm)

Valve lifter bore diameter:
Standard . . . . 0.787 - 0.788 in. (20.00 - 20.021 mm)
0.05 O/S . . . . 0.789 - 0.790 in. (20.050 - 20.071 mm)

Cylinder liners:
Outer dia. . . . . 3.114 - 3.115 in. (79.091 - 79.126 mm)
Inner dia. . . . . 2.930 - 2.936 in. (74.430 - 74.570 mm)
Block bore . . . . 3.111 - 3.114 in. (79.031 - 79.086 mm)
Interference fit . . . . 0.0015 - 0.0024 in.(0.04-0.06 mm)
Fitting pressure . . . . 4420-6620 lbs. (2000-3000 kg)

PISTONS, PISTON RINGS, PISTON PINS

Piston outer diameter:
Standard . . . . .2.951 - 2.953 in. (74.96 - 75.01 mm)
0.25 O/S . . . . .2.961 - 2.963 in. (75.21 - 75.26 mm)
0.50 O/S . . . . .2.971 - 2.973 in. (75.46 - 75.51 mm)
0.75 O/S . . . . .2.981 - 2.983 in. (75.71 - 75.76 mm)
1.00 O/S . . . . .2.991 - 2.993 in. (75.96 - 76.01 mm)

Piston running clearance at
20ºC . . . . 0.001 - 0.002 in. (0.03 - 0.05 mm)

Piston pin dia. . . . . 0.7086 - 0.7091 in. (17.999-18.011 mm)
Piston pin bore diameter in
piston . . . . .0.7085 - 0.7089 in. (17.995-18.007 mm)
Fitting temperature . . . . 70 - 80ºC (158 - 176ºF)
Ring gap . . . . 0.006 - 0.014 in. (0.15 - 0.35 mm)

Piston ring to groove clearance:
No.1 compression . . . . 0.0011-0.0027 in. (0.03 - 0.07 mm)
No.2 compression . . . . 0.0007 - 0.0023 in. (0.02 - 0.06 mm)
Oil ring . . . . .0.0006-0.0023 in. (0.015 - 0.060 mm)

CONNECTING RODS

Bend limit . . . . .0.002 in. (0.05 mm)
Twist limit . . . . .0.006 in. (0.15 mm)

Piston pin to small end bush clearance:
Standard . . . . .0.0002 - 0.0003 in. (0.004 - 0.008 mm)
Wear limit . . . . .0.002 in. (0.05 mm)

Connecting rod thrust clearance (side play):
Standard . . . . .0.004 - 0.008 in. (0.110 - 0.214 mm)
Wear limit . . . . 0.012 in. (0.3 mm)

Connecting rod to bearing running clearance:
Standard . . . . 0.0006 - 0.0015 in. (0.016 - 0.040 mm)
Wear limit . . . . 0.004 in. (0.1 mm)

Small end bush:
Inner dia. . . . . 0.7895 - 0.7903 in. (20.054 - 20.075 mm)
Outer dia. . . . . 0.7088 - 0.7093 in. (18.005 - 18.017 mm)

CRANKSHAFT

Max. run-out . . . . .0.001 in. (0.03 mm)

Crankshaft end float:
Standard . . . . 0.002 - 0.009 in. (0.04 - 0.22 mm)
Wear limit . . . . 0.011 in. (0.3 mm)

Thrust washer thickness:
Standard . . . . 0.096 - 0.098 in. (2.43 - 2.48 mm)
0.125 O/S . . . . 0.098 - 0.100 in. (2.49 - 2.54 mm)
0.250 O/S . . . . 0.100 - 0.102 in. (2.55 - 2.60 mm)

Crankshaft journals:
Running clearance . . . . . . .0.0005 - 0.0015 in. (0.016 - 0.040 mm)
Wear limit . . . . 0.004 in. (0.1 mm)
Max. taper . . . . 0.0003 in. (0.008 mm)
Max. out-of-round . . . . 0.0003 in. (0.008 mm)

Crankshaft journal diameters:
Standard . . . . .1.9675 - 1.9685 in. (49.976 - 50.000 mm)
0.25 U/S . . . . .1.9580 - 1.9584 in. (49.733 - 49.743 mm)
0.50 U/S . . . . .1.9481 - 1.9485 in. (49.483 - 49.493 mm)
0.75 U/S . . . . .1.9383 - 1.9387 in. (49.233 - 49.243 mm)

Crankpin diameters:
Standard . . . . .1.6525 - 1.6535 in. (41.976 - 42.000 mm)
0.25 U/S . . . . .1.6426 - 1.6430 in. (41.723 - 41.733 mm)
0.50 U/S . . . . .1.6328 - 1.6331 in. (41.473 - 41.483 mm)
0.75 U/S . . . . .1.6230 - 1.6233 in. (41.223 - 41.233 mm)

Crankshaft bearings undersizes
available . . . . .0.002 in. (0.05 mm), 0.01 in. (0.25 mm)
0.02 in. (0.50 mm), 0.03 in. (0.75 mm)

TIMING CHAIN, SPROCKETS AND TENSIONERS

Chain deflection . . . . 0.531 in. (13.5 mm) at 22 lbs. (5 kg)
Stretch limit . . . . .10.736 in. (272.7 mm

Timing chain sprocket wear limit:
Crankshaft sprocket . . . . .2.34 in. (59.4 mm)*
Camshaft sprocket . . . . 4.48 in. (113.8 mm)*

*This dimension is the outer diameter of the timing sprockets with the
timing chain wound around the wheels.

Thickness of tensioner/damper:
Tensioner . . . . .0.47 in. (12 mm)
Damper . . . . 0.28 in. (7 mm)

CAMSHAFT

Max. run-out . . . . .0.001 in. (0.03 mm)

Camshaft end float:
Standard . . . . 0.0028 - 0.0054 in. (0.070 - 0.138 mm)
Wear limit . . . . 0.012 in. (0.3 mm)

Bearing running clearance:
Standard . . . . 0.001 - 0.0026 in. (0.025 - 0.066 mm)
Wear limit . . . . 0.004 in. (0.1 mm)

Camshaft journals:
Max. taper . . . . .0.001 in. (0.02 mm)
Max. out-of-round . . . . .0.001 in. (0.02 mm)

Cam lobe height:
Inlet . . . . 1.436 - 1.439 in. (36.469 - 36.569 mm)
Exhaust . . . . 1.432 - 1.436 in. (36.369 - 36.469 mm)

Cam lobe height wear limit:
Inlet . . . . 1.424 in. (36.17 mm)
Exhaust . . . . 1.420 in. (36.07 mm)

Cam lift:
Inlet .0.225 in. (5.72 mm)
Exhaust . . . . .0.237 in. (6.02 mm)

Camshaft bearing journal diameters - Standard:
No.1 . . . . 1.701 - 1.702 in. (43.209 - 43.225 mm)
No.2 . . . . 1.691 - 1.692 in. (42.959 - 42.975 mm)
No.3 . . . . 1.681 - 1.682 in. (42.709 - 42.725 mm)
No.4 . . . . 1.671 - 1.672 in. (42.459 - 42.475 mm)

Camshaft bearing journal diameters - 0.25 mm U/S:
No.1 . . . . .1.6963 - 1.697 in. (43.087 - 43.097 mm)
No.2 . . . . 1.686 - 1.687 in. (42.837 - 42.847 mm)
No.3 . . . . 1.677 - 1.678 in. (42.587 - 42.597 mm)
No.4 . . . . 1.667 - 1.668 in. (42.337 - 42.347 mm)

VALVES

Valve head diameter:
Inlet . . . . .1.417 in. (36 mm)
Exhaust . . . . .1.141 in. (29 mm)

Valve stem diameter:
    Inlet . . . . 0.3139 - 0.3143 in. (7.975 - 7.986 mm)
    Exhaust . . . . 0.3134 - 0.3145 in. (7.960 - 7.975 mm)

Valve overall length . . . . 3.940 in. (100.1 mm)
Min. length . . . . .0.02 in. (0.5 mm) less

Valve head thickness limit:

    Inlet . . . . 0.031 in. (0.8 mm)
    Exhaust . . . . 0.035 in. (0.9 mm)

Valve seat width:
    Inlet . . . . 0.055 in. (1.4 mm)
    Exhaust . . . . 0.059 in. (1.5 mm)
Valve seat angle . . . . 45°

VALVE GUIDES

Guide overall length:
    Inlet . . . . 1.811 in. (46 mm)
    Exhaust . . . . 1.969 in. (50 mm)

Fitting temperature . . . . 80° (176°)
Protrusion from head .0.708 in. (18 mm)
Inner diameter . . . . 0.315 - 0.316 in. (8.01 - 8.03 mm)

VALVE TAPPETS

Valve tappet outer diameter:
    Standard . . . . .0.7864 - 0.7872 in. (19.974 - 19.995 mm)
    0.25 mm O/S . . . . .0.7883 - 0.7899 in. (20.024 - 20.065 mm)

Tappet running clearance:
    Standard . . . . 0.0007 - 0.0013 in. (0.019 - 0.033 mm)
    Wear limit . . . . 0.004 in. (0.1 mm)

VALVE SPRINGS

Free length . . . . .1.830 in. (46.5 mm)
    Limit . . . . .1.760 in. (45.1 mm)
Fitted length . . . . .1.512 in. (38.4 mm)
Fitted load:
    3K . . . . 55.2 lbs. (25 kg)
    3K-B, 3K-D . . . . .62.5 lbs. (28.3 kk)
Fitted load limit:
    3K . . . . .70.2 lbs. (31.8 kg)
    3K-B, 3K-D . . . . .77.0 lbs. (35.0 kg)

VALVE ROCKER SHAFT AND ARM

Shaft outer dia. . . . . 0.629 - 0.630 in. (15.976 - 15.994 mm)
Bush inner dia. . . . . 0.630 - 0.631 in. (16.000 - 16.018 mm)

Rocker arm running clearance:
    Standard . . . . 0.0002 - 0.0017 in. (0.006 - 0.042 mm)
    Wear limit . . . . .0.003 in. (0.08 mm)

Trouble Shooting

SYMPTOMS	PROBABLE CAUSE	ACTION TO BE TAKEN
Lack of power	1. Poor compression Incorrect valve clearance Intake valves leaking Sticking valves Valve springs broken Piston rings broken Rings or cylinders worn	 Adjust valve clearance Lap valve seats Replace valve and guides Replace valve spring Replace piston rings Overhaul engine
	2. Ignition improperly set Incorrect ignition timing Defective spark plugs Contact breakers defective	 Re-set Clean, re-set or renew Clean or replace, adjust gap
	3. Lack of fuel Clogged carburettor jet Clogged fuel pipe Dirty fuel tank Faulty fuel pump Fuel filter clogged	 Clean carburettor Clean fuel pipe Clean fuel tank Check fuel pump Clean or replace element
Overheating	Insufficient coolant Loose fan belt Fan belt worn or damaged Inoperative thermostat Defective water pump Clogged cooling system Incorrect ignition timing Incorrect valve clearance Incorrect oil used Radiator fins clogged	Top-up radiator Adjust fan belt Replace fan belt Replace thermostat Repair or replace Clean system Re-set timing Adjust clearance Refill with correct oil grade Clean radiator fins
Excessive oil consumption	Oil leaks Defective piston rings Piston rings worn or sticking in grooves Piston or cylinder worn Valve stem or guide worn	Find oil leak and rectify Replace piston rings Replace piston rings Replace piston or bore cylinder Replace as necessary
Difficult starting	Improper oil Discharged or defective battery Loose connections Defective ignition system Burnt valves Pistons, piston rings or cylinders badly worn	Change to proper viscosity Charge or replace battery Clean and tighten connections Adjust ignition, check plugs Repair or replace valves Overhaul engine
Engine noisy	Crankshaft bearings or journals worn Connecting rod bearings worn Connecting rod bent Piston, piston rings and pins damaged	Replace bearings and grind crankshaft or replace crankshaft Replace bearings and grind crankshaft or replace crankshaft Straighten or replace rod Check and replace parts as necessary

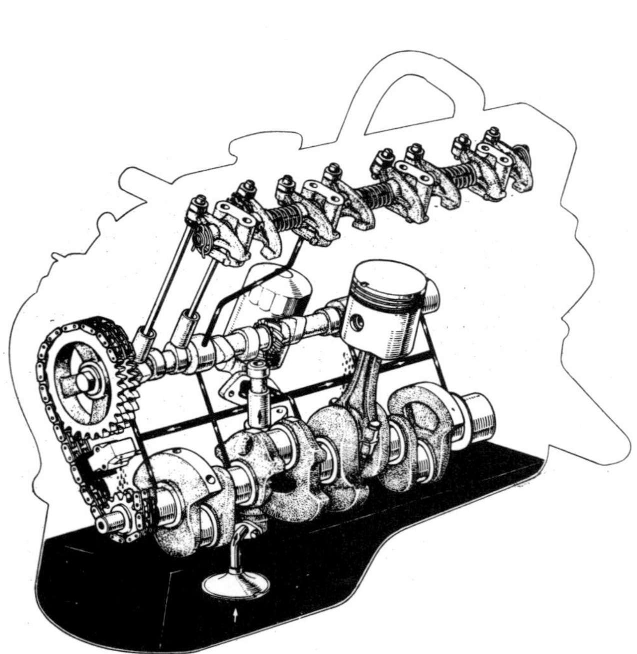

Fig.B.1. Engine lubricating diagram.

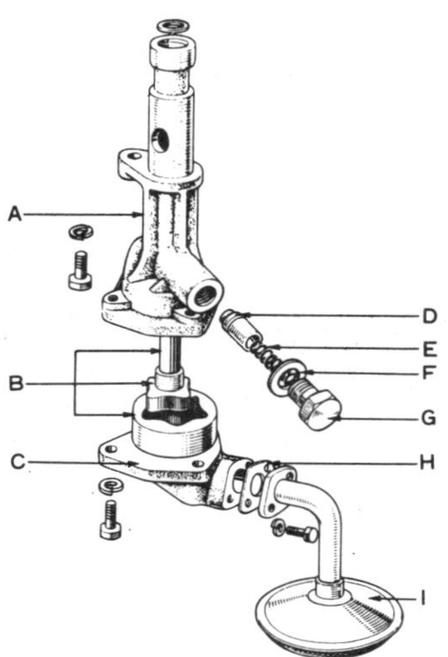

Fig.B.2. Exploded view of the oil pump.

A.   Oil pump body
B.   Oil pump rotor set
C.   Oil pump end cover
D.   Oil pressure relief valve
E.   Relief valve gasket
F.   Sealing washer
G.   Relief valve end plug
H.   Suction tube gasket
I.   Oil strainer with suction tube

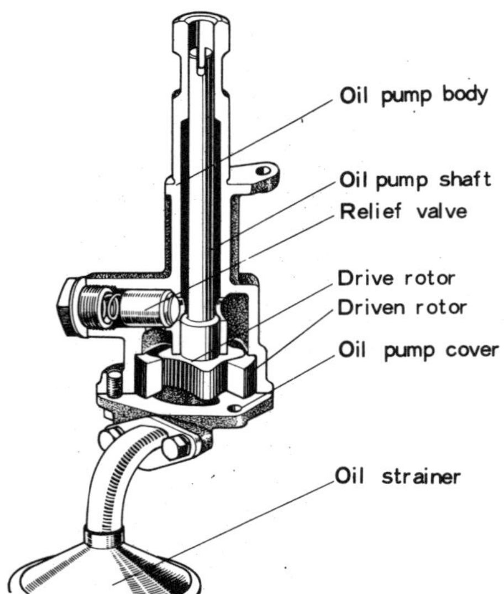

Fig.B.3. Sectional view of the oil pump.

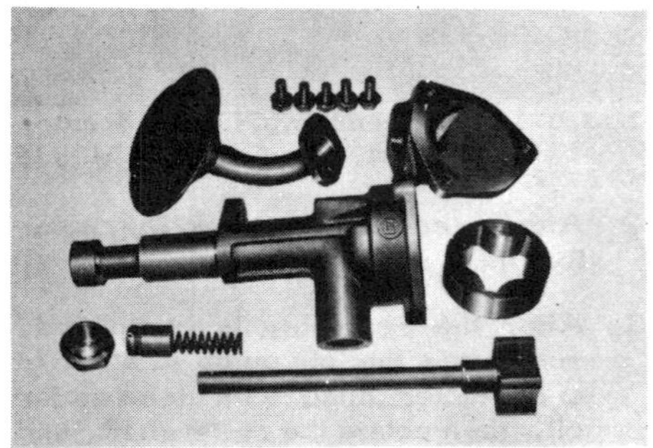

Fig.B.4. View of the dismantled oil pump.

Lubrication System

DESCRIPTION

The lubrication system of the Corolla Engine is a pressure-feed system with full-flow oil filter incorporating a rotor-type oil pump. The oil filter is fitted with a by-pass valve, allowing the oil to by-pass the filter element in case of a blocked filter. The oil pressure is controlled by a relief valve in the oil pump body. A diagram of the oil flow is shown in Fig.B.1.

OIL PUMP — Removal

Drain the oil, remove the engine oil sump, disconnect the oil pump outlet pipe and remove the oil pump together with the strainer from the crankcase. Fig.B.2 and Fig.B.3 show details of the removed oil pump.

OIL PUMP — Dismantling

Remove the oil strainer and unscrew the oil pump cover from the oil pump body. Lift out the driven rotor and the oil pump drive shaft with the drive rotor assembly. Unscrew the oil pressure relief valve plug from the oil pump body and withdraw the spring and the relief valve. The pump should be dismantled to the items shown in Fig.B.4.

OIL PUMP — Inspection and Overhaul

Thoroughly clean all parts in suitable cleaning solvent and check the following items:

The oil pump shaft for excessive wear or scores, replacing if necessary the shaft and rotor assembly as a set.

The drive and driven rotors for wear and damage and if necessary replace as a complete set. Measure the diameter of the rotors which should be as follows:

Drive rotor . . . . 1.169 - 1.171 in. (29.70 - 29.74 mm)
Driven rotor . . . . 1.595 - 1.597 in. (40.53 - 40.56 mm)

The tip clearance between the drive rotor and the driven rotor which should be 0.0016 - 0.006 in. (0.04 - 0.16 mm). If the clearance exceeds 0.008 in. (0.2 mm) replace the rotor as a set. Check the clearance as shown in Fig.B.5.

The end clearance between the rotor and the top of the oil pump body, which should be 0.0012 - 0.0035 in. (0.03 - 0.09 mm). If the clearance exceeds 0.006 in. (0.15 mm) replace the rotors and/or the cover. Check as shown in Fig.B.6.

The clearance between the driven rotor and the pump body bore. If the clearance exceeds 0.008 in. (0.2 mm) replace the body and/or the rotor set. Check as shown in Fig.B.7.

The oil pressure relief valve for proper fit and the sliding surfaces for scores. Also check the relief valve spring for weakness and damage. Replace parts as necessary. Relief valve data are as follows:

Free length . . . . .1.85 in. (47 mm)
Fitted length . . . . : . . . . 1.45 in. (36.8 mm)
Fitted load . . . . 13.2 - 14.6 lbs. (5.99 - 6.59 kg)

OIL PUMP — Assembly and Installation

The assembly of the oil pump is a reversal of the dismantling procedure. Note that there are punch marks on the drive rotor and the driven rotor. The driven rotor should be fitted so that the punch mark is facing the pump cover side, with the mark of the drive rotor being opposite the mark of the driven rotor.

After completed assembly, immerse the strainer into a container filled with engine oil and rotate the oil pump shaft. This lubricates the rotors for initial running and also shows if the oil flows from the outlet port.

The installation of the oil pump is carried out in reverse order to the removal procedure.

OIL FILTER — Removal

To remove the oil filter, use the filter band wrench 09228-22010 or make up a make-shift wrench from an old bicycle chain which is placed around the outer diameter of the oil filter body, locked in position so that it is snugly around the body. A metal bar should be attached to the free end of the chain. Using the bar as a lever, unscrew the oil filter body. The chain will grip the body, thereby unscrewing it. Disconnect the lead from the oil pressure switch and remove the oil filter bracket from the engine.

Check the by-pass valve (Fig.B.8) and the sliding surfaces for wear and replace if necessary. Replace the oil filter bracket if it is deformed in any way.

The oil filter element should be replaced every 6000 miles (10,000 km). Fig.B.9 shows a cut-away view of the full-flow oil filter.

OIL FILTER — Assembly and Installation

Refit the oil filter bracket to the engine. The filter element body should only be tightened by hand. Do not use the band wrench or the make-shift tool mentioned in the paragraph on removal.

Limit 0.2mm (0.0079″)

Fig.B.5. Checking the clearance between the inner and outer rotor.

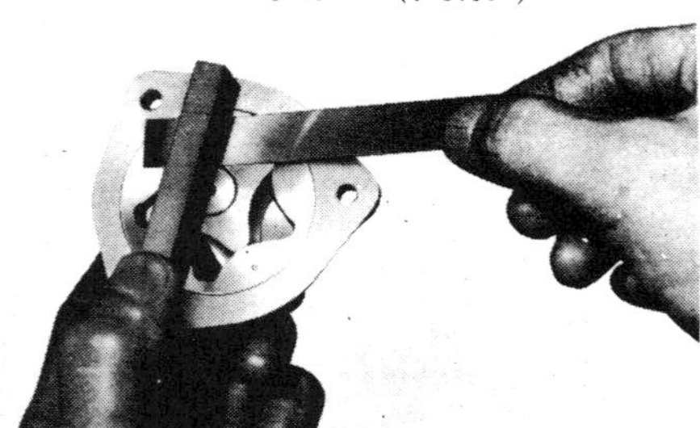

Limit 0.15mm (0.0059″)

Fig.B.6. Checking the end clearance of the rotor set.

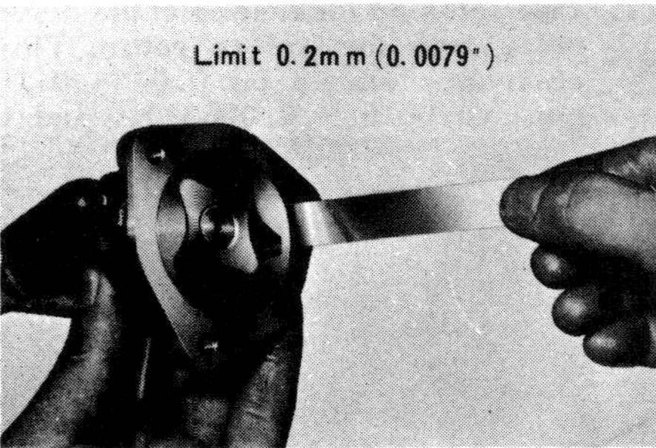

Limit 0.2mm (0.0079″)

Fig.B.7. Checking the clearance between outer rotor and body.

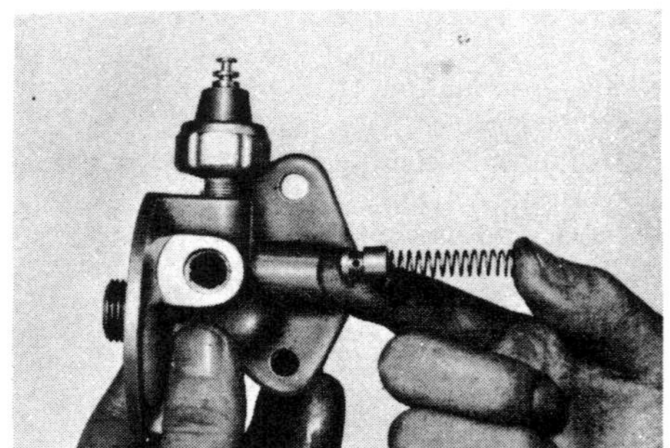

Fig.B.8. Fit the by-pass valve assembled as shown.

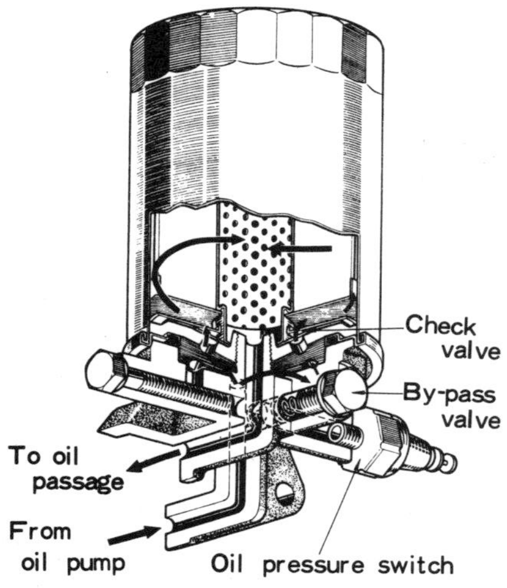

Fig.B.9. Sectional view of the oil filter.

Technical Data

OIL PUMP

Type . . . . Rotor-type oil pump

Tip clearance . . . . 0.04 - 0.16 mm (0.002 - 0.006 in.)
Limit . . . . 0.2 mm (0.008 in.)
Side clearance . . . . 0.03 - 0.09 mm (0.001 - 0.003 in.)
Limit .0.15 mm (0.006 in.)
Body clearance . . . . . . 0.10 - 0.16 mm (0.004 - 0.006 in.)
Limit . . . . .0.20 mm (0.008 in.)

Oil pressure relief valve spring:
   Free length . . . . .47 mm (1.85 in.)
   Fitted length . . . . 36.8 mm (1.45 in)
   Fitted load . . . . 5.99 - 6.59 kg (13.2 - 14.5 lbs.)

Relief valve opening
pressure . . . . 3.6 - 4.4 kg/sq.cm (51 - 63 psi.)

Delivery amount:
   The delivery amount at oil temperature of 100°C (212°F)
at 300 rpm. (pump) and oil pressure of 29 psi. (2
kg/sq.cm) should be greater than 2.6 Imp. pts. (3.2 U.S.
pts., 1.5 litres) per minute.

   The delivery amount at the same oil temperature, a pump
speed of 3000 rpm. and an oil pressure of 42.5 psi. (3
kg/sq.cm) should be greater than 37 Imp. pts. (44.4 U.S.
pts., 21 litres) per minute.

OIL FILTER

Type . . . . Full-flow filter with replaceable element
Capacity . . . . 0.53 Imp. pts (0.63 U.S. qts., 0.6 litres)
Valve opening pressure . . . . 0.8-1.2 kg/sq.cm (11-4-17.0 psi.)

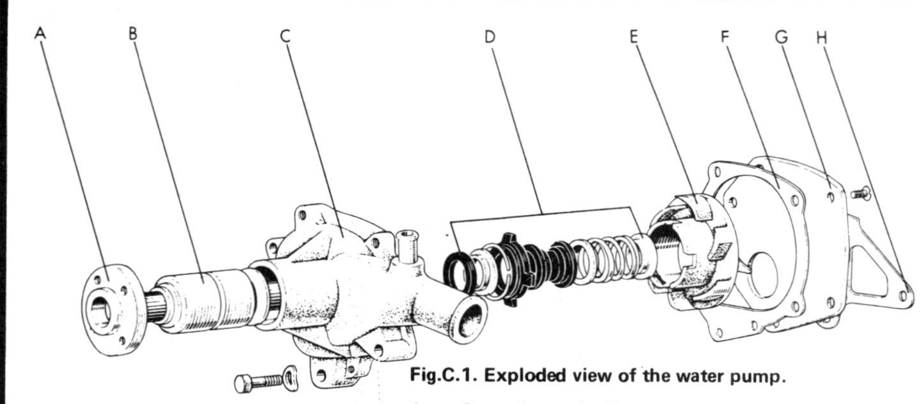

Fig.C.1. Exploded view of the water pump.

A. *Fan pulley seating flange*
B. *Water pump bearing*
C. *Water pump body*
D. *Water pump seal*
E. *Water pump impeller*
F. *Water pump body gasket*
G. *Water pump cover plate*
H. *Cover plate gasket*

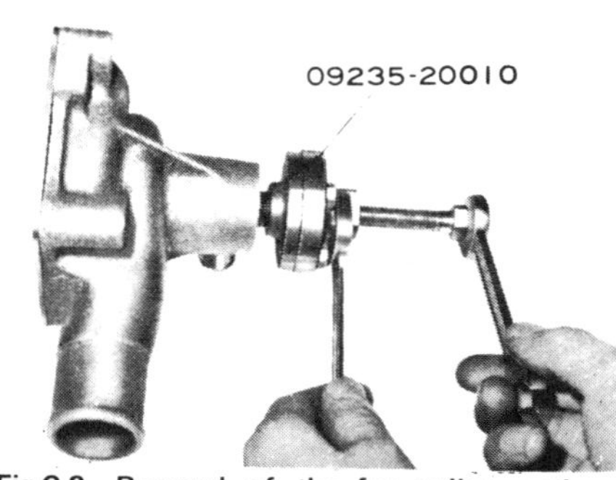

Fig.C.2. Removal of the fan pulley seating flange.

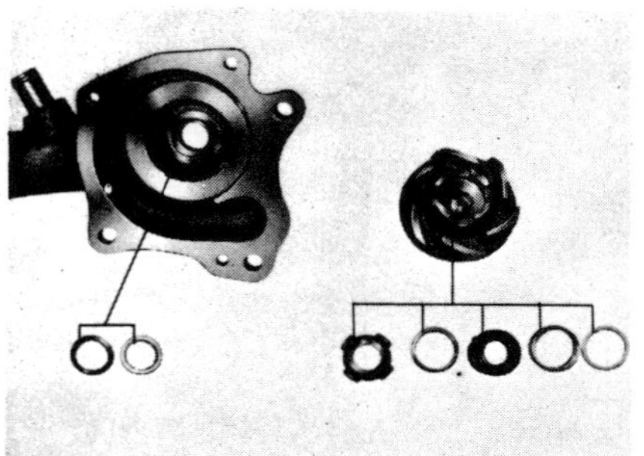

Fig.C.3. Exploded view of the water pump impeller components.

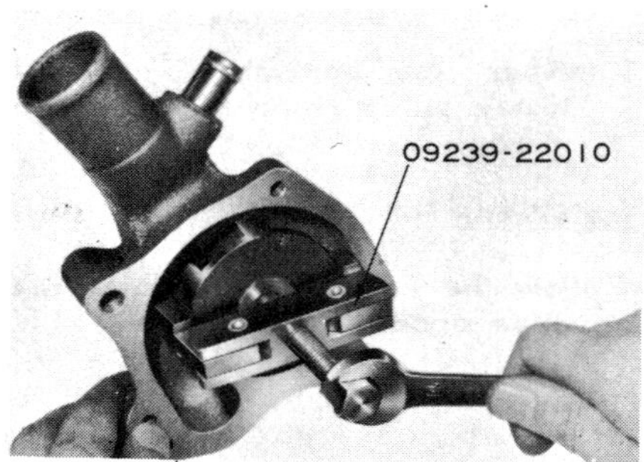

Fig.C.4. Removal of the water pump impeller.

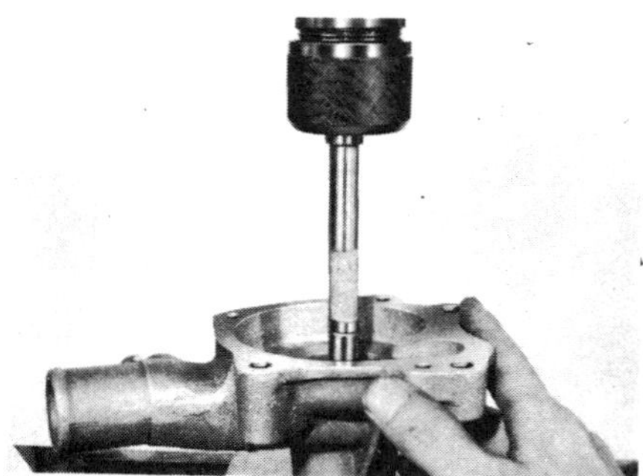

Fig.C.5. Removal of the water pump bearing.

Fig.C.6. Installation of the water pump bearing.

Fig.C.7. Installation of the fan pulley seating flange.

Fig.C.8. Installation of the impeller under a press.

Cooling System

DESCRIPTION

The cooling system is of the pressure-circulation type, ensuring positive cooling efficiency. The radiator is of the fin and tube type. The water pump is directly driven from the crankshaft pulley with the fan mounted to the front of the pump.

The radiator cap maintains a pressure of approx. 7 psi. (0.5 kg/sq.cm) in the cooling system when the engine has reached its operating temperature. The wax thermostat, fitted to the water outlet elbow, enables the engine to warm up quickly in cold weather and gives efficient regulation of the cooling water temperature.

NOTE: As cylinder head and water pump are made of aluminium alloy, take care only to use anti-freeze that will not damage the cylinder head and water pump material through corrosion. Anti-freeze to British Standard Specification 3150 is suitable for this engine.

WATER PUMP — Removal

Drain the coolant, disconnect the radiator hoses from the upper and the lower connections of the radiator, remove the radiator securing bolts and lift out the radiator. Remove the fan belt adjusting link bolt and lift off the fan belt.

Disconnect the water by-pass hose from the water pump and unscrew the water pump together with the pulley and the fan from the cylinder block.

WATER PUMP — Dismantling

The water pump pulley seat should be removed with the special puller 09235-20010 as shown in Fig.C.2. If this puller is not available and one tries to lever off the pulley seat by means of tyre levers or strong screwdrivers, remember that the water pump housing is made of aluminium alloy and therefore can crack very easily. From the rear of the water pump remove the cover plate together with the gasket and withdraw the pump impeller, using the impeller puller 09239-22010 as shown in Fig.C.4. This is a two-arm puller the legs of which are engaged under the impeller with the thrust bolt exerting pressure to the water pump shaft. The water pump seal can be removed at this stage.

The pump housing should be heated to 75 - 85°C (170 - 185°F) and the bearing pressed out, using a suitable press mandrel of the appropriate outer diameter.. An exploded view of the water pump is shown in Fig.C.1.

WATER PUMP — Inspection

With the exception of the permanently lubricated bearing and the water pump seal, wash all components of the water pump in suitable solvent. Inspect the bearing for roughness or excessive end float. Otherwise replace any worn or pitted parts. If the seat for the seal is damaged, replace the impeller.

WATER PUMP — Assembly

It is recommended that a new seal should be fitted into the impeller and the pump body (Fig.C.3). Press the bearing into the heated body until it is flush with the front face of the body. The pulley seat should be fitted to the bearing shaft, using a press, applying the pressure on to the pump shaft from the cover end of the pump body.

Fit the impeller to the water pump shaft, until it is flush with the end of the shaft. When correctly fitted, there should be a clearance of 0.012 - 0.024 in. (0.3 - 0.6 mm) between the impeller and the pump body. Refit the water pump cover plate with a new gasket and check the pump for freedom of rotation. The various stages of water pump assembly are shown in Figs.B.6, B.7 and B.8.

WATER PUMP — Installation

The installation is a reversal of the removal procedure. Adjust the fan belt tension to give a deflection of 0.3 - 0.5 in. (8 - 13 mm) on the longest run of the belt. To do this, slacken the adjusting link clamp bolt and push the alternator away from the engine, until the belt can be depressed to the value given. Hold the alternator in this position and tighten the link securing bolt and clamp bolt.

Finally refill the cooling system with plain water or anti-freeze solution, start the engine and check for leaks.

THERMOSTAT — Removal, Inspection and Installation

Drain the coolant and disconnect the upper radiator hose. Remove the water outlet and lift out the thermostat. Replace the thermostat when the valve is open under normal temperature.

To check the valve opening temperature, submerge the thermostat together with a thermometer in water, and heat up the water, but make sure that neither thermostat nor thermometer can touch the sides or the bottom of the water container as this will give false indications.

The valve should start to open at 82°C (180°F) and should be fully open at 95°C (198°F). The valve lift must exceed 0.315 in. (8.0 mm).

The installation of the thermostat is carried out in reverse order to the removal procedure. Refill the cooling system with plain water or anti-freeze, start the engine and check all connections for leaks.

RADIATOR — Removal and Installation

Drain the coolant. Remove the radiator inlet and outlet hoses from the radiator connection at the top and from the cylinder block connection at the bottom and unscrew the radiator mounting. Lift out the radiator with the lower hose attached to the radiator if desired.

The installation of the radiator is a reversal of the removal procedure. Check all connections for leaks after the engine has reached its normal operating temperature.

FLUSHING THE COOLING SYSTEM

After a considerable period of operation a fair amount of residue can build-up inside the cooling system, so it becomes necessary to flush the cooling system once a year, using water and compressed air. To achieve the best possible effects, this operation should be carried out in two stages:

Radiator: Connect an outlet pipe to the inlet pipe of the radiator, disconnect the lower radiator hose and plug the opening with a wooden plug with a hole in the centre to insert an air gun. Thoroughly flush the radiator with clean water and blow into the lower radiator tube with an air gun at regular intervals to force the water under pressure through the radiator. As soon as clean water emerges from the outlet hose, shut off the water and air supply and drain the radiator.

Engine: Connect an outlet hose to the water outlet and plug up the radiator hose connection on the cylinder block with a suitable plug with a hole in the centre. After removing the thermostat, flush the entire engine as described for the radiator.

Technical Data

WATER PUMP

Type . . . . . Centrifugal pump with impeller and six blade fan
Delivery . . . . 80 litres (21.1 U.S. gall.; 17.6 Imp.gall.)
per minute at 4600 rpm and 95°C (198°F)

RADIATOR

Type .Corrugated fin and tube
Radiation capacity . . . . 230 Kcal/min.
Radiator cap valve . . . . .7 psi. (0.5 kg/sq.cm)
Radiation area . . . . 37.6 sq.ft. (3.5 sq.m)
Radiator weight . . . . 9.5 lbs. (4.3 kg)
Radiator height . . . . .11.0 in. (280 mm)
Radiator width . . . . .16.5 in. (418 mm)
Radiator thickness . . . . 1.3 in. (32 mm)
Coolant capacity . . . . . 1.8 Imp.pts. (2.2 U.S. qts.,2.1 litres)

THERMOSTAT

Type . . . . Wax
Opens at . . . . 82°C (180°F)
Fully open at . . . . 95°C (198°F)
Valve lift . . . . 0.315 in. (8.0 mm)

CONVERSION TABLE

mm	ins	mm	ins	mm	ins	mm	Ins	mm	ins
.01	.000394	.51	.020079	1	.030370	51	2.007870	105	4.133848
.02	.000787	.52	.020472	2	.078740	52	2.047240	110	4.330700
.03	.001181	.53	.020866	3	.118110	53	2.086610	115	4.527550
.04	.001575	.54	.021260	4	.157480	54	2.125980	120	4.724400
.05	.001969	.55	.021654	5	.196850	55	2.165350	125	4.921250
.06	.002362	.56	.022047	6	.236220	56	2.204720	130	5.118110
.07	.002756	.57	.022441	7	.275590	57	2.244090	135	5.314950
.08	.003150	.58	.022835	8	.314960	58	2.283460	140	5.511800
.09	.003543	.59	.023228	9	.354330	59	2.322830	145	5.708650
.10	.003937	.60	.023622	10	.393700	60	2.362200	150	5.905500
.11	.004331	.61	.024016	11	.433070	61	2.401570	155	6.102350
.12	.004724	.62	.024409	12	.472440	62	2.440940	160	6.299200
.13	.005118	.63	.024803	13	.511810	63	2.480310	165	6.496050
.14	.005512	.64	.025197	14	.551180	64	2.519680	170	6.692900
.15	.005906	.65	.025591	15	.590550	65	2.559050	175	6.889750
.16	.006299	.66	.025984	16	.629920	66	2.598420	180	7.086600
.17	.006693	.67	.026378	17	.669290	67	2.637790	185	7.283450
.18	.007087	.68	.026772	18	.708660	68	2.677160	190	7.480300
.19	.007480	.69	.027165	19	.748030	69	2.716530	195	7.677150
.20	.007874	.70	.027559	20	.787400	70	2.755900	200	7.874000
.21	.008268	.71	.027953	21	.826770	71	2.795270	210	8.267700
.22	.008661	.72	.028346	22	.866140	72	2.834640	220	8.661400
.23	.009005	.73	.028740	23	.905510	73	2.874010	230	9.055100
.24	.009449	.74	.029134	24	.944880	74	2.913380	240	9.448800
.25	.009843	.75	.029528	25	.984250	75	2.952750	250	9.842600
.26	.010236	.76	.029921	26	1.023620	76	2.992120	260	10.236200
.27	.010630	.77	.030315	27	1.062990	77	3.031490	270	10.629900
.28	.011024	.78	.030709	28	1.102360	78	3.070860	280	11.032600
.29	.011417	.79	.031103	29	1.141730	79	3.110230	290	11.417300
.30	.011811	.80	.031496	30	1.181100	80	3.149600	300	11.811000
.31	.012205	.81	.031890	31	1.220470	81	3.188970	310	12.204700
.32	.012598	.82	.032283	32	1.259840	82	3.228340	320	12.598400
.33	.012992	.83	.032677	33	1.299210	83	3.267710	330	12.992100
.34	.013386	.84	.033071	34	1.338580	84	3.307080	340	13.385800
.35	.013780	.85	.033465	35	1.377949	85	3.346450	350	13.779500
.36	.014173	.86	.033858	36	1.417319	86	3.385820	360	14.173200
.37	.014567	.87	.034252	37	1.456689	87	3.425190	370	14.566900
.38	.014961	.88	.034646	38	1.496050	88	3.464560	380	14.960600
.39	.015354	.89	.035039	39	1.535430	89	3.503930	390	15.354300
.40	.015748	.90	.035433	40	1.574800	90	3.543300	400	15.748000
.41	.016142	.91	.035827	41	1.614170	91	3.582670	500	19.685000
.42	.016535	.92	.036220	42	1.653540	92	3.622040	600	23.622000
.43	.016929	.93	.036614	43	1.692910	93	3.661410	700	27.559000
.44	.017323	.94	.037008	44	1.732280	94	3.700780	800	31.496000
.45	.017717	.95	.037402	45	1.771650	95	3.740150	900	35.433000
.46	.018110	.96	.037795	46	1.811020	96	3.779520	1000	39.370000
.47	.018504	.97	.038189	47	1.850390	97	3.818890	2000	78.740000
.48	.018898	.98	.038583	48	1.889760	98	3.858260	3000	118.110000
.49	.019291	.99	.038976	49	1.929130	99	3.897630	4000	157.380000
.50	.019685	1 mm	.039370	50	1.968500	100	3.937000	5000	196.850000

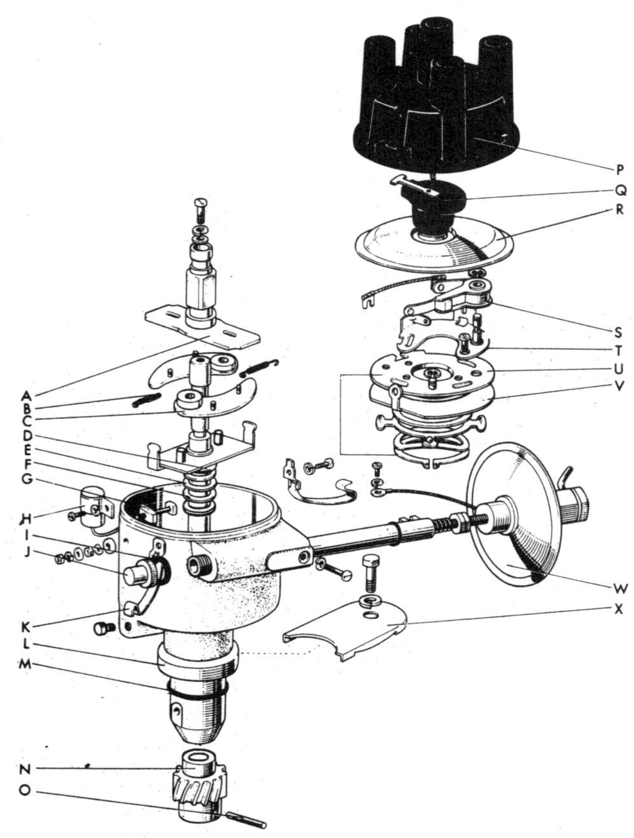

Fig.D.1. Exploded view of the ignition distributor.

A. Distributor cam
B. Flyweight spring
C. Flyweight
D. Washer
E. Bakelite washer
F. Adjusting shim
G. Terminal insulator
H. Condenser
I. Gasket washer
J. Adjusting cap
K. Spring clip for distributor cap
L. Distributor body
M. 'O' sealing ring
N. Distributor drive gear
O. Retaining pin for drive gear
P. Distributor cap
Q. Distributor rotor
R. Dust proof cover
S. Contact breaker arm
T. Fixed contact breaker
U. Contact breaker base plate
V. Stationary contact breaker plate
W. Vacuum unit
X. Distributor mounting clamp

Fig.D.2. Removal of the contact breaker set.

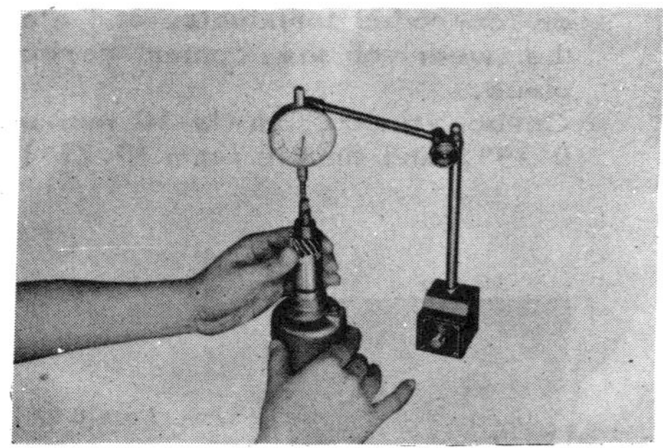

Fig.D.3. Checking the end clearance of the distributor shaft.

Fig.D.4. Checking the operating resistance between the two contact breaker plates.

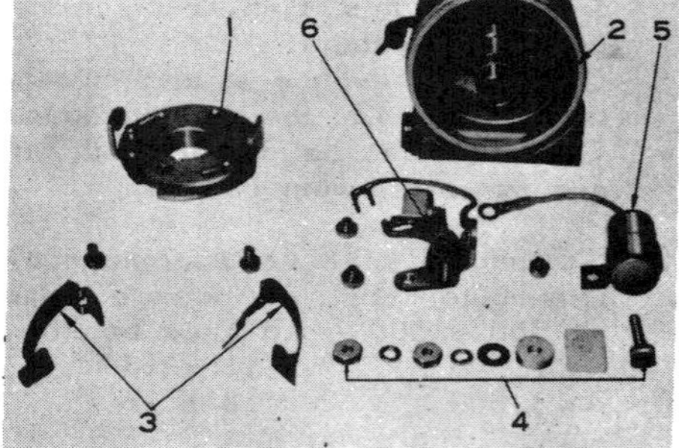

Fig.D.5. Exploded view of the ignition distributor.

1. Contact breaker plate
2. Distributor body
3. Spring clips
4. Terminal nut assembly
5. Condenser
6. Contact breaker points

Ignition System

DESCRIPTION

The battery ignition system consists of battery, leads, ignition coil, distributor with contact breaker and condensor, spark plugs and ignition switch. The current is taken from the battery which is charged by the alternator whilst the car is driven. In the case of poor engine performance, increased fuel consumption or abnormal overheating of the engine, test whether distributor, adjustment of ignition timing and the vacuum adjustment are in order.

THE IGNITION DISTRIBUTOR

The distributor has the purpose of supplying the ignition current in the correct order 1 - 3 - 4 - 2 and at the right moment (ignition timing) to the right spark plug. The distributor consists of the contact breaker set with condenser, centrifugal flyweight mechanism for spark advance according to the engine speed and the vacuum advance in accordance with the engine load.

DISTRIBUTOR — Removal

Disconnect the high tension cables from the spark plugs and the ignition coil and the primary lead from the distributor. Remove the vacuum pipe at the distributor connection. Remove the distributor cap.

Mark the distributor housing, the cylinder block and the rotor position as a guide for re-installation (if this is done, the crankshaft must not be turned before the distributor is refitted) and remove the distributor clamp. Withdraw the distributor from the cylinder block.

DISTRIBUTOR — Dismantling

Remove the rotor arm and the dust cover. Disconnect the vacuum advance unit wire and remove the snap ring that holds the diaphragm link to the contact breaker base plate. Remove the adjuster cap. Unscrew the vacuum unit retaining screws and withdraw the vacuum advance unit from the distributor body.

Disconnect the condenser lead at the terminal bolt, remove the bolt, the fixed contact securing screw and the condenser. Lift the fixed contact plate and the moveable contact arm from the distributor body (Fig.D.2). By removing the spring clip, lift out the breaker plate and the stationary plate. The cam can be detached from the distributor shaft after removing the securing screw from the centre of the shaft.

Mark one of the flyweight springs and the bracket associated with it and also one of the flyweights and the associated pivot pin. Remove the flyweight springs by unhooking them from their anchorage pins, using a pair of long-nosed pliers and remove the flyweights.

Release the drive gear from the distributor shaft by removing the roll pin, using a drift of suitable diameter and withdraw the distributor shaft from the housing. The dismantling of the distributor can be followed with reference to Fig.D.1.

DISTRIBUTOR — Inspection

Thoroughly clean all parts and inspect as follows:

Examine the distributor cap for cracks, carbon tracking and burnt or corroded terminals. The centre brush should be checked for wear. The brush should protrude at least 0.27 in. (7 mm). The normal protrusion of the brush is 0.39 in. (10 mm).

Inspect the rotor arm for damage or deterioration and the contact breaker points for pitting. Minor damage can be rectified by filing. Excessive wear will warrent replacement.

Check the distributor shaft for wear and fit in the body. The run-out of the shaft must not exceed 0.002 in. (0.05 mm). Check that the flyweights move freely on their pivot pin. Insert the shaft into the housing with all washers (the fibre washer is inserted between the metal washers) and secure the drive gear to the end of the shaft. Check that the end float of the shaft is between 0.006 - 0.197 in. (0.15 - 0.50 mm). This can be checked as shown in Fig.D.3 or it is possible to push the shaft as far as it will go towards the bottom of the distributor body and check the gap between body and drive gear with a feeler gauge. If necessary change the thickness of the metal washer (F in Fig.D.1) to correct the end float.

Check the force required to operate the breaker plate, holding the plate as shown in Fig.D.4 and using a spring scale. The resistance should not exceed 1.103 lb. (500 grams).

DISTRIBUTOR — Assembly

It is advisable to replace the contact breaker points and condenser every time the distributor is overhauled. To assemble the distributor, proceed as follows:

If the end float of the distributor shaft was found to be within the limits given, secure the retaining pin to the shaft and gear by peening over the pin end.

Re-assemble the flyweights and the flyweight springs in their marked position. Lightly oil the distributor shaft and fit the cam to the upper end of the shaft, using the retaining screw. Fill the groove in the upper part of the cam with grease. A dismantled view of the distributor is shown in Fig.D.5.

Fit the breaker plate (1, Fig.D.5) into the distributor body (2) and secure the plate with the spring clips (3) and the retaining screws. Fit the terminal post (4) and the insulation washers and connect the condenser lead to it. Fit the condenser in its correct position. Fit the contact breaker set (6) to the base plate (1) and tighten the securing screws. Coat the cam lobes lightly with lubricant.

Replace the vacuum advance unit, connect the operating link and wire and secure the retaining screws. Fit the washer and the adjusting cap.

Fit the rotor arm and check the centrifugal advance mechanism for freedom of movement by turning the rotor arm as far as it will go and releasing it. The drive gear must be held in one hand. The rotor arm should return to its original position. Also check

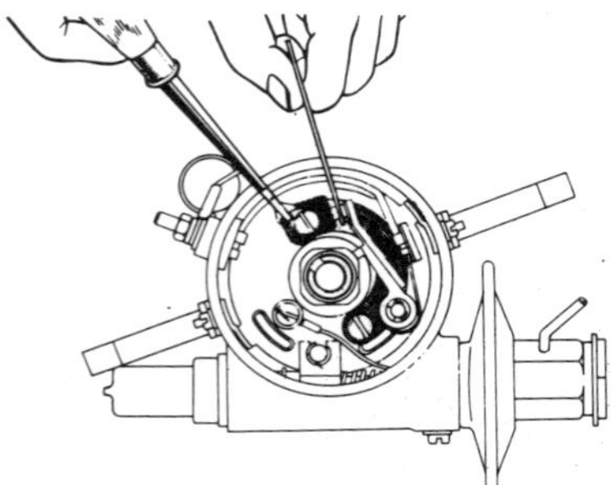

Fig.D.6. Adjusting the contact breaker gap.

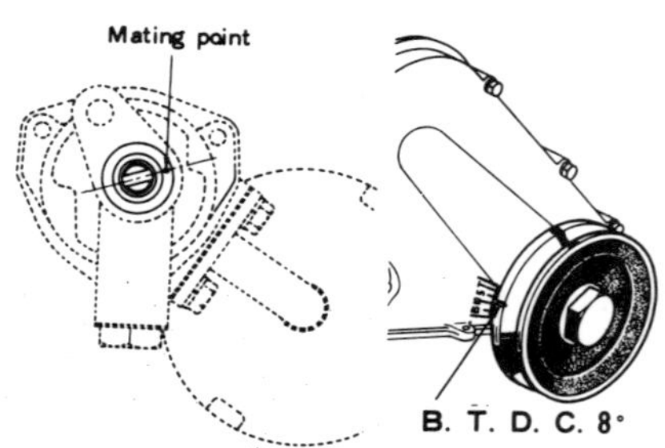

Fig.D.7. The position of the distributor driving slot in the oil pump (left) and the timing marks on the crankshaft pulley.

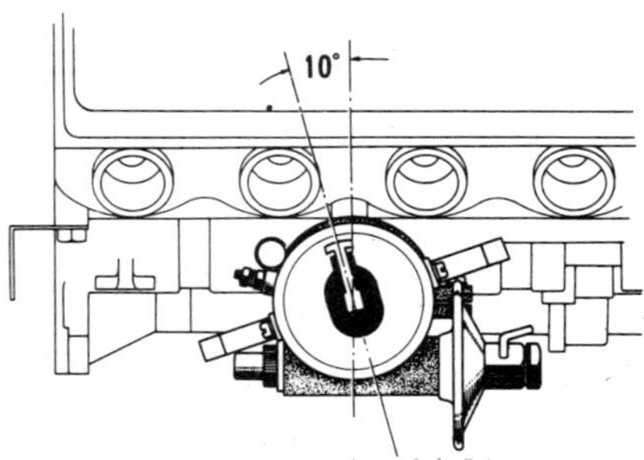

Fig.D.8. Position of the distributor rotor before installation of the distributor.

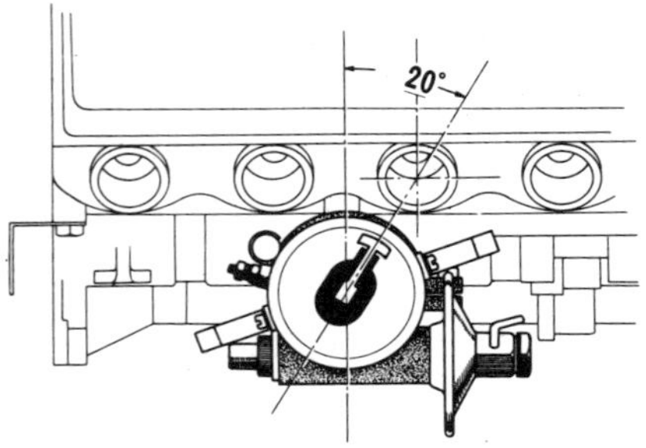

Fig.D.9. Position of the distributor rotor after installation of the distributor.

Fig.D.11. Dismantling of the vacuum retarder.

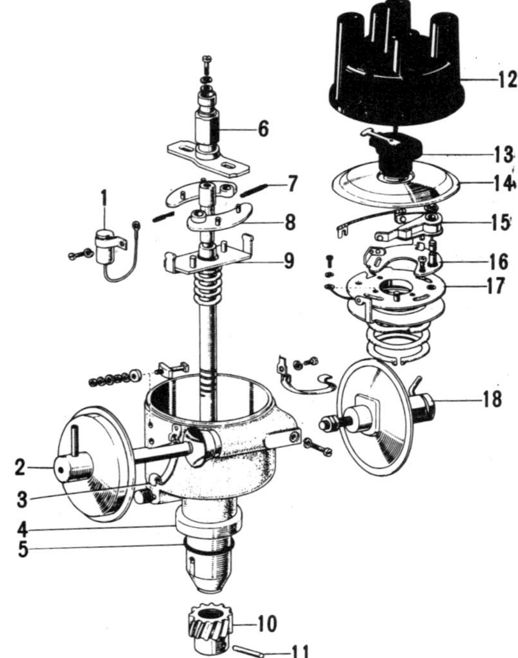

Fig.D.10. Exploded view of the distributor fitted to the K-C engine.

1. Condenser
2. Vacuum retarder
3. Spring clip
4. Distributor body
5. 'O' ring 6. Distributor cam
7. Flyweight spring
8. Flyweight
9. Flyweight shaft and plate
10. Drive gear
11. Retaining pin
12. Distributor cap
13. Rotor
14. Dust cover
15. Breaker contact
16. Breaker plate
17. Stationary plate
18. Vaccum advance unit

the vacuum advance mechanism, by moving the advance setting control. Finally fit the dust cover and the distributor cap.

DISTRIBUTOR — Adjustments and Tests

Contact Breaker Gap

Rotate the cam until the heel of the moveable contact is in its highest position on one of the cam lobes and adjust the contact gap, using a feeler gauge, to 0.016 - 0.020 in. (0.4 - 0.5 mm). To adjust the gap, slacken the contact plate retaining screw, insert the blade of a screwdriver into the slot of the breaker plate and turning the screwdriver in the required direction.The feeler gauge between the contacts must show a slight drag when withdrawn. The thickness of the feeler gauge, however, should not separate the contacts when inserted. Finally tighten the locking screw. (Fig.D.6).

Contact Breaker Arm Spring Tension

Check the contact breaker arm spring tension with a spring balance by pulling at right angles to the breaker arm point. The tension should be 18 - 24 ozs. (0.51 - 0.60 kg) when the points begin to open. If this is not the case, replace the contact breaker set.

Condenser

Check the correct capacity, the series resistance and the low insulation resistance of the condenser on a suitable test bench. If in doubt, replace the condenser. The capacity of the condenser is between 0.20 - 0.24 mfd.

Cam Dwell Angle

The cam dwell angle can only be tested on a distributor test bench. The angle should be between 50 and 54° and is adjusted by varying the point gap. The dwell angle increases when the gap is reduced.

Centrifugal Advance

The correct operation of the centrifugal advance mechanism can be checked on a distributor test bench. A visual inspection of the mechanical operation should suffice for normal means. Move the cam in the direction of rotation and release it in the end position. It must return to its original position through the action of the two springs.

If a distributor test bench is used, run the distributor at the various speeds given for the mechanical advance and compare the values obtained with the figures in section "Engine Tuning Data". If necessary, replace the flyweight springs to obtain the correct values.

Vacuum Advance

The correct operation of the vacuum advance mechanism can be checked on a distributor test bench. Check the values in accordance with the figures given in section "Engine Tuning Data" in this manual.

Ignition timing

If the crankshaft has not been rotated, align the various components with the markings made on removal and insert the distributor. Fit the distributor clamp and the cap.

If the position of the crankshaft is uncertain, proceed as follows and re-adjust the ignition timing: Turn the crankshaft until No.1 cylinder is at T.D.C. compression stroke. Align the 8° B.T.D.C. graduation on the timing chain cover with the 'V'

shaped groove in the crankshaft pulley (Fig.D.7).

Align the oil pump shaft slot with the mating slot in the oil pump body and set the octane selector to the normal position. The rotor should face in the direction shown in Fig.D.8. Insert the distributor into the cylinder block and observe that the rotor arm rotates to turn in the position shown in Fig.D.9. Check that the oil pump shaft has engaged properly with the distributor shaft.

Turn the distributor body until the contact breaker points begin to open. Fit the distributor clamp and the retaining screw.

The alignment of the 'V' groove in the crankshaft pulley with the 8° graduation on the timing chain cover can be checked with a stroboscopic lamp with the engine running at 600 rpm.

NOTE: The 8° setting applies to the standard K-Engine only. The setting for the K-B Engine is 10° B.T.D.C. and the setting for the K-C engine is 5° A.T.D.C. at 600 rpm. The setting for all 1200 c.c. engines is 8° B.T.D.C. at 6000 rpm.

IGNITION COIL

The ignition coil is readily removed or refitted by unscrewing (or refitting) the securing bolt. Check the primary resistance with a suitable tester. The correct value is 3.6 ohms. The secondary resistance is 7,500 ohms. The insulation resistance of the primary terminal should exceed 10 megaohms to the case.

When the engine is idling, remove the high tension wire from the spark plug. Hold it about 1/4 in. (6 mm) from a good earthing point on the cylinder head. A strong spark should be visible. If this is not the case, the ignition coil must be replaced, assuming that the condenser is in good condition.

SPARK PLUGS — Removal, Inspection and Installation

Remove the spark plug cables from the plug ends and unscrew the spark plugs, using the spark plug wrench.

Check the spark plugs for cracks and chips on the insulators and check the electrodes for wear. If the carbon deposit is excessive, this is an indication of burning engine oil, so install a hotter plug. If the plug faces are excessively white or rapid electrode wear is noted, fit a colder spark plug.

Clean the plugs with a sand blaster and adjust the electrode gaps to 0.027 - 0.031 in. (0.7 - 0.8 mm), by bending the side electrode.

When refitting the spark plugs take care not to damage the thread in the cylinder head. (Aluminium alloy).

TESTING THE IGNITION CIRCUIT

Before testing the ignition circuit with a 0 - 20 volt voltmeter, check that the battery is in a fully charged state. Then proceed as follows in the order given:

Wiring - Ignition switch to coil

Connect the voltmeter between the cable connected to the positive terminal of the ignition coil and a good earthing point.

Switch on the ignition and note the voltmeter reading. A voltmeter reading of approx. battery voltage indicates that the wiring between the ignition switch and the coil is in good order. No voltmeter reading indicates an open circuit. A reading between "0" and battery voltage indicates a voltage drop somewhere in the wiring (loose connection).

Coil primary winding

Disconnect the cable from the coil and connect the voltmeter between the terminal and a good earthing point. Switch on the ignition and note the voltmeter reading. A voltmeter reading of approx. the battery voltage indicates a good primary winding. No reading indicates an open circuit in the winding.

Distributor contacts, L.T. wiring and earth

With the original connections restored to the coil, connect the voltmeter between the coil terminal and a good earthing point. Remove the distributor cap. Switch on the ignition and whilst observing the voltmeter reading, open the contact breakers. With the points open a voltmeter reading of approx. the battery voltage should be registered, indicating that the low tension wiring, earth connection and the contacts are in satisfactory condition. If no reading is registered when the points are closed check the distributor for good earth connection and check the L.T. cable between distributor and coil for continuity. Check the condenser by fitting a condenser, known to be in good condition.

Coil secondary winding and condenser

Withdraw the high tension cable from the distributor cap and remove the cap. With the ignition switched on, hold the lead 1/4 in. (6 mm) away from the cylinder head and "snap" the points open. A spark should occur with each "snap" between the cable end and the cylinder head. A weak spark or no spark could be caused by a faulty condenser.

Rotor arm insulation

Switch on the ignition and hold the high tension lead 1/8 in. (3 mm) away from the rotor electrode. "Snap" the points open. If no spark occurs the rotor arm insulation is satisfactory. If a spark occurs, the rotor arm must be replaced.

VACUUM ADVANCER AND VACUUM RETARDER
(K-C Engine)

The K-C engine is fitted with a vacuum advancer and vacuum retarder to comply with the regulations of certain countries. To dismantle the units, remove the cap, rotor and dust cover, remove the advancer retaining screw and remove the advance unit from the distributor body. The nuts at the end of the advance unit must not be removed.

Remove the snap ring from the pivot pin and disconnect the retarder rod. Withdraw the retarder from the distributor body.

When refitting the advance unit, screw in the advance unit fully and then unscrew it until the lock holes make the first alignment. As it is rather difficult to spring the distributor cap in position, great care is required when pressing the clips home with a suitable tool in order not to distort the retarder.

Technical Data

	K-Engine	K-B Engine	K-C Engine
Condenser cap.	0.20 - 0.24 mfd.	Same	Same
Breaker point pressure	510 - 690 grams (18 - 24 ozs.)	Same	Same
Breaker point gap	0.4 - 0.5 mm (0.016-0.020 in.)	Same	Same
Cam dwell angle	50 - 54°	Same	Same
Vacuum adv.	See under ENGINE TUNING DATA in this manual		
Centrif. adv.	See under ENGINE TUNING DATA in this manual		
Vacuum retarder: Starts			100-140 mm Hg. (3.94-5.51 in. Hg)
5.5 - 7.5° (max.)			200-290 mm Hg (9.84-11.42 in.Hg)

IGNITION COIL

Primary voltage . . . . 12 volts
Secondary voltage:
The sparking distance from the centre to the negative electrodes should be more than 8 mm (0.315 in.) at a distributor speed of 1,500 rpm. with 8 volts applied. The same distance should be more than 6 mm (0.236 in.) at 3,000 rpm with 12 volts applied.

Primary resistance . . . . 3.6 ohms
Secondary resistance .7,500 ohms

Trouble Shooting

SYMPTOMS	PROBABLE CAUSE	ACTION TO BE TAKEN
Starter turns, but engine will not start	Weak battery Excessive moisture on spark plugs or high tension wires Cracked or leaky distributor cap or rotor Broken wire in primary circuit Burned or improperly adjusted points Defective condenser	Recharge battery Remove moisture and dry Replace cap or rotor Repair or replace wire Adjust or replace points Replace condenser
Difficult starting	Defective spark plugs Defective breaker points Loose connection in primary circuit Defective condenser Defective ignition coil Defective rotor or distributor cap	Clean, adjust or replace plugs Replace breaker points Tighten or repair Replace condenser Replace ignition coil Replace cap or rotor
Engine misfires	Dirty or faulty spark plugs Loose ignition wire or faulty insulation Cracked distributor cap Breaker points not correctly adjusted	Clean, adjust or replace plugs Tighten, repair or replace wires Replace cap Adjust breaker points
Ignition circuit interrupted and voltage drop in primary circuit	Burnt or incorrectly adjusted contact breaker gap Defective leads, loose or dirty connections Ignition switch defective Ignition coil defective	Adjust contact breaker gap Check leads, clean connections Check or replace switch Check or replace ignition coil
Secondary circuit interrupted and no current	Spark plugs wet, worn or incorrect gap Defective condenser Defective or broken ignition cable Tracking between coil, distributor cap and rotor Defective ignition coil	Clean and adjust or replace plugs Replace condenser Replace ignition cable Clean and check parts or replace Check or replace coil

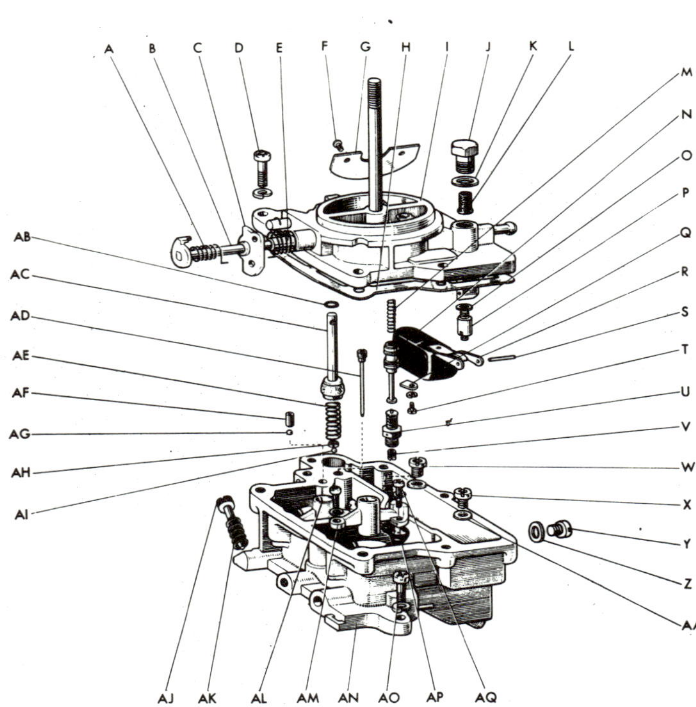

Fig.E.1. Exploded view of the carburettor (upper body half).

A. Choke valve relief spring
B. Choke valve shaft
C. Choke valve lever
D. Screw
E. Choke valve return spring
F. Screw
G. Choke valve
H. Top cover gasket
I. Top cover
J. Main passage plug
K. Inlet gauze filter gasket
L. Inlet gauze filter
M. Power piston spring
N. Power piston
O. Needle valve seat gasket
P. Float needle valve
Q. Power piston stop plate
R. Float
S. Float lever pivot pin
T. Screw
U. Power valve
V. Power jet
W. Primary main jet
X. Secondary main jet
Y. Drain plug
Z. Gasket
AA. Main jet gasket
AB. 'O' sealing ring
AC. Pump plunger
AD. Slow-running jet
AE. Pump damping spring
AF. Pump discharge weight
AG. Check ball
AH. Check ball retainer
AI. Check ball
AJ. Throttle valve adjusting screw
AK. Spring
AL. Primary small venturi
AM. Secondary small venturi
AN. Main body
AO. Screw
AP. Gasket
AQ. Screw

Fig.E.1a. Exploded view of throttle valve body and linkages.

A. Pump linkage spring
B. Connecting link
C. High speed valve shaft
D. Fast idle connecting link
E. Pump lever securing screw
F. Pump operating lever
G. Pump connecting link
H. Retaining clip
I. Shim
J. High speed valve
K. Screw
L. Slow-running adjusting screw
M. Spring
N. Retaining clip
O. Shim
P. Body flange gasket
Q. Throttle valve body
R. High speed valve stop lever
S. Spring
T. Screw
U. Fast idle lever
V. Screw
W. Snap ring
X. Throttle arm
Y. Throttle valve link
Z. Primary throttle valve shaft
AA. Secondary throttle valve shaft
AB. Throttle valve return spring
AC. Screw
AD. Primary throttle valve plate
AE. Screw
AF. Secondary throttle valve plate
AG. Screw
AH. Screw

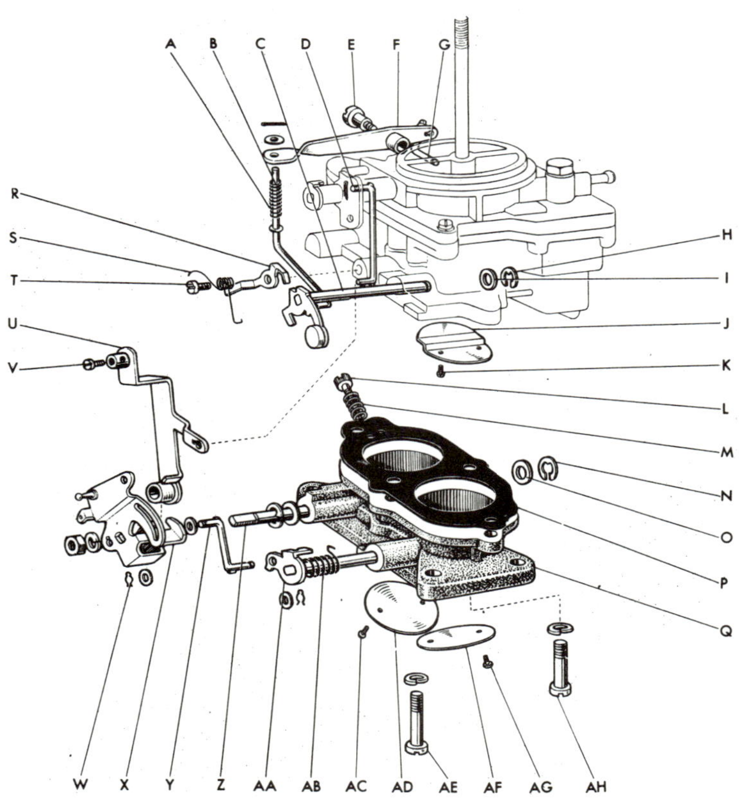

Fuel System

DESCRIPTION

The fuel system consists of carburettor, fuel pump, fuel filter, fuel tank, fuel lines, accelerator control cable and the air cleaner. The fuel tank is installed in the luggage compartment from where the fuel is sucked by means of the fuel pump through the fuel pipes into the fuel filter and from there into the carburettor, where it is mixed with the incoming air to form the fuel-air mixture needed for the combustion.

CARBURETTOR — Removal

When carrying out service repairs on the carburettor, it is recommended that the special screwdriver set 09860-00010 is used which comprises all necessary tools. To remove the carburettor, proceed as follows:

Remove the air cleaner, disconnect the fuel and vacuum pipes from the carburettor connections, and detach the accelerator and choke control cables from the carburettor. Remove the carburettor securing nuts and lift off the carburettor. It is wise to place a clean cloth over the manifold opening to prevent dust or dirt or other foreign matter from entering the engine.

CARBURETTOR — Dismantling

Disconnect the fast idle connector and the pump lever connecting link (1) in Fig.E.3. Unscrew the pump lever securing screw (3) and remove the pump lever (2) and the pump connecting link (4).

Loosen and remove the six securing screws for the carburettor cover and lift off the cover together with the gasket. Take care not to damage the float. Remove the pump plunger and the damping spring. Invert the carburettor main body over the palm of the hand and shake out the pump discharge weight and the check ball (AF, AG, Fig.E.1). Remove the four screws, securing the throttle valve body to the main body and separate the two parts. The carburettor should now be dismantled to the three parts shown in Fig.E.5. Further dismantling is carried out as follows, giving details for every sub-assembly of the carburettor, to facilitate the repair of one particular carburettor part, if this is needed:

Carburettor Cover

With reference to Fig.E.6 remove the float lever spindle (1) and the float (2). Take out the needle valve (3) with the push pin and the spring and unscrew the float needle valve seat (4). Remove the seat gasket.

With reference to Fig.E.7 remove the power piston stopper (1) by removing the retaining screw. Take out the power piston (2) and the springs (3). Remove the main passage plug (J in Fig.E.1) and the strainer (L).

Main Body

With reference to Fig.E.1 remove the primary small venturi (AL) together with the gasket by unscrewing the securing screws and also remove the secondary small venturi (AM). Remove the check ball retainer, invert the carburettor over the palm of the hand and shake out the check ball (AI).

Remove the slow-running jet (AD) (the exact location of which is also shown in Fig.E.8), taking care not to damage the thread of the jet and the slot. Then remove the primary (W) and secondary (X) main jets and gaskets and unscrew the drain plug with the gasket (Y & Z). Unscrew the power valve (U) with the special spanner included in the repair tool set and remove the jet (V) from the power valve. This operation is also shown in Fig.E.9.

Throttle Valve Body

At the moment it is only necessary to unscrew the idle adjusting screw with the spring from the throttle valve body. Any further dismantling (of throttle valves and throttle valve shafts) should be carried out after the various parts have been checked as described below.

CARBURETTOR — Inspection and Repair

Before any repairs are carried out on the carburettor, it should be considered if it is more economical to fit a replacement carburettor. Otherwise proceed as follows:

General

Clean all parts of the carburettor in petrol (gasoline), using a soft brush. Clean out the passage ways with compressed air. Jets must not be cleaned with wire.

Carburettor Cover

Assumed that the carburettor cover is free of cracks, nicks or burrs, check the operation of the power piston by blowing and sucking on the tube fitted in the air hole in the centre of the carburettor, using a suitable length of tube. (Fig.E.11). The piston should move smoothly without showing any signs of air leaks.

Check for damage and replace parts if necessary, float, float tab, lever pin bore, 'O' ring, needle valve and seating and strainer. The choke valve should be checked for smooth movement and excessive play. If replacement is necessary file off the rivetted screw ends and remove the valve (A) from the choke valve shaft (B) (Fig.E.13), return spring (C) and the relief valve (D). When checking the choke valve for excessive play in the bores, make sure to check in all directions indicated by the arrow heads in Fig.E.12. The assembly of the choke valve is carried out in reverse order to the removal procedure. Lubricate the sliding portions of the choke valve shaft with grease and adjust the valve position so that it will close correctly. Tighten the securing screws and slightly rivet the screw ends to secure the screws in position.

Main Body

Check all parts for wear, free operation of the power valve (by blowing and sucking), pump plunger for wear, defective leather and weak spring. The smooth movement of the high speed valve and the high speed valve shaft should be checked. If the latter requires replacement, file off the rivetted parts of the securing screws and remove the high speed valve (A) from the high speed shaft (B), remove the retaining ring (C) and withdraw the shaft (Fig.E.14). The assembly is carried out in reverse order. Use

Fig.E.2. Removal of the carburettor.

Fig.E.3. Removal of the connecting links.

1. Pump lever connecting link   3. Lever securing screw
2. Pump operating lever   4. Pump connecting link

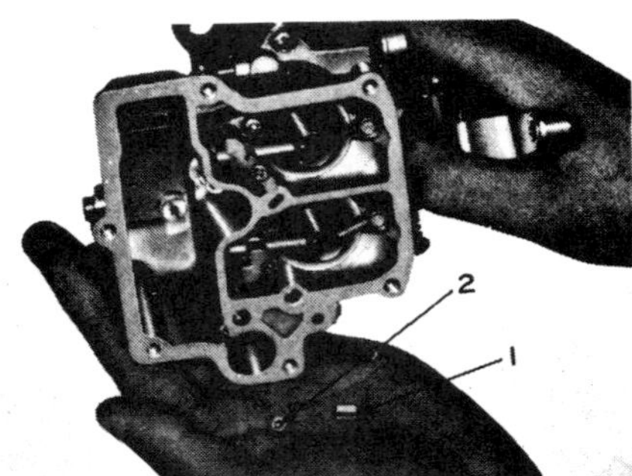

Fig.E.4. Tilt the carburettor as shown to remove the discharge weight (1) and the check ball (2).

Fig.E.5. The carburettor dismantled to show the three carburettor main sections. Left — throttle valve body, Centre — Main body, — Right — Cover.

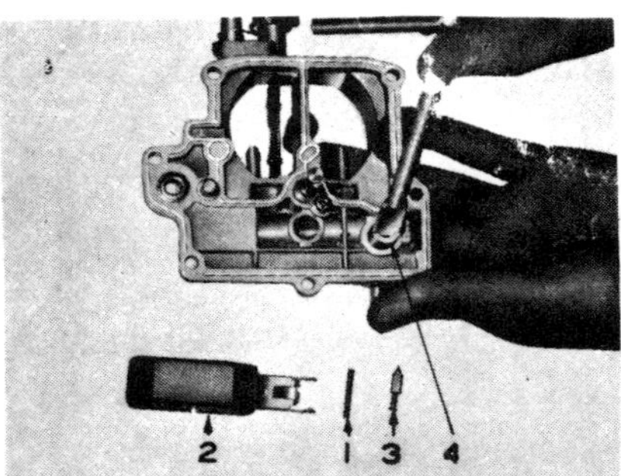

Fig.E.6. Removal of float and float needle valve.

1. Float pivot pin 3. Float needle valve
2. Float   4. Float needle valve seat

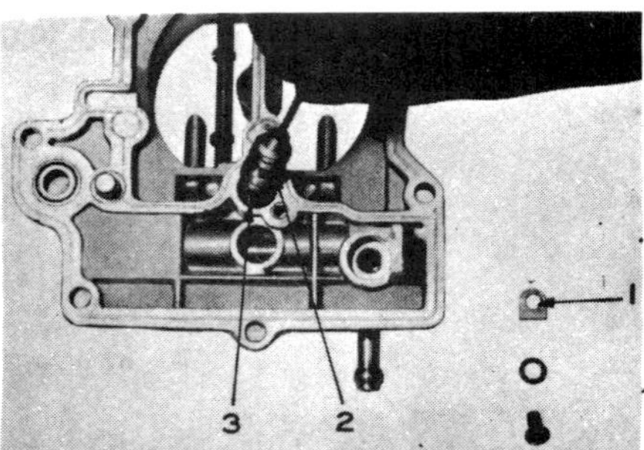

Fig.E.7. The removal of the power piston.

1. Piston stop plate
2. Power piston
3. Spring

Fig.E.8. Removal of the slow-running jet (1).

Fig.E.9. Removal of the power valve.

1. Primary main jet   3. Drain plug
2. Secondary main jet 4. Special wrench for power jet

Fig.E.10. Removal of the slow-running adjusting screw.

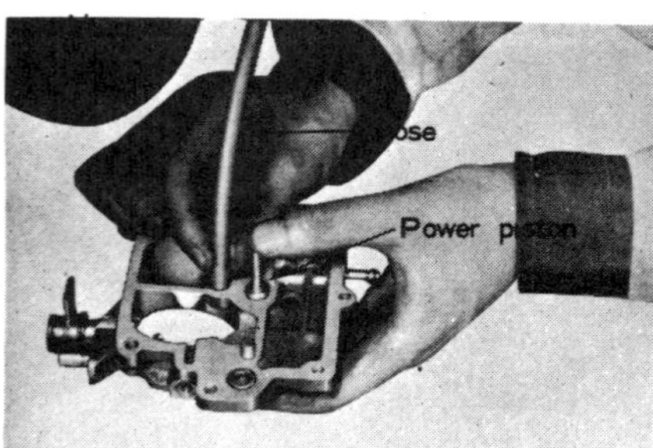

Fig.E.11. Checking the operation of the power piston.

Fig.E.12. Checking the operation of the choke valve shaft. Move the shaft in the direction of the arrow heads to check for excessive clearance.

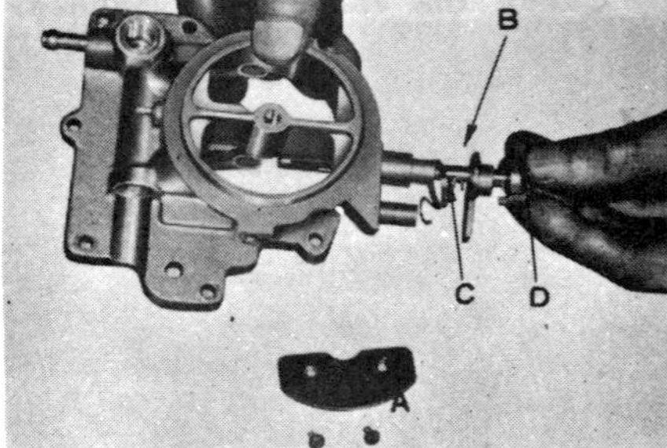

Fig.E.13. Removal of the choke valve shaft.

A. Choke valve plate
B. Choke valve shaft
C. Choke valve return spring
D. Choke relief spring

Fig.E.14. Removal of the high speed valve shaft.

A. High speed valve plate
B. High speed valve shaft
C. Retaining clip

Fig.E.15. Checking the throttle valve shaft. Move the shaft in the direction of the arrow heads, to check for excessive clearance.

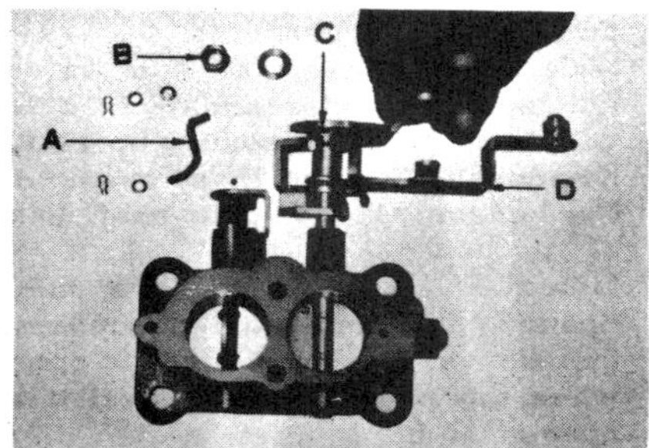

Fig.E.16. Removal of the throttle valve shaft.

A. Throttle valve link *C. Primary throttle shaft arm*
B. Securing nut *D. Fast idle lever*

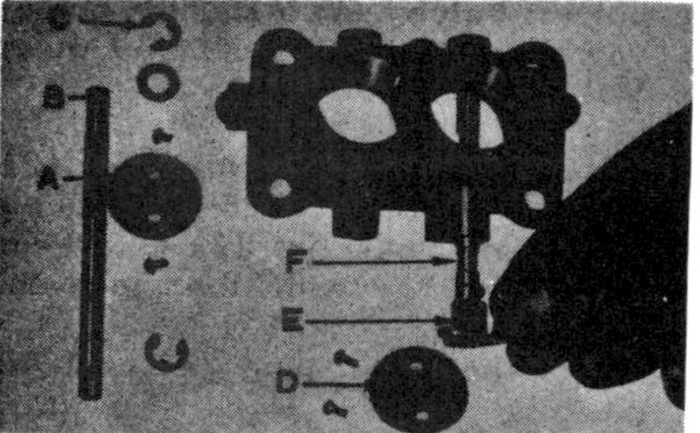

Fig.E.17. Removal of the secondary throttle valve plate.

A. Primary throttle valve plate *D. Secondary throttle valve plate*
B. Primary throttle valve shaft *E. Throttle valve return spring*
C. Retaining clip *F. Secondary throttle valve shaft*

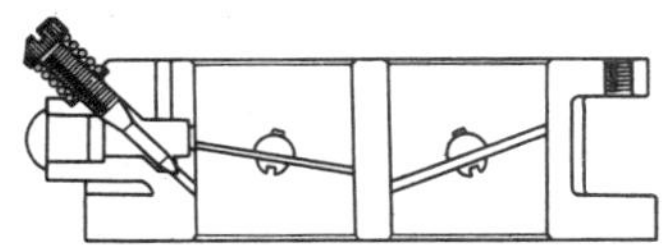

Fig.E.18. The correct assembly of the throttle valve shafts.

Fig.E.19. The correct closed position of the two throttle valve plates.

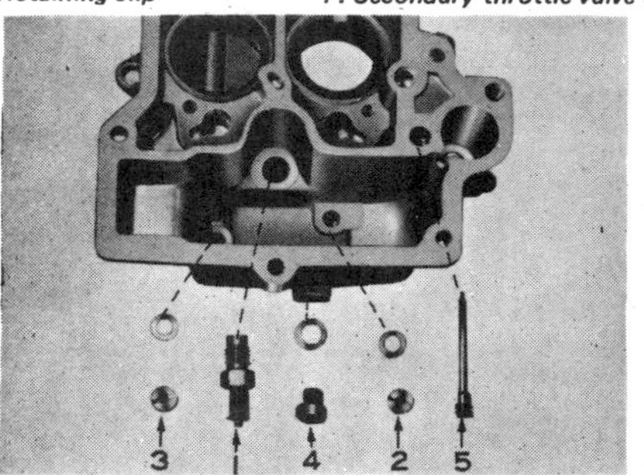

Fig.E.20. The location of the carburettor jets.

1. Power valve *4. Carburettor drain plug*
2. Primary main jet *5. Slow-running jet*
3. Seondary main jet

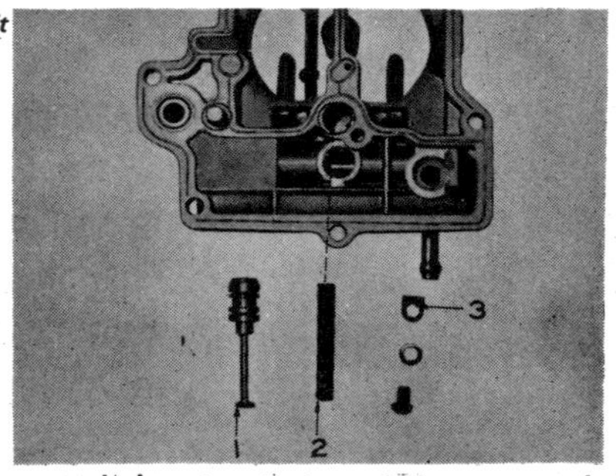

Fig.E.21. The installation of the power valve components.

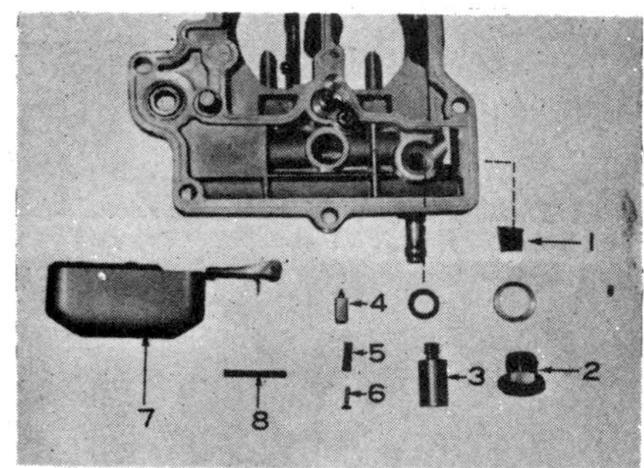

Fig.E.22. The installation of the float and float needle valve components.

1. Fuel strainer *5. Spring*
2. Main passage plug *6. Pin*
3. Valve needle seat *7. Float*
4. Float needle valve *8. Float pivot pin*

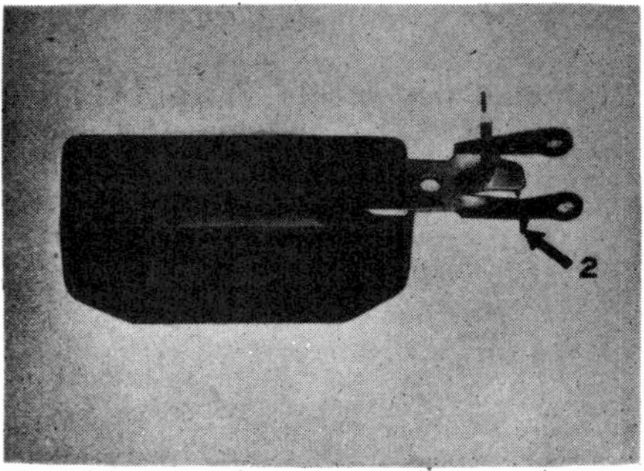

Fig.E.23. Bed the tab (1) of the float to adjust the fuel level in the raised position and the tab (2) in the lowered position.

Fig.E.24. Checking the float position (fuel level) in the raised position.

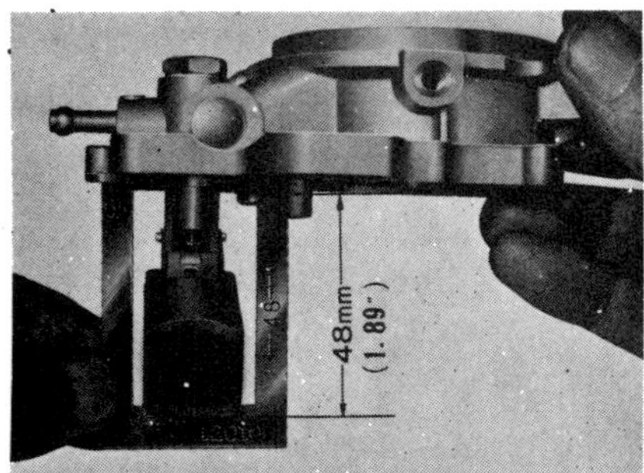

Fig.E.25. Checking the float position (fuel level) in the lowered position.

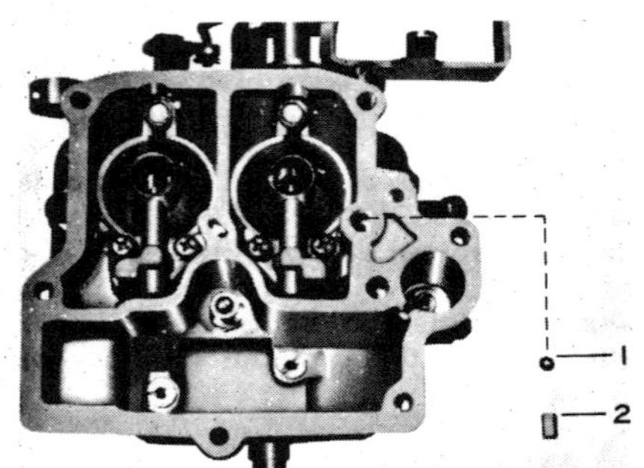

Fig.E.26. The location of the check ball (1) and the discharge weight (2).

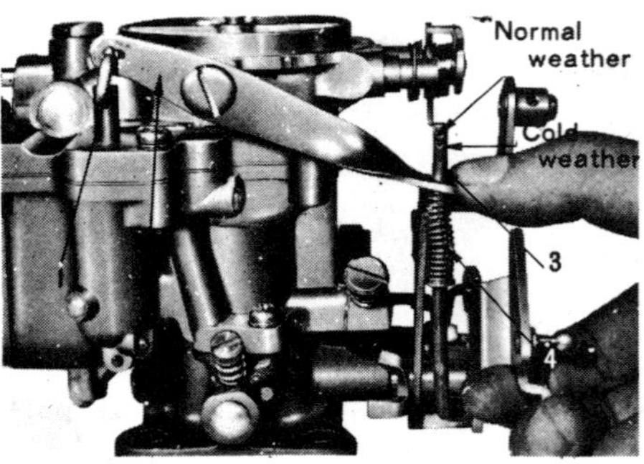

Fig.E.27. Assembly of the pump operating linkage assembly.

1. Pump connecting link
2. Pump operating lever
3. Connecting link
4. Pump lever spring

Fig.E.28. Adjustment of the secondary throttle stop lever. A clearance of 0.5 mm (0.02 in.) should be obtained between high speed valve shaft arm (1) and stop lever (2).

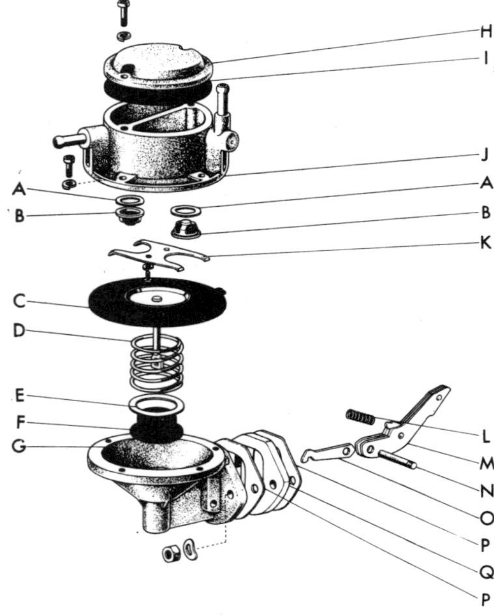

Fig.E.30. Exploded view of the fuel pump.

A.   Valve gasket
B.   Valve
C.   Pump diaphragm
D.   Diaphragm spring
E.   Oil seal retainer
F.   Oil seal
G.   Lower pump body half
H.   Pump body cover
I.   Cover gasket
J.   Upper pump body half
K.   Valve retainer
L.   Rocker arm spring
M.   Rocker arm
N.   Rocker arm pivot pin
O.   Rocker arm link
P.   Fuel pump gasket
Q.   Fuel pump insulating flanges,

Fig.E.29. Adjustment of the fast idle setting by inserting a 1.0 mm (0.04 in.) drill. Bend the tab (1) to correct the setting.

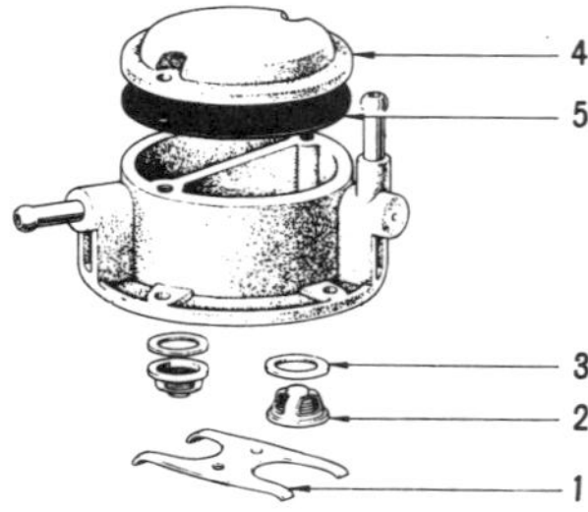

Fig.E.31. Exploded view of the upper pump body half.

1. Valve retainer
2. Valves
3. Valve gasket
4. Pump cover
5. Pump cover gasket

shims on one or both sides of the high speed valve shaft to limit excessive play. Shims are available in thicknesses of 0.0039 in. (0.1 mm) (Part No. 21681-21060) and 0.0079 in. (0.2 mm) (Part No. 21682-21060). The high speed valve is adjusted so that it cannot touch the main body bore and should operate smoothly without binding. Finally tighten the securing screws and slightly rivet the screw ends.

Throttle Valve Body

Check the parts for damage, weak springs and throttle valve operation. When checking the play of the throttle valve shafts, move the shafts as indicated by the arrow heads in Fig.E.15. End float in the direction of the shaft axis can be taken up with shims. The throttle valve shafts can be replaced if necessary. To dismantle proceed as follows:

Disconnect the shaft link (A) in Fig.E.16, unscrew the lever retaining nut (B) and remove the primary shaft arm (C) and the fast idle lever (D). File off the rivetted ends of the screws and remove the securing screws for the primary throttle valve from the corresponding shaft. With reference to Fig.E.17 remove the securing clip (C) and extract the primary valve shaft (B). The secondary throttle valve shaft is removed in the same way.

To assemble the throttle valves reverse the dismantling procedure. Select shims to obtain the correct shaft play. Shims are available in three thicknesses of 0.004, 0.008 and 0.012 in. (0.1, 0.2 and 0.3 mm). The thinner valve plate is fitted to the primary side. Adjust both throttle valve plates to close completely in the fully closed position and then rivet the securing screw ends. Fig.E.18 shows the correct location of shims and securing clip. Fig.E.19 shows the correct adjustment of both valves.

CARBURETTOR — Assembly

Use new gaskets and packings on assembly. Check that all fuel passages are clear. Lightly grease all moving parts and check for smooth operation at all stages of assembly.

Throttle Valve Body

Fit the adjusting screw and the spring and turn the screw gently until it is felt to be seating and then turn back by 2 1/2 turns.

If necessary, bend the throttle shaft link until the secondary throttle valve plate is fully open at the same time as the primary valve. When the throttle valves are correctly adjusted, the primary valve should be open by 60° when the secondary valve begins to open.

Main Body

Fit the following parts in this order: The power jet to the power valve (Fig.E.20) and the whole assembly to the main body, using the special wrench. Install the primary main jet (1.08 mm) and the secondary main jet (1.75 mm) together with the gaskets and the drain plug with the gasket. Then refit the slow-running jet, primary small ventury and gasket, secondary small venturi and gasket.

The check balls and the retainers are fitted to the pump cylinder. The ball on the inlet side is the smaller one.

Carburettor Cover

With reference to Fig.E.21 fit the power piston and the spring and retain the parts with the power piston stop. Install the strainer (1) and the main passage plug (2) in Fig.E.22 to the carburettor cover, followed by the needle valve seat and gasket (3). Fit the needle valve (4), compression spring (5) and the pin (6) into the needle valve seat and insert the float (7), securing it with the float spindle (8).

The float is adjusted to suit float level gauge 09240-22010 (09240-22011 for later cars) by bending the tabs on the lever (Fig.E.23) so that in the raised position the gap between the end of the float and the carburettor cover is 0.256 in. (6.5 mm). To correct the setting, adjust tab No.1 in Fig.E.23. The gauge is inserted as shown in Fig.E.24. The tab No.2 is adjusted so that the lower side of the float is in contact with the gauge as shown in Fig.E.25.

Fit the throttle valve body and the gasket to the main body. One of the four securing screws is drilled and MUST be inserted on the float chamber side. The drilled hole is a vacuum passage.

Fit the check ball and the discharge weight in the locations shown in Fig.E.26 and the pump damping spring and the plunger to the pump body.

Assemble the carburettor cover with gasket to the main body. Now fit pump connecting link, pump lever, connecting link and pump lever spring to the carburettor (Fig.E.27). The pump stroke is controlled by the position of the connecting link in the lever. The upper hole is for normal and the lower hole for cold weather. Fit the fast idle lever connection.

Adjust the stop for the secondary throttle valve to give a clearance of 0.02 in. (0.5 mm) between the high speed shaft arm and the stop lever. (Fig.E.28). Set the gap between the primary throttle valve edge and the barrel bore to 0.04 in. (1 mm), using a drill bit of suitable diameter by bending the fast idle lever (Fig.E.29). The choke valve should be fully closed in this position.

CARBURETTOR — Installation

Reverse the removal procedure. Check that the primary throttle valve opens fully when the accelerator pedal is depressed to the floor panel. Adjust the slow-running speed with the engine fully warmed up as described below.

Slow-running adjustment

Remove the plug from the inlet manifold and connect a vacuum gauge. Connect a revolution counter to the ignition coil. Start the engine.

Turn the throttle valve stop screw in or out until the engine operates smoothly without stalling at the lowest possible speed. Turn the slow-running adjusting screw to obtain the highest steady vacuum at idle speed. Then turn the slow-running volume screw and the throttle stop screw to obtain a steady and high vacuum with the engine running smoothly at idling speed. When the idling speed is 600 rpm. the vacuum reading should be more than 430 mm Hg. (17 in.Hg.).

FUEL PUMP — Removal

Disconnect the fuel hoses, remove the securing bolts and lift off the fuel pump.

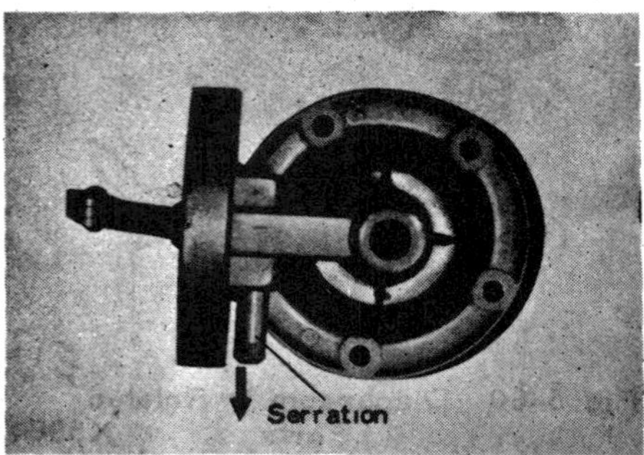

Fig.E.32. Drive out the rocker arm pivot pin in the direction of the arrow. Insert the pin with the plain end first.

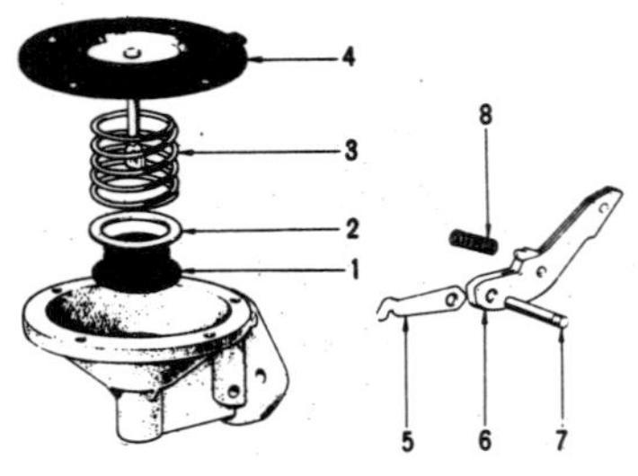

Fig.E.33. Exploded view of the lower pump body half.

1. *Oil seal*
2. *Oil seal retainer*
3. *Diaphragm spring*
4. *Pump diaphragm*
5. *Rocker arm link*
6. *Rocker arm*
7. *Pivot pin*
8. *Rocker arm spring*

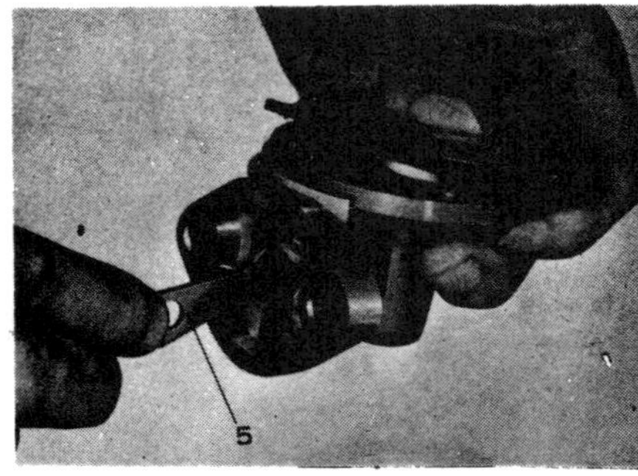

Fig.E.34. Insert the rocker arm link (5) in the position shown.

Fig.E.35. The correct installation of the pump valves.

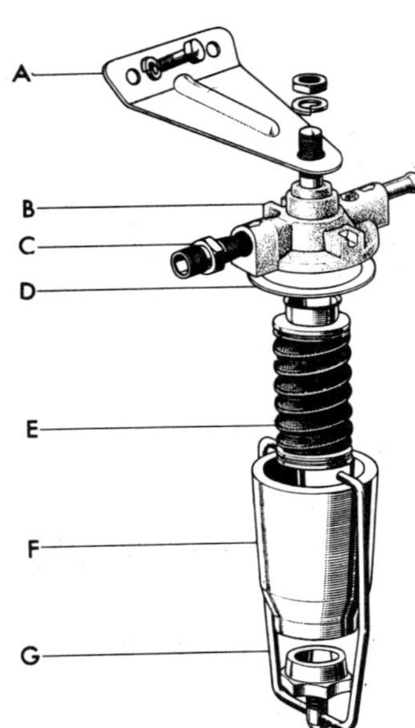

Fig.E.36. Exploded view of the fuel filter.

A. *Fuel filter bracket*
B. *Fuel filter head*
C. *Union connector*
D. *Filter bowl gasket*
E. *Filter element*
F. *Filter bowl*
G. *Retaining clamp*

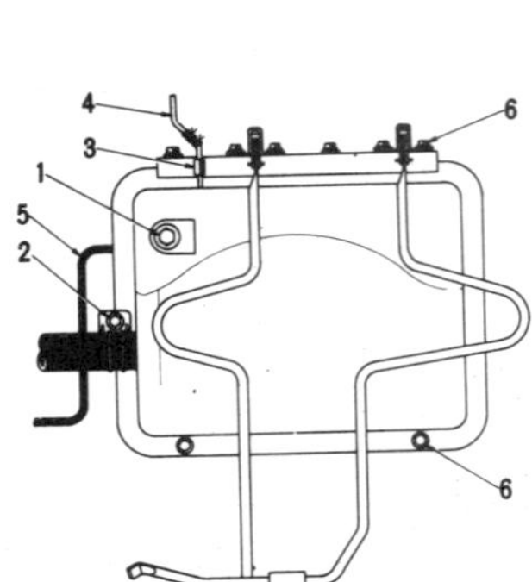

Fig.E.37. Removal of the fuel tank on Saloon Models.

Fig.E.38. Removal of the fuel tank on Estate Car Models.

Fig.E.39. Removal of the ASS unit.

1. *Inlet pipe*
2. *Connecting hose*
3. *Securing screws*

FUEL PUMP — Dismantling

·An exploded view of the fuel pump is shown in Fig.E.30. Remove the upper part of the body from the lower part, having removed the securing screws. Remove the valve retainer, valves and gasket washers and the pump cover with gasket from the upper pump half. (Fig.E.31).

Using a suitable drift, drive out the rocker arm pin in the direction of the serration (Fig.E.32) and remove the rocker arm and the spring. Press down the diaphragm into the body and unhook the rocker arm link from the diaphragm pull-rod. Remove the oil seal, packing retainer, diaphragm and spring. (Fig.E.33).

All parts should be cleaned, inspected and if necessary replaced. All gaskets must be renewed.

FUEL PUMP — Assembly

Insert the rocker arm and the link into the lower body and hold in place while fitting the pivot pin from the non-serrated side of the pin. Install the rocker arm spring.

Install the oil seal packing retainer, the oil seal packing, the oil seal spring retainer and the diaphragm to the lower body half. Press down the diaphragm and engage it with the rocker arm link. Fit the cover to the upper body half.

Install the gaskets and the valves correctly into the upper body half and secure the valves with the valve retainer and the screws. (Fig.E.35). Position the upper body onto the lower body and insert the screws. Make sure the screws pass through the diaphragm without tearing the material. Tighten the screws evenly and securely.

FUEL PUMP — Installation

The fuel pump should be refitted to the engine with a new gasket and checked for petrol and oil leaks with the engine running. The pump should deliver not less than 1.6 pints/min. (900 c.c./min.). The delivery pressure of the pump should be between 3.0 - 4.5 psi. (0.2 - 0.3 kg/sq.cm.).

FUEL FILTER
(Fig.E.36)

The filter is of the replaceable element type but the element should be cleaned at frequent intervals. If the element is excessively dirty it should be replaced. A new gasket should be fitted.

FUEL TANK — Removal and Installation

Drain the fuel, disconnect the hose clamps from inlet pipe and bleeder hose and the fuel gauge wire and the flare nut. Remove the retaining nuts and the tank may then be lifted out.

WARNING: Repairs to a fuel tank should only be attempted by an experienced person after adequately steaming to remove trapped vapour.

In the case of KE16V Estate Car models it is necessary to remove the spare wheel from the spare wheel carrier. The tank is removed together with the spare wheel carrier.

The installation in both cases is a reversal of the removal procedure. Make sure that all connections are securely tightened.

Technical Data

CARBURETTOR

Type . . . . Down-draught, two-barrels
Air intake diamater . . . . .63 mm (2.480 in.)
Main choke tube diameter:
Main choke tube diameter - Primary:
  K & K-C . . . . .21 mm (0.827 in.)
  K-B .19 mm (0.75 in.)
Main choke tube diameter - Secondary:
  All engines . . . . .24 mm (0.94 in.)
Small choke tube diameter:
  Primary . . . . 7 mm (0.28 in.)
  Secondary . . . . 8 mm (0.31 in.)
Throttle bore diameter:
  Primary . . . . .28 mm (1.10 in.)
  Secondary . . . . .28 mm (1.10 in.)
Main jet diameter - Primary:
  K . . . . .1.08 mm (0.0425 in.)
  K-B . . . . .0.875 mm (0.034 in.)
  K-C . . . . .1.12 mm (0.044 in.)
Main jet diameter - Secondary:
  K . . . . .1.75 mm (0.0689 in.)
  K-B . . . . 1.3 mm (0.051 in.)
  K-C . . . . .1.75 mm (0.0689 in.)
Slow-running fuel jet diameter:
  K & K-B . . . . .0.47 mm (0.0185 in.)
  K-C . . . . .0.525 mm (0.021 in.)
Power jet diameter:
  K & K-C . . . . .0.70 mm (0.0276 in.)
  K-B . . . . .0.65 mm (0.026 in.)
Pump jet diameter:
  K & K-C . . . . 0.5 mm (0.020 in.)
  K-B . . . . .0.40 mm (0.016 in.)
Main air bleed:
  Primary . . . . 0.5 mm (0.020 in.)
  Secondary . . . . 0.5 mm (0.020 in.)
Slow-running air bleed:
  Primary . . . . .1.10 mm (0.0433 in.)
  Secondary . . . . 1.225 mm (0.0482 in.)
Economizer jet . . . . .1.02 mm (0.040 in.)
Accelerator pump stroke:
  Normal . . . . 3.0 - 3.5 mm (0.12 - 0.14 in.)
  Cold . . . . 4.0 - 4.5 mm (0.16 - 0.18 in.)
Float level setting:
  Float raised . . . . 6.5 mm (0.256 in.)
  Float lowered . . . . .48 mm (1.89 in.)
Slow-running screw - initial setting:
  K . . . . .2 1/2 turns from fully closed
  K-B . . . . .2 1/4 turns from fully closed
  K-C . . . . .2 1/3 turns from fully closed

CARBURETTOR — Corolla 1200

Main choke tube diameter - Primary:
  3K . . . . .21 mm (0.827 in.)
  3K-D, 3K-B . . . . .18 mm (0.709 in.)

Main choke tube diameter - Secondary:
  Both .24 mm (0.905 in.)

Small choke tube diameter:
  Primary . . . . .7 mm (0.276 in.)
  Secondary . . . . .8 mm (0.315 in.)

Throttle bore diameter:
  Primary . . . . .28 mm (1.102 in.)
  Secondary . . . . 28 mm (1.102 in.)

Main jet diameter - Primary:
  3K . . . . .1.00 mm (0.039 in.)
  3K-D, 3K-B . . . . .0.825 mm (0.033 in.)

Main jet diameter - Secondary:
  3K . . . . .1.74 mm (0.069 in.)
  3K-D, 3K-B . . . . .1.40 mm (0.055 in.)

Main nozzle diameter:
  Primary . . . . 2.0 mm (0.08 in.)
  Secondary . . . . 2.0 mm (0.08 in.)

Slow-running fuel jet . . . . .0.47 mm (0.019 in.)
Pump jet . . . . .0.47 mm (0.019 in.)
Economizer jet . . . . .1.02 mm (0.040 in.)

Power jet diameter:
  3K . . . . 0.775 mm (0.030 in.)
  3K-D, 3K-B . . . . .0.55 mm (0.023 in.)

Slow-running air bleed - Primary:
  3K . . . . 0.825 mm (0.032 in.)
  3K-D, 3K-B . . . . .1.10 mm (0.043 in.)

Slow-running air bleed - Secondary:
  3K . . . . 1.225 mm (0.048 in.)
  3K-D, 3K-B . . . . 1.225 mm (0.048 in.)

Main air bleed . . . . 0.5 mm (0.02 in.)

Accelerator pump stroke:
  Normal . . . . 3.5 mm (0.138 in.)
  Cold . . . . 4.5 mm (0.177 in.)

Float level:
  Raised . . . . 6.5 mm (0.26 in.)
  Lowered . . . . .48 mm (1.90 in.)

FUEL PUMP

Type . . . . Diaphragm pump
Delivery . . . . .900 c.c. at 2,900 camshaft rpm.
Delivery pressure . . . . 0.2 - 0.3 kg/sq.cm (2.8 - 4.3 psi.)
Vacuum . . . . 400 mm Hg. (15.7 in. Hg.)

Trouble Shooting

SYMPTOMS	PROBABLE CAUSE	ACTION TO BE TAKEN
CARBURETTOR Flooding	Improper seating or damaged float needle valve or seat Incorrect float level Fuel pump has excessive pressure	Check and replace parts as necessary Adjust float level Check fuel pump
Excessive fuel consumption	Float level too high Loose plug or jet Defective gasket Fuel leaks at pipes or connections Choke valve operates improperly Obstructed air bleed	Adjust float level Tighten Replace gaskets Trace leak and rectify Check choke valve Check and clear
Stalling	Main jet obstructed Incorrect throttle opening Slow-running adjustment incorrect Slow-running fuel jet blocked Incorrect float level	Clean main jet Adjust throttle Adjust slow-running Clean jet Adjust float level
Poor acceleration	Defective accelerator pump Float level too low Incorrect throttle opening Defective accelerator linkage Blocked pump jet	Overhaul pump Adjust float level Adjust throttle Adjust accelerator linkage Clean pump jet
Spitting	Lean mixture Dirty carburettor Clogged fuel pipes Manifold draws secondary air	Clean and adjust carburettor Clean carburettor Clean or replace pipes Tighten or replace gasket
Insufficient fuel supply	Clogged carburettor Clogged fuel pipe Dirty fuel Air in fuel system Defective fuel pump Clogged fuel filter	Dismantle and clean carburettor Clean fuel pipe Clean fuel tank Check connections and tighten Repair or replace fuel pump Clean or replace filter
FUEL PUMP Loss of fuel delivery	Slotted body screws loose Diaphragm cracked Loose fuel pipe connections Defective valves Cracked fuel pipes	Tighten body screws Overhaul fuel pump Tighten fuel pipe connections Replace valves Replace fuel pipes
Noisy pump	Loose pump mounting Worn or defective rocker arm Broken rocker arm spring	Tighten mounting bolts Replace rocker arm Replace spring

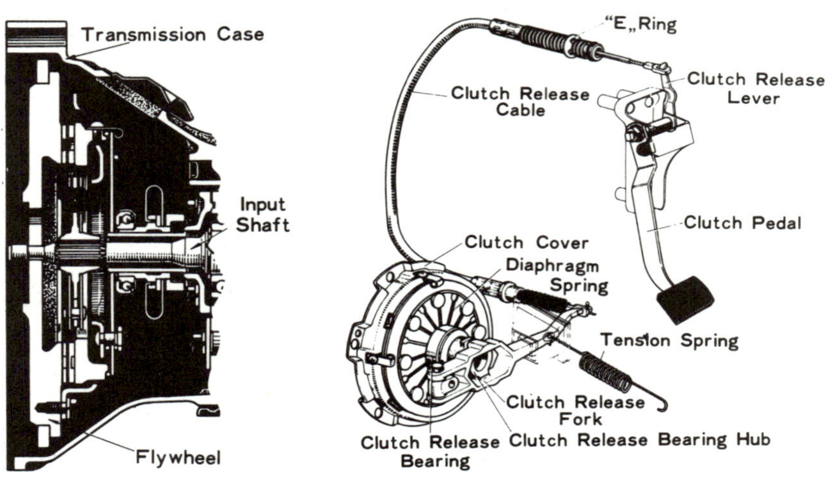

Fig.F.1. View of clutch and clutch operating mechanism.

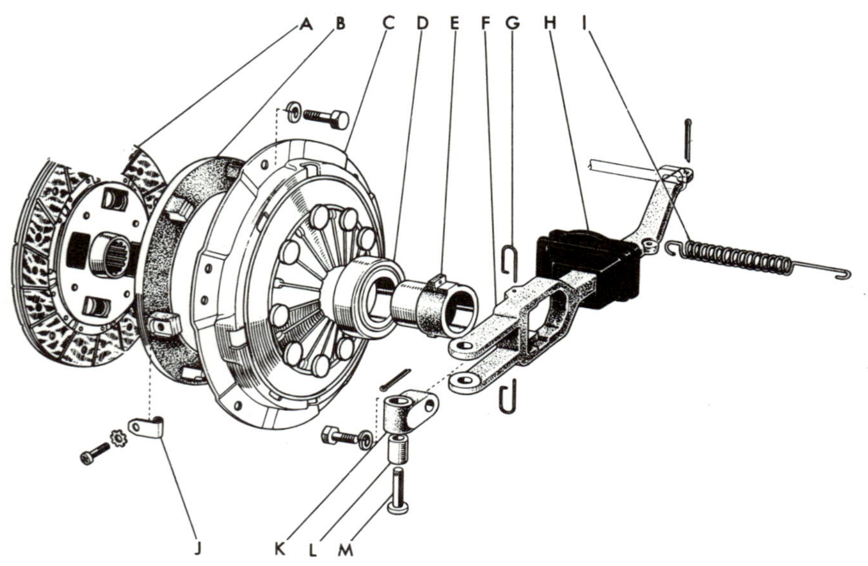

Fig.F.2. Exploded view of the clutch and clutch release mechanism.

A. Clutch driven plate
B. Clutch pressure plate
C. Clutch cover with spring
D. Clutch release bearing
E. Release bearing hub
F. Clutch withdrawal fork
G. Withdrawal fork clip
H. Rubber boot
I. Return spring
J. Clutch retracting spring
K. Withdrawal fork support
L. Bush
M. Pivot pin

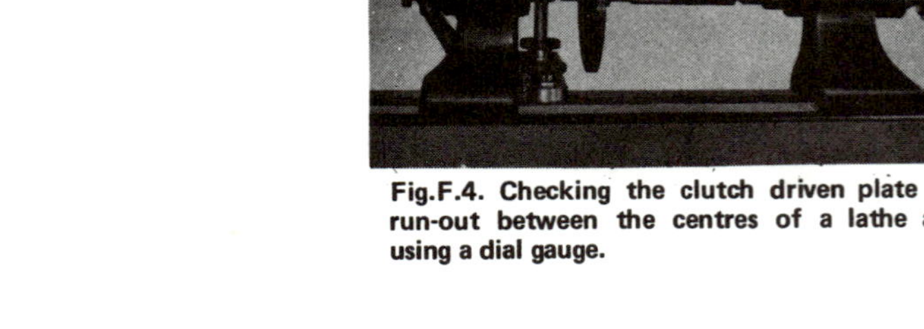

Fig.F.3. Checking diagram for clutch driven plate. (1). Clutch facing, (2). Cushion, (3) Hub splines.

Fig.F.4. Checking the clutch driven plate for run-out between the centres of a lathe and using a dial gauge.

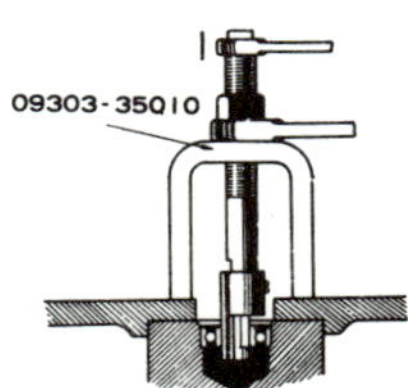

Fig.F.5. Removal of the clutch shaft pilot bearing.

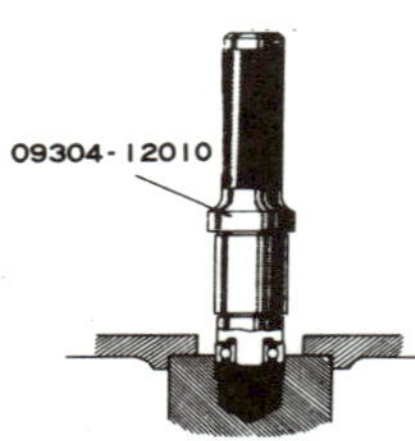

Fig.F.6. Installation of the clutch shaft pilot bearing.

Clutch

CLUTCH — Removal
(Fig.F.1)

Remove the gearbox as described in section "GEARBOX" and remove the clutch cover securing bolts in a diagonal pattern.

Mark the location of the clutch cover in the flywheel and lift out the cover and the driven plate.

Check the clutch pressure plate with a suitable tester to make sure the clutch pressure is not less than 180 kg (400 lbs.). If less, replace the diaphragm spring.

CLUTCH — Dismantling
(Fig.F.2)

Suitably mark the clutch cover and the pressure plate and remove the four retracting spring securing bolts. Remove the springs and pressure plate. Next remove the diaphragm securing bolts and the two pivot rings and lift off the diaphragm spring.

From inside the clutch housing remove the two release bearing hub clips and remove the release hub.

CLUTCH — Inspection
(Fig.F.3 & Fig.F.4)

Check the clutch driven plate for worn friction linings. The lining minimum thickness is 0.6 mm (0.024 in.). If the linings appear glazed, remove glaze by lightly rubbing with sand paper. If traces of oil have reached the linings or torsion rubbers are distorted in any way or the hub splines of the clutch driven plate are worn beyond limits, the driven plate should be renewed. Check the run-out of the driven plate between the centres of a lathe and if excessive, replace the plate (Fig.F.4).

Check the pivots of the clutch cover and the pressure plate for wear or discolouration. Inspect the retracting springs for breaks or damage.

Replace the diaphragm spring if the release bearing contact face or the pivot ring contact face is badly worn or cracks can be detected.

Examine the clutch release bearing for wear, roughness and noise and replace if necessary. If it is necessary to replace the clutch shaft front bearing, remove the old bearing by means of the puller 09303-35010 (Fig.F.5), pack the new bearing with grease and install it into the crankshaft, using the bearing replacer 09304-12010. (Fig.F.6).

CLUTCH — Assembly

Assemble clutch cover, pressure plate and retracting springs in accordance with the marks made on dismantling. Tighten the retracting spring bolts to a torque reading of 0.4 - 0.7 kgm (3 - 5 lb.ft.). (Fig.F.7). Grease the inside of the release bearing hub and the hub to release fork contact area and fit the release fork (withdrawal fork), the bearing hub and the two clips. (Fig.F.8).

Using special tool 09301-12010 (or a spare clutch shaft), fit the clutch driven plate and the clutch cover assembly on to the flywheel (Fig.F.9). The longer end of the driven plate hub must face towards the gearbox. (Fig.F.10). Tighten the clutch securing bolts to a torque reading of 1.0 - 1.5 kgm (7 - 11 lb.ft.).

Refit the gearbox as described in section "GEARBOX".

CLUTCH PEDAL — Removal
(Fig.F.11)

Remove the circlip from the upper end of the outer clutch cable, disconnect the inner cable (1) in Fig.F.12 from the lever (2), remove the clutch pedal return springs (3) and finally remove the nut (4), the pedal (5) and the two bushes (6).

Check the following parts and repair or replace as necessary:

Clutch pedal rubber pad for wear, pedal for damage or cracks, bump stop cushion for damage, lever shaft for wear and lever for wear. Check the bushes and the pedal support shaft boss for wear and the return springs for weakness.

CLUTCH PEDAL — Installation

The installation of the clutch pedal is a reversal of the removal procedure, observing the following points:

Grease the bushes (2) and the release lever (1) in Fig.F.13. Tighten the release lever securing nut to 5 - 7 kgm (35 - 50 lb.ft.). Adjust the pedal height and clutch free-play as decribed later on.

CLUTCH RELEASE CABLE — Removal and Installation

Remove the circlips from the pedal end of the outer clutch cable and the clevis pin from the inner cable at the top of the clutch withdrawal fork and the lower end of the cable from the withdrawal fork. Remove the cable from the gearbox. Disconnect the inner cable from the release lever (clutch pedal) and remove the cable completely.

The installation is a reversal of the removal procedure. Grease both ends of the clutch cable and adjust the pedal height and the clutch free-play.

CLUTCH PEDAL — Height adjustment

The clutch pedal height is adjusted by means of a bolt with locknut. Bolt and nut should be adjusted until the distance between the floor mat and the clutch pedal is 140 - 150 mm (5.5 - 5.9 in. (Fig.F.15).

CLUTCH FREE-PLAY — Adjustment

With the circlip (item G, Fig.F.11) removed, pull the clutch release cable through the cable support flange until resistance is

Fig.F.7. Assembly of the clutch cover.

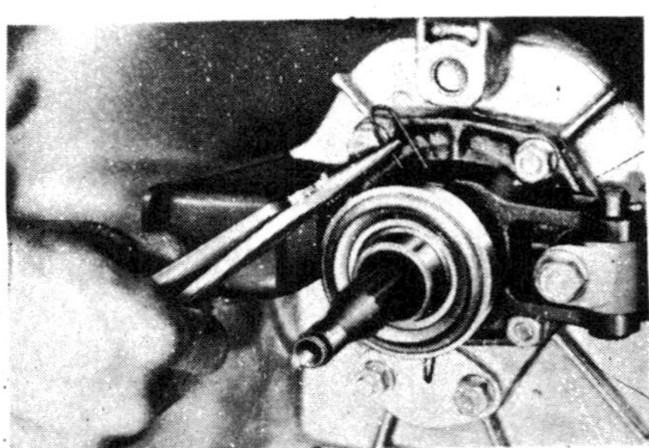
Fig.F.8. Fitting the clutch withdrawal fork to the clutch shaft.

Fig.F.9. Installation of the clutch.

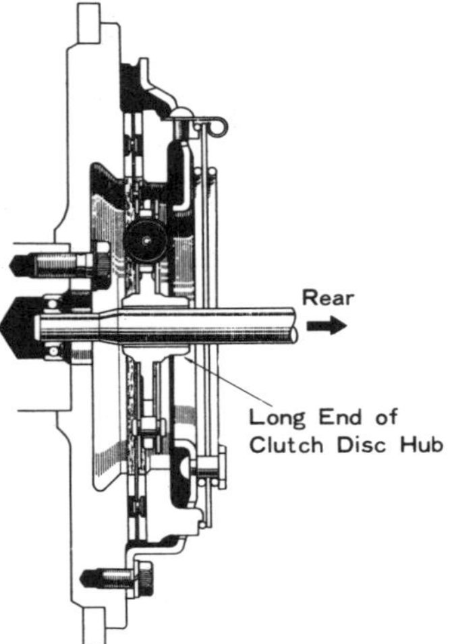

Fig.F.10. View through the clutch to show the correct installation of the clutch driven plate.

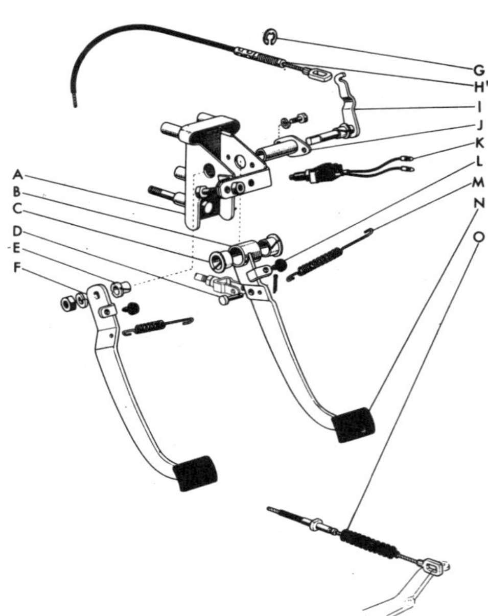

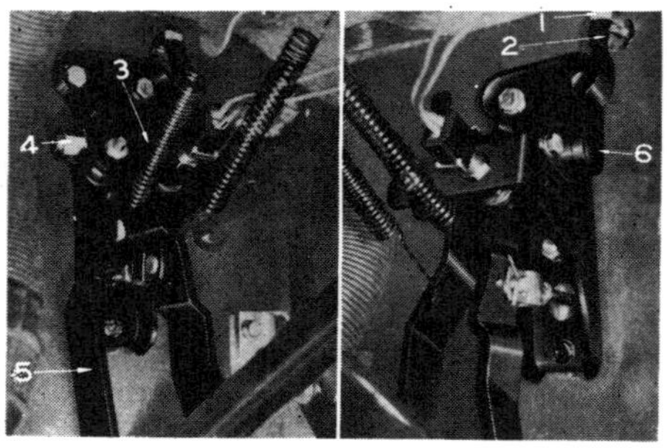

Fig.F.11. Exploded view of clutch and brake pedal assembly.

A.	Pedal support
B.	Brake pedal
C.	Bush
D.	Clevis pin
E.	Bush
F.	Clutch pedal
G.	"E" clip
H.	Clutch operating cable
I.	Clutch release lever
J.	Pedal support shaft boss
K.	Brake light switch
L.	Rubber stop
M.	Return spring
N.	Pedal rubber pad
O.	Clutch cable boot

Fig.F.12. Removal of the clutch pedal (For annotations see text).

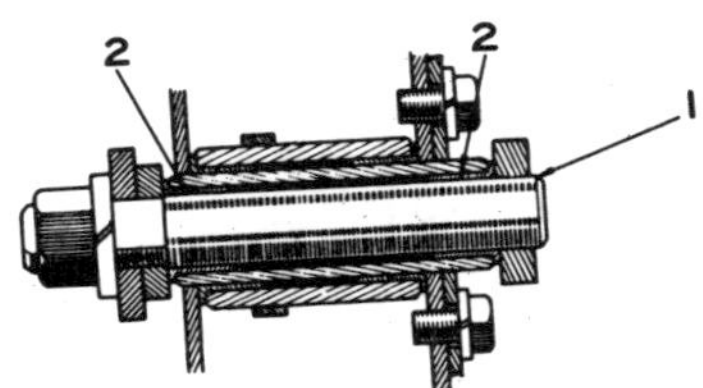

Fig.F.13. Installation of the clutch pedal. (1). Clutch release lever, (2). Bushes.

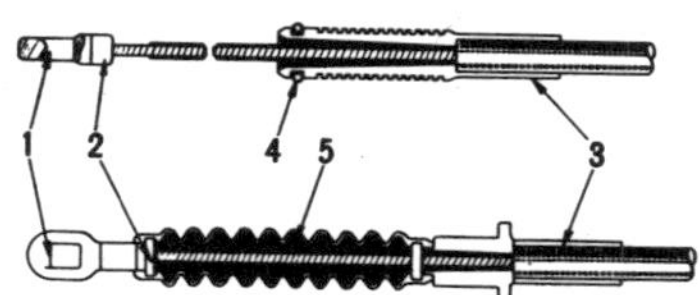

Fig.F.14. View of the clutch release cable.

1. Hooks
2. End piece
3. Outer sleeve
4. 'O' ring
5. Rubber boot

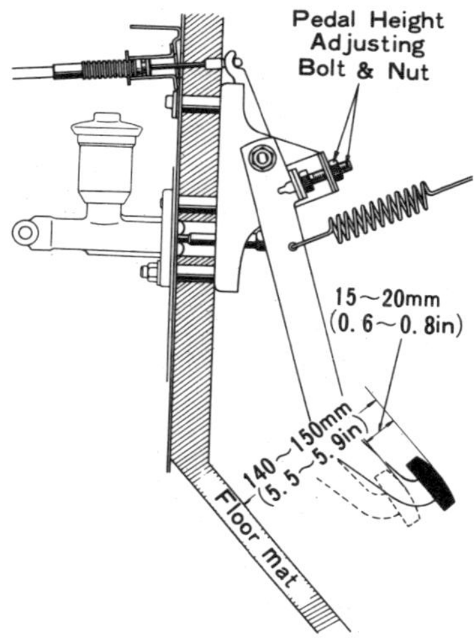

Fig.F.15. The clutch pedal adjustment.

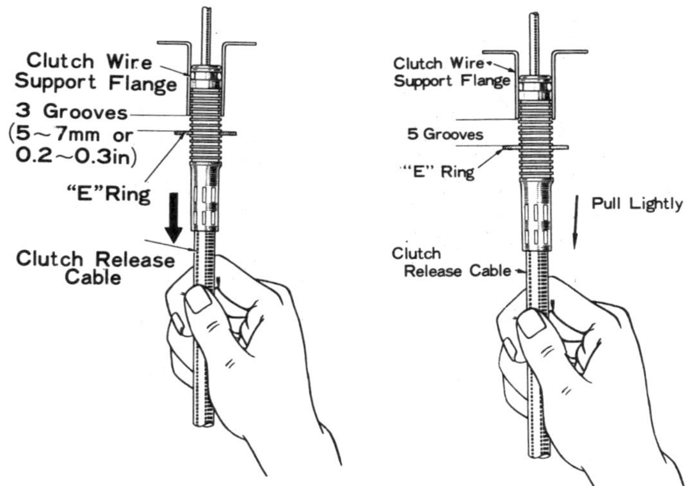

Fig.F.16. Checking the pedal free play on earlier 1100 (left) and later 1100 and 1200 (right).

felt (release bearing in contact with diaphragm spring). With the cable held in this position, replace the circlip 5 - 7 mm (0.2 - 0.3 in.) back from the support flange (about 3 grooves) as shown in Fig.F.16. Check that the clutch pedal free-play is about 15 - 20 mm (0.6 - 0.8 in.).

NOTE: Later 1100 models and the 1200 models should have the circlip inserted about 5 grooves after the support flange. (See Fig.F.17).

Modifications on later 1100 models and 1200 models

When checking the clutch pressure plate load, the following results should be obtained:

Models K, K-C . . . . More than 240 kg (530 lbs.)
Models K-B, 3K, 3K-B, 3K-D . . . . 300 kg (662 lbs.)

Clutch Pedal

The clutch pedal assembly on later 1100 models and the 1200 models is slightly modified. The removal and installation of the pedal is carried out in a similar manner as described for the previous type. Any changes can be taken from Fig.F.18.

Technical Data

Type .Dry, single disc clutch

Clutch linings:
  Outer diamater . . . . 180.0 mm (7.087 in.)
  Inner diamater . . . . 125.0 mm (4.921 in.)
  Thickness . . . . 3.4 mm (0.14 in.)

Clutch diaphragm spring:
  Thickness:
    K, K-C, K-B, 3K . . . . .1.95 mm (0.078 in.)
    3K-D, 3K-B . . . . .2.05 mm (0.081 in.)
  Fitted load:
    K, K-C, K-B, 3K . . . . .240 kg (530 lbs.)
    3K-D, 3K-B . . . . .300 kg (660 lbs.)

Clutch release cable:
  Inner cable length . . . . 934 mm (36.8 in. — R.H.D.
                        1659 mm (65.3 in.) — L.H.D.
  Inner cable diameter . . . . . 3.7 - 4.0 mm (0.15 - 0.16 in.)
  Outer cable diameter . . . . . . 9.0-10.0 mm (0.19 - 0.20 in.)
  Adjustable free play length:
    R.H.D. . . . . .160.5 mm (6.32 in.)
    L.H.D. . . . . .885.5 mm (34.9 in.)

Trouble Shooting

SYMPTOMS	PROBABLE CAUSE	ACTION TO BE TAKEN
Noises	Damaged or worn release bearing Damaged or worn pilot bearing Loose driven plate hub Driven plate distorted Damaged pressure plate	Replace Replace Replace driven plate Replace driven plate Renew clutch assembly
Chatter or vibration	Gearbox case loose in mountings Uneven contact of pressure plate Loose rivets in clutch driven plate Oil or grease on clutch linings	Tighten mounting bolts Renew clutch assembly Replace linings Replace linings or driven plate
Clutch does not release completely	Excessive pedal free-play Driven plate has run-out Sticky friction linings Clutch friction linings worn Splines on drive shaft or clutch shaft dirty Deformed pressure plate or flywheel Clutch cable defective	Check and rectify Replace driven plate Replace linings or plate Replace linings or plate Clean splines, remove burrs Check and rectify as necessary Check and replace cable if necessary
Clutch slips	No clutch pedal free-play Badly worn friction linings Pressure plate faulty Friction linings oil-soaked Weak clutch pressure springs	Check and rectify Replace linings or friction plate Check and if necessary renew clutch Replace linings or driven plate Replace clutch assembly

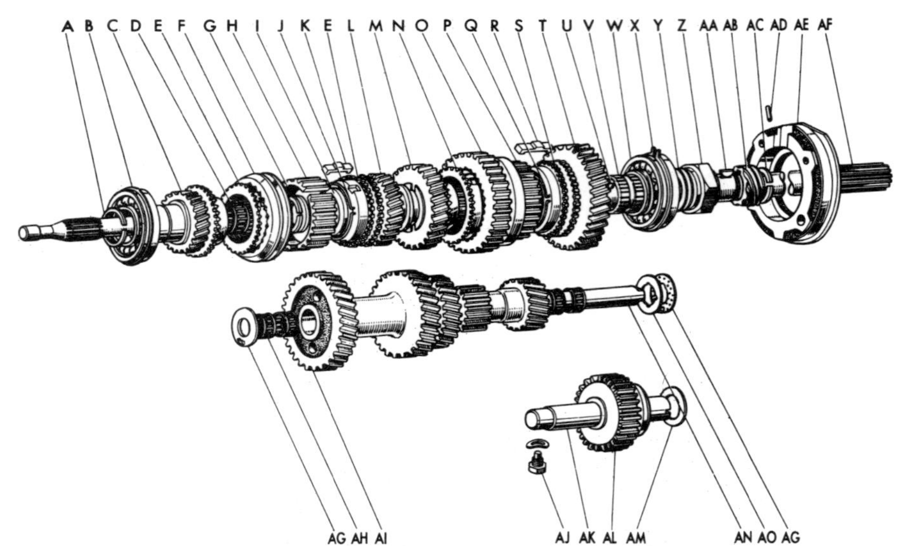

EXPLODED VIEW OF THE GEAR TRAIN

A.	Shaft snap ring	L.	Third speed gearwheel	V.	Bush for 1st speed gearwheel
B.	Front mainshaft bearing	M.	Second speed gearwheel	W.	Rear shaft bearing
C.	Main drive shaft (clutch shaft)	N.	Synchroniser ring (2nd speed)	X.	Shaft snap ring
D.	Needle roller bearing	O.	Reverse gearwheel	Y.	Shim
E.	Synchroniser ring (3rd speed)	P.	Synchroniser hub (1st/2nd speeds)	Z.	Mainshaft nut
F.	Synchroniser operating sleeve	Q.	Shifting key	AA.	Woodruff key
G.	Shaft snap ring	R.	Shifting key	AB.	Speedometer drive worm
H.	Synchroniser hub (3rd/4th speeds)	S.	Synchroniser ring (1st speed)	AC.	Shaft snap ring
I.	Hub spacer	T.	First speed gearwheel	AD.	Roll pin
J.	Shifting key	U.	Locating ball	AE.	Rear bearing retainer
K.	Shifting key				

AF.	Mainshaft
AG.	Thrust washer
AH.	Needle roller bearing
AI.	Countershaft gear cluster
AJ.	Shaft securing bolt
AK.	Reverse idler shaft
AL.	Reverse idler gear
AM.	Spacer
AN.	Countershaft
AO.	Thrust washer

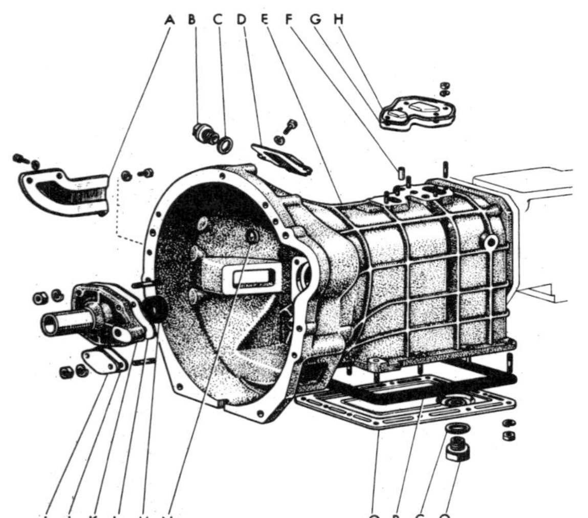

EXPLODED VIEW OF THE GEARBOX MAIN CASE

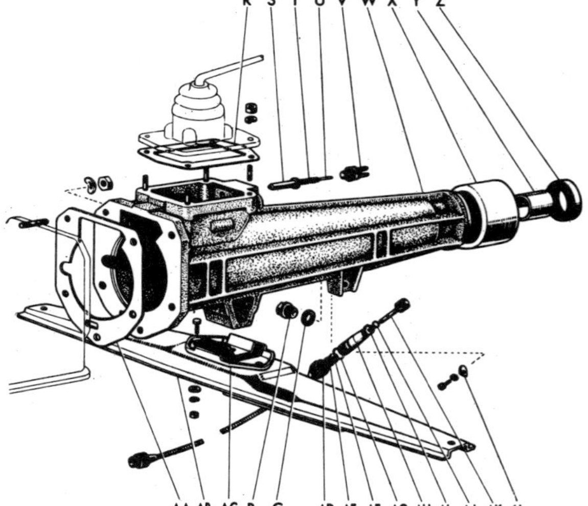

EXPLODED VIEW OF THE GEARBOX EXTENSION HOUSING

A.	Reinforcement plate	J.	Cover gasket
B.	Filler plug	K.	Front bearing retainer
C.	Drain plug gasket	L.	Gasket
D.	Clutch inspection cover	M.	Oil seal
E.	Gearbox case	N.	Screw plug
F.	Spring seat for detent ball	O.	Gearbox bottom cover
G.	Gearbox cover gasket	P.	Gasket
H.	Gearbox cover	Q.	Oil drain plug
I.	Countershaft cover		

R.	Gearchange lever cover gasket	AC.	Engine mounting rubber
S.	Reverse gear lock pin	AD.	Speedometer drive cable
T.	Spring	AE.	Speedometer inner drive cable
U.	Pin	AF.	Speedometer drive outer drive
V.	Reversing light switch	AG.	'O' sealing ring
W.	Extension housing	AH.	Speedometer pinion bearing sleeve
X.	Extension housing dust deflector	AI.	Bush
Y.	Bush	AJ.	'O' sealing ring
Z.	Oil seal	AK.	Speedometer driven gear
AA.	Extension housing gasket	AL.	Lock plate for bearing sleeve
AB.	Engine rear mounting crossmember		

Gearbox

DESCRIPTION

The gearbox contains four forward speeds and one reverse speed. All forward speeds are fully synchronised, while the reverse gear operates with a sliding gearwheel. The gearchange mechanism is directly controlled by means of a floor-change gear lever, which engages in the gear selector mechanism in the extension housing. The selector cover incorporates three selector shafts. The extreme right-hand shaft is for the 1st and 2nd speeds, the centre shaft for the 3rd and 4th speeds and the left-hand shaft for the reverse speed.

GEARBOX — Removal

Remove or disconnect the following parts: Front floor mats, gear lever boot, gear lever retainer (using special gear lever remover 09305-12010) (Fig.G.1) and plug up the opening with a clean cloth.

Disconnect the reversing light connector from the right-hand side at the rear of the engine, the positive battery lead and the radiator inlet hose. Bring the fan blades in a horizontal position and disconnect the exhaust pipe from the manifold.

Jack up the car and place on suitable stands. The stands at the front should be placed under the body behind each front wheel. The stands at the rear should be placed under the axle housing.

Disconnect the propeller shaft from the drive pinion flange and remove the shaft from the gearbox extension housing. The gearbox oil plug 09325-12010 should be inserted in the extension housing (Fig.G.2) in order to prevent loss of oil. If this plug is not available, plug the gearbox end with a spare sleeve yoke or in some other suitable manner.

Remove the exhaust securing bracket (1, Fig.G3) and the nut (2) and the speedometer drive cable (3) from the extension housing. Support the gearbox with a jack at the forward end and remove the bolts (4), securing the rear engine mounting insulator on to the rear support crossmember. Remove the bolts (5), holding the rear support crossmember to the body and remove this part and the jack.

NOTE: With the parts disconnected or removed as described above, it is possible to replace the reversing light switch, if this operation is required.

Remove the starter motor bolts (1, Fig.G.4) and the starter motor and unscrew the bolts (2) and the reinforcement plate from the gearbox case. Remove the clevis pin and the clutch operating cable from the clutch withdrawal fork and remove the cable with the rubber boot. Remove the two lower bolts (3) holding the gearbox to the rear engine plate and the four bolts (4) holding the gearbox to the cylinder block. Slide the gearbox carefully backwards until the main drive shaft (clutch shaft) is clear of the clutch driven plate. Then lower the gearbox and remove from under the car.

GEARBOX — Dismantling

Drain the oil and clean the magnetic drain plug. Remove the clutch release bearing hub clips and the withdrawal fork boot and remove the fork and the release bearing hub. (Fig.G.5). Remove the bottom cover (oil pan), speedometer drive sleeve lock plate and remove the shaft sleeve and the driven gear for the speedometer drive from the extension housing (Fig.G.6). Remove the gearchange lever retainer (Fig.G.7) and after unscrewing the nuts, remove the extension housing from the gearbox, taking care not to damage the oil seal in the rear of the housing (Fig.G.8).

Remove the countershaft cover and the front bearing retainer (Fig.G.9), taking care not to damage the oil seal in the inside of the bearing retainer. Remove the gearbox case cover and lift out the detent balls and springs. Unscrew the reverse idler shaft securing bolt from the gearbox case and remove the reverse idler gear and the spacer (if fitted).

Using a dial gauge (Fig.G.10) with the plunger resting on a tooth of the layshaft and with the main drive shaft locked, measure and note the backlash by rotating the countershaft. Also measure and note the end clearance of the countershaft gear cluster (Fig.G.11).

Using a brass drift, knock out the countershaft (Fig.G.12) and remove the gear cluster, thrust washer and the four needle roller bearings. With the 1st/2nd speed selector rod pushed towards the rear of the gearbox and the reverse gear and the second gear engaged remove the roll pins, inserted in the selector rods and selector forks with a suitable drift (Fig.G.13). Make sure that only a drift of the dimensions shown is used.

Remove the selector rods for reverse speed, 1st/2nd speeds and 3rd/4th speeds and lift out the interlock balls from the gearbox case. (Fig.G.14). Lift the selector forks from the gearbox case and remove the mainshaft.

Remove the needle roller bearing and the 4th speed synchroniser ring from the main drive shaft and remove the shaft through the front of the gearbox housing (Fig.G.15).

Clamp the assembled mainshaft into a vice and measure and record the end float of 1st, 2nd and 3rd speed gearwheels. (Fig.G.16). The measured values should be retained for assembly reference.

Remove the mainshaft retaining circlips and slide off the 3rd/4th speed synchroniser, synchroniser hub spacer and the 3rd speed gearwheel. (Fig.G.17). Keep the synchroniser ring with the synchroniser unit. Remove the speedometer drive worm circlip and drive the drive worm off the shaft.

Taking care not to damage the thread, straighten the peened over part of the mainshaft nut (Fig.G.18) and holding the shaft by clamping the reverse gear into a vice (with soft-metal jaws), slacken the nut with the special wrench 09326-12010 and remove together with the shims from the shaft. Remove the rear bearing retainer, 1st speed gearwheel, bush for 1st speed gearwheel, locating ball, 1st and 2nd speed synchroniser unit assembly, synchroniser rings and the second speed gearwheel in the order shown in Fig.G.19. Dismantle the synchroniser units.

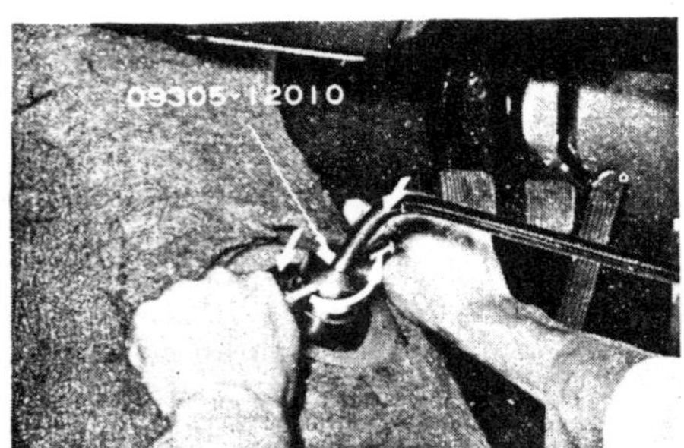

Fig.G.1. Removal of the gearchange lever.

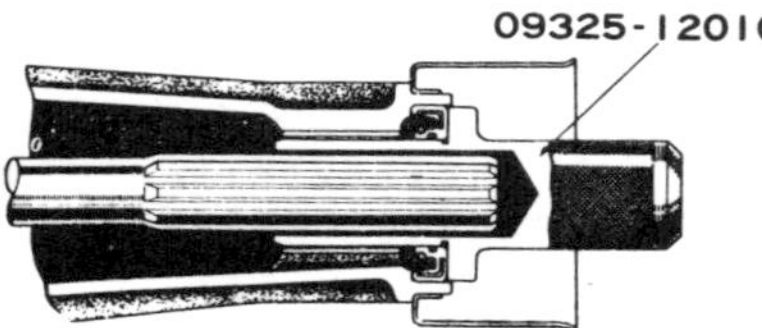

Fig.G.2. The special oil plug fitted to the extension housing to prevent loss of oil.

Fig.G.3. Removal of the rear engine mounting crossmember.

1. Exhaust pipe bracket
2. Nut
3. Speedometer drive cable
4. Mounting bolts
5. Crossmember bolts

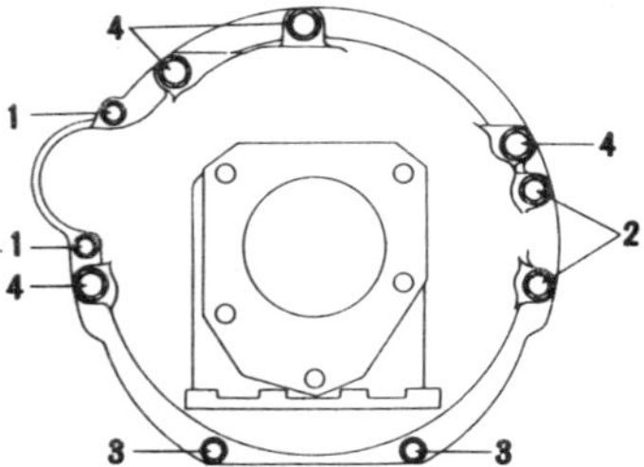

Fig.G.4. Gearbox securing bolts.

1. Bolts for starter motor
2. Bolts for reinforcement plate
3. Bolts to rear end plate
4. Bolts to cylinder block

Fig.G.5. Removal of the clutch withdrawal fork.

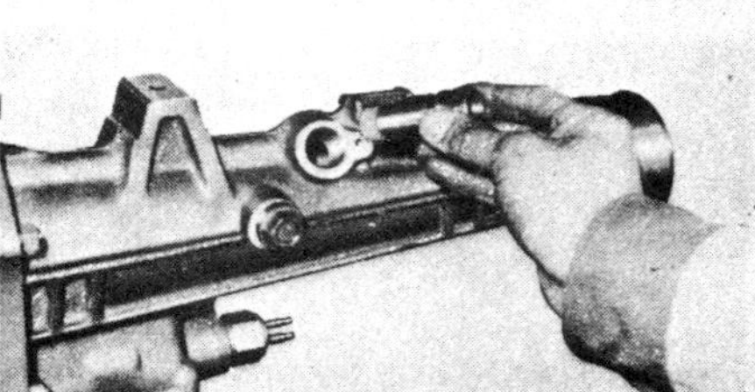

Fig.G.6. Removal of the speedometer driven pinion bearing sleeve.

Fig.G.7. Removal of the gearchange lever retainer.

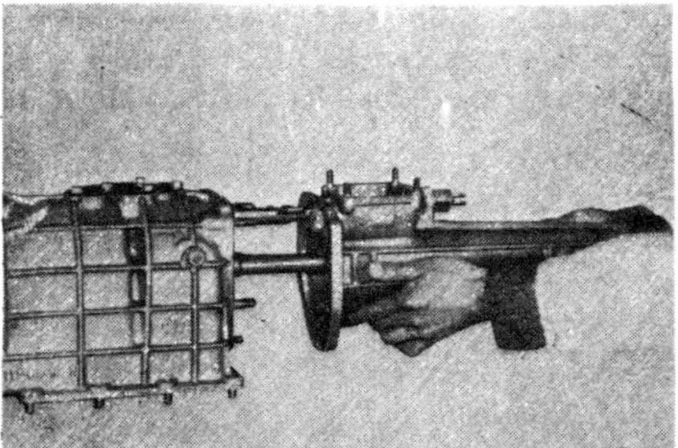

Fig.G.8. Removal of the extension housing.

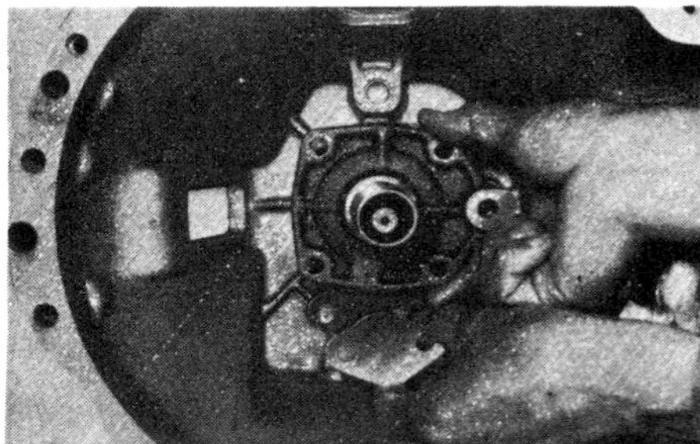

Fig.G.9. Removal of the front bearing retainer.

Fig.G.10. Measuring the backlash of the gearwheels as reference for assembly.

Fig.G.11. Measuring the end clearance of the countershaft gear cluster.

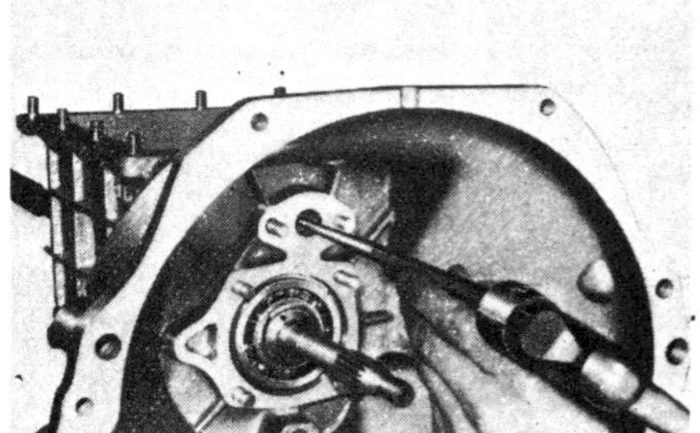

Fig.G.12. Removal of the countershaft from the front of the gearbox case.

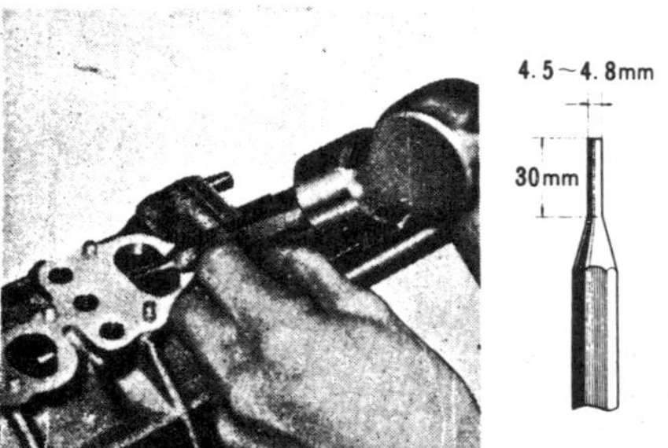

Fig.G.13. Removal of the selector fork retaining pins by means of the drift shown.

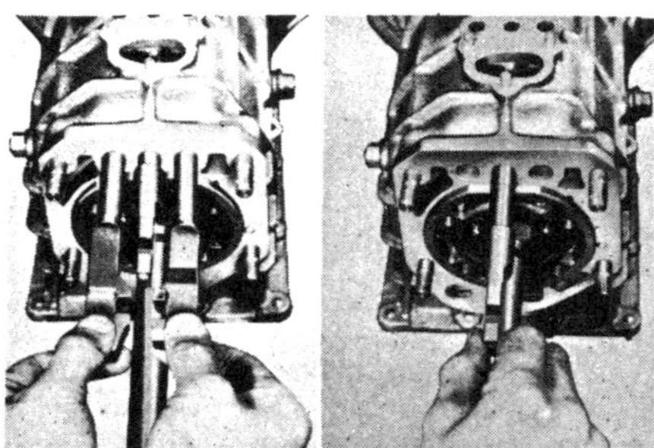

Fig.G.14. Removal of the selector shafts.

Fig.G.15. Removal of the main drive shaft (clutch shaft).

Fig.G.16. Measuring the end clearance of the mainshaft gearwheels.

Fig.G.17. Removal of the 3rd/4th speed synchroniser and third speed gearwheel.

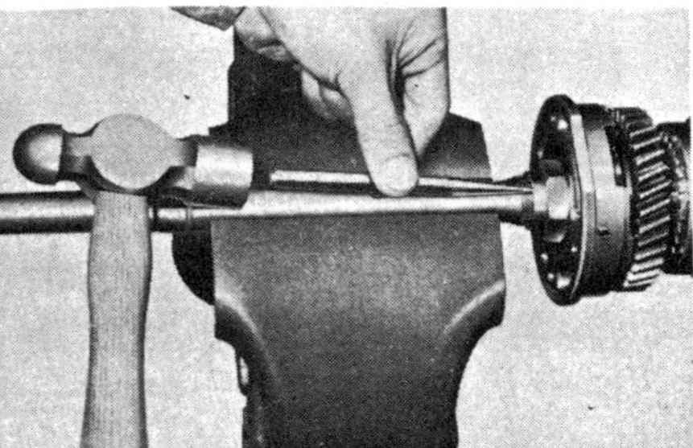

Fig.G.18. Unlocking the mainshaft nut locking plate.

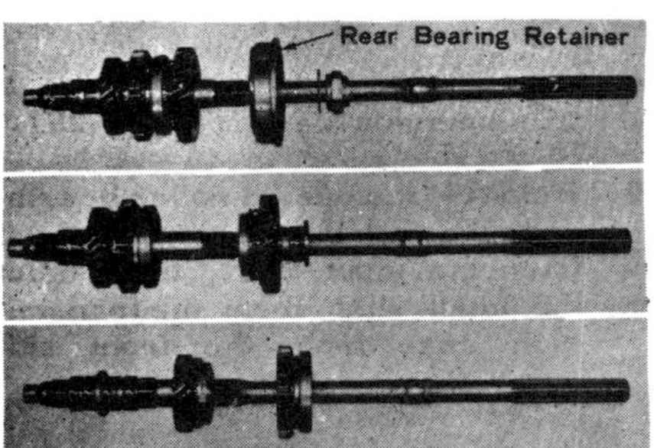

Fig.G.19. Removal sequence for the 2nd speed gearwheel.

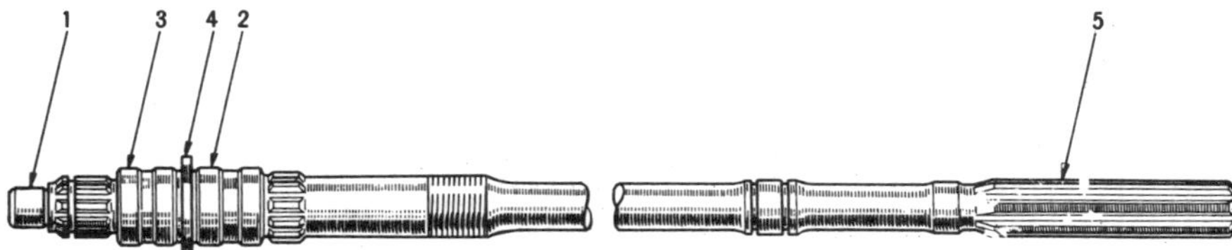

Fig.G.20. The surfaces shown should be checked on the mainshaft.

1. Spigot for main drive shaft
2. 2nd speed gearwheel running area
3. 3rd speed gearwheel running area
4. Flange
5. Splines

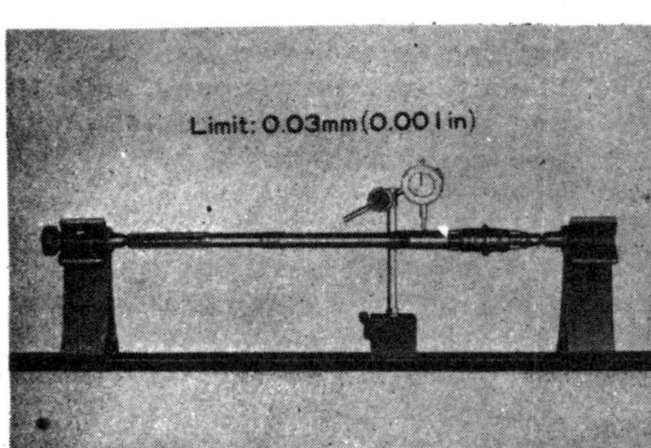

Fig.G.21. Checking the mainshaft for run-out.

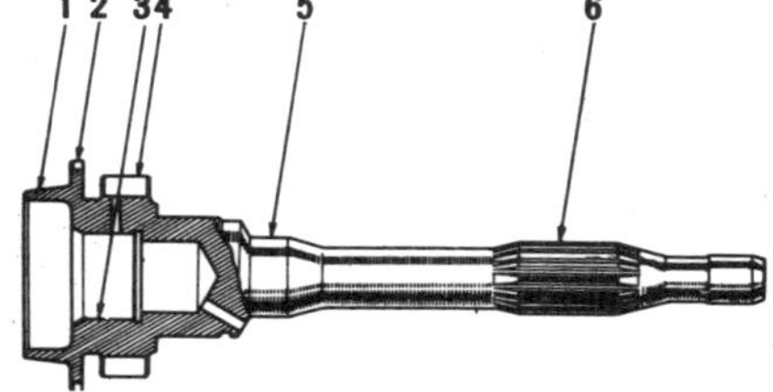

Fig.G.22. The surfaces of the main drive shaft (clutch shaft) to be checked.

1. Cone face for synchroniser ring
2. Synchomesh gear (4th speed)
3. Needle roller bearing running area
4. Main drive gear teeth
5. Bearing seat
6. Driven plate splines

Fig.G.23. Replacement of the main drive shaft bearing.

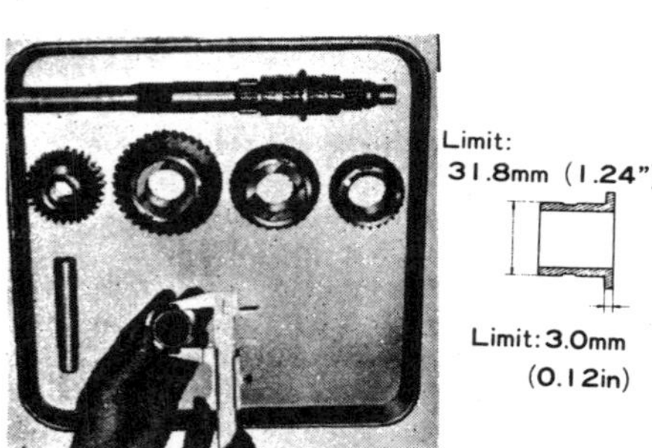

Fig.G.24. Checking the bush for the 1st speed gearwheel.

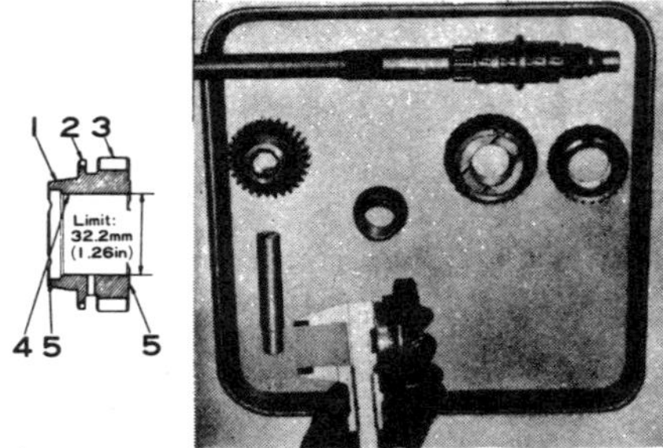

Fig.G.25. Checking the gearwheels for wear.

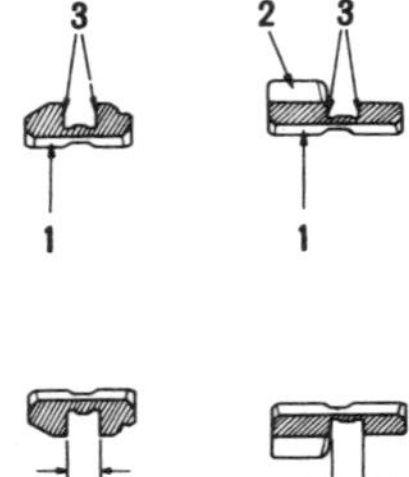

Fig.G.26. Checking of synchroniser operating sleeves and reverse gearwheel.

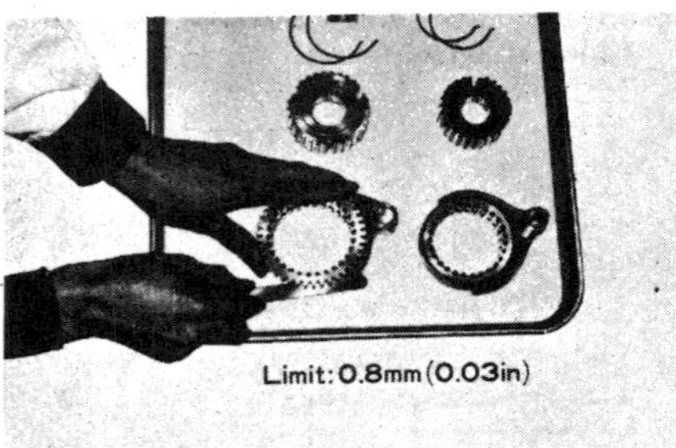

Fig.G.27. Checking the clearance between selector fork and operating sleeves.

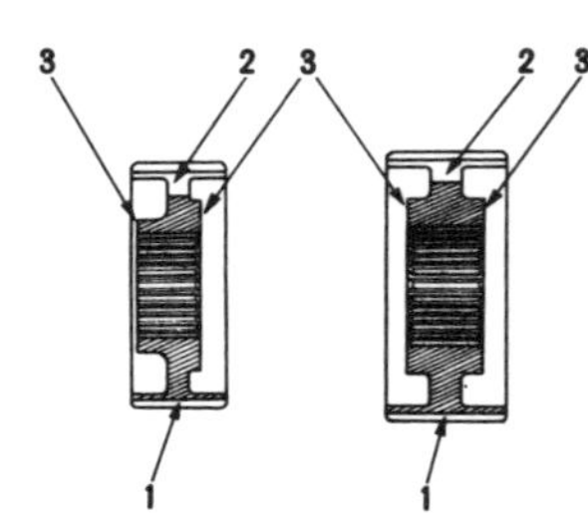

Fig.G.28. Checking the synchroniser hubs. (1). Splines, (2). Contact face with shifting keys, (3). Contact face with gears.

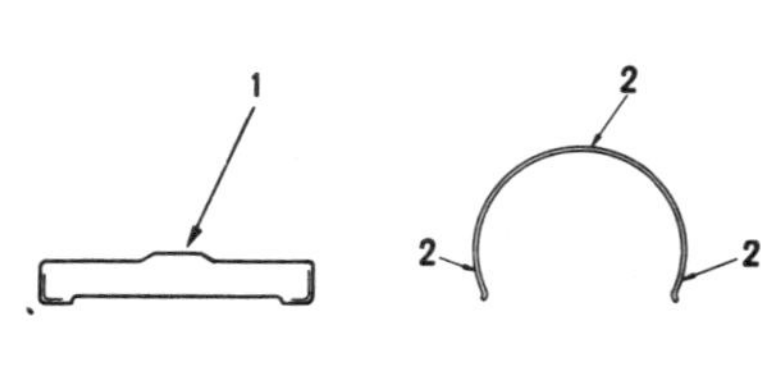

Fig.G.29. Check the shifting keys (1) and the synchroniser springs (2) for wear.

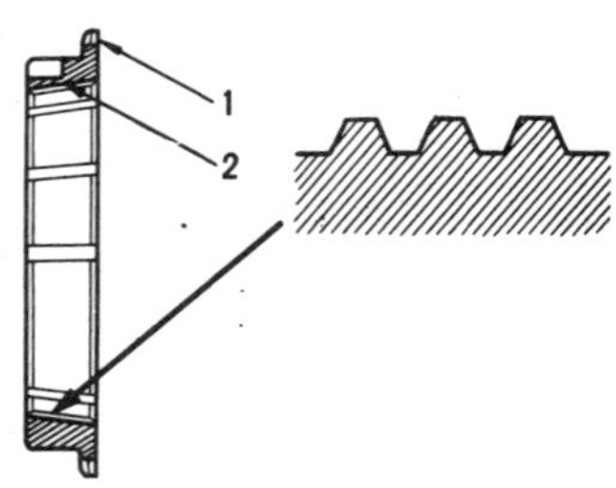

Fig.G.30. Check the synchroniser ring for wear at the teeth (1) and the cone (2).

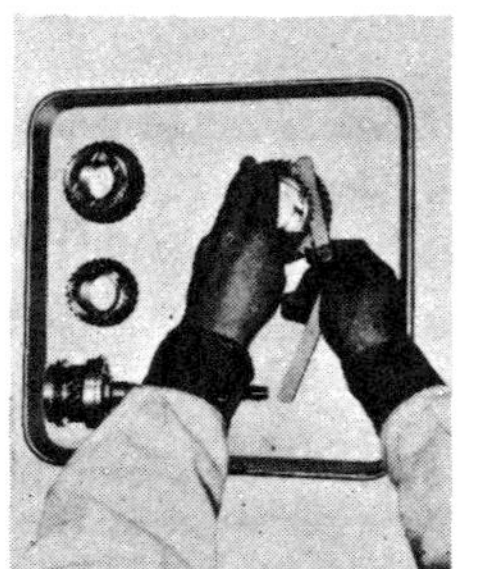

Fig.G.31. Checking the synchroniser ring clearance when fitted to the gearwheel.

Fig.G.32. Replacement of the rear bearing.

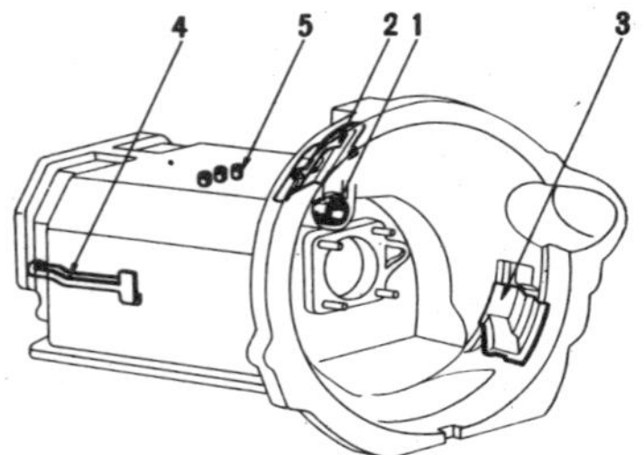

Fig.G.33. Check the numbered areas of the gearbox case for wear or damage.

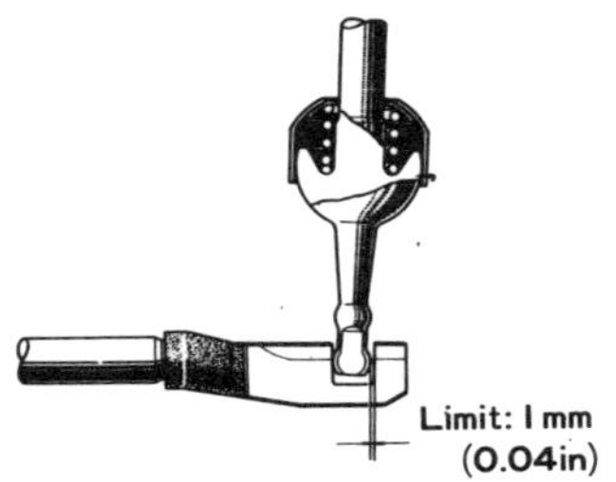

Fig.G.34. Checking the clearance of the gearchange lever for wear in its recess.

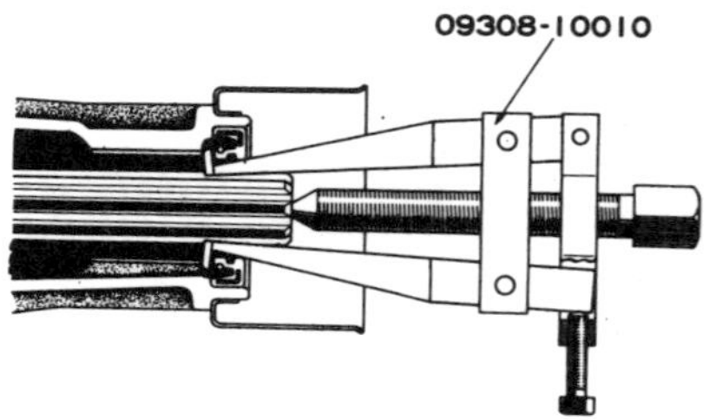

Fig.G.35. Removal of the extension housing oil seal.

GEARBOX — Inspection and Overhaul

Thoroughly clean all parts and replace parts showing signs of wear or damage or repair any defective parts if possible.Check the backlash and end clearance measurement obtained during dismantling with the standard values and replace or repair parts where they fall outside the limits given. Backlash and end clearance should be as follows:

Backlash of gearwheels

Main drive gear to countershaft:
    Standard . . . . 0.1 mm (0.004 in.)
    Limit . . . . 0.2 mm (0.008 in.)
Third speed gear to countergear:
    Standard . . . . .0.11 mm (0.004 in.)
    Limit . . . . 0.2 mm (0.008 in.)
Second speed gear to countergear:
    Standard . . . . .0.11 mm (0.004 in.)
    Limit . . . . 0.2 mm (0.008 in.)
Fourth speed gear to countergear:
    Standard . . . . .0.11 mm (0.004 in.)
    Limit . . . . 0.2 mm (0.008 in.)
Reverse speed gear to countergear:
    Standard . . . . .0.16 mm (0.006 in.)
    Limit . . . . : . . . 0.3 mm (0.012 in.)
Reverse idler gear to countergear:
    Standard . . . . .0.18 mm (0.007 in.)
    Limit . . . . 0.3 mm (0.012 in.)

End clearance of gears

Countergear:
    Standard . . . . 0.05 - 0.25 mm (0.002 - 0.010 in.)
    Limit . . . . 0.5 mm (0.02 in.)
First speed gearwheel:
    Standard . . . . 0.10 - 0.30 mm (0.004 - 0.012 in.)
    Limit . . . . 0.5 mm (0.02 in.)
Second speed gearwheel:
    Standard . . . . 0.15 - 0.30 mm (0.006 - 0.012 in.)
    Limit . . . . 0.5 mm (0.02 in.)
Third speed gearwheel:
    Standard . . . . 0.10 - 0.25 mm (0.004 - 0.25 mm)
    Limit . . . . 0.5 mm (0.02 in.)

Check the following parts for wear or damage:

1. **Mainshaft:** (Fig.G.20). Check the contact surface (1) for the needle roller bearings, the flange (4) and surfaces (2) & (3) (for second and third speed gears) for damage. The flange thickness is 3.5 mm (0.14 in.) min. Contact faces (2) & (3) should be more than 31.8 mm (1.24 in.) in diameter. Check the mainshaft splines for wear or damage and the mainshaft for run-out. If the run-out is in excess of 0.03 mm (0.001 in.) (Fig.G.21), replace the shaft.

2. **Main drive shaft and front bearing:** Check the tapered part (1), synchromesh gear (2) of the main drive shaft, contact face (3) for the needle roller bearing, main drive shaft gear (4) and the surface (5) where it contacts the oil seal and the splines (6) for wear and damage. Check the front bearing by holding the outer race stationary and rotating the inner race while applying pressure. If the bearing is rough or noisy, remove the circlip from the shaft and press off the bearing. Fit a new bearing (Fig.G.23), using replacer set 09608-12010, No.11. Insert the circlip.

3. **Bush for 1st speed gearwheel:** The first speed gearwheel bush should be replaced if it falls outside the dimensions shown in Fig.G.24.

4. **Gearwheels:** Check the cone faces of 1st, 2nd and 3rd speed gearwheels (1), synchroniser gear (2), teeth (3), inside surface (4) and thrust face (5) in Fig.G.25 and check that the inner diameter is not less than 32.2 mm (1.26 in.).

5. **Operating sleeve with reverse gear:** (Fig.G.26). Check the splines (1) of the operating sleeve/reverse sliding gear, the reverse gear (2), operating sleeve and reverse gear to selector fork contact faces (3) for wear and damage and the width of the groove in the synchroniser operating sleeve and reverse gear. (Less than 7.5 mm (0.30 in.).

6. **Selector forks:** Fig.G.27. Check the clearance between the operating sleeve grooves and the selector forks by means of feeler gauges and inspect the surfaces for wear and damage. The thickness of the fork ends must be no less than 6.5 mm (0.26 in.). The max. clearance between groove and fork end must not exceed 0.8 mm (0.03 in.).

7. **Synchroniser hub:** (Fig.G.28). Check the synchroniser hub splines (1), the surface (2) of the hub in contact with the synchroniser shifting keys and the surface (3) of the hub in contact with the thrust faces of the gears for wear and damage.

8. **Shifting keys and synchroniser springs:** (Fig.G.29). Check the shifting keys (1) and the synchroniser springs (2) for wear and damage.

9. **Synchroniser rings:** (Fig.G.30 & G.31). Check the ring gear (1), and the cone face (2) for wear and damage. Place the synchroniser ring onto the gear cone and check the clearance between ring and gear. If the clearance is less than 0.4 mm (0.016 in.), replace the synchroniser ring. The standard clearance is 1.5 mm (0.06 in.). If the contact surface is poor or a new ring is fitted, lap the ring on the gear cone until a dull appearance of the surface is obtained. Thouroughly clean all traces of lapping paste.

10. **Countershaft, gear cluster and thrust washers:** Check the teeth of the gear cluster for wear or damage and the countershaft at the running area for the needle roller bearings for grooves or scoring. The min. thickness of the thrust washers is 1.7 mm (0.067 in.).

11. **Reverse idler gear and reverse idler shaft:** Check the reverse idler gear teeth and the gear bush for damage or wear. The inner diameter of the bush should be 18.2 mm (0.71 in.). Check the groove for the reverse selector arm on the idler gear for wear or damage. The gear shaft diameter should be 17.9 mm (0.70 in.).

12. **Speedometer gears:** Check the speedometer drive worm, the speedometer driven gear and the drive gear shaft for wear or damage. The outer diameter of the shaft should be 9.4 mm (0.37 in.). The max. inner diameter of the bush should be 9.8 mm (0.39 in.). Replace the 'O' sealing rings if worn.

13. **Gearbox rear bearings:** Check the gearbox rear bearing by rotating the inner race while applying pressure by hand and holding the outer race stationary. If the bearing is noisy or rough, it should be replaced. Using the special tools shown in the left-hand illustration of Fig.G.32, press the bearing out of its retainer whilst holding the circlip in the open position with the pliers. Press the new bearing

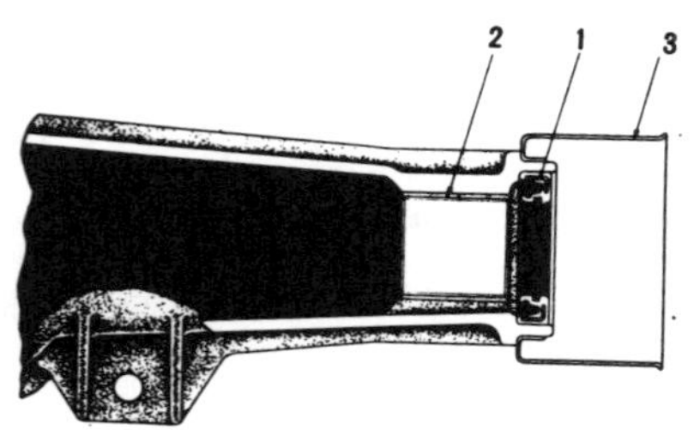

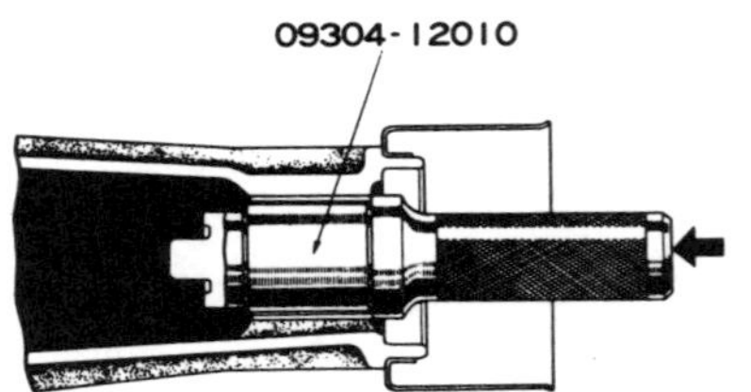

09304-12010

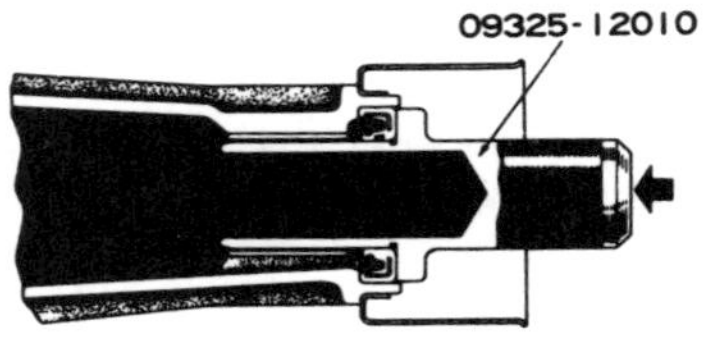

09325-12010

Fig.G.36. Check the rear extension housing at the numbered areas for wear and damage.

Fig.G.37. Replacement of the extension housing bush.

Fig.G.38. Installation of the extension housing oil seal.

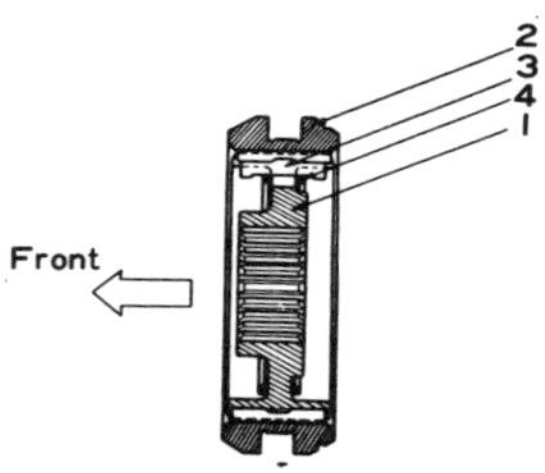

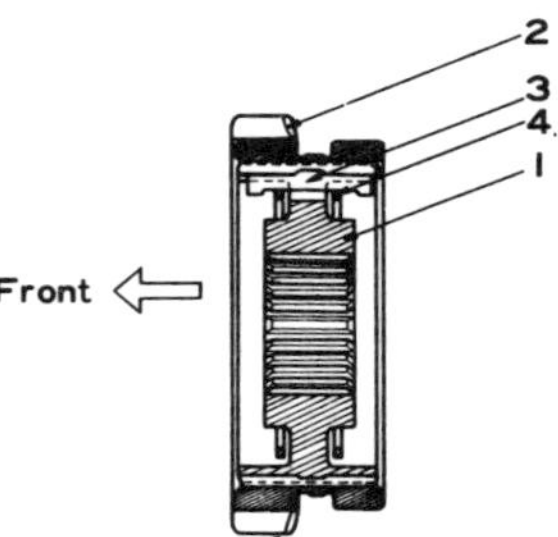

Fig.G.39. The correct assembly of the 3rd/4th speed synchroniser. (1). Hub, (2). Operating sleeve, (3). Shifting keys, (4). Synchroniser springs.

Fig.G.40. Assembly of the 1st/2nd speed synchroniser. (1). Hub, (2). Operating sleeve, (3). Shifting keys, (4). Synchroniser springs.

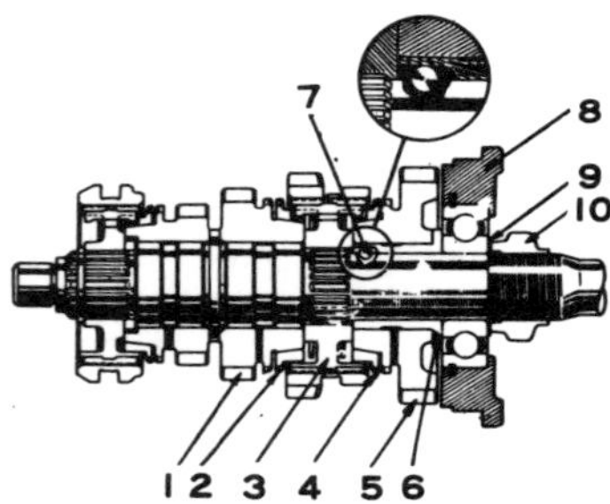

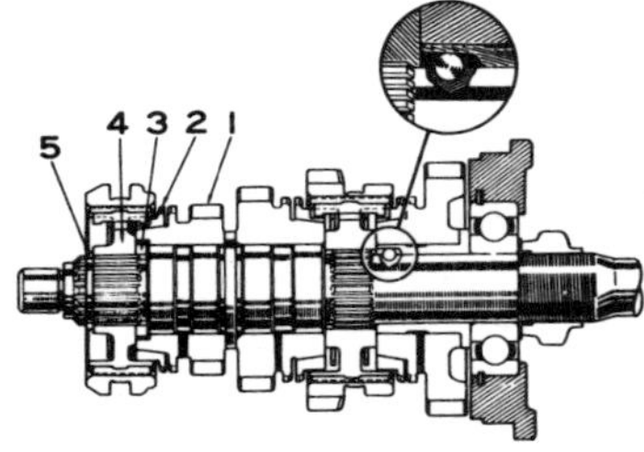

Fig.G.41. Assembly of the mainshaft.

1. Second speed gearwheel
2. Synchroniser ring (2nd speed)
3. Synchroniser unit
4. Synchroniser ring (1st speed)
5. First speed gearwheel
6. Bush for 1st speed gearwheel
7. Locating ball
8. Rear bearing
9. Shims
10. Nut

Fig.G.42. Assembly of mainshaft.

1. 3rd speed gearwheel
2. Synchroniser ring (3rd speed)
3. Hub spacer
4. Synchroniser unit
5. Snap ring

into the retainer as shown in the right-hand illustration of Fig.G.32.

14. **Gearbox case:** (Fig.G.33). Check the screw plug (1), clutch housing covers (2 & 3) ,oil receiver (4), detent ball spring seat (5) and all studs for wear or damage. Check the gearbox case for cracks.

15. **Gearbox front cover (bearing retainer):** Check the oil seal in the front cover and measure the outer diameter of the cover sleeve, which should be 27.9 mm (1.09 in.). This diameter is important in order to obtain a play-free fit of the clutch release bearing.

16. **Selector mechanism:** (Fig.G.34). Check the selector rod surfaces where they contact the detent balls and the gear lever recess in the selector rods. A clearance of 1.0 mm (0.04 in.) should be present. The width of the gear lever end should be more than 9.3 mm (0.36 in.). Check the contact surface of the gear lever with the gear lever cap pin for wear. The groove width should have a maximum of 6.3 mm (0.25 in.). The diameter of the pin should be more than 5.5 mm (0.21 in.)

17. **Extension housing:** If the oil seal in the rear of the extension housing is damaged, remove the seal from the housing, using oil seal puller 09308-10010 when the extension housing is fitted to the gearbox case (mainshaft fitted). (Fig.G.35). If the bi-metal bush is worn above 32.2 mm (1.27 in.) in diameter, or is damaged, it should be replaced as follows:

Heat the rear end of the extension housing to 80 - 100°C (180 - 210°F) and remove the bush, using the special tool 09304-12010 (Fig.G.37). (It is assumed that the oil seal was already removed). Fit a new bush with the same tool, with the split in the bush uppermost after the housing has been re-heated to the temperature given above. Ream the bush to an inner diameter of 32.00 - 32.03 mm (1.260 - 1.261 in.) to obtain a running clearance of 0.01 - 0.06 mm (0.0004 - 0.0024 in.). Fit a new oil seal with special driver 09325-12010 or any other suitable drift. (Fig.G.38). Check the correct position of the dust deflector.

GEARBOX — Assembly

It is recommended that new gaskets and sealing compound are used and that all parts are thinly coated with oil prior to assembly.

Assemble the 3rd/4th speed synchroniser assembly (Fig.G.39). Fit the two equal shifting key springs (4) on to the synchroniser hub (1) with the ends of the springs at 120° and insert the shifting keys (3) into the slots in the hub. Push the hub into the sleeve, making sure that the hub is facing the mainshaft as shown in the illustration. In similar manner fit the synchroniser hub assembly into the reverse gear (2) (Fig.G.40), again noting the installation of the shifting key springs and the correct assembly of the hub.

Fit the 2nd speed gearwheel (1) and the synchroniser ring for the 2nd speed (2) on to the mainshaft from the rear (Fig.G.41). Slide the 1st/2nd speed synchromesh unit on to the mainshaft with the shifting keys aligned with the grooves in the synchroniser ring. Now fit the 1st speed synchroniser ring (4), the 1st speed gearwheel (5) together with its bush (6), the locating ball (7), rear bearing (8), shims (9) and the nut (10).

Tighten the mainshaft nut, using special spanner 09326-12010 to a torque reading of 8 - 11 kgm (60 - 80 lb.ft.). Lock the nut by bending the metal over one of the flats, using a blunt chisel.

From the front of the mainshaft (Fig.G.42) fit the 3rd speed gearwheel (1), the 3rd speed synchroniser ring (2), the hub spacer (3) and the 3rd/4th speed synchroniser assembly (4). Fit a circlip (5) of correct thickness to reduce the end float of the operating sleeve. Circlips are available in the following thicknesses:

Spare part number 90520-23088
Thickness . . . . 2.0 mm (0.079 in.)

Spare part number 90520-23089
Thickness . . . . 2.1 mm (0.083 in.)

Spare part number 90520-23090
Thickness . . . . 2.2 mm (0.087 in.)

Fit the circlip, the Woodruff key, speedometer drive worm and the second circlip on to the rear end of the mainshaft and check the end float of each gearwheel. The end float values for each gear are given earlier on in the text under "GEARBOX — Inspection".

NOTE: The end float values for the new Corolla 1100 (after April 1968) and the Corolla 1200 are different from the values given under the mentioned heading, and can be found at the end of this section.

Fit the main drive shaft (clutch shaft) into the gearbox case, using the replacer shown in Fig.G.43. If the bearing protrudes in front of the gearbox case, use a bearing retainer gasket of 0.5 mm (0.02 in.) in thickness, if not use a 0.3 mm (0.01 in.) thick gasket. The part number for the first gasket is 33132-12010 and for the second gasket 33133-12010.

Grease the lip of the oil seal in the front bearing retainer and fit the retainer on to the gearbox case. Both sides of the gasket should be coated with sealing compound. Tighten the bearing retainer securing bolts to a torque reading of 1.0 - 1.6 kgm (7 - 12 lb.ft.).

Fit the needle roller bearing into the recess in the main drive shaft and the synchroniser ring over the main drive shaft gear and insert the mainshaft from the rear into the gearbox case, aligning the slotted pin in the rear bearing retainer with the groove in the gearbox case (Fig.G.44) and the synchroniser ring with the shifting keys.

Engage the reverse gear with the second gear and fit the 1st/2nd speed selector fork (1) into the groove of the reverse sliding gear. Turn the fork half a turn and fit the corresponding selector fork (2) from the rear of the gearbox case and into the selector fork (1). Fit 3rd/4th speed selector fork (3) into the groove of the operating sleeve for the 3rd/4th speed synchroniser assembly (3), rotate the fork half a turn and insert the selector rod for the 3rd/4th speeds through the gearbox case and the selector fork (3). Fit the reverse selector fork (5) into the gearbox case by engaging it with the centre of the reverse selector arm and fit the selector rod (6) into the gearbox case and the selector fork (5). The selector fork and rod assembly is shown in Fig.G.45 in assembled condition.

Align the holes in selector rods and forks and fit the slotted spring pins. This is carried out through the opening on the top of the gearbox case.

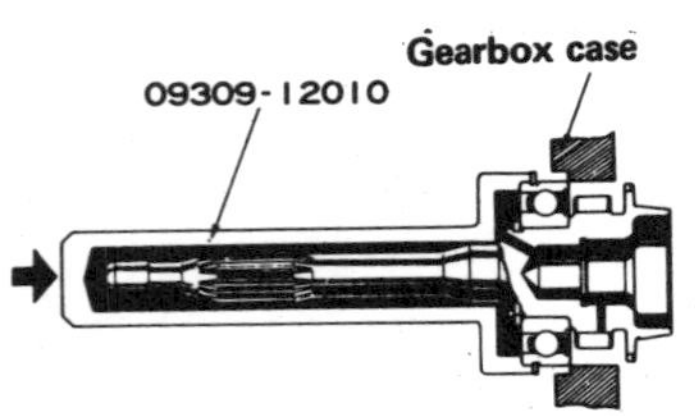

Fig.G.43. Assembly of the main drive shaft (clutch shaft).

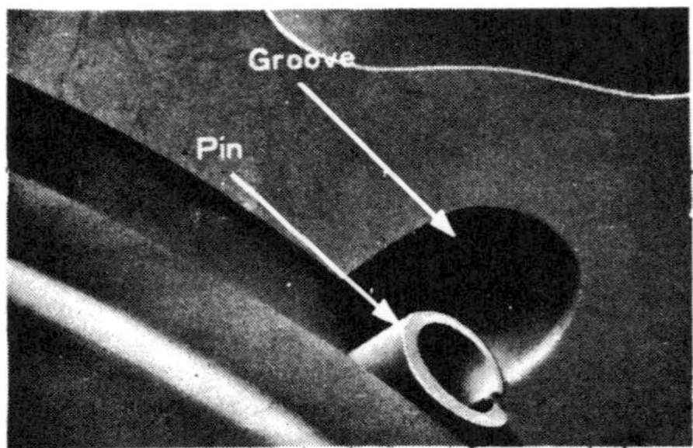

Fig.G.44. Aligning the roll pin with the groove in the bearing retainer.

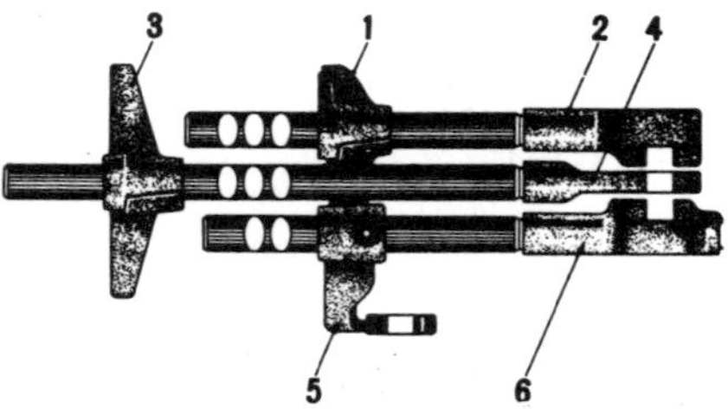

Fig.G.45. Assembly of the selector shafts and forks.

1. 1st/2nd speed selector fork
2. 1st/2nd speed selector shaft
3. 3rd/4th speed selector fork
4. 3rd/4th speed selector shaft
5. Reverse selector fork

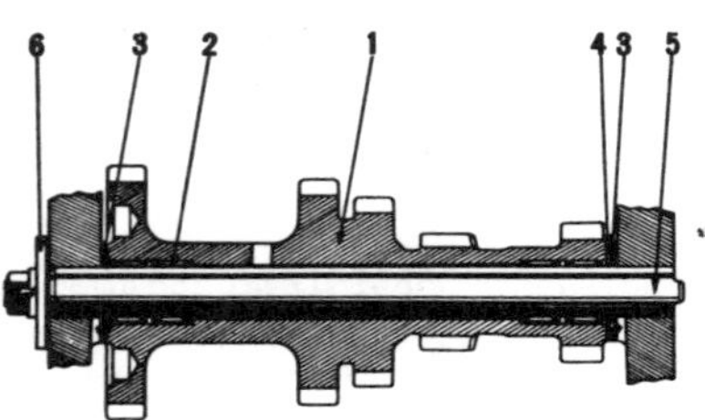

Fig.G.46. Installation of the countershaft gear cluster.

1. Gear cluster
2. Needle roller bearings
3. Side thrust washer
4. Thrust washer
5. Countershaft
6. Countershaft cover

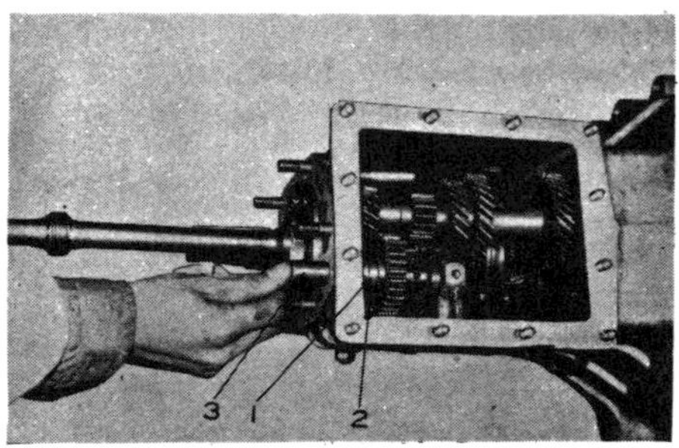

Fig.G.47. Installation of the reverse idler gear. (1). Groove of idler gear, (2). Selector fork pin, (3). Reverse idler shaft.

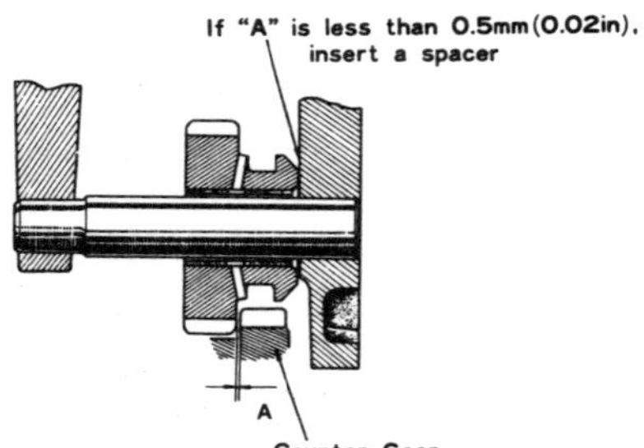

Fig.G.48. Checking the reverse idler gear position.

Fig.G.49. Installation of the reverse idler shaft securing bolt.

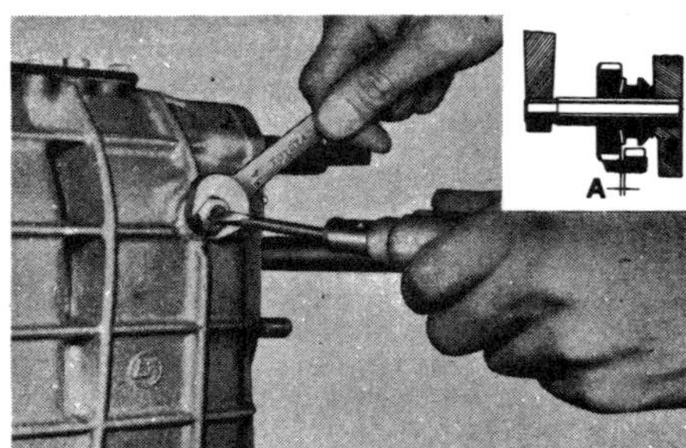

Fig.G.50. Adjustment of the reverse selector arm pivot.

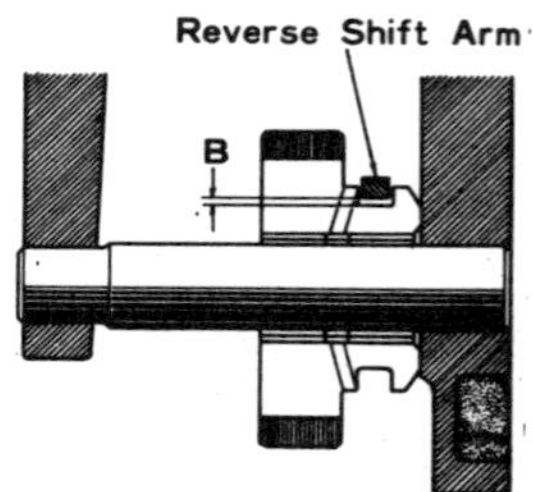

Fig.G.51. Adjustment of the reverse selector arm pivot.

Insert the needle roller bearings (2) into the countershaft gear cluster (1). Fit the gearbox case side thrust washer (3) and (4) at the front of the housing and the other thrust washer (3) at the rear of the housing with the raised parts of the washers engaged in the gearbox case recesses.. Fit the countershaft gear cluster and check that the end float of the cluster is 0.05 - 0.25 mm (0.002 - 0.010 in.). If necessary change the thickness of the thrust washers to obtain the required end float. Thrust washers are available in the following thicknesses:

Part number	Mark	Thickness
33441-12010	0	1.30 - 1.35 mm (0.051 - 0.053 in.)
33442-12011	1	1.40 - 1.45 mm (0.055 - 0.057 in.)
33443-12011	2	1.50 - 1.55 mm (0.059 - 0.061 in.)
33444-12010	3	1.60 - 1.65 mm (0.063 - 0.065 in.)

NOTE: Two needle roller bearings are fitted at each end of the countershaft gear cluster on Corolla 1100 models before April 1968. The countershaft of these models has a diameter of 20 mm. After April 1968, Corolla 1100 and the Corolla 1200 were fitted with one needle roller bearing at each end and the diameter of the countershaft was increased to 21 mm

Fit the countershaft (5) from the rear of the gearbox case so that the flats at the rear of the shaft are in a horizontal position. Fit the countershaft cover together with the gasket (6) and tighten the securing bolts to 1.0 - 1.6 kgm (7 - 12 lb.ft.).

Engage the groove (1) of the reverse idler gear with the reverse selector arm (2) (Fig.G.47) and fit the reverse idler gear into the case together with the idler shaft (3). Position the retaining boss of the shaft to the top in order to insert the locating bolt. Check the clearance "A" in Fig.G.48 between the teeth of the reverse idler gear and the teeth of the countershaft gear cluster. If this clearance is less than 0.5 mm (0.02 in.) insert a spacer (Part Number 90560-19198) at the rear of the reverse idler gear. Align the retaining boss with the locating bolt and tighten the shaft locating bolt to a torque reading of 1.3 - 1.8 kgm (9.5 - 13.0 lb.ft.). (Fig.G.49).

Fit detent balls and springs, gearbox cover and gasket and tighten the nuts to a torque reading of 0.4 - 0.9 kgm (3 - 7 lb.ft.).

Slacken the reverse selector arm pivot (Fig.G.50) and adjust the clearance "A" between the reverse idler gear and the countershaft gear cluster to 1.5 mm (0.06 in.) by turning the pivot with the selector rod in neutral position. Check the clearance "B" (Fig.G.51) between the bottom of the reverse idler gear groove and the upper end of the reverse selector arm. Adjust the pivot if the clearance is not between 1.5 - 0.5 mm (0.06 - 0.02 in.) to obtain clearances "A" and "B" within the specified values.

With the first gear engaged, check that the reverse gear does not touch the reverse idler. Grease the lips of the oil seal inside the extension housing and fit the extension housing and the gasket to the gearbox case. Tighten the securing nuts to 2.0 - 3.0 kgm (14.5 - 22 lb.ft). Oil and install the speedometer driven gear and shaft bearing sleeve into the extension housing. Fit the interlock plate (the sliding faces greased) into the gear lever retainer and fit the retainer to the gearbox case, with all gears in neutral position.

Again check the end float of all gearwheels before fitting the bottom gearbox cover (oil sump) with the embossed part of the gasket to the rear. Tighten nuts to 0.6 - 0.7 kgm (4.5 - 5.0 lb.ft.). Fit the drain plug with sealing washer and tighten to 3.7 - 4.3 kgm (27 - 31 lb.ft.).

Coat the moving parts of the clutch release bearing hub with grease and fit the hub and the withdrawal fork to the gearbox case. Tighten the bolts to 1.9 - 3.1 kgm (14 - 22 lb.ft.). Check the operation of the reversing light switch by means of a voltmeter (by moving the plunger of the switch) and reconnect the wiring.

GEARBOX — Installation

The installation of the gearbox is a reversal of the removal procedure, noting the following points:

All sliding faces should be lightly oiled or greased. All bolts should be tightened to the specified tightening torques. Fill the gearbox with 1.7 litres (1.85 U.S. qts.; 3 Imp. pts.) of the recommended oil. Tighten the oil filler plug to a torque reading of 3.7 - 4.3 kgm (27 - 31 lb.ft.).

MODIFICATIONS AFTER APRIL 1968
(Corolla 1100 and Corolla 1200)

The following modifications and changes were made on the Corolla 1100 after April 1968 and also incorporated in the Corolla 1200. The details given are different from the ones described in the previous text.

Synchroniser ring

The clearance between the synchroniser ring and the cone of the gearwheel must now be of a minimum of 0.6 mm (0.023 in.). This clearance was of a minimum of 0.4 mm (0.016 in.) in case of the earlier models.

Dismantling the gearbox

As already mentioned in the text, the countershaft has been altered. The shaft runs now in two bearings, instead of the former four and was increased in diameter from 20 mm to 21 mm.

Extension housing bush

A new special tool is needed for the installation of the extension housing rear bush.

Old special tool .09304-12010
New special tool 09307-12010

End float of gearwheels

The end float of the gearwheels and the countershaft gear cluster should be as follows:

Countergear:
    Standard . . . . 0.05 - 0.20 mm (0.002 - 0.008 in.)
    Limit . . . . 0.3 mm (0.012 in.)
1st and 2nd gear:
    Standard . . . . 0.10 - 0.25 mm (0.004 - 0.010 in.)
    Limit . . . . 0.3 mm (0.012 in.)
3rd gear:
    Standard . . . . 0.10 - 0.25 mm (0.004 - 0.010 in.)
    Limit . . . . 0.3 mm (0.012 in.)

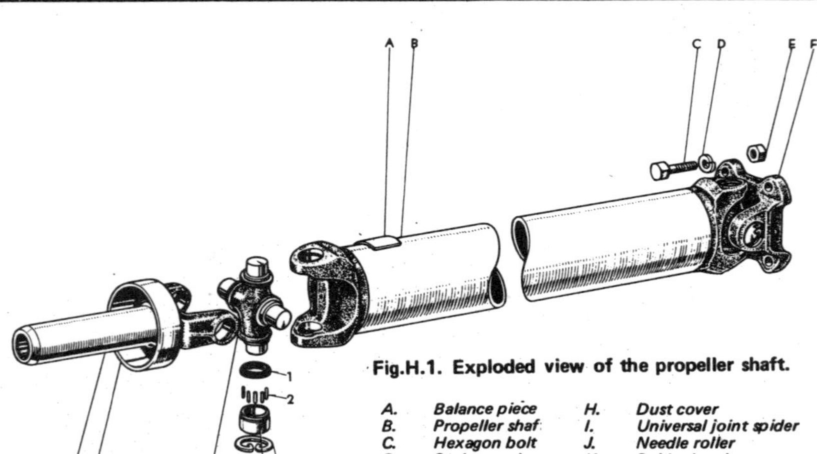

Fig.H.1. Exploded view of the propeller shaft.

A.	Balance piece	H.	Dust cover
B.	Propeller shaft	I.	Universal joint spider
C.	Hexagon bolt	J.	Needle roller
D.	Spring washer	K.	Spider bearing
E.	Nut	L.	Hole snap ring
F.	Yoke flange	M.	Seal ring
G.	Sleeve yoke		

Fig.H.2. Marking the propeller shaft (1) and the yoke flange (2) before dismantling.

Fig.H.3. Removal of the universal joint bearings (A & B).

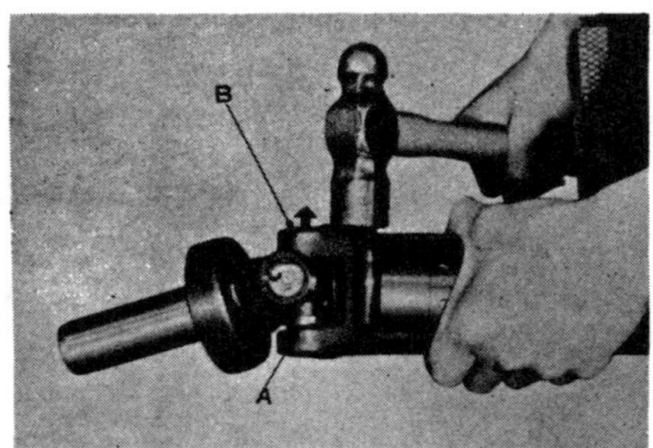

Fig.H.4. Removal of the universal joint bearings (A & B).

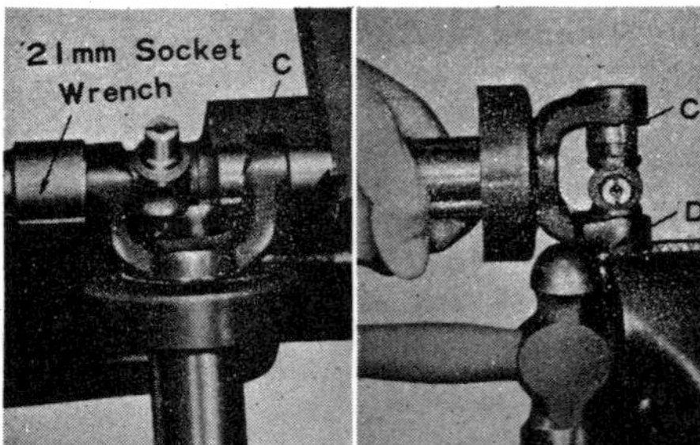

Fig.H.5. Removal of the universal joint bearings (C & D).

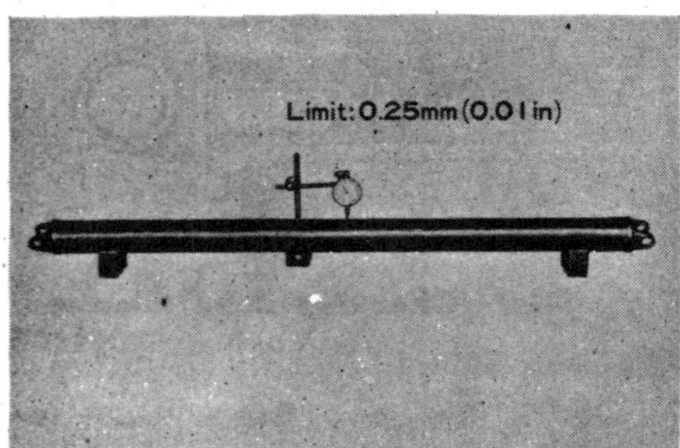

Fig.H.6. Checking the propeller shaft tube for run-out.

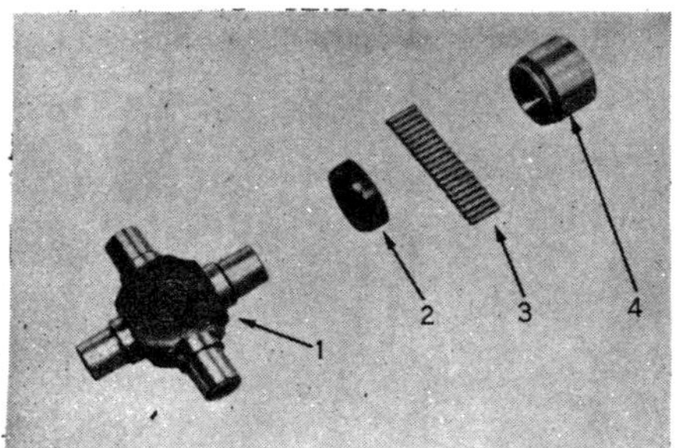

Fig.H.7. Dismantled universal joint.

1. Spider
2. Seal
3. Needle rollers
4. Spider bearing

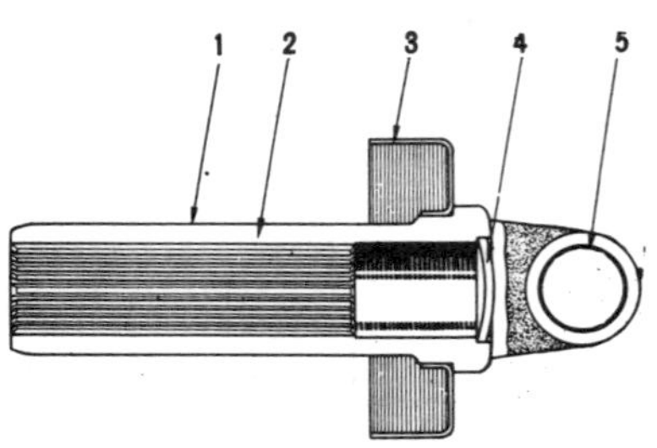

Fig.H 8. Checking the joint sleeve yoke.

1. Yoke
2. Splines
3. Dust cover
4. Expansion plug
5. Yoke bore

Rear Axle and Rear Suspension

GENERAL

The rear axle is a semi-floating axle with hypoid bevel drive. The centre line of the drive pinion is mounted below the centre line of the crown wheel. The drive pinion is mounted in taper roller bearings.

The rear suspension consists of leaf springs and double-acting, hydraulic, telescopic shock absorbers.

The propeller shaft consists of the propeller shaft tube with two universal joints, sliding joint and universal joint yoke flange. The universal joints are of conventional construction with joint spider, needle roller bearings and bearing caps.

PROPELLER SHAFT — Removal
(Fig.H.1)

With the rear of the car resting on suitable stands, remove the bolts securing the rear propeller shaft flange to the axle drive flange, lower the shaft end and withdraw the yoke from the rear of the gearbox extension housing. Fit a spare yoke into the extension housing to prevent loss of oil.

PROPELLER SHAFT — Dismantling

Punch mating marks into the shaft yoke and the sliding joint yoke (Fig.H.2), using a centre punch. Using a suitable drift, tap one end of the spider bearing and remove the circlip from the hole. Repeat this operation for the other three circlips. Using a 14 mm socket, press bearing "A" in a vice until bearing "B" touches the vice as shown in Fig.H.3. Then tap against the shaft as shown in Fig.H.4 until bearing "B" protrudes at the top and remove the bearing. Now clamp the spider into a vice with the socket until bearing "A" touches and again tap the shaft until bearing "A" protrudes and can be withdrawn. Remove the spider from the yoke.

Using a 21 mm and a 14 mm socket in a vice, press on the bearing "C" until bearing "D" protrudes. Then place the yoke over the vice as shown in Fig.H.5 (soft-metal jaws fitted to the vice), clamp bearing "D" carefully between the jaws and tap the yoke off the bearing. Remove bearing "C" in a similar manner and remove the yoke. Remove the spider at the other end of the propeller shaft in the same way. Remove the seal and the needle roller bearings from the spider bearing.

PROPELLER SHAFT — Inspection and Assembly

Check the propeller shaft for signs of unbalance, run-out or wear at the spider bearings, yoke bores. The max. run-out is 0.25 mm (0.01 in.). To check the run-out, place the propeller shaft into two V-blocks and check by means of a dial gauge as shown in Fig.H.6. Check the spider journal (1, Fig.H.7), seal (2), needle rollers (3) and the bearing outer races (4) for corrosion, damage or wear.

Check the sliding joint yoke splines (2, Fig.H.8), yoke (1), spider bearing bores (5), joint dust cover (3) and the expansion plug (4) for wear, damage or leaks. If any of the bearings are to be replaced, check on the yoke concerned if there is a drill mark, which is located as shown in Fig.H.9. In this case fit the oversize spider bearing with the red identification mark. Bearing details are as follows:

Spider Bearing Outer diameter

Part Number	Size	Marking
37402-10010	20.008 - 20.021 mm	No
	(0.7877 - 0.7882 in.)	Marking
37402-10020	20.029 - 20.042 mm	Red
	(0.7885 - 0.7892 in.)	Marking

Yoke Bore Diameters

Size	Marking
20.000 - 20.021 mm	No
(0.7874 - 0.7882 in.)	Marking
20.011 - 20.042 mm	Drilled
(0.7882 - 0.7892 in.)	Marking

Ensure that the parts are correctly matched (check mating marks). Pack the spider bearing outer races with grease, insert 20 needle rollers into each race and fit the seal. Fit the spider and one bearing into the sliding joint yoke and then press in the bearing in a vice, using a 14 mm socket, until the spider touches the yoke. (Fig.H.10). Fit the other bearing and press into the yoke until the spider is in the centre of the yoke. Then, using two 14 mm sockets, press in both bearings and select new circlips to allow the spider 0.05 mm (0.002 in.) side play. The circlips should have the same thickness on both sides. Having fitted the circlips, check the universal joint for freedom of movement. Circlips are available as follows:

Part Number	Thickness
90521-22011	1.20 mm (0.047 in.)
90521-22012	1.25 mm (0.049 in.)
90521-22013	1.30 mm (0.050 in.)

Fit the spider into the corresponding yoke of the shaft and fit the spider and the sliding joint yokes to the shaft (Fig.H.12). Fit spider, bearings and circlips in the above manner to both ends of the shaft and the rear flange.

PROPELLER SHAFT — Installation

The installation of the propeller shaft is a reversal of the removal procedure. The splines of the sliding joint should be lubricated with oil prior to installation. Tighten the flange bolts to a torque reading of 1.5 - 2.2 kgm (11.0 - 16.0 lb.ft.).

DIFFERENTIAL — Removal and Dismantling

Remove the differential carrier as described in the next section (see also Fig.I.5) and clamp the differential carrier into a vice. Without damaging the thread of the drive pinion, straighten the flange securing nut with a chisel and holding the flange by suitable means, remove the nut from the flange. Withdraw the flange from the differential carrier and withdraw the pinion oil seal as shown in Fig.H.14. Any two-arm puller is also suitable to

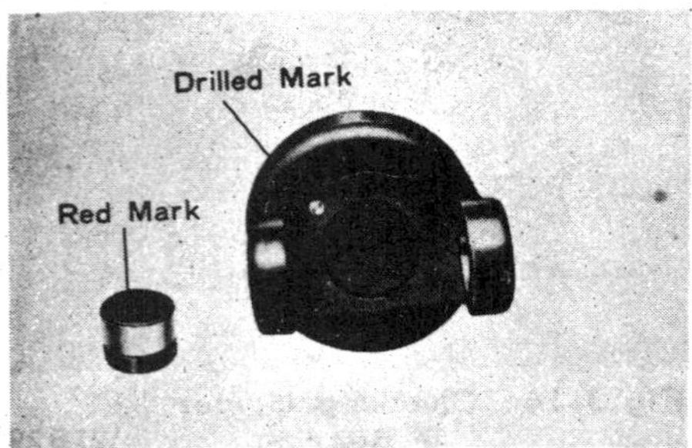

Fig.H.9. The markings of spider bearings and yoke flange.

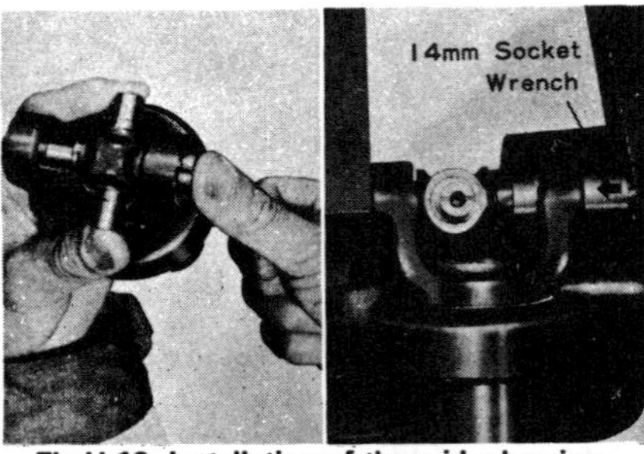

Fig.H.10. Installation of the spider bearings.

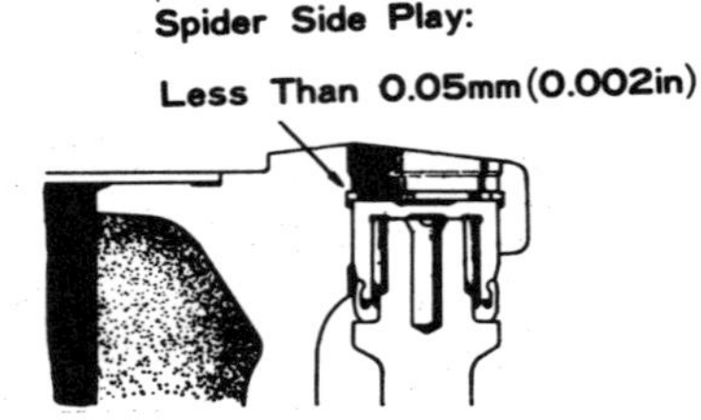

Fig.H.11. Selecting a bearing snap ring of suitable size.

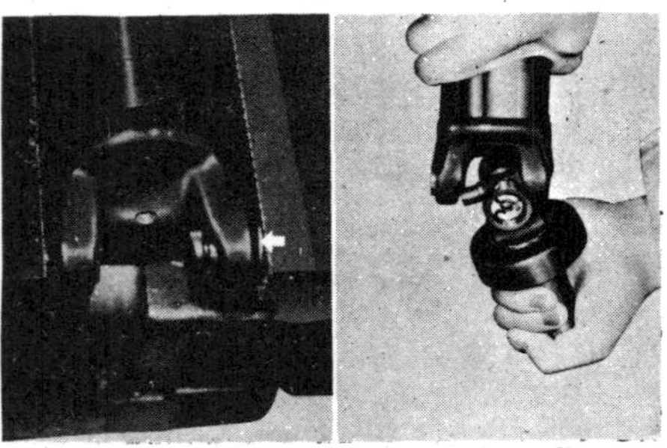

Fig.H.12. Installation of the yoke sleeve flange.

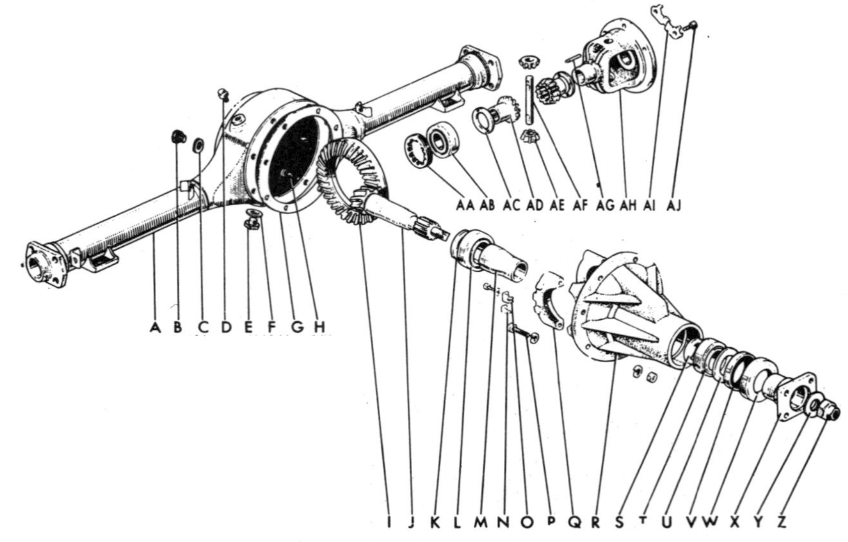

Fig.H.13. Exploded view of the rear axle assembly

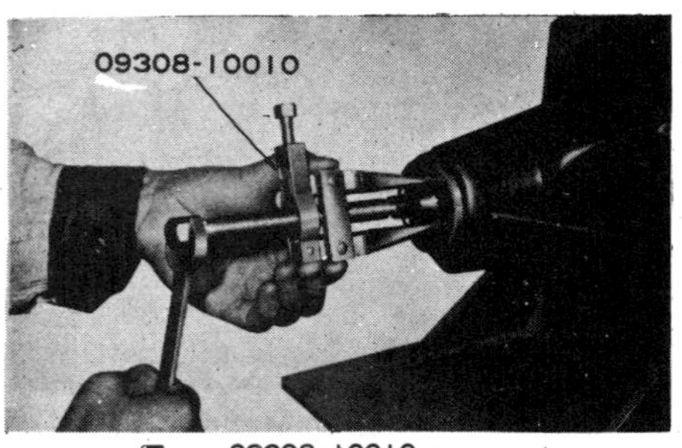

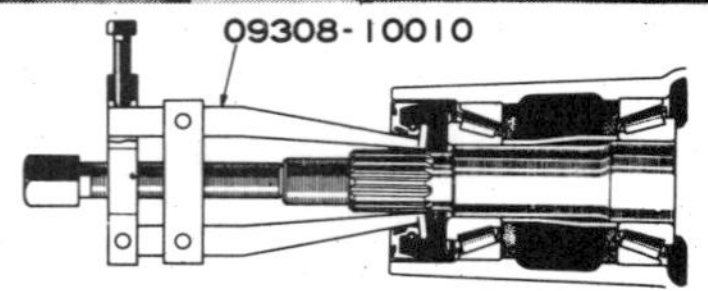

Fig.H.14. Removal of the drive pinion oil seal.

A.	Rear axle case	R.	Differential carrier
B.	Filler plug	S.	Shim
C.	Filler plug seal washer	T.	Taper roller bearing
D.	Breather plug	U.	Oil deflector
E.	Drain plug	V.	Oil seal
F.	Drain plug seal washer	W.	Dust deflector
G.	Differential carrier gasket	X.	Drive pinion flange
H.	Bolt	Y.	Plain washer
I.	Crown wheel	Z.	Pinion nut
J.	Drive pinion	AA.	Differential bearing adjusting nut
K.	Washer	AB.	Taper roller bearing
L.	Taper roller bearing	AC.	Thrust washer
M.	Drive pinion bearing spacer	AD.	Differential side gear
N.	Bearing cap nut lock plate	AE.	Differential pinion
O.	Bearing cap nut lock plate	AF.	Differential pinion shaft
P.	Hexagon bolt	AG.	Securing pin
Q.	Differential bearing cap	AH.	Differential cage
		AI.	Lock plate (crown wheel)
		AJ.	Bolt (crown wheel)

Fig.H.15. Checking the crown wheel for run-out.

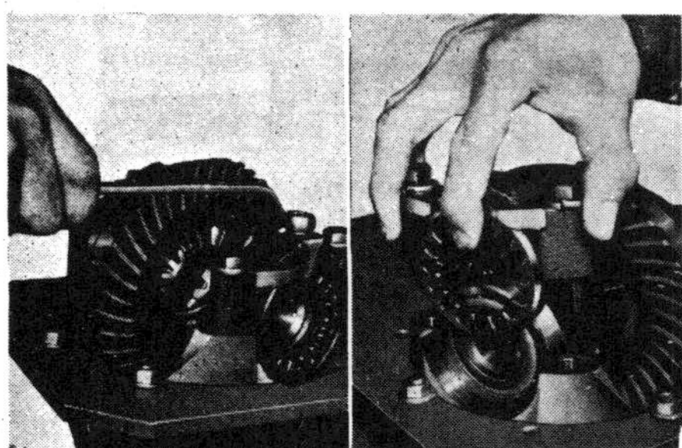

Fig.H.16. Removal of the differential bearing caps.

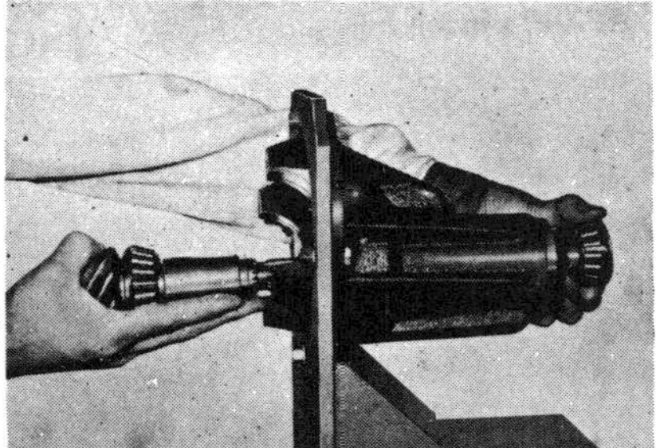

Fig.H.17. Removal of the drive pinion.

Fig.H.18. Removal of the differential side bearings.

Fig.H.19. Checking the backlash of the differential side gears.

Fig.H.20. Removal of the securing pin for the differential pinion shaft.

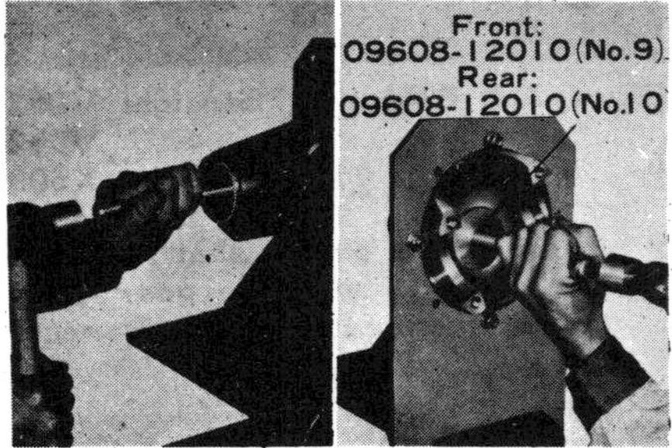

Fig.H.21. Replacing the outer pinion bearing races.

Fig.H.22. Installation of the securing pin for the differential pinion shaft.

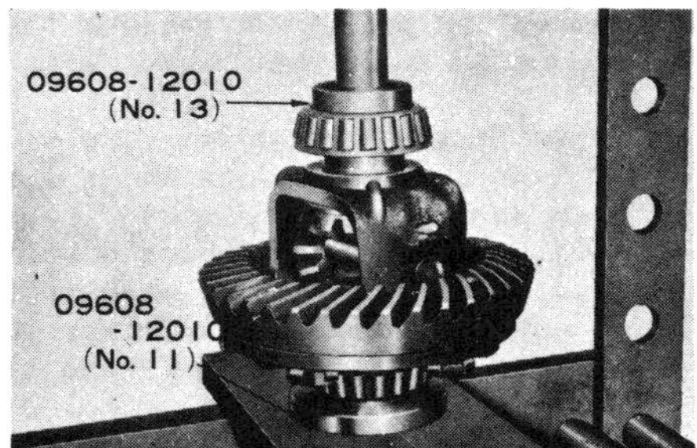

Fig.H.23. Installation of differential side bearings.

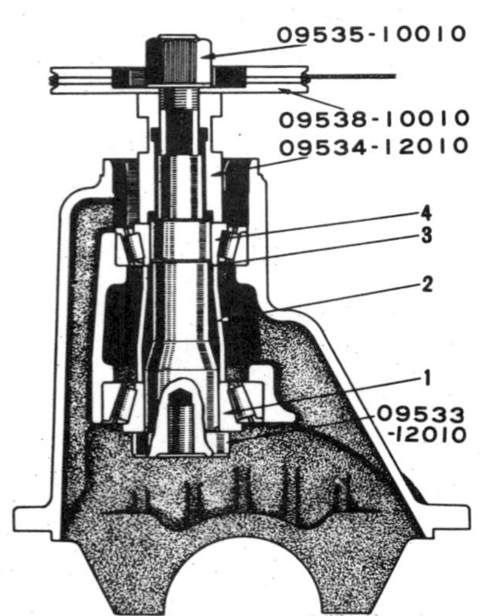

Fig.H.24. The drive pinion setting gauge in fitted position.

Fig.H.25. Checking the pre-load of the drive pinion bearings.

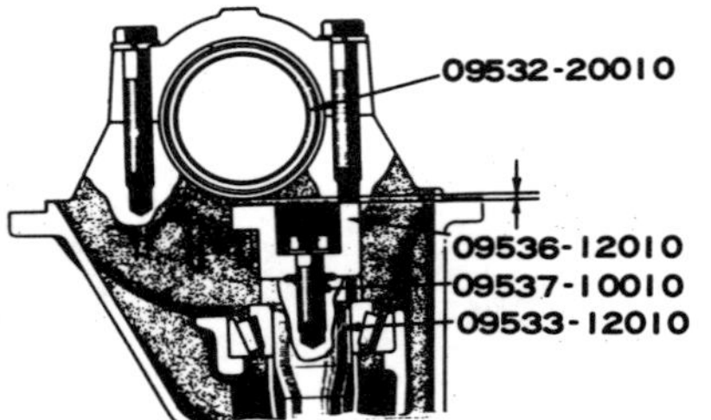

Fig.H.26. The master checking gauge in fitted position.

Fig.H.27. Selection of the drive pinion bearing spacer.

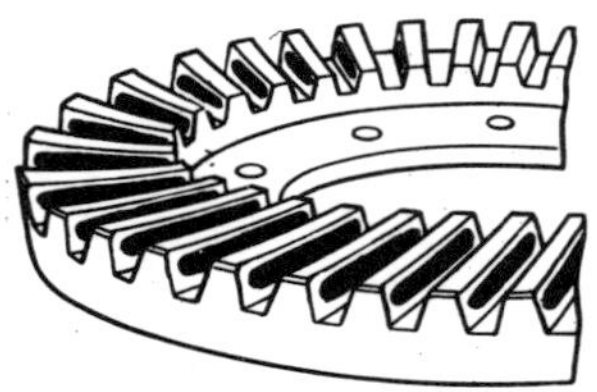

Fig.H.28. The correct tooth contact pattern.

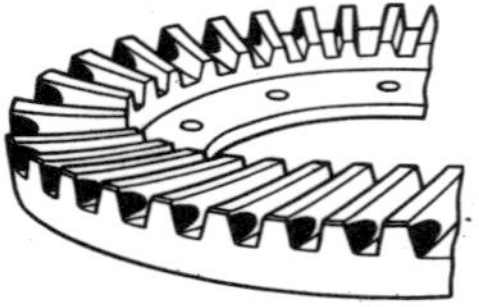
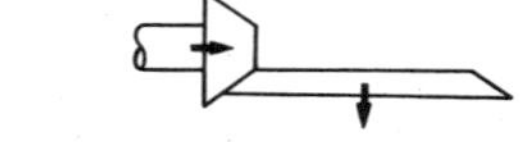

Fig.H.29. Heel contact.

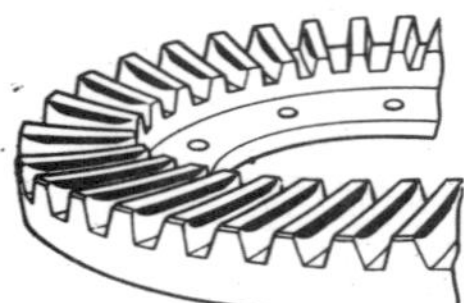
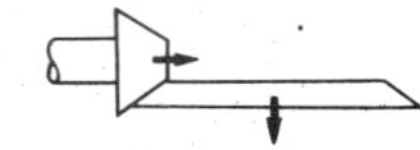

Fig.H.30. Face contact.

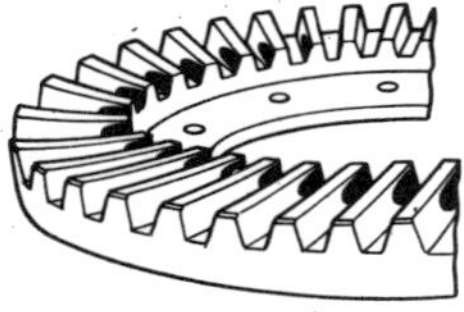
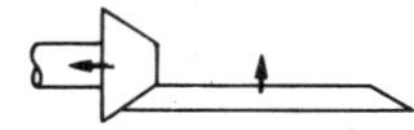

Fig.H.31. Toe contact.

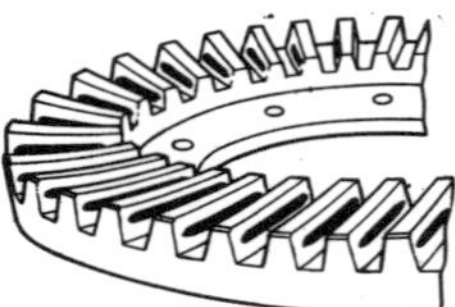
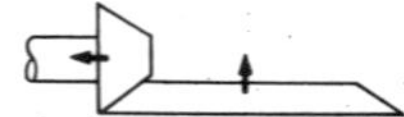

Fig.H.32. Flank contact.

remove the oil seal. If the oil seal is to be replaced, lever it out by means of a strong screwdriver. When the oil seal is removed, refit the flange with the nut to the pinion shaft for the following check:

Check the crown wheel for run-out (max. 0.04 mm; 0.0016 in.) as shown in Fig.H.15. The crown wheel must be turned one complete revolution to find the total deflection.

Punch mating marks into the differential carrier and the bearing caps, remove the adjusting nut lock washers, bearing cap bolts, the caps and the adjusting nuts (Fig.H.16). Remove the differential case assembly from the differential carrier together with the bearings. Remove the flange and the nut from the pinion shaft end and withdraw the drive pinion, front bearing and oil slinger, spacer and adjusting shims. The rear bearing will remain with the pinion shaft. If necessary tap the pinion out of the carrier, using a rubber mallet. (Fig.H.17). To remove the drive pinion rear bearing, special tool 09950-20010 is available, which is a two-arm puller the arms of which are to be inserted under the inner bearing race. Also remove the differential side bearings. This operation is shown together with the special tool in Fig.H.18. A suitable two-arm puller can also be used.

Bend back the crown wheel bolt lock plates and remove the crown wheel from the differential case. Check the backlash of the differential side gears and bevel pinions in similar manner as shown in Fig.H.19, and record the measured values. Remove the securing pin for the differential pinion shaft, supporting the differential case as shown in Fig.H.20 and withdraw the shaft. Differential side gears and bevel pinions can now be removed from the case. Collect the thrust washers.

Inspection of Parts

Thoroughly clean all parts and check for wear, damage or deformation. When it is necessary to replace one of the gear wheels, all gears that are in mesh with this gear must also be replaced.

Check the drive pinion bearing outer races and if necessary replace the races by driving them out with a brass drift. Fit new bearing races with the special tools shown in Fig.H.21 or use suitable drifts, the outer diameters of which must be the same as the diameter of the race in question.

Check all bearings for noise or roughness. Inspect the drive pinion and crown wheel teeth for excessive wear or damage. Crown wheel and pinion are matched and must be replaced as a set. Check the differential side bearing adjusting nuts for thread damage and replace if necessary.

The drive pinion flange must show little wear on the splines and on the running area for the drive pinion oil seal. Check the inside of the differential case for wear where the case is in contact with the differential side gears and bevel pinions. The crown wheel run-out must not exceed 0.04 mm (0.0016 in.).

Check the differential side gears for tooth wear, spline damage and measure the outside diameter of the outside boss, which must not be less than 29.9 mm (1.20 in.). Inspect the bevel pinions in similar manner, measuring the bore diameter (15.15 mm; 0.5965 in.) and the pinion shaft diameter (14.95 mm; 0.5886 in.).

DIFFERENTIAL — Assembly and Adjustment

Lubricate all parts with oil prior to assembly. Insert the differential side gears and the bevel pinions into the differential case and check the backlash of the gear wheels by holding the bevel pinions and moving the side gears as shown in Fig.H.19. Read off the indication of the dial gauge. If the backlash is not within 0.02 - 0.15 mm (0.0001 - 0.006 in.) adjust the backlash by altering the thickness of the side gear thrust washers (using the same thickness on both sides) to obtain the correct reading. The oil groove in the thrust washers must face the wheels. Fit the bevel pinion shaft, insert the securing pin and peen over the end of the hole to retain the securing pin in position. (Fig.H.22).

Fit the crown wheel to the differential case using new lock plates and tighten the bolts to 6.0 - 7.5 kgm (45 - 55 lb.ft.). Make sure that both mating faces are clean and free from any foreign matter. If this is not the case, run-out will be "build-in". Bend over the lock plates.

Using a press and a suitable press mandrel (or special tool 09608-12010, No.11 and No.13) press on the differential side bearings as shown in Fig.H.23.

With reference to Fig.H.24 fit the drive pinion rear bearing (1), bearing spacer (2) and shim (3), removed during dismantling, onto the differential pinion adjusting gauge 09530-12010 and insert the tool together with the assembled parts from the rear into the differential carrier. Then fit the pinion front bearing (4) and attach the collar, the pre-load flange and the nut to the drive pinion, tightening the nut to a torque reading of 13 - 15 kgm (95 - 110 lb.ft.). Wind a cord around the flange and using a spring scale as shown in Fig.H.25, pull slowly until the shaft turns and read off the pull required. If the pre-load exceeds the limits given below, change the bearing spacer and shims to obtain the correct values.

Pre-load new bearings . . . . 1.2 - 2.2 kg (2.7 - 4.8 lb.)
Pre-load (used bearings) . . . . 0.4 - 1.3 kg (0.9 - 2.8 lb.)

The shim is available in one thickness only (0.25 mm (0.01 in.). Spacers are selective as follows:

Drive pinion bearing spacers

Part Number	Length in mm	Length in inches
41231-12010	49.70 mm	1.957 in.
41232-12010	49.74 mm	1.958 in.
41233-12010	49.78 mm	1.960 in.
41233-12010	49.78 mm	1.960 in.
41234-12010	49.82 mm	1.961 in.
41235-12010	49.86 mm	1.963 in.
41236-12010	49.90 mm	1.965 in.

Fit the base rod head of the adjusting gauge to the base rod and fit the master mandrel into the side bearing housings. Tighten the bearing cap bolts to 5.5 - 6.5 kgm (40 - 47 lb.ft.) The mating marks on the carrier and the bearing caps must correspond. Select a pinion spacer washer that will give the minimum clearance between gauge and washer. The correct washer can be selected by inserting the washer directly as shown in Fig.H.27 or the gap can be measured with feeler gauges. Spacer washers are available in thicknesses from 2.33 mm (0.092 in.) to 2.57 mm (0.101 in.) in steps of 0.3 mm (0.012 in.).

Remove the differential/drive pinion adjusting gauge and slide the spacer washer over the drive pinion shaft. Then fit the rear pinion bearing to the shaft, using a press, so that the smaller diameter of the bearing is facing to the threaded end of the shaft. Fit the selected bearing spacer with the shim on to the pinion shaft and insert the assembly into the differential carrier. From the front of the carrier insert the front bearing, the oil slinger, drive flange, washer and a new nut. Tighten the nut to 13 - 15 kgm (95 - 110 lb.ft.), holding the flange by suitable means whilst tightening the nut.

Fit the side bearing outer races to the respective bearing cones and place the differential case into the differential carrier so as to obtain minimum pinion to crown wheel backlash. Fit the bearing adjusting nuts, place the respective bearing caps over the adjusting nuts on to the differential carrier and insert the bolts. Tighten the bolts only enough so that the adjusting nut threads seat snugly in the bearing caps and the differential arrier.Then tighten the bearing cap bolts to 5.5 - 6.5 kgm (40 - 47 lb.ft.).

Slacken the pinion side adjusting nut and tighten the crown wheel side adjusting nut until all backlash disappears. Back off the crown wheel side adjusting nut by four notches so that one of the notches aligns with the lock washer. Firmly tighten the pinion side nut until it forces the opposite side bearing to contact its adjusting nut. Slacken the pinion side adjusting nut until it is free from the bearing and re-tighten the nut until it just contacts the outer bearing race. From this position tighten the pinion side nut from 1 to 1 1/2 notches, so that the lock washer can be inserted in the notch, in order to pre-load the differential side bearings.

To check the backlash between the drive pinion and the crown wheel proceed as follows:

Using a dial gauge, placed with the plunger at right angles against one of the crown wheel teeth, check that the backlash is between 0.10 - 0.15 mm (0.004 - 0.006 in.). If the measured value is found to be outside the limits given, obtain the correct setting by using the adjusting nuts (the bearing cap bolts must be slightly slackened for this purpose). If the backlash is more than 0.15 mm (0.006 in.) slacken the pinion side nut; if the backlash is less than 0.10 mm (0.004 in.), slacken the crown wheel nut. In both cases the nut opposite to the one slackened, must be tightened by the same amount. One notch of the adjusting nut represents a change of approx. 0.04 mm (0.0016 in.) in backlash.

Fit the pre-load flange on to the pinion flange and check the pre-load as shown in Fig.H.25.This reading represents the total pre-load and should be 1.6 - 3.0 kg (3.5 - 6.6 lb.) for new bearings or 0.6 - 1.9 kg (1.3 - 4.2 lb.) for used bearings.

To check the tooth contact pattern of crown wheel and pinion mesh, apply red lead or mechanic's blue to the crown wheel teeth and rotate the crown wheel several times backwards and forwards by means of the drive pinion. If the tooth pattern is not as shown in Fig.H.28 adjust as follows:

Heel contact (Fig.H.29): Move the drive pinion towards the crown wheel by increasing the spacer washer thickness between pinion head and rear bearing and/or adjust the backlash by moving the crown wheel away from the drive pinion.

Face contact (Fig.H.30): The adjustment procedure for face contact patterns is the same as described above for the heel contact.

Toe contact (Fig.H.31): Move the drive pinion away from the crown wheel by decreasing the spacer washer thickness between pinion head and rear bearing and/or adjust the backlash by moving the crown wheel towards the drive pinion.

Flank contact (Fig.H.32): The adjustment procedure for this type of tooth pattern is the same as decribed above for the toe contact.

Fit the bearing cap adjusting nut lock washers to the bearing caps (two differnt types) and tighten the securing bolts to 0.4 - 0.7 kgm (3 - 5 lb.ft.). Remove the drive pinion flange and fit a new oil seal with a suitable mandrel. Fit the flange washer, the flange and a new nut and tighten to 13 - 15 kgm (95 - 110 lb.ft.). Peen the material of the nut into the pinion shaft to lock it.

DIFFERENTIAL — Installation

The installation of the differential assembly is described in the next section.

REAR AXLE — Removal

With the rear of the car supported on stands and the rear wheels removed, mark the fitting position of the brake drums on the rear axle half shafts and remove the brake drums. From the inside of the axle remove the bearing outer retainer nuts (Fig.I.3) and from the ourside of the brake assembly remove the brake shoe return springs. Align the holes in the half shaft flange and in the bearing retainer and fit the rear axle shaft remover bolts 09520-10010. Alternately tighten the bolts and pull the shaft out of the axle tube. (Fig.I.4). Remove the propeller shaft as detailed in the relevant section and drain the rear axle lubricant. Unscrew the differential carrier from the banjo housing of the rear axle and lift the complete carrier out of the axle (Fig.I.5).Disconnect and plug the flexible brake pipes, remove the handbrake cable clevis pin and disconnect the rigid brake pipes. Unscrew the brake back plates from the rear axle.

If the car is jacked up under the axle casing, change the stands so that the car is supported under the jacking plate between floor sidemember and the door and rear wheel housing and disconnect the shock absorber (1), handbrake cable (2) and remove the rear spring 'U'-bolts (3). Remove the rear axle from the leaf springs, by first pushing the axle to one side to clear one side of the axle from the spring and then freeing the other side.

REAR AXLE — Inspection

Rear axle half shafts

With reference to Fig.I.7 check the wheel studs (1), the outer face of the inner bearing retainer (2) and the splines (3) for damage and wear. Check the shaft and the shaft flange for run-out. Run-out values of 0.2 mm (0.008 in.) for the flange and 2.0 mm (0.08 in.) for the shaft must not be exceeded.

Check the axle shaft bearing for roughness or noise by holding the half shaft in one hand as shown in Fig.I.8 and applying a pressure to the outer race as it is rotated.

To replace a wheel securing stud, fit one of the wheel nuts and drive out the stud, using a brass drift and hammer. Install the new wheel stud into the shaft flange and using a piece of tube of about 15 mm (0.06 in.) inner diameter,clamp the shaft flange into a vice as shown in Fig.I.9 to press in the stud.

To replace the axle shaft bearing, fit one of the nuts to the serrated stud and drive out the stud with a brass drift and a hammer in a similar manner as described for the wheel studs. Then grind the inner bearing retainer and split the retainer, using a cold chisel. (Fig.I.10 and Fig.I.11). Using a press and suitable press plates (special plates 09232-10010) remove the bearing together with the outer bearing retainer from the axle shaft.

Refit the removed serrated stud to the outer bearing retainer and press the retainer and a new bearing on to the shaft, using bearing replacer set 09608-12010, No.11. If using other suitable press plates, take care that the thrust of the press is applied as near as possible to the axle shaft. Heat a new inner bearing retainer to 150ºC (302ºF) and fit the retainer quickly over the shaft so that it can shrink in position. (Fig.I.12).

Rear axle casing

With reference to Fig.I.13 check the rear axle casing (1 & 2) for damage and deformation, the differential carrier securing bolts (3) and the breather plug (4) for damage. If the breather plug is removed, re-tighten it on installation to a torque reading of 1.0 - 1.3 kgm (7 - 9 lb.ft.). If the oil seals in the axle tube ends are worn or damaged, remove the seal in question from the rear axle, using a strong screwdriver or another suitable tool and drive in a new oil seal, using the special drift 09517-12010 or if this is not available, a drift, the outer diameter of which is the same as that of the oil seal.

REAR AXLE — Assembly and Installation

The assembly and the installation of the rear axle is a reversal of the removal procedure noting the following points:

a.   All sliding or moving parts are to be lubricated with rear axle oil. When fitting the differential carrier gasket make sure that the protruding part of the gasket is located as shown in Fig.I.14.

b.   When refitting the brake drums to the rear axle, take care that the marks made during dismantling are in line. Bleed the brake system as described in section "BRAKES" under the same heading.

c.   Refill the rear axle with 1.0 litres (1.1 U.S.qts;0.9 Imp. pts.) of the recommended oil (hypoid-type). Before inserting the filler plug, check that the oil level has reached the lower edge of the filler plug hole. Then insert the filler plug and tighten to a torque reading of 2.7 - 3.3 kgm (20 - 24 lb.ft.

NOTE: It is advisable to check the axle drain plug for security before the car is taken on the road. Experience has shown that drain plugs are sometimes removed to drain the oil, then replaced and left untightened. To avoid this, therefore, re-check the plug.

d.   All nuts and bolts should be tightened to the recommended tightening torques in accordance with the values given in the "Tightening Torque Table" in this manual.

REAR SUSPENSION — Removal
(Fig.I.15)
(Later models see Fig.I.22)

With the rear end of the car resting on stands and the rear wheels removed, place a jack under the centre of the rear axle casing. From the inside of the luggage compartment remove the upper shock absorber mountings (nuts, dished washers, rubber bushes). Then remove the lower shock absorber mountings (bolt and nut) and remove the shock absorbers. (Fig.I.16).

Remove the rear spring "U"-bolt nuts and the "U"-bolt spring plate and the lower spring pad. From the rear of the rear springs remove the shackle plate nuts and the shackle plate and insert a tyre lever or strong screwdriver between the opposite shackle plate and the spring hanger in order to remove the shackle plate bolts. From the front of the rear spring remove the two bolts and nut securing the spring bracket pin and push out the pin by inserting a strong screwdriver between the pin and the spring bracket. This operation should be carried out with greatest care, as the spring will drop to the ground as soon as the spring pin is clear of its locations.

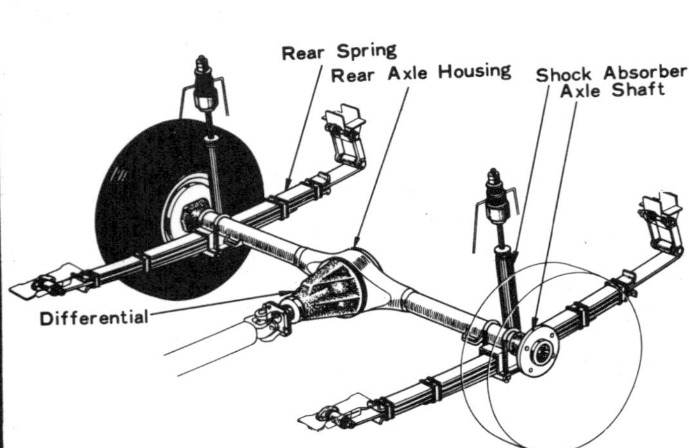

Fig.I.1. View of the rear suspension.

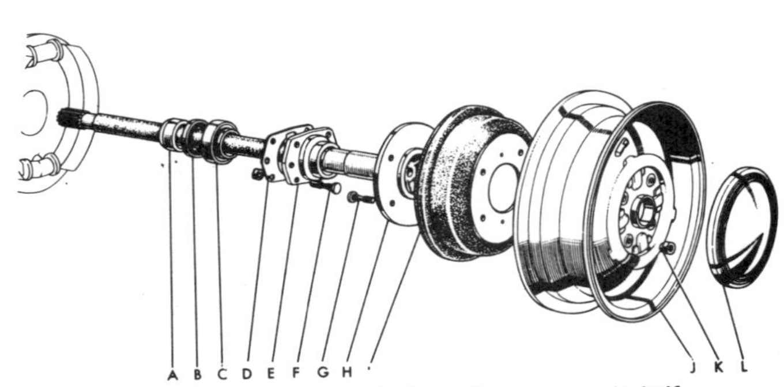

Fig.I.2. Exploded view of the rear axle half shaft.

A.	Inner bearing retainer	G.	Hub stud
B.	Oil seal	H.	Rear axle half shaft
C.	Bearing	I.	Brake drum
D.	Retainer gasket	J.	Disc wheel
E.	Outer retainer	K.	Hub nut
F.	Bolt	L.	Wheel cap

Fig.I.3. Removal of the outer bearing retainer nuts from the inside of the axle.

Fig.I.4. Removal of the rear axle shaft.

Fig.I.5. Removal of the differential carrier.

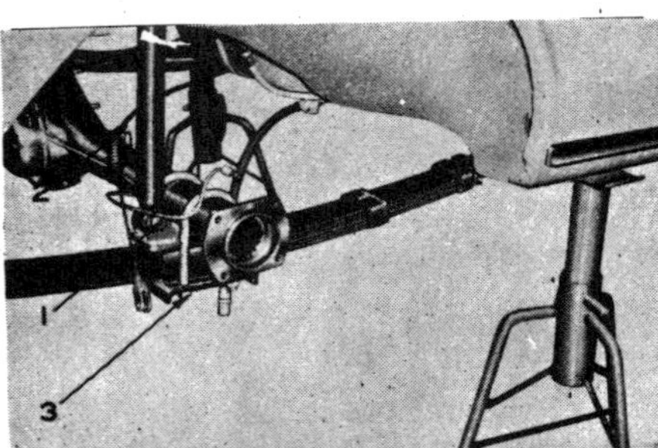

Fig.I.6. Removal of the rear axle.

1. Shock absorber mounting
2. Clip
3. Spring bolt nuts

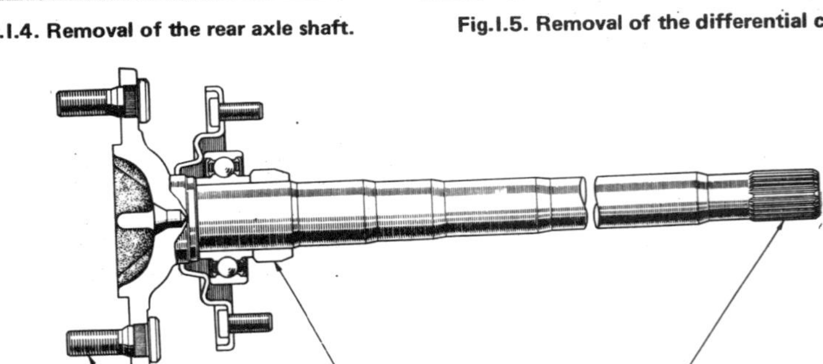

Fig.I.7. Check the wheel studs (1), the contact area for the inner bearing retainer (2) and the splines (3) of the axle shaft.

Fig.I.8. Checking the axle shaft bearing for damage.

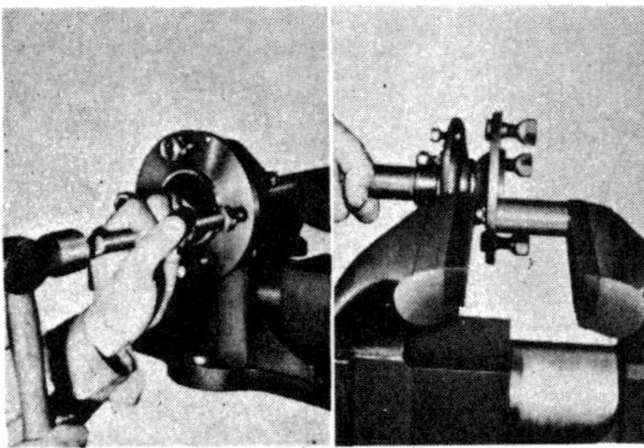

Fig.I.9. Replacement of the hub studs.

Fig.I.10. Removal of the inner bearing retainer.

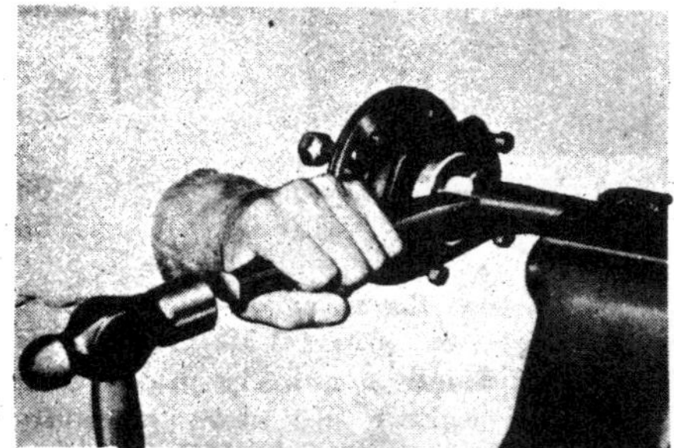

Fig.I.11. Removal of the inner bearing retainer with a chisel.

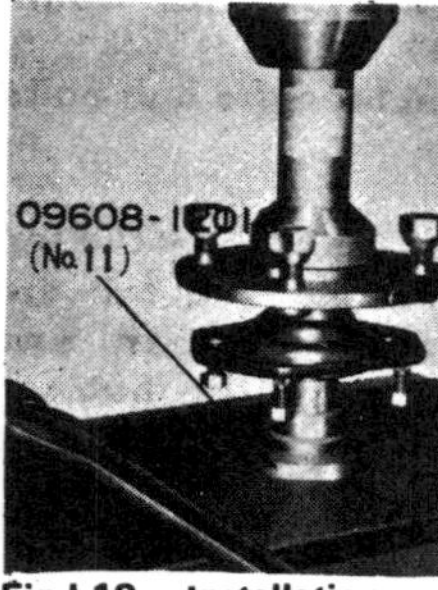

Fig.I.12. Installation of the inner bearing retainer.

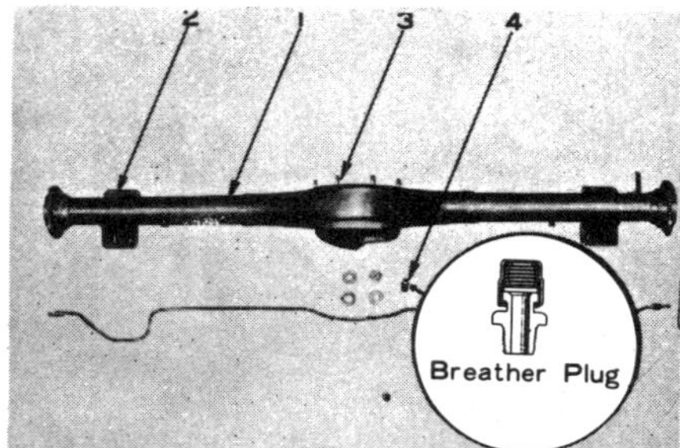

Fig.I.13. Check the rear axle housing at the areas shown.

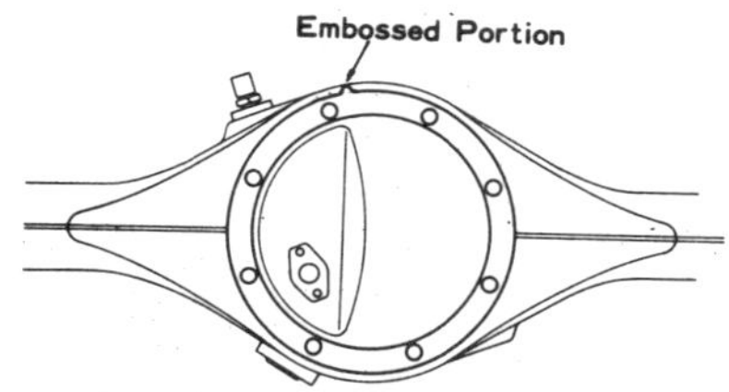

Fig.I.14. The correct installation of the differential carrier gasket.

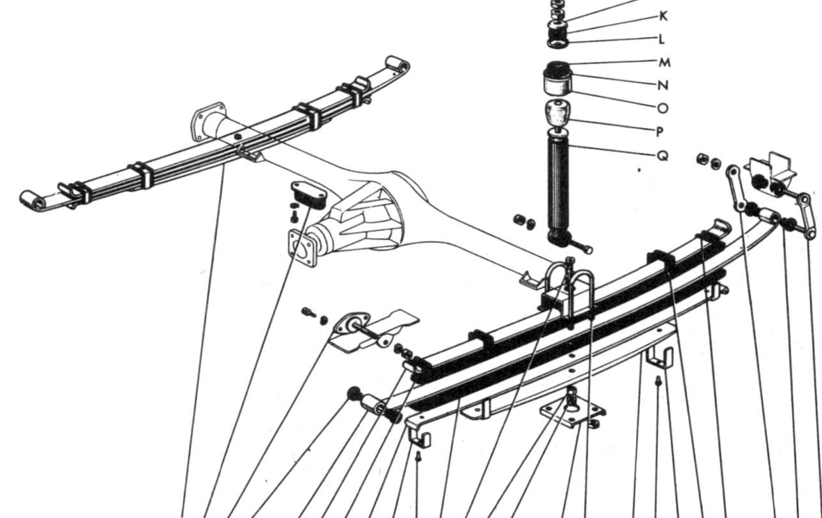

Fig.I.15. Exploded view of the rear suspension.

A.	Rear spring	Q.	Rear shock absorber
B.	Differential carrier bump stop	AA.	1st spring leaf
C.	Spring bracket pin	AB.	Tensioning leaf
D.	Bush	AC.	Inter-leaf
E.	Rear spring U-bolt seat	AD.	2nd rear spring leaf
F.	U-bolt	AE.	Spring clip
G.	Outer plate of spring shackle	AF.	Rivet
H.	Bush	AG.	Inter-leaf
I.	Spring shackle with pins	AH.	Spring centre bolt
J.	Cup washer for shock absorber	AI.	Distance piece
K.	Rubber bearing	AJ.	Nut
L.	Cup washer	AK.	3rd rear spring leaf
M.	Rubber bearing	AL.	Rivet
N.	Rubber bearing seat	AM.	Spring clip
O.	Bump stop cover	AN.	Clip insert
P.	Rear spring bump stop	AO.	Clip insert

Fig.I.16. Removal of the upper shock absorber mounting (left) and lower shock absorber mounting (right).

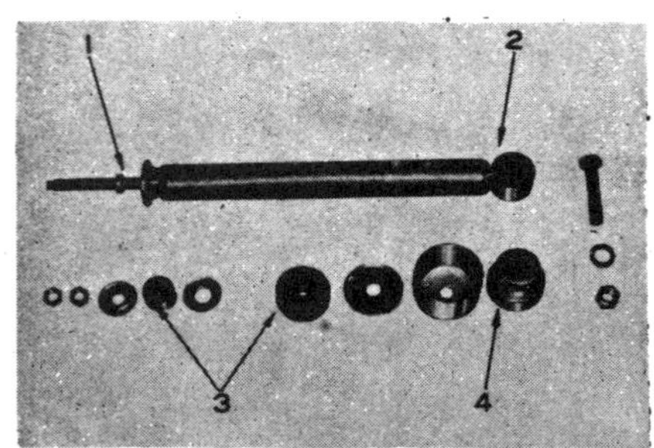

Fig.I.17. Checking the shock absorber parts.

1. Piston rod
2. Bush
3. Rubber bushes
4. Spring bump stop

Fig.I.18. Installation of the front spring hanger bolt.

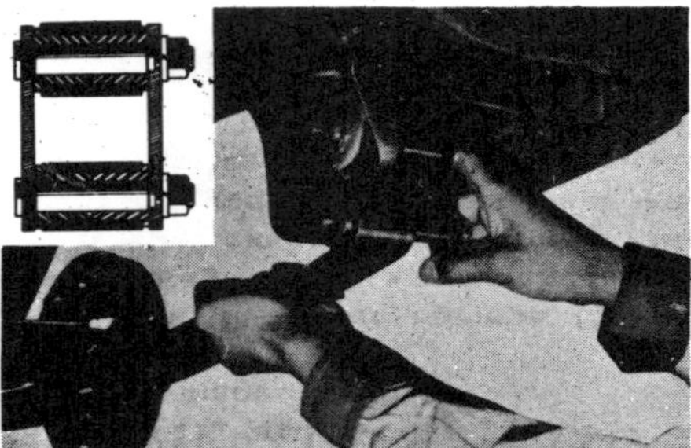

Fig.I.19. Installation of the rear shackle plate.

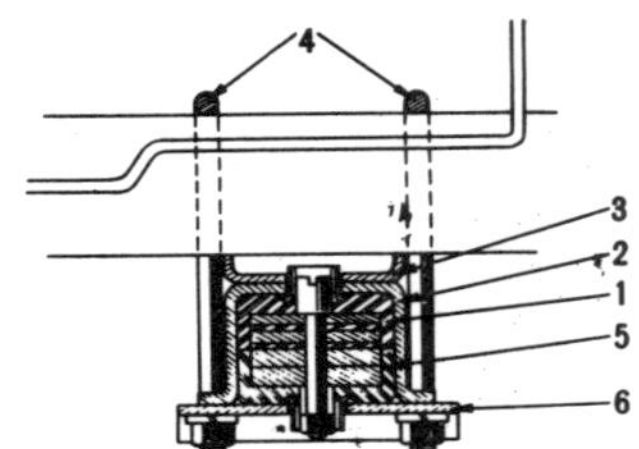

Fig.I.20. Section through the fitted spring mounting.

1. Upper pad   *4. U-bolts*
2. Pad retainer   *5. Lower pad*
3. Rear axle seat *6. U-bolt seat*

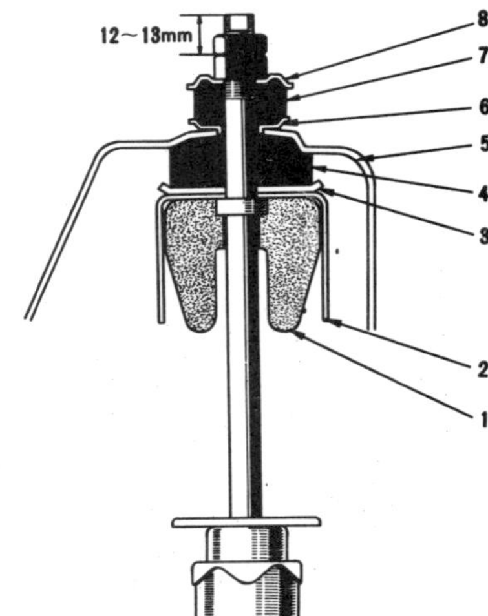

Fig.I.21. Section through the upper shock absorber mounting.

1. Bump rubber   *5. Mounting bracket*
2. Bump rubber cover   *6. Cup washer*
3. Rubber bush retainer *7. Rubber bush*
4. Rubber bush   *8. Cup washer*

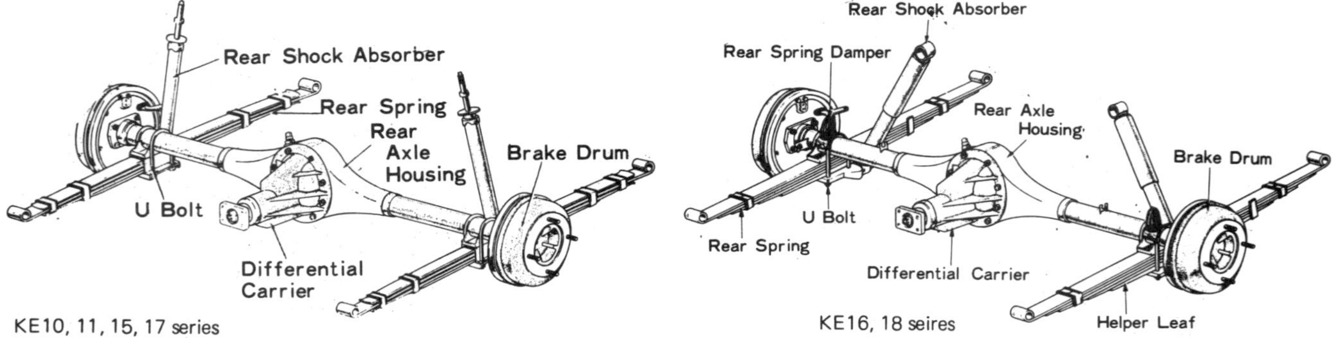

Fig.I.22. View of the rear suspension assemblies fitted to later Corolla 1100 and 1200 Saloon and Estate Car Models.

REAR SUSPENSION — Inspection

Shock Absorbers

With reference to Fig.I.17 check the shock absorber piston rod (1), bushes (2), rubber bearings (3) and the spring bump rubber (4) for wear or damage. Check the shock absorbers by gripping the upper and the lower end with the hands and moving the shock absorber several times to and fro. Any air present in the shock absorber is normally indicated by lack of resistance. If air is present in the shock absorber hold it in a vertical position for a few minutes so that the air can escape to the top. Then pump the shock absorber a few times to force the air from the pressure chamber. A shock absorber in good condition must show an equal resistance over the entire working range.

Rear Springs

Check the shackle pin bushes, the shackle, bracket pin and bracket pin bushes and the "U" bolts for wear or damage. Examine the rear spring leaves for breakage, cracks, rust or weakness. Whilst it is possible to replace a single leaf in a spring it is generally more satisfactory to renew the complete spring. To dismantle a spring, open the four spring clips with a suitable tool, clamp the spring into a vice and remove the centre bolt. Slowly open the vice to release the spring tension and take the spring apart. If the spring leaf with the clips is to be replaced, drill out the rivet head from the clip, using a 8.5 mm (0.33 in.) drill and rivet the clip to the new spring leaf.

Assemble the spring by placing the spring leaves in their order of assembly over a rod, the diameter of which should be the same as the centre bolt. Then clamp the spring leaves into a vice, slowly close the vice until the leaves are compressed and withdraw the pilot rod. Insert the centre bolt into the leaf holes and tighten the nut. Finally, bend the clips over the spring leaves.

REAR SUSPENSION — Installation

Fit the rubber bushes into the front spring eye and fit the front of the spring to the body with the bracket pin. Finger-tighten the two bolts and the nuts. Install the rubber bushes into the rear eye of the spring and the rear bracket, insert the shackle pins into the spring eye and the bracket, fit the shackle plate and tighten the nuts finger-tight. (Fig.I.19).

Fit the upper spring pad (1) and the pad retainer (2) (Fig.I.20) between the rear spring and the rear axle housing seat (3), insert the "U"-bolts and from below the axle fit the lower pad (5) and the "U"-bolt seat (6). Tighten the "U"-bolt nuts to a tightening torque of 3.0 - 4.5 kgm (22 - 32 lb.ft.).

Support the rear end of the car under the rear axle casing by means of stands and tighten the spring securing bolts and nuts as follows:

Bracket pin bolts . . . . .1.0 - 1.6 kgm (7 - 12 lb.ft.)
Bracket pin nut . . . . 2.0 - 3.0 kgm (15 - 22 lb.ft.)
Shackle nuts . . . . 2.0 - 3.0 kgm (15 - 22 lb.ft.)

On to the shock absorber rod fit the bump stop (1, Fig.I.21), bump stop cover (2), dished washer (3), rubber bush (4) and insert the piston rod through the opening in the body bracket (5). From the inside of the luggage compartment fit the second dished washer (6), the rubber bearing (7) and a dished washer (8). Secure the assembly with the nut. Tighten the nut so that the end of the piston rod protrudes 12 - 13 mm (0.47 - 0.51 in.) above the end face of the nut as shown in the illustration and fit and tighten the locknut to a torque reading of 1.9 - 3.1 kgm (14 - 22 lb.ft.).

Fit the lower end of the shock absorber to the rear axle casing, tightening the securing nut to a torque reading of 3.5 - 5.5 kgm (25 - 40 lb.ft.). Finally refit the wheels, lower the car to the ground and tighten the wheel nuts to 9 - 12 kgm (65 - 90 lb.ft.).

MODIFICATIONS ON LATER MODELS

Corolla Series KE10, 11, 15, 17, and KE16 and 18 have been fitted with a different rear suspension as the one illustrated in Fig.I.15. The rear suspension fitted to these models is shown in Fig.I.22. The removal and installation of this rear suspension is practically the same as described for the previous suspension. Any detail changes can be taken from the illistrations. Note the upper mounting of the shock absorber and the additional rear spring damper on the KE16 and 18 series.

Technical Data

REAR AXLE

	KE 10, 11, 15, 17	KE 16, 18
Type	Semi-floating	Semi-floating
Design of casing	Banjo	Banjo
Reduction gears:		
Gear type	Hypoid	Hypoid
Ratio	4.222:1	4.444:1
Drive pinion	9 teeth	9 teeth
Crown wheel	38 teeth	40 teeth

DIFFERENTIAL

Gear type	Bevel gear	Bevel gear
Pinion gears	Two - 10 teeth	Two - 10 teeth
Side gears	Two - 16 teeth	Two - 16 teeth

REAR SPRINGS

Type	Asymmetrical semi-elliptic leaf springs	Asymmetrical semi-elliptic leaf springs
Number of leaves	4	5
Thickn. of leaves	KE10 & 15:	1 x 5 mm
	1 x 4 mm	3 x 6 mm
	2 x 6 mm	1 x 13 mm
	1 x 7 mm	
	KE11 & 17:	
	1 x 4 mm	
	3 x 6 mm	
Width of leaves	50 mm (2.0 in.)	(50 mm (2.0 in.)

SHOCK ABSORBERS

Type	Double-acting, hydraulic, telescopic	Double-acting, hydraulic, telescopic
Stroke	206 mm (8.24 in.)	170 mm (6.7 in.)
Damping force:		
Rebound	45 kg (0.3 m/sec.)	75 kg (0.3 m/sec.)
	(100 lbs. (12 in./sec)	(165 lbs. (12 in./sec.)
Compression	25 kg (0.3 m/sec.)	34 kg (0.3 m/sec.)
	(55 lbs. (12 in./sec.)	(75 lbs. (12 in./sec.)

WHEELS AND TYRES

Tyre size:
  Saloon . . . . 6.00 - 12 4-ply
  Estate . . . . 5.00 - 12 6-ply
Tyre pressures:
  Front . . . . 1.3 kg/sq.cm (18 psi.)
  Rear . . . . 1.3 kg/sq.cm (18 psi.) — Saloon
  2.1 kg/sq.cm (30 psi.) — Estate

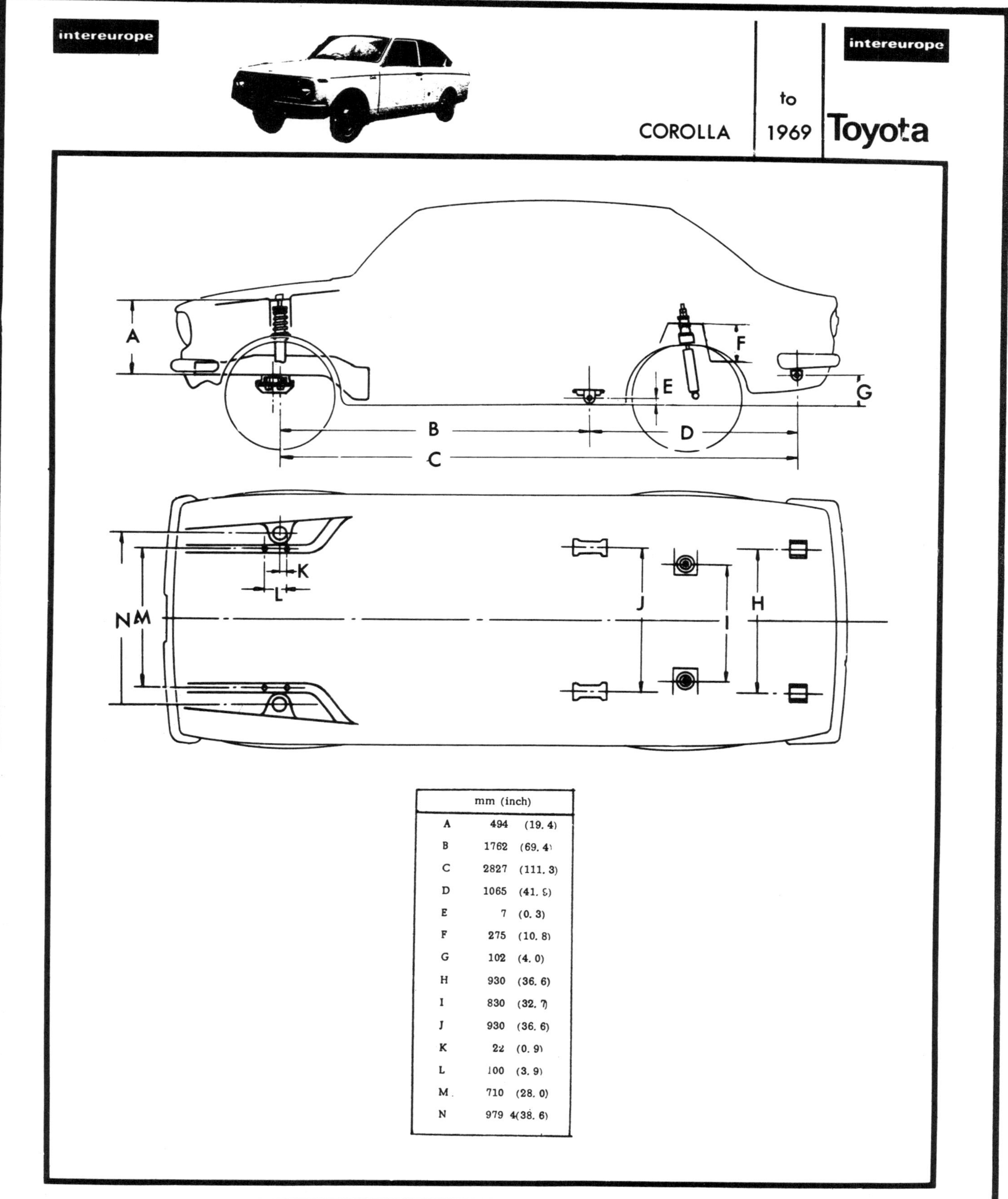

mm (inch)		
A	494	(19. 4)
B	1762	(69. 4)
C	2827	(111. 3)
D	1065	(41. 9)
E	7	(0. 3)
F	275	(10. 8)
G	102	(4. 0)
H	930	(36. 6)
I	830	(32. 7)
J	930	(36. 6)
K	22	(0. 9)
L	100	(3. 9)
M	710	(28. 0)
N	979 4	(38. 6)

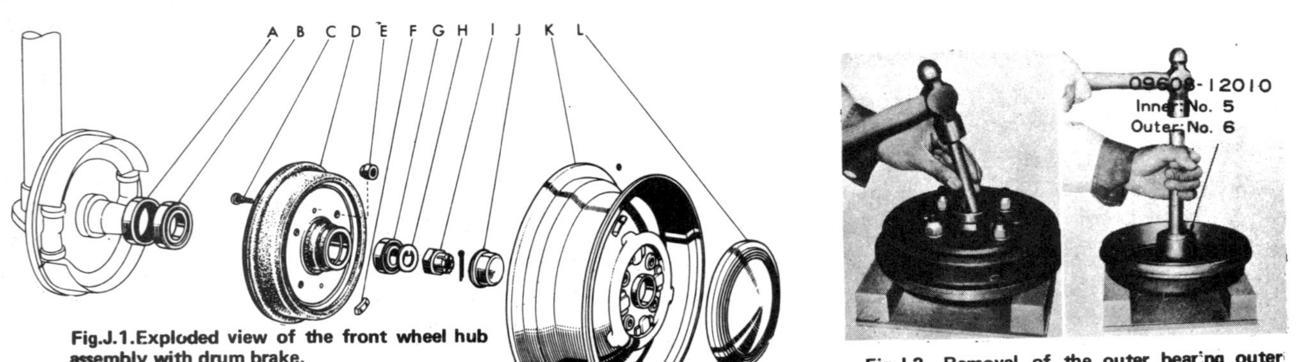

Fig.J.1. Exploded view of the front wheel hub assembly with drum brake.

Fig.J.2. Removal of the outer bearing outer race (left) and the inner bearing outer race.

A.	Oil seal	G.	Outer wheel bearing
B.	Inner wheel bearing	H.	Locating washer
C.	Wheel securing stud	I.	Castellated nut
D.	Hub and drum assembly	J.	Grease cap
E.	Wheel securing nut	K.	Disc wheel
F.	Balance weight	L.	Hub cap

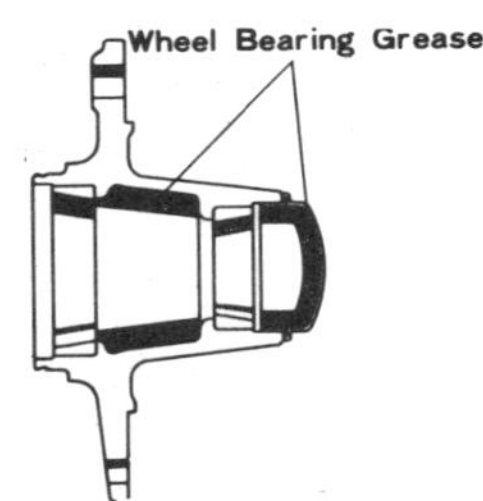

Fig.J.3. The shaded areas should be filled with grease as shown after assembly of the hub.

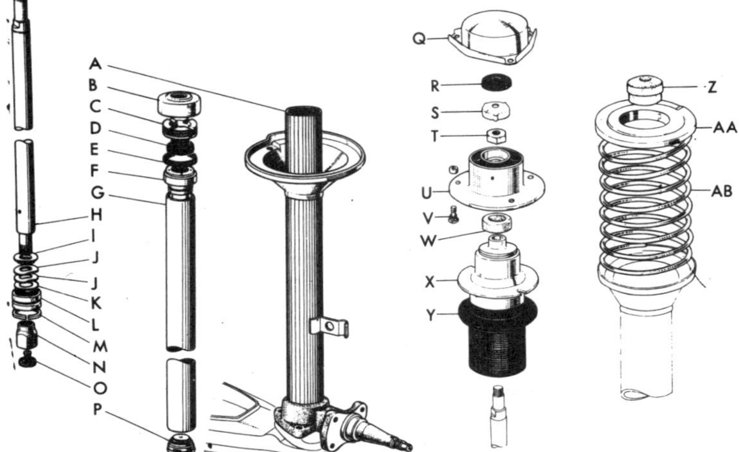

Fig.J.4. Exploded view of the front suspension unit assembly.

A.	Outer tube	O.	Piston valve
B.	Shock absorber upper cap	P.	Check valve
C.	Shock absorber ring nut	Q.	Suspension support cover
D.	Oil seal	R.	Rubber cushion
E.	Gasket	S.	Dust cover
F.	Shock absorber rod guide	T.	Nut
G.	Shock absorber cylinder	U.	Front suspension mount
H.	Shock absorber piston rod	V.	Stud
I.	Stop washer for non-return valve	W.	Dust seal for mount
J.	Spring for non-return valve	X.	Bumber seat
K.	Non-return valve	Y.	Shock absorber dust cover
L.	Shock absorber piston	Z.	Front spring bumper
M.	Shock absorber piston ring	AA.	Front spring upper seat
N.	Piston nut	AB.	Front coil spring

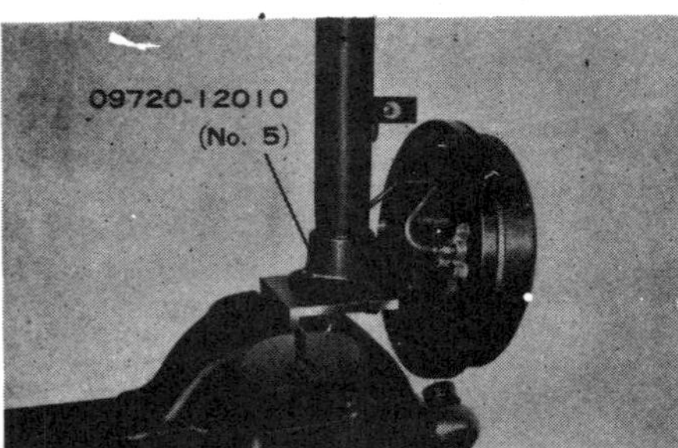

Fig.J.5. Removal of the front shock absorber upper mounting (left) and withdrawal of the shock absorber assembly (right).

Fig.J.6. Removal of the dust cover.

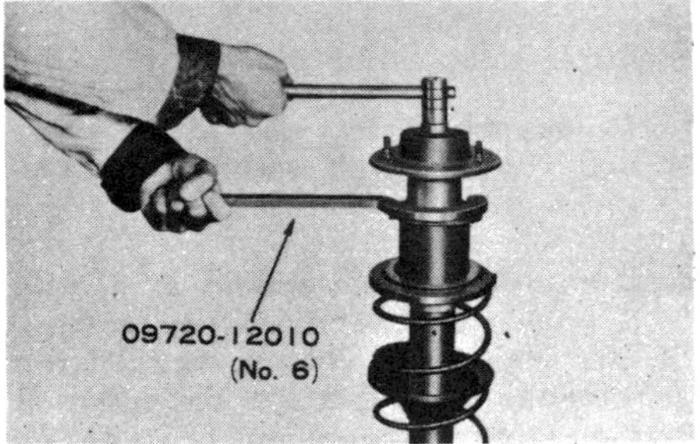

Fig.J.7. Removal of the nut securing the shock absorber rod to the suspension mount.

Front Axle and Front Suspension

The front suspension assembly consists of vertical shock absorbers, surrounded by coil springs and integrally built with the steering knuckle, a travers leaf spring and the lower suspension arms. The front shock absorbers serve at the same time as upper mounting for the suspension, being attached by means of a rubber bearing to a reinforcement on the wing apron. The lower end of the shock absorbers carry the steering knuckles, attached to which are the steering levers by means of three bolts.

The lower suspension arms are connected to the suspension units by ball joints at their outer ends and by means of rubber bushes and a fulcrum shaft to the front suspension crossmember. Both ends of the travers leaf spring are connected with the ends of the lower suspension arms. The front leaf spring has the function of a stabiliser bar.

Camber, castor and king-pin inclination are not adjustable.

FRONT HUB — Removal
(Fig.J.1)

With the front end of the car resting on suitable stands and the front wheel removed, remove the front hub grease cap and withdraw the split pin. Unscrew the castellated nut and the locating washer. Remove the brake drum, the wheel hub and the outer wheel bearing as one assembly from the wheel spindle. Withdraw the inner bearing race, the inner bearing and the oil seal with a suitable brass drift from the inside of the hub.

Inspection of parts
Thoroughly clean all parts and check as follows: Brake drums for wear and cracks, bearing rollers and races for wear, cracks or pitting and discolouration.To replace a bearing race, drift out the old race, using a brass drift and fit a new one, using either the special tools Nos. 09608-12010 Nr.5 for the inner bearing and No.6 for the outer bearing or a suitable mandrel, the outer diameter of which is the same as that of the bearing races.

FRONT HUB — Installation

Pack the bearings, the inside of the hub and the grease cap with wheel bearing grease. After assembly of the hub, the grease should bedistributed as shown by the shaded areas in Fig.J.3. Fit the inner bearing into the wheel hub and install the grease seal, using the same tool as for the replacement of the outer bearing race for the inner bearing.

Fit the brake drum and the hub assembly to the stub axle (wheel spindle) and insert the outer bearing into the end of the hub. Fit the locating washer and the castellated nut and adjust the front wheel bearings as follows:

Tighten the castellated nut to a torque reading of 2.6 - 3.2 kgm (19 - 23 lb.ft.), at the same time rotating the hub backwards and forwards to settle the bearings in their races. Check the wheel hub for end float. Then unscrew the castellated nut until it can be turned with the fingers only and re-tighten the nut,

using a tube spanner without tommy bar. Insert a split pin in this position.

Check the bearing pre-load by winding a cord around the brake drum and pulling with a spring scale. Read the force required to rotate the hub. The pre-load should be 160 - 135 grams (5.6 - 13.2 ozs.). Finally refit the wheels and tighten the wheel nuts to a torque reading of 9.0 - 12.0 kgm (65 - 86 lb.ft.)

SHOCK ABSORBER — Removal
(Fig.J.4)

With the front end of the car resting on suitable stands and the wheels removed, support the suspension arm at the leaf spring eye and lift the outer end of the suspension arm within the deflection capabilities of the springs. Disconnect and plug the brake hose and remove the three bolts holding the steering arm to the steering knuckle. Remove the three support securing bolts from the wing apron (the cover will come loose and can be removed after slowly lowering the jack).

Shock absorber and brake drum can now be removed as one assembly.

Using the special repair tool kit 09720-12010 (Nr. 5) clamp the shock absorber into a vice. Fig.J.5 shows the shape of the tool which is bolted to the lower end of the shock absorber. If the tool is not available it is possible to make-up a similar holding device or the shock absorber can be clamped carefully into a vice, using soft-metal jaws.

Remove the bearing dust cover (Fig.J.6) and remove the coil spring by disengaging the lower end of the coil spring lower seat and turning the coil spring clockwise towards the lower side. Remove the nut holding the shock absorber rod to the support, holding the front bumper stop seat with the tool set shown in Fig.J.7. Lift off the suspension support, the dust seal, front bumper stop seat, spring upper seat, coil spring and bump stop.

Remove the front hub as described under "Front Hub - Removal" and unscrew the brake back plate together with the brake shoe assembly from the steering knuckle. (In the case of disc brakes at the front, remove the disc brake assembly.).

SHOCK ABSORBER — Dismantling

The dismantling of the shock absorber is only possible if special tool set 09720-12010 (Fig.J.8) is available. Remove the top cap with a punch and straighten the end of the outer tube. Loosen the ring nut with the ring nut wrench (2 in Fig.J.8) taking care not to damage the oil seal in the inside of the nut. Remove the gasket between the rod guide and the tube and slowly withdraw the piston rod and the guide.

Remove the cylinder from the outer tube and knock out the base valve with a 450 mm (18 in.) long brass drift (Fig.J.9). Unclamp the outer tube from the vice and empty the fluid. Pry the base valve assembly from the base valve case. Hold the top end of the piston in a vice with soft-metal jaws and remove the piston valve in the piston nut with the piston valve wrench (4 in Fig.J.8) as shown in Fig.J.10.

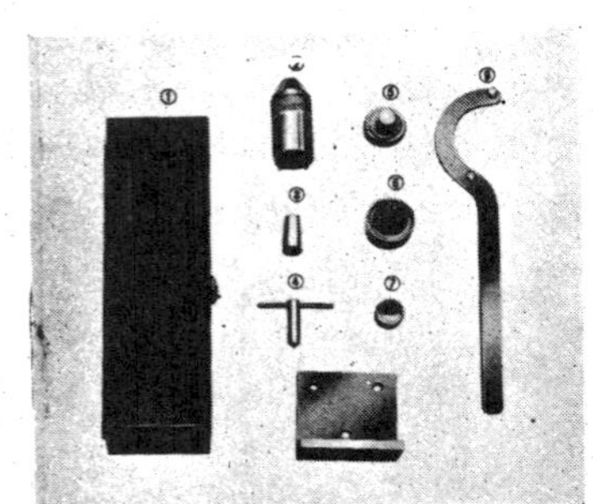

Fig.J.8. View of the shock absorber service tool set.

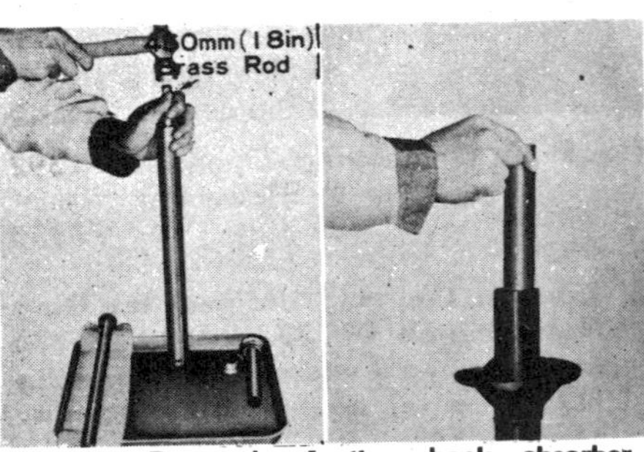

Fig.J.9. Removal of the shock absorber compression valve (see text).

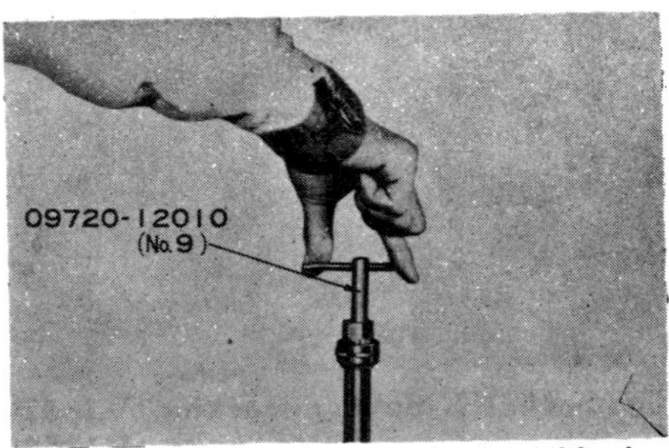

Fig.J.10. Remove the piston valve with the special wrench shown.

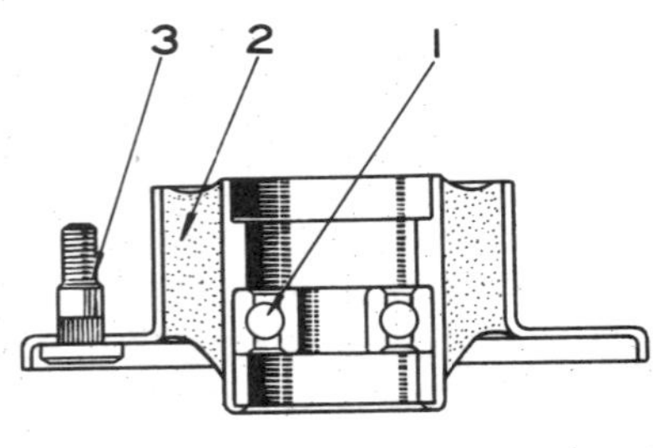

Fig.J.11. Sectional view of the suspension upper mount. 1. Bearing, 2. Rubber bush, 3. rod stud.

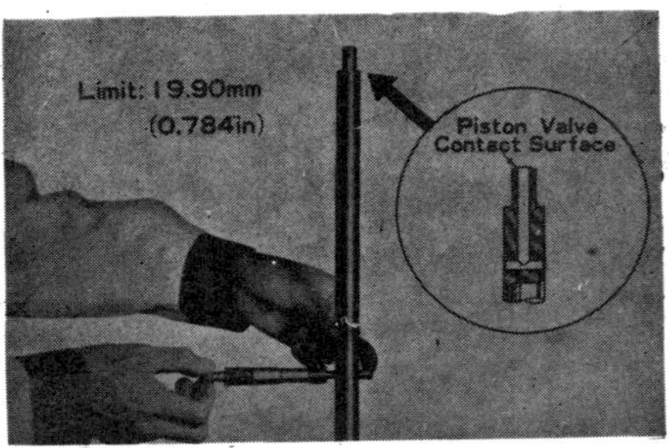

Fig.J.12. Checking the diameter of the piston

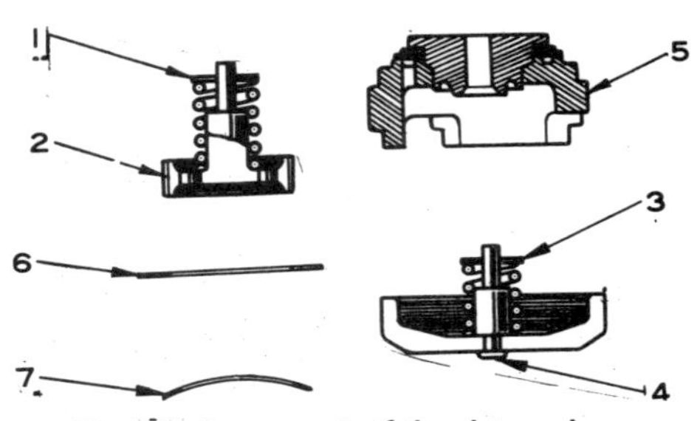

Fig.J.13. Components of the piston valve.

1. Piston valve
2. Valve thread
3. Compression valve
4. Rivetted portion
5. Valve case
6. Non-return valve
7. Non-return valve spring

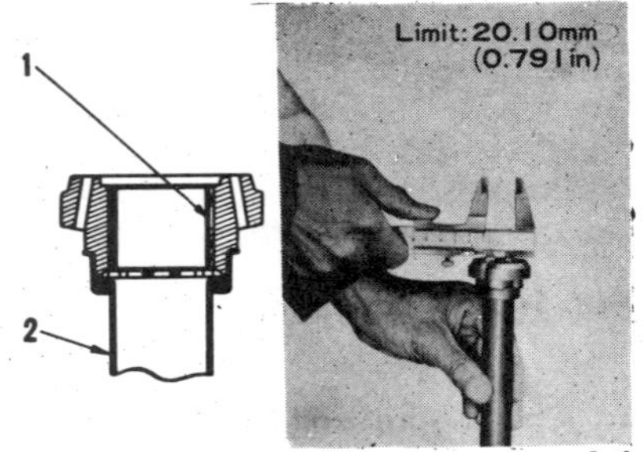

Fig.J.14. Checking the inner diameter of the bush (1) and the outer face of the rod guide for wear.

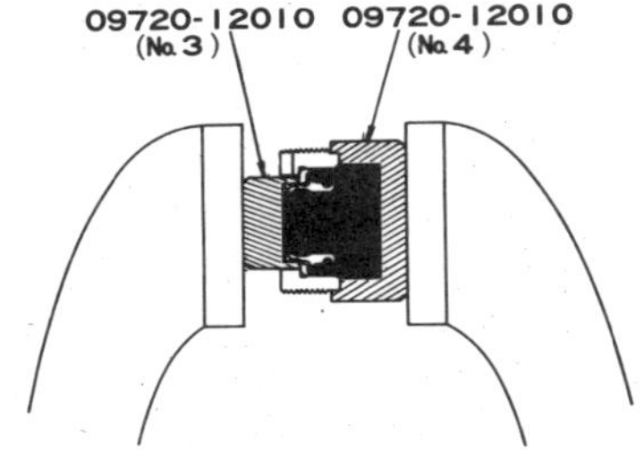

Fig.J.15. Removal of the ring nut oil seal in a vice.

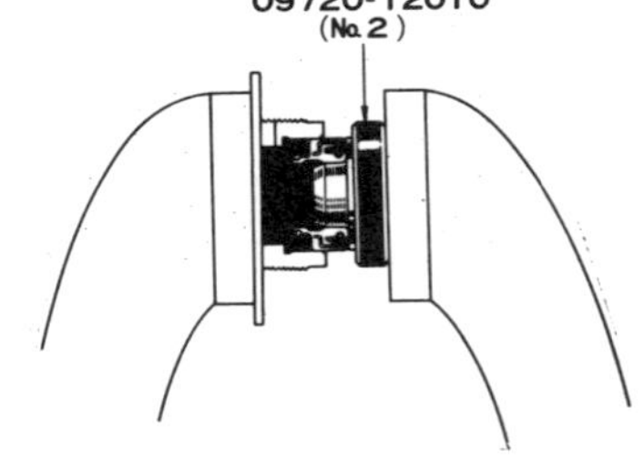

Fig.J.16. Installation of the ring nut oil seal in a vice.

Fig.J.17. The components of the piston rod.

1. Piston rod
2. Stop washer for non-return valve
3. Valve springs
4. Non-return valve
5. Piston
6. Piston nut

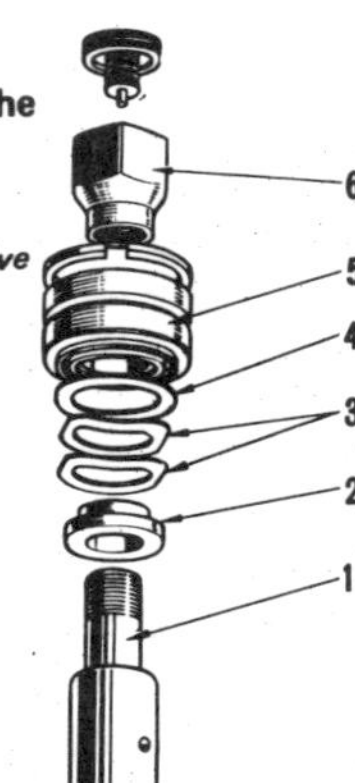

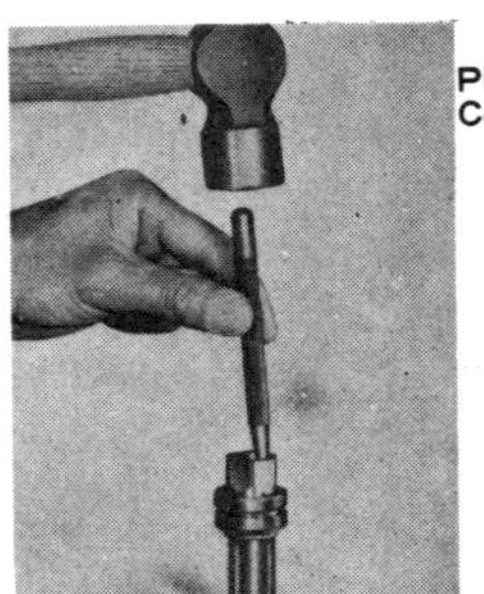

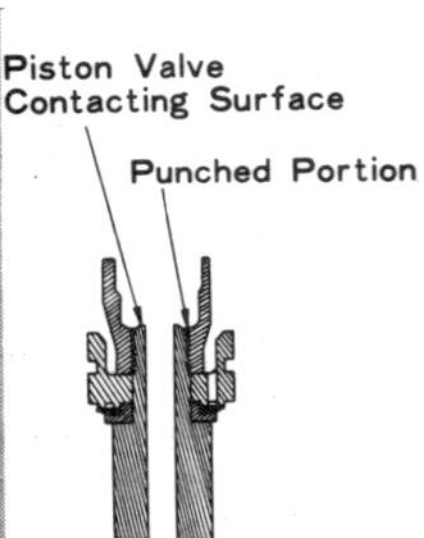

Fig.J.18. Securing the piston nut to the piston rod.

Remove the piston nut, piston, non-return valve, spring and non-return valve stopper from the piston rod and remove the piston ring from the piston.

Inspection of parts

Inspect as follows and repair or replace parts as necessary:

Check the outer tube for leaks or distortion, steering knuckle for damage or cracks, coil springs for weakness, spring bump stop and dust cover for damage. Check the suspension support for deterioration of the rubber bearing (2), the bearing (1) for roughness and the serration bolts for damage. (See Fig.J.11).

Check the piston rod for run-out (max. 0.30 mm (0.012 in.) or wear. The piston rod should have a diameter of 19.90 mm (0.784 in.) (Fig.J.12). There should be no damage at the valve contact surface. The diameter of the piston should be 30.05 mm (1.183 in.). Check the mating surface with the non-return valve for wear or damage.

Check the piston valve (1, Fig.J.13) and the valve threaded portion (2), non-return valve (6) and non-return valve spring (7), base valve (3), the rivetted portion (4) and the base valve case (5) for damage, wear or spring weakness.

Check the cylinder bore for wear or scores. The max. internal diameter should be 30.00 mm (1.193 in.). The cylinder run-out should not exceed 0.10 mm (0.004 in.).

Check the bush (1, Fig.J.14) and the oil lock tube (2) of the piston rod guide for wear or damage. The inner bush diameter should be less than 20.10 mm (0.791 in.). Check the ring nut for thread damage and the oil seal in the inside of the nut for damage or wear. To replace the oil seal, use the special tools shown in Fig.J.15, with the ring nut and the oil seal clamped between the jaws of a vice. Slightly oil the seal and install as shown in Fig.J.16.

SHOCK ABSORBER — Assembly

Thoroughly clean all parts in automatic transmission fluid. Hold the upper end of the piston rod (1, Fig.J.17) in a vice, using soft-metal jaws and fit the non-return valve stop (2), two non-return valve springs (3), non-return valve (4), piston (5) and the piston nut (6) to the piston rod. Tighten the nut to a torque reading of 5.0 - 6.0 kgm (36 - 43 lb.ft.). Using a punch, lock the piston nut to the piston rod as shown in Fig.J.18.

Screw the piston valve into the piston nut until the centre of the piston valve touches the top of the piston rod and then unscrew the piston valve by two complete turns. Punch two portions of thread in the same manner as for the piston rod and piston nut and fit the piston ring to the piston.

Press the base valve case (2, Fig.J.19) on to the base valve assembly (2) and fit the valve into the cylinder (3) with a hide or rubber mallet.

Taking care not to damage the piston ring, fit the piston rod into the cylinder and the cylinder into the outer tube. Fill the outer tube with 270 c.c. of automatic transmission fluid, Type A, Suffix A. Insert the piston rod guide into the outer tube and insert a new gasket between rod guide and outer tube. Grease the lip of the oil seal and fit the ring nut, using the special wrench shown in Fig.J.20 on to the piston rod. Tighten the ring

nut to 10 - 15 kgm (75 - 110 lb.ft.), using the ring nut wrench and peen over the top of the outer tube to lock the ring nut.

NOTE: In the case of shock absorbers used in cars after April 1968, tighten the ring nut as follows:

Withdraw the piston rod as far as it will go and in this condition tighten the ring nut with the special wrench 09728-12010. Then push down the piston rod and tighten the ring nut to the torque setting given above, using the special wrench 09720-12010, No.7. The top of the outer tube should be peened into the nut as for the previous models.

Finally refit the upper cap on to the outer tube.

SHOCK ABSORBER — Installation

The installation of the shock absorber is a reversal of the removal procedure, noting the following points:

Grease the support dust seal, use a new nut for the attachment of the suspension support to the piston rod, check the front wheel bearing pre-load as described at the beginning of the section. When connecting brake hoses, make sure that they are not twisted. Tighten nuts and bolts to the recommended values. (See Torque setting table).

FRONT AXLE — Removal
(Fig.J.21)

With the front end of the car resting on stands and the front wheels removed, remove the track rod ball joint stud from the steering lever, using the special puller 09611-12010 or any other suitable ball stud puller. Raise the lower suspension arm with a jack and disconnect the steering lever from the steering knuckle. Slowly lower the suspension arm and remove the bolt holding the leaf spring eye and the two bolts securing the lower suspension arm pivot to the front crossmember. Remove the suspension arm and the leaf spring seat from the crossmember. (Fig.J.22). When both suspension arms are removed, remove the leaf spring from the crossmember.

Inspection of parts

Check the lower suspension arm (1, Fig.J.23) and the lower arm shaft (2) for damage, deformation or cracks and check the bushes (3) for wear. If necessary replace the bushes as follows:

Remove the bolts securing the lower suspension arm shaft and remove the bushes with the special puller 09725-12010. Using Fig.J.24 as reference, fit the thrust bush (2) on to the shaft (1) and fit the shaft to the suspension arm (3). Take care that the shaft is fitted in the correct direction. Insert the bush (4) into the front end of the suspension arm, using the bush replacer 09726-12010 Nos. 1 & 2, clamped in a vice and fit the rear bush (5) in a similar manner using the adaptors Nos. 1 & 3 of the same tool set. Fit the plate washer, lock washer and the bolts on both ends of the lower arm shaft and tighten the bolts to a torque setting of 0.5 kgm (3.6 lb.ft.). The bolts should be tightened fully after the suspension arm has been refitted to the car and the weight of the car is resting on its wheels.

Check the ball joint in the lower suspension arm for wear or slackness at the ball joint stud. If the turning torque of the stud without dust cover is less than 3 kgcm (2.6 lb.ft.) or if any other defects are visible, replace the ball joint as follows:

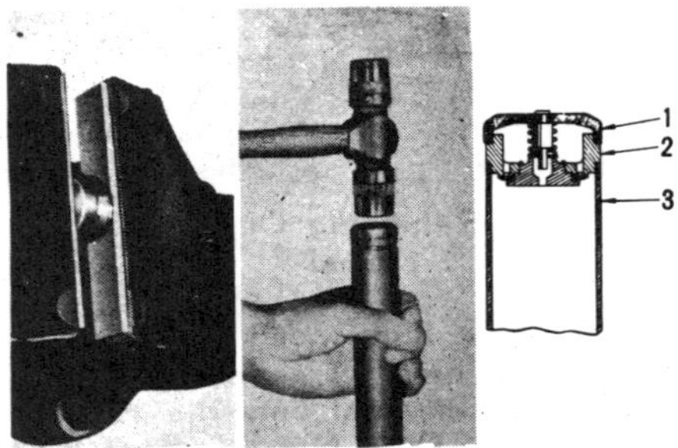

Fig.J.19. Installation of the compression valve (1) into the case (2). (3) is the cylinder.

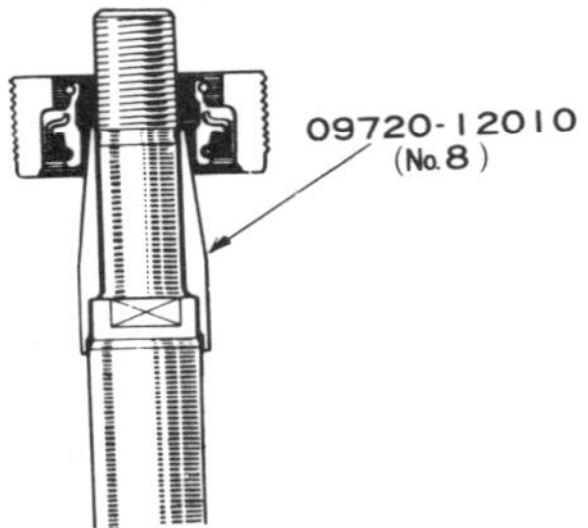

Fig.J.20. Installation of the ring nut.

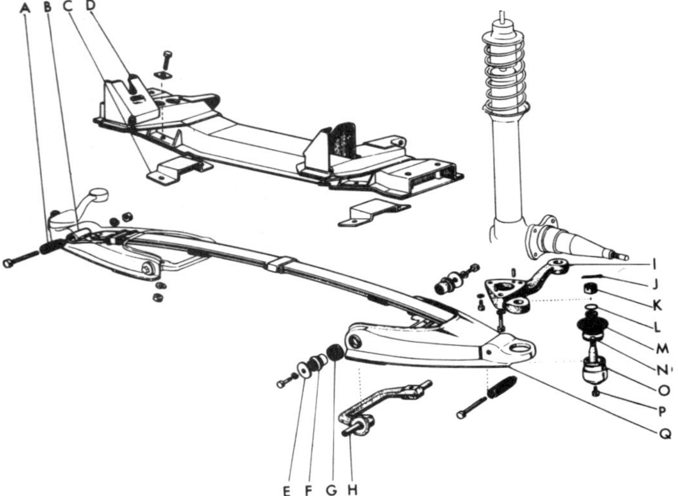

Fig.J.21. Exploded view of the front suspension.

A.	Front spring bush	J.	Split pin
B.	Front spring	K.	Castellated nut
C.	Front spring seat	L.	Ring
D.	Suspension crossmember	M.	Ball joint dust cover
E.	Plain washer	N.	Retaining ring
F.	Suspension arm bush	O.	Suspension ball joint
G.	Suspension arm bush	P.	Screw plug
H.	Suspension arm shaft	Q.	Lower suspension arm
I.	Steering lever		

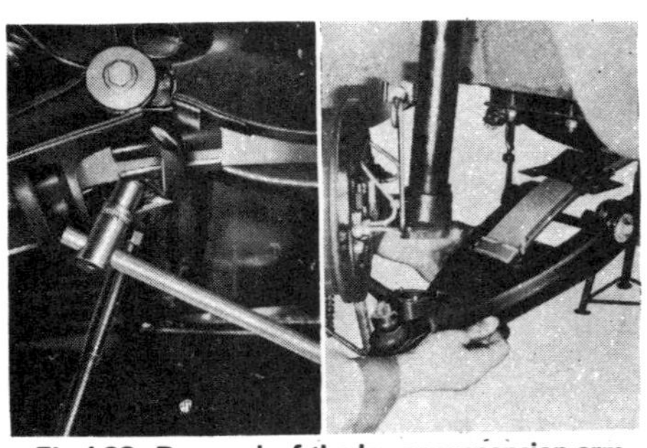

Fig.J.22. Removal of the lower suspension arm.

Fig.J.23. Areas of the lower suspension arms which may have suffered damage.

1. Suspension arm
2. Suspension arm shaft
3. Suspension arm bushes

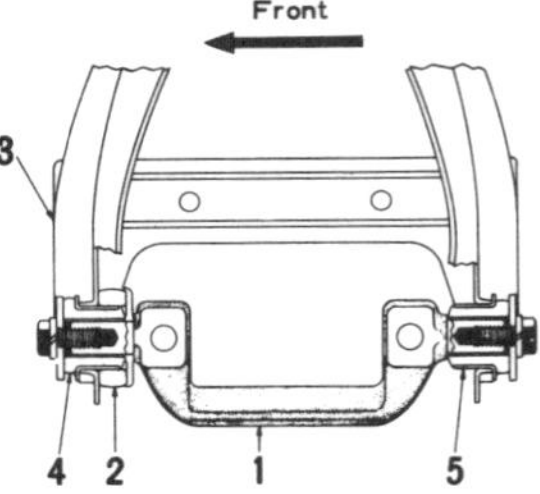

Fig.J.24. The correct installation of the lower suspension arm.

1. Suspension arm shaft
2. Bush
3. Suspension arm
4. Bush
5. Bush

Remove the split pin and the castellated nut from the ball joint stud and remove the steering lever from the suspension arm, using the track rod ball joint puller 09611-12010 as shown in Fig.J.25. Remove the dust cover and press out the ball joint with the special remover/replacer set 09628-12010. Fit a new ball joint, using a press and the same tools. Place a 2 mm (0.08 in.) diameter piece of wire between the ball joint stud and the cover and then fit the securing ring and the rubber ring on to the cover (Fig.J.26). This wire allows the air to escape whilst the ball joint is lubricated with grease. Remove the grease plug and fit a grease fitting. Fill the ball joint with grease until the dust cover is more than 3/4 full of molybdenum disulphide lithium grease. Remove the grease fitting, fit the plug and tighten the plug to 0.4 - 0.7 kgm (3.0 - 5.0 lb.ft.). Remove the wire. Fit the steering lever on to the ball joint and tighten the mounting bolts to a torque setting of 5.0 - 7.0 kgm (36.0 - 53.0 lb.ft.). Fit a new split pin.

Check the leaf spring for wear and damage or weakness and inspect the spring clips (1) and the rubber pads (2) in Fig.J.27. Also check the spring bushes (3) and the spring seats (4).

Check the front crossmember for damage or deformation and if necessary replace as follows:

Disconnect the engine mounting brackets from the crossmember and support the engine from underneath with a jack (wooden block between jack head and engine). Remove the nuts securing the crossmember to the body and lift out the crossmember. The installation of the new crossmember is a reversal of the removal procedure. The tightening torque for the mounting nuts is 4.0 - 5.5 kgm (30.0 - 40.0 lb.ft.). The tightening torque for the engine mounting bolts is 3.5 - 5.5 kgm (25.0 - 40.0 lb.ft.). When a new crossmember is fitted, it becomes necessary to check the turning angle setting as described under "Front Wheel Alignment".

FRONT AXLE — Installation

The installation is a reversal of the removal procedure, noting the following points: The leaf spring seat must be fitted to the car as shown in Fig.J.28. Grease the ball joint studs of the track rod end before fitting to the steering lever. If the bushes of the lower suspension arm have been replaced, tighten the suspension arm shaft mounting bolts (which were previously tightened with 0.5 kgm (3.6 lb.ft.) to the correct tightening torque of 4.0 - 5.5 kgm (30 - 40 lb.ft.) when the car is resting on its wheels. To ensure that the suspension arm bushes are settled properly without stress, it is advisable to bounce the front end of the car several times up and down before the bolts are tightened. All bolts of the front suspension must be tightened in accordance with the figures given in the tightening torque table in this manual.

FRONT WHEEL ALIGNMENT

Before attempting to check the front wheel alignment, check the following points:

1. Check the tyres for correct pressures.
2. Check if wheels and tyres are properly balanced.
3. Check the wheel rims for run-out.
4. Check the wheel bearing for correct adjustment.
5. Check ball joints and track rods for excessive slackness.
6. Check the front coil springs for correct seating.
7. Check the steering gear for correct adjustment and secure mounting.

Checking the toe-in setting

Check the toe-in setting with a suitable gauge with the front wheels in the straight-ahead position. The measurements should be taken at the same height at the front and the rear of the wheels. If the setting is outside the specified value of 2 - 6 mm (0.08 - 0.24 in.), adjust as follows:

Slacken the track rod clamp nuts at each end of the track rods and check that the length of the track rods is the same on both sides. To adjust, rotate the track rod tubes in the same direction until the required setting is obtained. Re-check the setting as shown in Fig.J.29. Fig.J.30 shows which way the track rods should be turned to increase or descrease the setting. Tighten the track rod clamp nuts to 3.5 - 5.5 kgm (25 - 40 lb.ft.), taking care that the track rod tubes cannot move whilst the nuts are tightened.

Checking the turning angles

Check the inside and outside turning angles and adjust the angles by loosening or tightening the bolts on the rear of the suspension crossmember. Tighten the locknuts to a torque reading of 1.5 - 2.2 kgm (11 - 16 lb.ft.). The correct values are as follows:

Inner wheel	37 - 38°
Outer wheel	32 - 33°

Camber, Castor, King-pin inclination

Using suitable equipment (either mechanical or optical) check the castor, camber and king-pin inclination angles. If these values are not within the specified limits, this indicates damage to suspension or misalignment of the body, as these angles are not adjustable. The correct values, set during manufacture, are as follows:

Castor (unloaded)	15 - 45'
Camber (unloaded)*	1°30' - 2°30'
King-pin inclination	6.0 - 7.0°

*On later models, the effective Chassis No. of which are given below, the camber has been altered by modifying the shape of the steering knuckle arm and should be 30' - 1° 30' in the unloaded condition.

Effective Chassis Nos. for new camber angle

KE10	290392
KE15	103923
KE16 (Estate)	169001
KE16 (Van)	170000

MODIFICATIONS AFTER APRIL 1968
(Corolla 1100 and Corolla 1200)

The following modifications and changes were made on the Corolla 1100 after April 1968 and were also incorporated in the Corolla 1200. The details given are different from the ones described in the text.

Shock Absorber - Installation

The refitting procedure for the upper shock absorber mounting differs from the previous models. This operation is decribed under the heading "Shock Absorber - Installation".

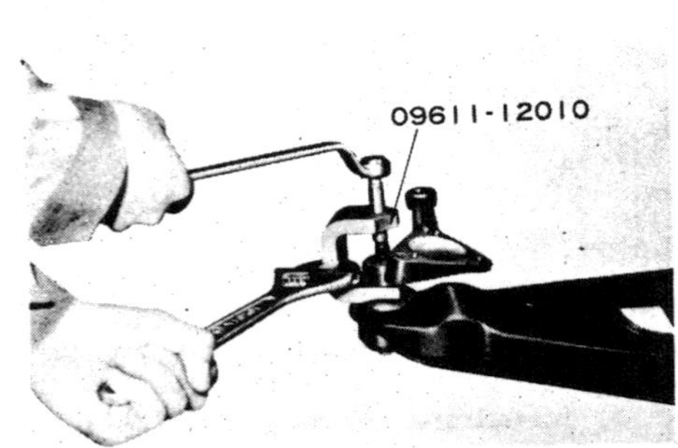

Fig.J.25. Removal of the steering lever from the suspension arm.

Fig.J.26. Lubrication of the suspension ball joint.

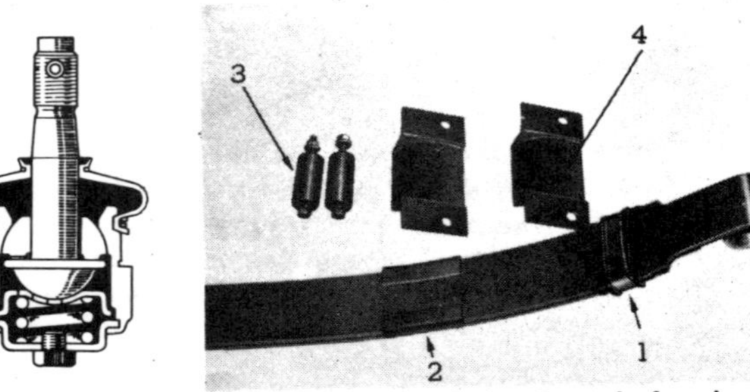

Fig.J.27. View of the front leaf spring. 1. Spring clip, 2. Rubber pad, 3. Bushes, 4. Seat.

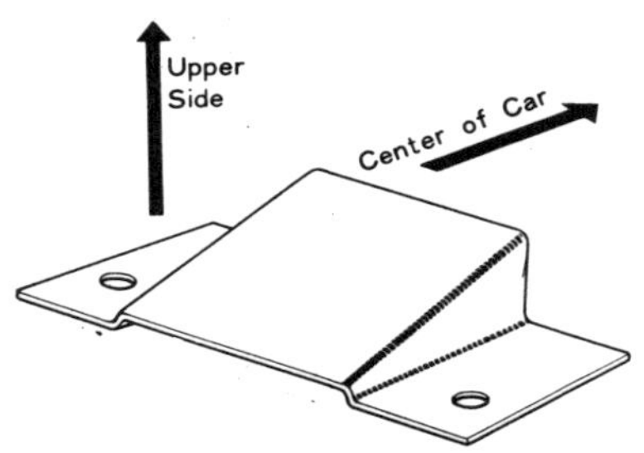

Fig.J.28. Install the spring seat as shown in the illustration.

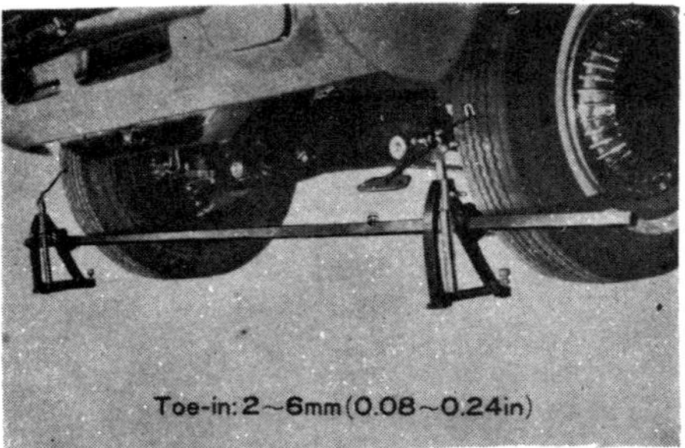

Fig.J.29. Checking the toe-in setting.

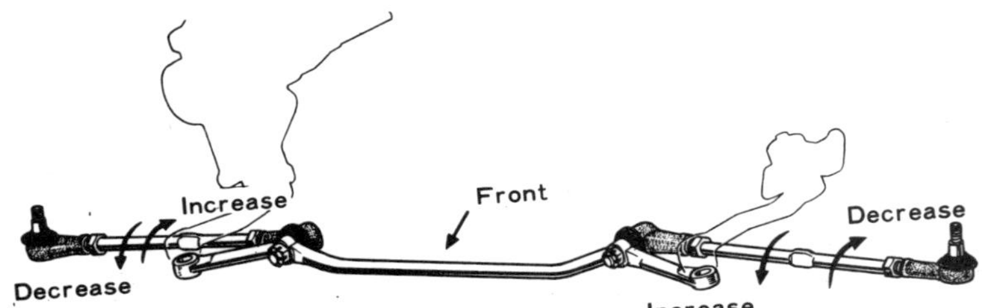

Fig.J.30. Adjusting diagram for toe-in setting.

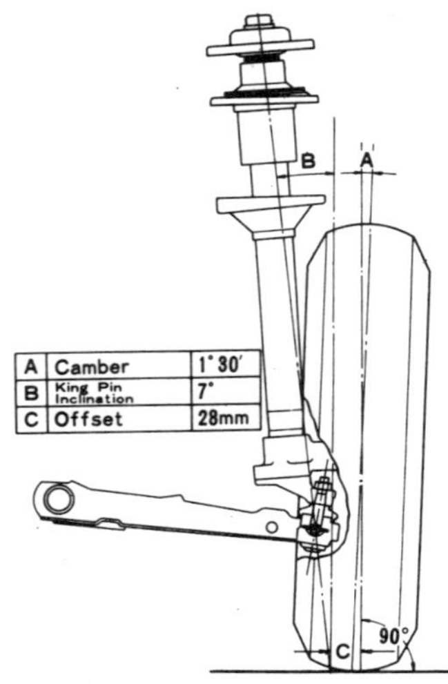

Fig.J.31. Castor diagram.

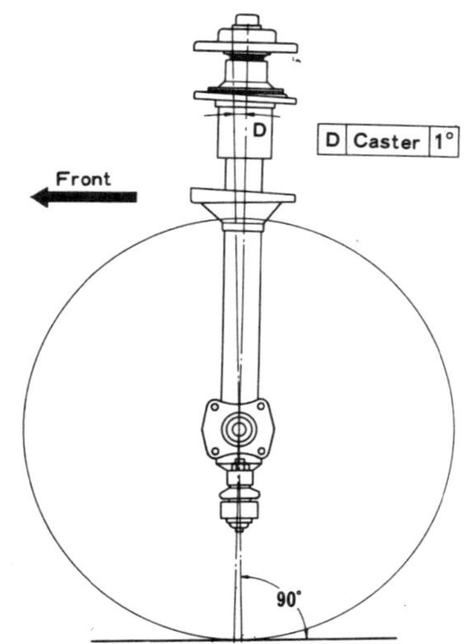

Fig.J.32. Camber and king-pin inclination diagram.

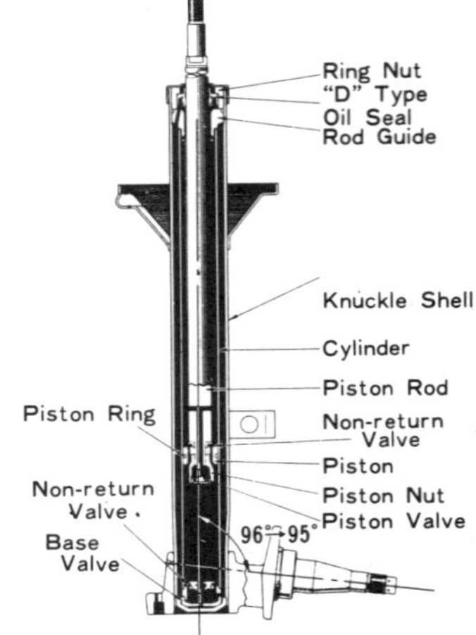

Fig.J.33. Sectional view of the front suspension as fitted to later 1100 models and 1200 models.

Front Axle – Installation

When refitting a front axle on these models note that the tightening torques are different from the previous models. The tightening table shows the new values.

Front Wheel Alignment

To prevent abnormal tyre wear, the camber has been changed by modifying the shape of the steering knuckle arm. The new values are given under the same heading earlier in the text.

For trouble shooting of "Front Suspension" see section "Steering".

Technical Data

FRONT LEAF SPRING

```
Length (loaded) . . . . . . . . . . . . . . 1022 mm (40.25 in.)
Camber (loaded) . . . . . . . . . . . . . . 33.0 mm (1.30 in.)
                                          Before April 1968
Camber (loaded) . . . . . . . . . . . . . . 32.8 mm (1.29 in.)
                                          After April 1968
Width . . . . . . . . . . . .60 mm (2.36 in.) - Before April 1968
                             70 mm (2.75 in.) - After April 1968
Thickness . . . . . . . 6.0 mm (0.24 in.) - Before April 1968
                        7.0 mm (0.275 in.) - After April 1968
Number of leaves . . . . . . . . . . . Two - Before April 1968
                                       One - After April 1968
Deflection rate . . . . . . . . . . . . .1.65 kg/mm (92 lb./in.)
                                         Before April 1968
                          1.40 kg/mm (78.5 lb./in.)
                                         After April 1968
```

FRONT COIL SPRING

Models before April 1968

```
Free length:
  KE10-B . . . . . . . . . . . . . . . . .305 mm (12.0 in.)
  KE10L- B R.H.D. . . . . . . . . . . . .295 mm (11.6 in.)
  KE10L-B L.H.D. . . . . . . . . . . . .318 mm (12.5 in.)
Fitted length . . . . . . . . . . . . . .145 mm (5.71 in.)
Fitted load . . . . . . . . . . . . . . . . .72 kg (155 lb.)
Coil wire diameter . . . . . . . . . . . . . 8 mm (0.3 in.)
Number of coils . . . . . . . . . . . . . . . . . . . . . . .4
Deflection rate . . . . . . . . . . . . .0.59 kg/mm (33 lb./in.)
```

Models after April 1968 - Driver's side

```
Free length . . . . . . . . . . . . . . . . .399 mm (15.7 in.)
Wire diameter . . . . . . . . . . . . . . . 8.5 mm (0.34 in.)
Coil diameter . . . . . . . . . . . . . . . .120 mm (4.8 in.)
Number of coils . . . . . . . . . . . . . . . . . . . . . . .7
Number of effective coils . . . . . . . . . . . . . . . . . .5.5
Fitted length . . . . . . . . . . . . . . . .145 mm (5.71 in.)
Fitted load . . . . . . . . . . . . . . . . . 134 kg (296 lb.)
Deflection rate . . . . . . . . . . . .0.55 kg/mm (30.9 lb./in.)
Colour identification . . . . . . . . . . . . . . . . . . . Green
```

Models after April 1968 - Passenger side

```
Free length . . . . . . . . . . . . . . . . .365 mm (14.4 in.)
Wire diameter . . . . . . . . . . . . . . . 8.2 mm (0.32 in.)
Coil diameter . . . . . . . . . . . . . . . .120 mm (4.8 in.)
Number of coils . . . . . . . . . . . . . . . . . . . . . . .6.4
Number of effective coils . . . . . . . . . . . . . . . . . .4.8
Fitted length . . . . . . . . . . . . . . . .145 mm (5.71 in.)
Fitted load . . . . . . . . . . . . . . . . . 114 kg (251 lb.)
Deflection rate . . . . . . . . . . . .0.55 kg/mm (30.9 lb./in.)
Colour identification . . . . . . . . . . . . . . . . . . Orange
```

SHOCK ABSORBERS

```
Type . . . . . . . . . . . .Double-acting, hydraulic, telescopic
Max. length . . . . . . . . . . . . . . . . . 644 mm (25.37 in.)
Min. length . . . . . . . . . . . . . . . . . 453 mm (17.95 in.)
Stroke . . . . . . . . . . . . . . . . . . . .191 mm (5.53 in.)
Damping force in compression:
  Before April 1968 . . . . . . . . . . .27 - 43 kg at 0.6 m/sec.
                                         (60 - 95 lb. at 24 in./sec.)
  After April 1968 . . . . . . . . . . . . 67 kg at 0.6 m/sec.
                                         (148 lb. at 24 in./sec.)
Damping force in rebound:
  Before April 1968 . . . . . . . . . . .50 - 70 kg at 0.6 m/sec.
                                         (110 - 150 lb./sec.)
  After April 1968 . . . . . . . . . . . . 50 kg at 0.6 m/sec.
                                         (110 lb. at 24 in./sec.)
Fluid capacity . . . . . . . . . . . . . . . . . . . . . .270 c.c.
Fluid type . . . . . . . . . . . . .Automatic transmission fluid
                                    Type A, Suffix A
```

FRONT WHEEL ALIGNMENT

```
Toe-in (loaded) . . . . . . . . . . . . . . 3.5 mm (0.14 in.)
Castor (loaded) . . . . . . . . . . . . . . . . . . . . . . . .1°
Camber (loaded) . . . . . . . . . .1° 30' - Before April 1968
                                   0° 30' - After April 1968
```

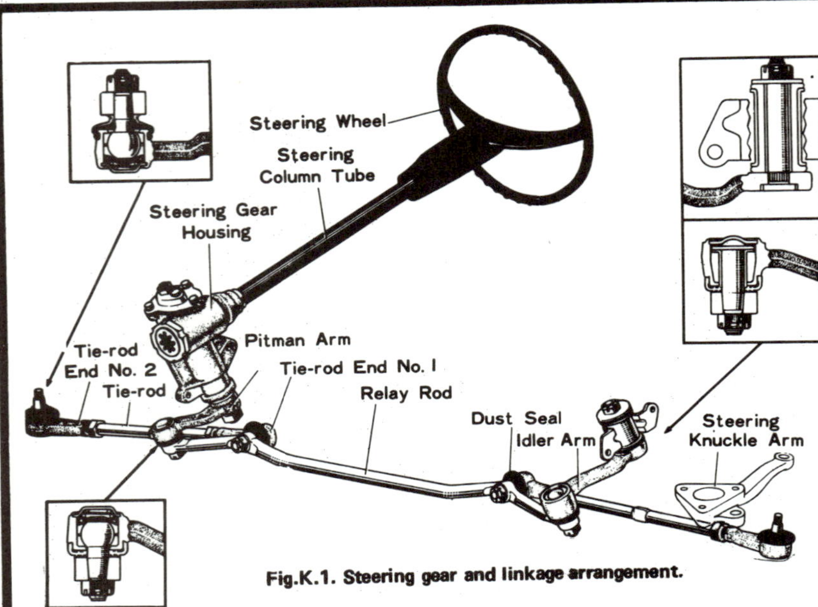

Fig.K.1. Steering gear and linkage arrangement.

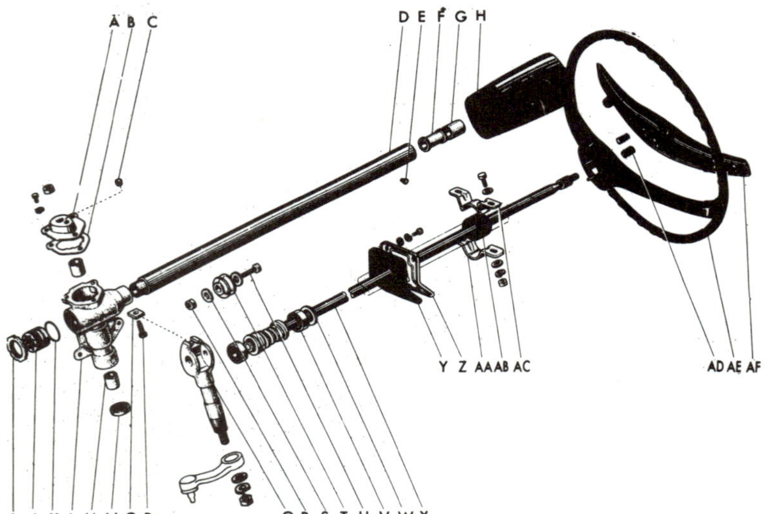

Fig.K.2. Exploded view of steering box with column assembly.

A.	Rocker shaft cover		Q.	Rocker shaft
B.	Cover gasket		R.	Nut
C.	Oil filler plug		S.	Shim
D.	Steering column outer tube		T.	Steering roller
E.	Locating screw		U.	Steering roller pivot bolt
F.	Upper bush		V.	Worm shaft bearing
G.	Collar		W.	Shim
H.	Steering column shroud		X.	Steering main shaft (spindle)
I.	Locknut for bearing adjusting screw		Y.	Draught excluder
J.	Bearing adjusting screw		Z.	Cover plate for column
K.	'O' ring		AA.	Lower column clamp
L.	Steering gear housing		AB.	Grommet
M.	Bush		AC.	Column upper clamp
N.	Oil seal		AD.	Compression spring
O.	Rocker shaft thrust washer		AE.	Steering wheel
P.	Rocker shaft adjusting screw		AF.	Horn push

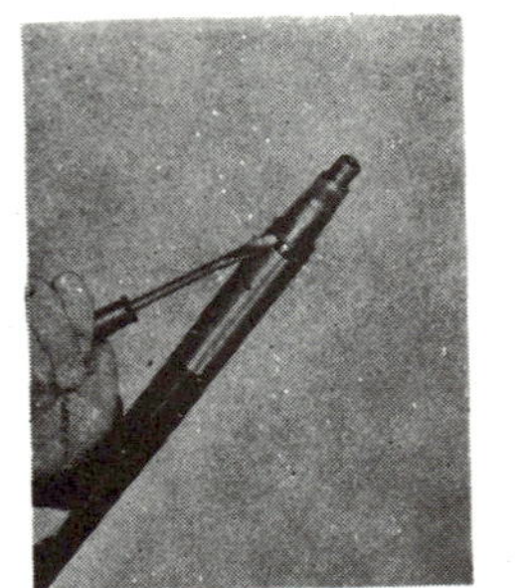

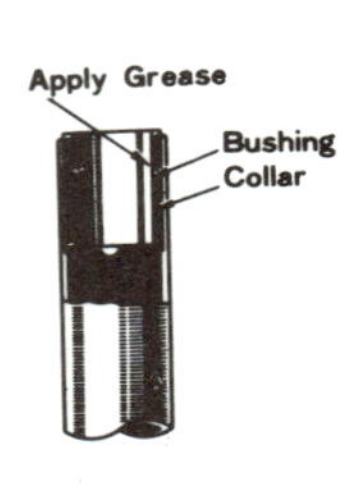

Fig.K.3. Replacement of the upper column bush.

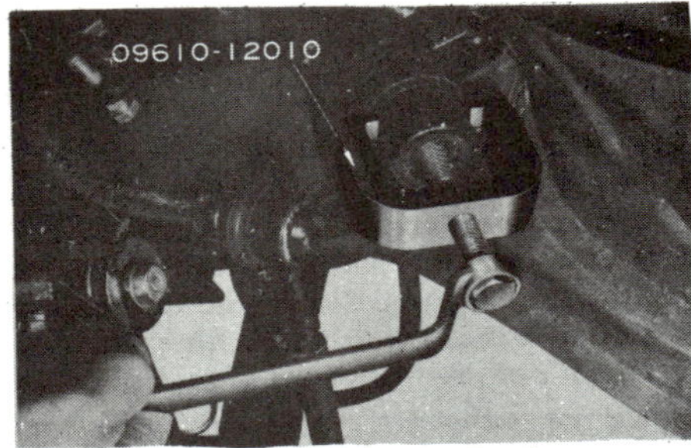

Fig.K.4. Location of speedometer cable (1) and water temperature sender unit (2).

Fig.K.5. Removal of the steering drop arm.

Fig.K.6. Removal of steering gear with column.

Steering

DESCRIPTION

The steering gear is of the worm and sector roller type with a gear ratio of 18:1. The steering box is attached to the front right-hand sidemember of the body, with the steering column secured to the instrument panel.

Bushes are used for the sector shaft, whereas the steering worm shaft is supported in ball thrust bearings. Bearing pre-load is adjusted by altering the thickness of the shims between the steering housing and the upper outer bearing race of the worm bearings.

STEERING WHEEL AND STEERING BOX — Removal

Disconnect the horn wire at the connector and pull off the horn push. In the case of the 10S, 15S and 15 models, the horn push is removed by pushing it towards the inside, at the same time rotating it in an anti-clockwise direction. Fig.K.22 and K.23 show the different manners of horn push removal.

Remove the steering wheel securing nut and punch mating marks into steering wheel hub and steering spindle. The steering wheel should be removed with the special puller 09609-20010. If any other puller is used, take care not to damage the steering wheel in any way.

Diconnect the direction indicator switch wires at the connector under the facia panel. Move the indicator switch into the position for a right turn (downwards), remove the switch securing screws and lift off the switch.

Remove steering column securing screw under the indicator switch and remove the steering column cover. Slacken the steering cover clamp from the column outer tube, but do not remove completely. It is now possible to replace the bush and the collar in the top of the steering column tube if this is intended. Using a punch, inserted in the two holes at the upper end of the outer tube, push the collar and the bush towards the end of the tube and pry out the two parts by means of a screwdriver. (Fig.K.3). Apply a thin coat of grease on the new bush and fit the bush and the collar into the tube.

Remove the instrument parcel tray (if fitted) and unscrew the steering column clamp. Disconnect the speedometer drive cable (1) and oil pressure and water temperature sender wires (2) in Fig.K.4.

With the front end of the car supported on stands, turn the steering wheel to the left lock and disconnect the steering drop arm from the rocker shaft (sector shaft), using the special puller 09610-12010 (as shown in Fig.K.5) or any other suitable puller.

Remove the engine undercover and the three steering box mounting bolts from the body sidemember. Remove the steering box together with the steering column from underneath the car at the angle shown in Fig.K.6.

STEERING BOX — Dismantling

Clamp the steering box into a vice and remove the three bolts (2) holding the end cover, the rocker shaft adjusting screw locknut (1) and remove the steering end cover by screwing in the rocker shaft adjusting screw, until the cover is lifted from the housing. (Fig.K.7). Hold the steering column in one hand and withdraw the rocker shaft from the steering housing.

Remove the worm shaft bearing adjusting screw locknut with the special wrench 09617-12010 and using another special wrench (09616-12010) remove the bearing adjusting screw. Remove the 'O' ring that is inserted between the adjusting screw and the outer race of the thrust bearing.

Screw a nut on to the end of the steering shaft and tap the end of the shaft with a mallet to remove the steering shaft (steering worm and spindle) together with the bearings from the steering box housing. Take care that inner races, outer races and ball cages are kept together for their respective bearing position. Remove the bush and the collar from the top end of the outer column tube, as already described under "Steering Wheel and Steering Box - Removal"

STEERING BOX — Inspection

Inspect the parts as follows and replace if necessary:

Check the steering wheel boss for cracks and damage. Check the steering spindle and the steering worm for wear, cracks or other damage. Check the ball bearings for wear or damage. To replace the bearings, remove the inner bearing race from the steering spindle using a chisel and replace by means of a brass drift and a hammer. Remove the outer bearing race from the steering housing with the special puller 09612-10011 (Fig.K.8) and fit a new outer race with the special drift 09562-10010 or any other drift that can be inserted through the opening in the steering housing and has the same outer diameter as the bearing outer race.

Check the rocker shaft surfaces (1) and (3) in Fig.K.9 where they are in contact with the bearing bushes and the oil seal. The diameter should be more than 24.9 mm (0.98 in.). Also check the gear contact surfaces (2) for wear or damage or bearing damage.

To replace the rocker shaft, grind the welded portion of the rocker shaft and loosen the nut and then remove the sector roller from the rocker shaft. Fit a new sector roller into the rocker shaft and tighten the nut to a torque reading of 1.5 - 2.0 kgm (11 - 14 lb.ft.). Insert shims until there is no clearance on the sector roller. The roller must still turn freely. Tighten the nut to the torque reading given above and weld the nut to the rocker shaft to lock it in position. (See also Fig.K.10).

Check the bushes (1) in Fig.K.11 for wear. The max. inner diameter must not exceed 25.1 mm (0.989 in.). The running clearance between bush and rocker shaft should have a value of max. 0.1 mm (0.004 in.). Check the oil seal (2) and the steering column outer tube for wear, cracks or damage.

To replace the bushes, remove the oil seal and using the special puller 09633-12010, remove the upper rocker shaft bush towards the top of the housing. The lower bush should be removed in the opposite direction. (Fig.K.12). Insert the new

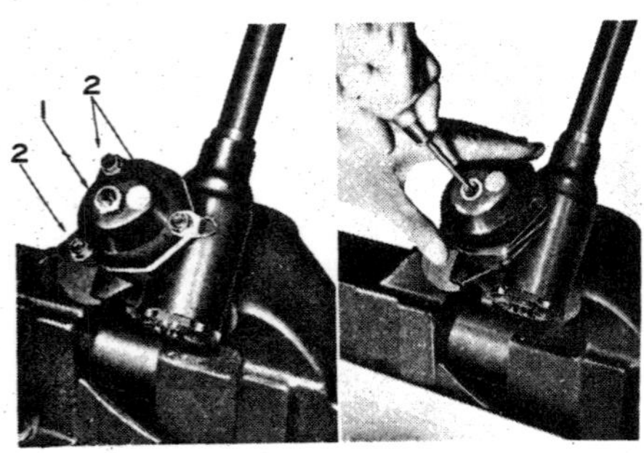
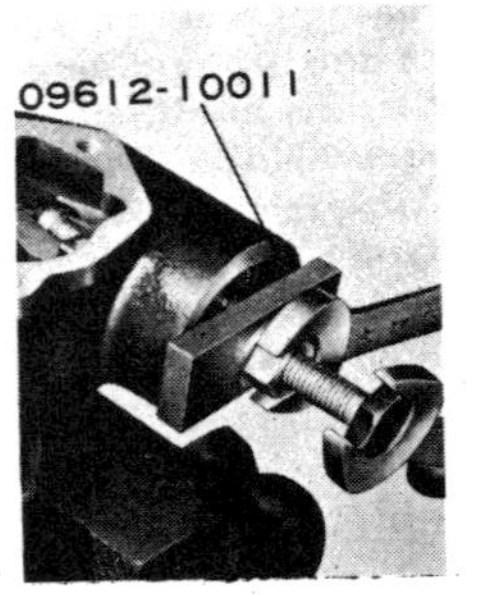

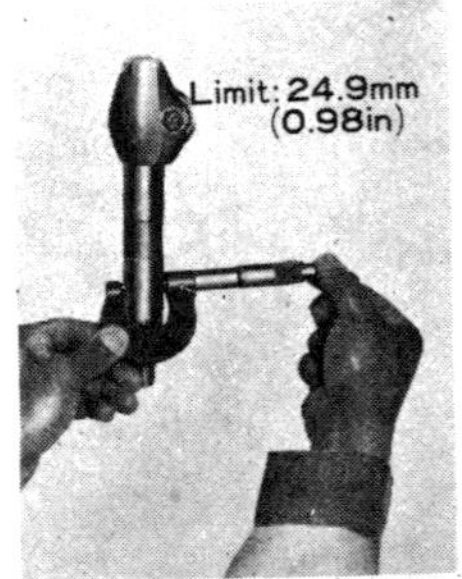
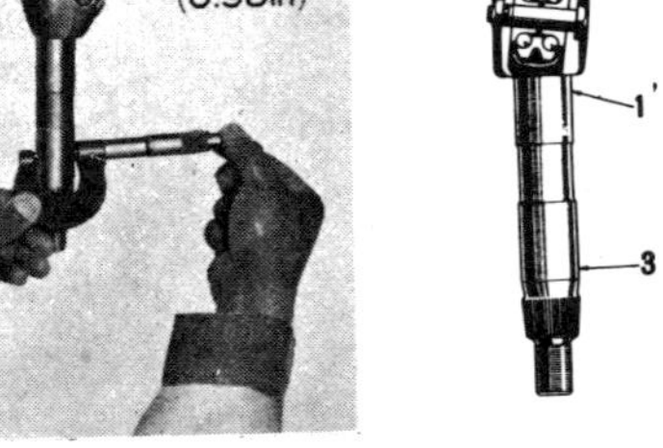

Fig.K.7. Removal of the steering cover. 1. Locknut, 2. Securing bolts.

Fig.K.8. Removal of the bearing outer race.

Fig.K.9. Inspection of the rocker shaft. 1. Bearing surface, 2. Gear teeth, 3. Bearing surface.

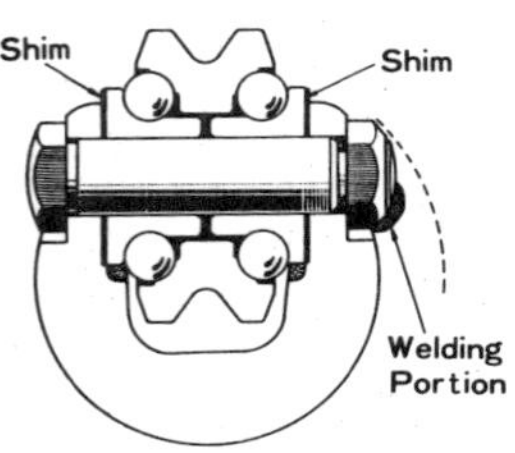

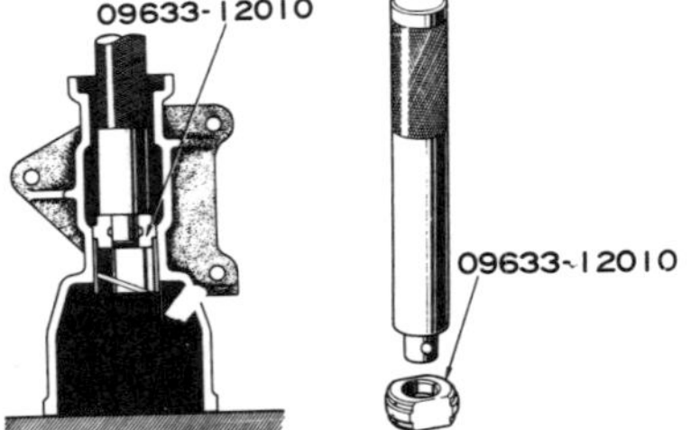

Fig.K.10. Assembled rocker shaft.

Fig.K.11. Inspection of the steering housing. 1. Bushes, 2. Oil seal, 3. Column outer tube.

Fig.K.12. Removal of the rocker shaft bushes.

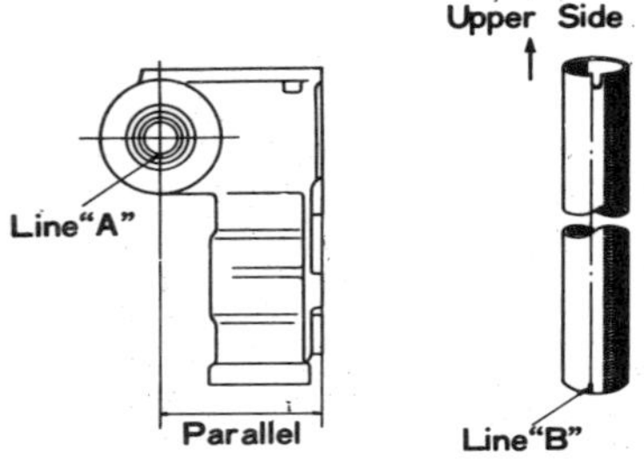

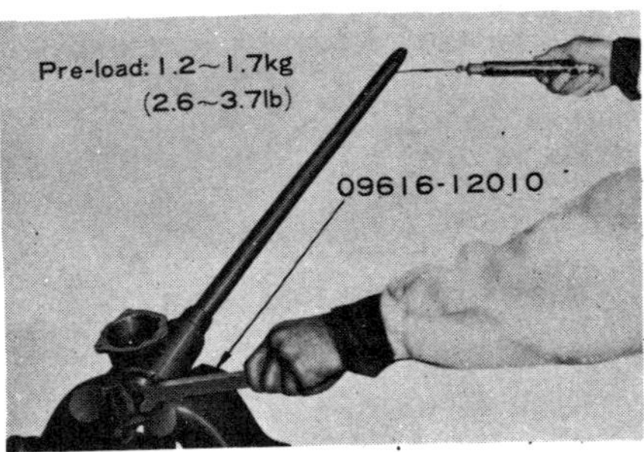

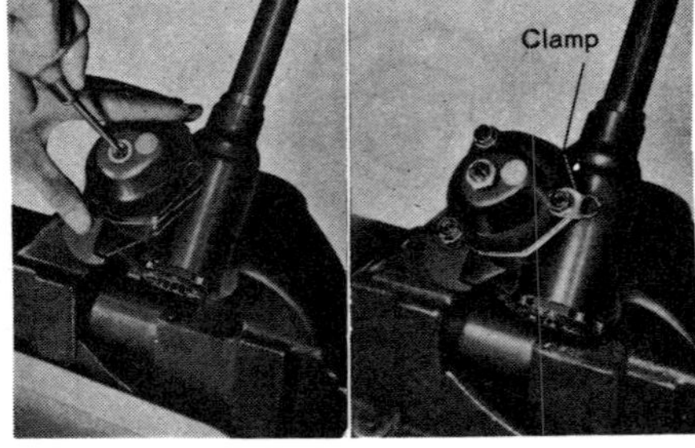

Fig.K.13. Installation direction of steering column outer tube (see text).

Fig.K.14. Checking the pre-load of the steering column bearings.

Fig.K.15. Installation of the steering box cover.

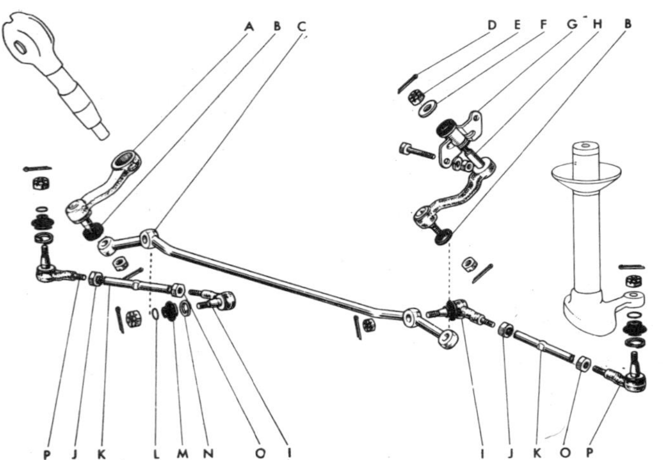

Fig.K.16. Exploded view of the steering linkage.

A.	Steering drop arm
B.	Idler arm dust seal
C.	Centre track rod
D.	Split pin
E.	Castellated nut
F.	Plain washer
G.	Idler arm bracket
H.	Steering idler arm
I.	Track rod (R.H. thread)
J.	Clamp nut (RH. thread)
K.	Track rod centre tube
L.	Ring
M.	Dust cap
N.	Clip
O.	Nut (L.H. thread)
P.	Track rod end (L.H. thread)

bushes with the oil grooves in the bushes towards the top and press in the bushes with special press mandrel 09633-12010 (the same tool as used for removal). Any other mandrel with the appropriate outer diameter and a pilot spigot is also suitable. Finally ream the bushes to an inner diameter of 25.00 - 25.021 mm (0.9843 - 0.9851 in.). The running clearance between bushes and rocker shaft should be 0.007 - 0.041 mm (0.0003 - 0.0016 in.). Fit the new oil seal with a drift of suitable outer diameter.

To replace the column outer tube, clamp the tube into a vice and using a wooden or rubber mallet tap the steering housing off the steering shaft. Mark a line "A" on the steering housing parallel to the mounting surface and a line "B" on the column tube in line with the left-hand side of the slot at the top of the tube (Fig.K.13).

Clamp the column tube into a vice (with soft-metal jaws) and fit the worm bearing adjusting screw. Lock the nut into the steering housing. Now assemble the steering housing to the column tube by tapping the housing on to the tube until the lines "A" and "B" are in line and the length from the top of the tube to the bottom of the steering housing is 788 mm (31.05 in.). Finally check the bush and collar at the upper end of the steering column tube for wear or damage, if the tube was not replaced.

STEERING — Assembly

Lubricate the steering worm and the worm bearings with gear oil. Fit the bearing to both sides of the steering worm and insert the steering spindle with the worm into the steering housing. Using the steering worm bearing replacer 09562-10010, fit the lower bearing outer race. Grease and fit a new 'O' seal ring to the worm bearing adjusting screw and screw the adjusting screw and the locknut to the steering housing. Adjust the bearing pre-load to 1.2 - 1.7 kg (2.6 - 2.7 lb) (Fig.K.14) by tightening the adjusting screw with the special wrench 09617-12010. The pre-load can be checked by means of a piece of string attached to the end of the steering spindle and a spring scale attached to the end of the string. With the pre-load correctly adjusted, tighten the locknut to a torque reading of 8 - 10 kgm (60 - 70 lb.ft.), using the special wrench 09617-12012. This operation must be carried out with the greatest of care in order not to disturb the setting of the adjusting screw.

Select and fit a thrust washer that will give the minimum clearance between rocker shaft and washer. Thrust washers are available in the following thicknesses:

NOTE: The thrust washer thickness for Corolla 1100 models after April 1968 and for Corolla 1200 models are different to the sizes given below. For these models, refer to heading "MODIFICATIONS" at the end of this section..

Part number	Thickness
45352-10011	2.01 mm (0.079 in.)
45353-10011	2.07 mm (0.082 in.)
45354-10010	2.11 mm (0.083 in.)
45355-10010	2.15 mm (0.085 in.)

Oil the rocker shaft and the oil seal and fit the shaft together with the rocker shaft adjusting bolt and the thrust washer into the steering housing. Fit the end cover and gasket to the housing and tighten the three cover bolts to 1.5 - 2.2 kgm (11 - 16 lb.ft.). (Fig.K.15).

Fit the steering drop arm and the securing nut to the rocker shaft and with the rocker shaft in the centre of the steering worm, turn the adjusting screw to obtain a backlash of 0.16 - 0.19 mm (0.006 - 0.007 in.) at the end of the drop arm. Tighten the locknut of the adjusting screw to 2.5 - 4.0 kgm (18 - 29 lb.ft.). Fully turn the steering spindle clockwise all the way and back by 180º and check that the backlash has a value of 0.9 - 1.6 mm (0.04 - 0.06 in.). Then check the backlash on the other side by turning the shaft fully anti-clockwise and back by 180º. The backlash should be within 0.7 mm (0.03 in.) of the value measured on the other side. If not, adjust by changing the worm adjusting shim. If the backlash was greater when the steering shaft was turned clockwise, increase the shim thickness. If the backlash was greater when the shaft was turned anti-clockwise, decrease the shim thickness. Washers are available in the following thicknesses:

Part Number	Thickness
90564-34052	0.1 mm (0.004 in.)
90564-34053	0.2 mm (0.008 in.)
90564-34054	0.3 mm (0.012 in.)
90564-34055	0.4 mm (0.016 in.)

If shims have been removed or added, it becomes necessary to re-adjust the steering worm bearing pre-load.

Grease the steering column upper bush and install the bush and the collar into the upper end of the outer tube.

STEERING — Installation

The installation of the steering gear is a reversal of the removal procedure, noting the following points:

Fit the column outer tube temporarily to the facia panel prior to fitting the steering gear, in order to obtain the correct fitting position of the steering. Align the mating marks on rocker shaft and drop arm when re-connecting the parts.

The clearance between the steering cover and the indicator switch should be 0.4 mm (0.016 in.). There should be a gap of 2.7 mm (0.12 in.) between the indicator switch and the steering wheel after installation. Align the steering wheel and steering shaft mating marks. Tighten all bolts and nuts of the steering gear to the recommended tightening torques. Finally fill the steering box with 0.16 litres (0.17 U.S. qts.; 0.3 Imp. pts.) of gear oil.

NOTE: When referring to the tightening torque table in this manual, note that the tightening torque for the steering column clamp to the instrument panel is different for models before April 1968 and after.

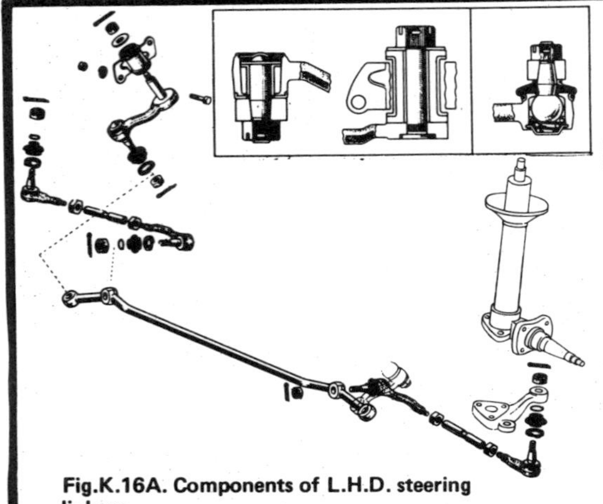

Fig.K.16A. Components of L.H.D. steering linkage.

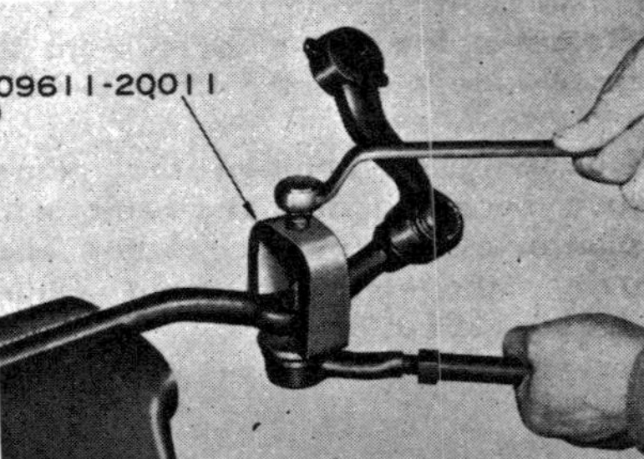

Fig.K.17. Removal of the track rod end.

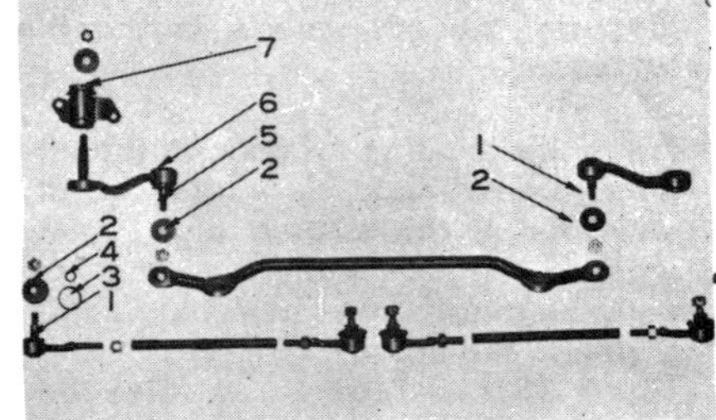

Fig.K.18. View of the dismantled steering linkage.

1. Ball joint   5. Idler arm joint
2. Dust cap   6. Steering idler arm
3. Retaining clip   7. Idler arm bracket
4. Retaining ring

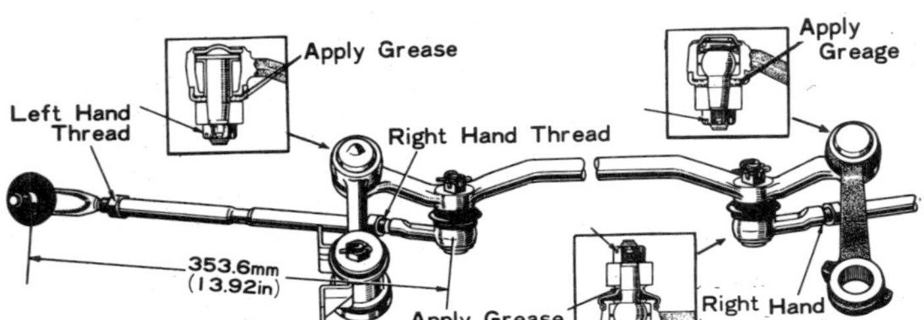

Fig.K.19. View of the assembled steering linkage.

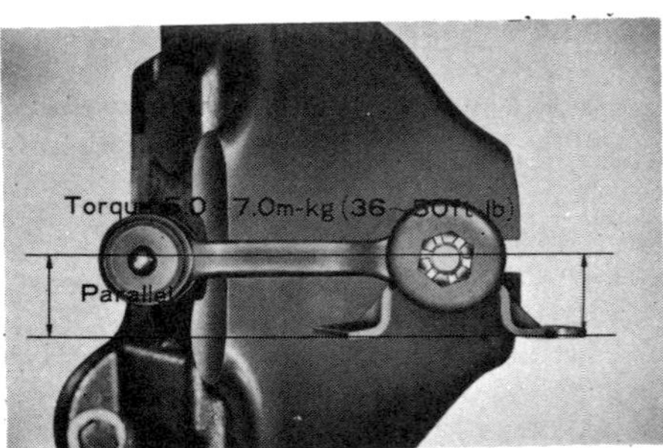

Fig.K.20. The correct installation of the steering idler arm.

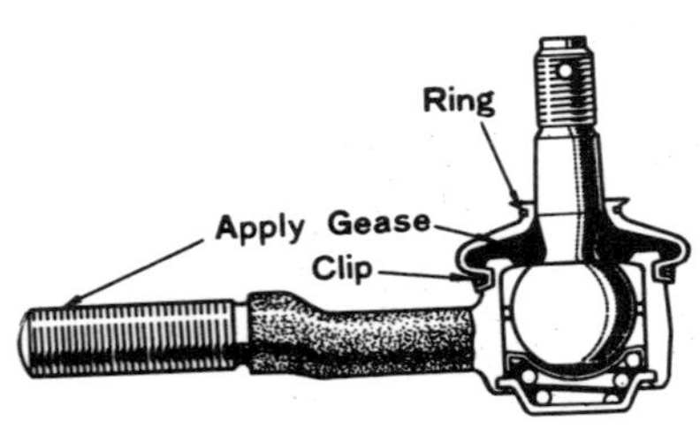

Fig.K.21. Correct assembly of the track rod end.

Fig.K.22. Removal of horn push on Saloon Models.

Fig.K.23. Removal of horn push on Sprinter and Coupe Models.

STEERING LINKAGE — Removal
(Fig.K.16)

With the front end of the car resting on stands and the front wheels removed, remove the idler arm (H in the illustration) from the front side member. Remove the nut, holding the steering drop arm (A) to the rocker shaft and withdraw the drop arm by means of the special puller 09610-12010 or another suitable extractor. Remove the castellated nut from the track rod end ball joint on the steering knuckle after withdrawing the split pin and disconnect the track rod end with a suitable puller. Special tool 09611-12010 is available. The steering linkage can now be removed from the car.

STEERING LINKAGE — Dismantling
(Fig.K.16)

Remove the track rod ends from the centre track rod with the special puller 09611-20011 or any suitable puller as shown in Fig.K.17 after having removed the castelleted nut and the split pin. Slacken the track rod end locknuts and unscrew both track rod ends from the side track rods. Remove the steering drop arm and steering idler arm (A and H) from the centre track rod in a similar manner as described above.

The steering idler arm is held in position in its bracket by means of a washer, castellated nut and split pin and can be withdrawn after removal of the mentioned parts. Finally remove the rubber boots from track rod ends, drop arm and idler arm.

STEERING LINKAGE — Inspection
(Fig.K.18)

Inspect the parts as follows and replace as necessary:

1. Check the track rod ball joints (1) for roughness, excessive movements or oil leaks.

2. Check the rubber boots (4) and the securing clips (3) for wear, deterioration or other damages. Weak securing clips should always be renewed.

3. Check the idler arm ball joint (5) and the seat in the idler arm (6) for roughness and leaks and the bush in the inside of the idler arm bracket for excessive wear.

STEERING LINKAGE — Assembly
(Fig.K.19)

Fit the steering idler arm pivot pin into the idler arm bracket and fit the washer and the castellated nut. Tighten the nut to a torque reading of 5.0 - 7.0 kgm (36 - 50 lb.ft.), with the bracket face parallel to the idler arm (Fig.K.20) and fit the split pin.

Clean the rubber boots and pack them with grease. Fit the boots over the track rod ball joint studs and all other ball joint studs and secure the boots in position with the securing clips and the retaining rings as shown in the sectional view of Fig.K.21. Grease the track rod end threads and fit the track rod ends into the centre tubes. Screw in both track rod ends by the same amount so that the distance between the track rod ball joint studs is 353.6 mm (13.92 in.) (see Fig.K.19) and temporarily tighten the locknuts.

Fit the steering drop arm and the steering idler arm to the centre track rod and tighten the castellated nut to a torque reading of 5.0 - 7.0 kgm (36 - 50 lb.ft.). Fit the split pin. Fit the two track rod ends of the side track rods to the centre track rod and tighten the castellated nuts to a torque reading of 3.0 - 4.5 kgm (22 - 32 lb.ft.). Fit the split pin.

STEERING LINKAGE — Installation

Grease the track rod end rubber boots and fit the ball joint studs into the steering levers on the steering knuckle arms. Tighten the castellated nuts to 3.0 - 4.5 kgm (22 - 32 lb.ft.) and secure with the split pins. Align the mating marks of the steering drop arm and the rocker shaft and fit the drop arm, washer, lock washer and the castellated nut to a torque reading of 7.0 - 11.0 kgm (50 - 80 lb.ft.). Secure the nut with the split pin. Fit the idler arm bracket to the side member and tighten the bolts to a tightening torque of 1.0 - 1.4 kgm (7.0 - 10.0 lb.ft.) in the case of cars before April 1968 or 1.0 - 1.6 kgm (7.0 - 11.0 lb.ft.) in the case of cars after April 1968.

Fit the front wheels, lower the car and tighten the wheel nuts. **NOTE:** Wheel nuts of cars before April 1968 are tightened to 9.0 - 12.0 kgm (65 - 87 lb.ft.). Wheel nuts of cars after this date are tightened to 8.0 - 11.0 kgm (58 - 80 lb.ft.). Finally adjust the front wheel alignment (toe-in) as described in section "Front Axle and Front Suspension".

Trouble Shooting

SYMPTOMS	PROBABLE CAUSE	ACTION TO BE TAKEN
Hard steering	Low tyre pressure Incorrect wheel alignment Stiff track rod ends Steering box needs adjustment	Correct pressure Correct alignment Check and replace if necessary Adjust if necessary
Steering wheel shimmy	Tyre pressure incorrect Incorrect wheel alignment Wheels and tyres need balancing Wheel hub nut loose Wheel bearings damaged Front suspension distorted Steering box needs adjustment	Correct Correct alignment Balance as necessary Adjust wheel bearings Replace wheel bearings Check, repair or replace Adjust as necessary
Steering wheel pulls to one side	Uneven tyre pressure Improper wheel alignment Wheel bearings worn or damaged Brakes improperly adjusted Shock absorbers faulty Suspension distorted Steering box worn	Correct Correct Replace and adjust Adjust brakes Check and rectify Check and rectify Adjust or replace
Wheel tramp	Over-inflated tyres Unbalanced tyre and wheel Defective shock absorber Defective tyre	Correct pressure Check and balance if necessary Check and rectify Repair or replace
Abnormal tyre wear	Incorrect tyre pressure Incorrect wheel alignment Excessive wheel bearing play Improper driving	Correct Correct Adjust Avoid sharp turning at high speeds, rapid starting and braking, etc.
Tyre noises	Improper tyre inflation Incorrect wheel alignment	Correct Correct

TIGHTENING TORQUES

ENGINE

Main bearing caps	39 - 47 lb.ft. (5.4 - 6.6 kgm)
Big end bearing caps	29 - 37 lb.ft. (4.0 - 5.2 kgm)
Oil pump	7 - 11 lb.ft. (1.0 - 1.5 kgm)
Front end plate	4 - 6 lb.ft. (0.6 - 0.9 kgm)
Camshaft thrust plate	4 - 6 lb.ft. (0.6 - 0.9 kgm)
Camshaft sprocket	16 - 22 lb.ft. (2.3 - 3.1 kgm)
Chain tensioner	4 - 6 lb.ft. (0.6 - 0.9 kgm)
Vibration damper	4 - 6 lb.ft. (0.6 - 0.9 kgm)
Timing cover	4 - 6 lb.ft. (0.6 - 0.9 kgm)
Rear oil seal retainer	4 - 6 lb.ft. (0.6 - 0.9 kgm)
Oil sump	2 - 3 lb.ft. (0.25 - 0.35 kgm)
Crankshaft pulley	29 - 43 lb.ft. (4.0 - 6.0 kgm)
Cylinder head	36 - 48 lb.ft. (5.4 - 6.6 kgm)
Rocker supports	13 - 16 lb.ft. (1.8 - 2.2 kgm)
Fuel pump	7 - 11 lb.ft. (1.0 - 1.5 kgm)
Engine mountings	14 - 22 lb.ft. (2.0 - 3.0 kgm)
Oil filter bracket	7 - 11 lb.ft. (1.0 - 1.5 kgm)
Alternator bracket	7 - 11 lb.ft. (1.0 - 1.5 kgm)
Manifold	14 - 22 lb.ft. (2.0 - 3.0 kgm)
Water pump	7 - 11 lb.ft. (1.0 - 1.5 kgm)
Fan pulley	4 - 6 lb.ft. (0.6 - 0.9 kgm)
Alternator	11 - 14 lb.ft. (1.5 - 2.0 kgm)
Rear end plate	4 - 6 lb.ft. (0.6 - 0.9 kgm)
Flywheel	39 - 48 lb.ft. (5.4 - 6.6 kgm)
Clutch cover	7 - 11 lb.ft. (1.0 - 1.5 kgm)
Gearbox to engine	36 - 51 lb.ft. (5.0 - 7.0 kgm

The tightening torques given are listed in the order of engine assembly.
This list, therefore, is at the same time a guide for the fitting sequence of
the individual parts.

GEARBOX

Main shaft nut	60 - 80 lb.ft. (8 - 11 kgm)
Front bearing retainer	7 - 12 lb.ft. (1.0 - 1.6 kgm)
Countershaft cover	7 - 12 lb.ft. (1.0 - 1.6 kgm)
Idler shaft bolt	9.5 - 13 lb.ft. (1.3 - 1.8 kgm)
Gearbox cover	3 - 7 lb.ft. (0.4 - 0.9 kgm)
Extension housing	15 - 22 lb.ft. (2.0 - 3.0 kgm)
Bottom cover	4.5 - 5.0 lb.ft. (0.6 - 0.7 kgm)
Drain plug	27 - 31 lb.ft. (3.7 - 4.5 kgm)
Clutch fork bolt	14 - 22 lb.ft. (1.9 - 3.1 kgm)
Gearbox to engine	36 - 50 lb.ft. (5.0 - 7.0 kgm)
Gearbox to rear end plate	11 - 16 lb.ft. (1.5 - 2.2 kgm)
Gearbox to stiffener	25 - 32 lb.ft. (3.5 - 4.5 kgm)
Starter motor	7 - 11 lb.ft. (1.0 - 1.5 kgm)
Extension to mounting rubber	15 - 22 lb.ft. (2.0 - 3.0 kgm)
Mounting rubber to member	22 - 32 lb.ft. (3.0 - 4.5 kgm)
Member to body	25 - 40 lb.ft. (3.5 - 5.5 kgm)
Gearbox filler plug	27 - 31 lb.ft. (3.7 - 4.3 kgm)

REAR AXLE AND REAR SUSPENSION

Spring "U" bolts	22 - 32 lb.ft. (3.0 - 4.5 kgm)
Shock absorber (bottom)	25 - 40 lb.ft. (3.5 - 5.5 kgm)
Shock absorber (top)	14 - 22 lb.ft. (1.9 - 3.1 kgm)
Brake line to hose	9 - 13 lb.ft. (1.3 - 1.8 kgm)
Brake line to cylinder	6 - 9 lb.ft. (0.8 - 1.3 kgm)
Differential carrier (axle)	15 - 22 lb.ft. (2.0 - 3.0 kgm)
Differential carrier (shaft)	11 - 16 lb.ft. (1.5 - 2.2 kgm)
Outer bearing retainer	15 - 22 lb.ft. (2.0 - 3.0 kgm)
Wheel nuts	65 - 85 lb.ft. (9.0 - 12.0 kgm)
Axle filler plug	20 - 24 lb.ft. (2.7 - 3.3 kgm)
Breather plug	7 - 9 lb.ft. (1.0 - 1.3 kgm)
Crown wheel bolts	45 - 55 lb.ft. (6.0 - 7.5 kgm)
Pinion nut	95 - 110 lb.ft. (13 - 15 kgm)
Diff. bearing caps	40 - 47 lb.ft. (5.5 - 6.5 kgm)
Adjusting nut locks	3 - 5 lb.ft. (0.4 - 0.7 kgm)

Spring bracket pin bolts	7 - 12 lb.ft. (1.0 - 1.6 kgm)
Spring bracket nut	15 - 22 lb.ft. (2.0 - 3.0 kgm)
Shackle nuts	15 - 22 lb.ft. (2.0 - 3.0 kgm)

FRONT AXLE AND FRONT SUSPENSION

Hub adjusting torque	19 - 23 lb.ft. (2.6 - 3.2 kgm)
Piston rod nut	36 - 43 lb.ft. (5.0 - 6.0 kgm)
Ring nut	75 - 110 lb.ft. (10 - 15 kgm)
Piston rod to support	30 - 50 lb.ft. (4.0 - 5.5 kgm)
Support to front wing	11 - 16 lb.ft. (1.5 - 2.2 kgm)
Steering arm	15 - 22 lb.ft. (2.0 - 3.0 kgm)
Brake hose to pipe	9 - 13 lb.ft. (1.3 - 1.8 kgm)
Wheel nuts	65 - 85 lb.ft. (9.0 - 12.0 kgm)
Ball joint grease plug	3 - 5 lb.ft. (0.4 - 0.7 kgm)
Steering lever to ball joint	36 - 53 lb.ft. (5 - 7 kgm)
Crossmember to body	30 - 40 lb.ft. (4.0 - 5.5 kgm)
Crossmember to engine mounting	25 - 40 lb.ft. (3.5 - 5.5 kgm)
Fulcrum shaft to crossmember	50 - 60 lb.ft. (7.0 - 8.5 kgm)
Front spring bush to arm	11 - 16 lb.ft. (1.5 - 2.2 kgm)
Steering lever to damper	15 - 22 lb.ft. (2.0 - 3.0 kgm)
Track rod ends	22 - 32 lb.ft. (3.0 - 4.5 kgm)
Steering angle locks	11 - 16 lb.ft. (1.5 - 2.2 kgm)

Cars after April 1968:

Wheel nuts	58 - 80 lb.ft. (8 - 11 kgm)
Fulcrum shaft to crossmember	68 - 87 lb.ft. (9 - 12 kgm)
Steering lever to damper	16 - 26 lb.f.t (2.0 - 3.5 kgm)

STEERING

Adjusting screw locknut	60 - 70 lb.ft. (8 - 10 kgm)
Steering cover	11 - 16 lb.ft. (1.5 - 2.2 kgm)
Steering cover locknut	18 - 29 lb.ft. (2.5 - 4.0 kgm)
Steering box bolts	- 16 lb.ft. (1.5 - 2.2 kgm)
Steering drop arm	50 - 80 lb.ft. (7.0 - 11.0 kgm)
Column clamp to instrument panel:	
Before April 1968	15 - 22 lb.ft. (2.0 - 3.0 kgm)
After April 1968	29 - 36 lb.ft. (4.0 - 5.0 kgm)
Steering wheel nut	15 - 22 lb.ft. (2.0 - 3.0 kgm)
Idler arm nut	36 - 50 lb.ft. (5.0 - 7.0 kgm)
Drop arm to centre rod	36 - 50 lb.ft. (5 - 7 kgm)
Idler arm to centre rod	36 - 50 lb.ft. (5 - 7 kgm)
Track rods to centre rod	22 - 32 lb.ft. (2 - 3 kgm)
Track rods to steering arm	22 - 32 lb.ft. (2 - 3 kgm)
Idler arm to sidemember	7 - 10 lb.ft. (1.0 - 1.4 kgm)
Track rod locknuts	25 - 40 lb.ft. (3.5 - 5.5 kgm)

BRAKES

Master cylinder to reservoir	10 - 13 lb.ft. (1.4 - 1.8 kgm)
Master cylinder to bulkhead	11 - 16 lb.ft. (1.5 - 2.2 kgm)
Master cylinder connection	20 - 25 lb.ft. (2.7 - 3.5 kgm)
'A' type union nut	6 - 9 lb.ft. (0.8 - 1.3 kgm)
'B' type union nut	9 - 13 lb.ft. (1.3 - 1.8 kgm)
Brake hose	9 - 13 lb.ft. (1.3 - 1.8 kgm)
Brake drum to hub	7 - 12 lb.ft. (1.0 - 1.6 kgm)
Back plate to knuckle	11 - 16 lb.ft. (1.5 - 2.2 kgm)
Wheel cylinder to back plate	7 - 12 lb.ft. (1.0 - 1.6 kgm)
Back plate to rear axle	15 - 20 lb.ft. (2.0 - 3.0 kgm)
Adjuster cylinder to back plate	7 - 12 lb.ft. (1.0 - 1.6 kgm)
Wheel cylinder to back plate	3 - 5 lb.ft. (0.4 - 0.7 kgm)
Handbrake lever to floor	7 - 12 lb.ft. (1.0 - 1.6 kgm)

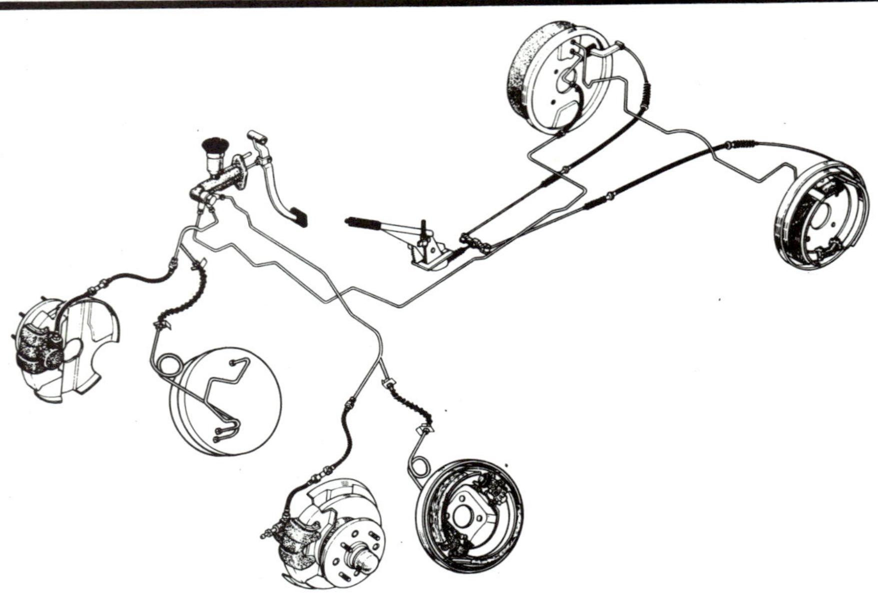

Fig.L.1. Layout of the brake system with drum brakes and disc brakes at the front.

Fig.L.2. Brake pedal adjustment.

Fig.L.3. Adjustment of the front brake assembly (drum brakes).

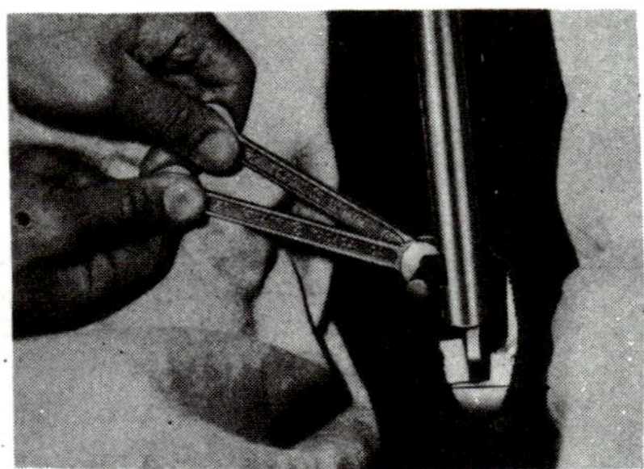

Fig.L.4. Handbrake adjustment.

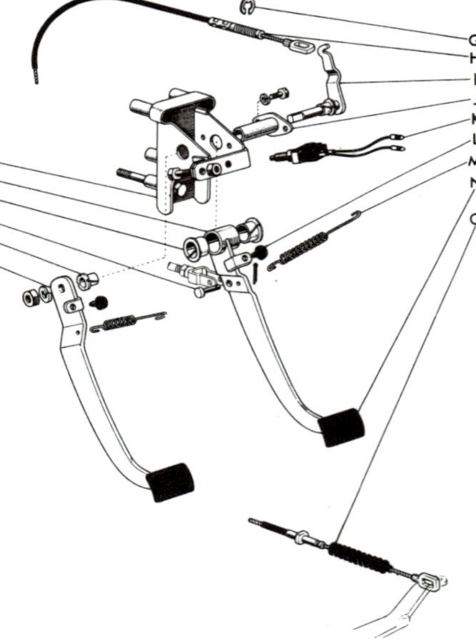

Fig.L.5. Exploded view of brake and clutch pedal assembly.

A. Pedal support
B. Brake pedal
C. Bush
D. Clevis pin
E. Bush
F. Clutch pedal
G. 'E' clip
H. Clutch operating cable
I. Clutch release lever
J. Pedal support bearing tube
K. Brake light switch
L. Rubber stop
M. Return spring
N. Pedal rubber pad
O. Clutch cable boot

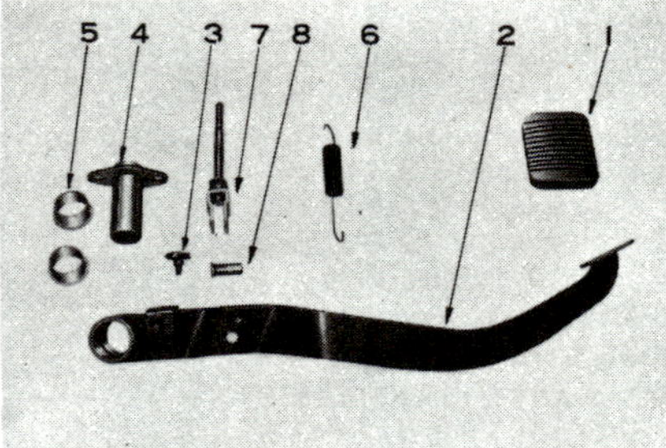

Fig.L.6. Details for brake pedal removal. (for annotations see text).

Fig.L.7. Dismantled view of clutch pedal. (For annotations see text).

Brakes

DESCRIPTION

The brake system is hydraulically operated, acting on all four wheels. The front wheels are fitted with drum brakes of the two leading shoe type with two wheel cylinders for each wheel or can be equipped with disc brakes. The rear wheels are fitted with drum brakes of the leading and trailing shoe type with one wheel cylinder for each wheel.

The handbrake, independent of the hydraulic pressure, operates the brake shoes of the rear wheels through cables and linkages. Handbrake adjustment is effected by adjusting the length of the primary handbrake cable. The layout of the brake systems is shown in Fig.L.1.

BRAKE PEDAL — Adjustment
(Fig.L.2)

Disconnect the stop light switch leads, slacken the locknut (1) and adjust the pedal height to140 - 150 mm (5.5 - 6.0 in.) by turning the stop light switch (2) in the appropriate direction. Tighten the locknut (1) to 1.9 - 3.1 kgm (14 - 22 lb.ft.).

By turning the push rod (4) after slackening the locknut (3) obtain a clearance of 0.5 - 3.0 mm (0.02 - 0.12 in.) between the master cylinder piston and push rod. Tighten the locknut to 1.0 - 1.6 kgm (7 - 11 lb.ft.). Reconnect the stop light switch leads.

BRAKE SHOE ADJUSTMENT

Front Brakes

Support the front end of the car on stands and remove the shoe adjusting plug from the rear of the brake back plate. Expand one brake shoe by rotating the adjusting nut with the brake adjusting tool 09704-10010 until the wheel is locked to the shoe. Pump the brake pedal several times and check that the wheel is still locked, if not expand the shoe further until the wheel is locked once more. Back off the nut about 4 notches so that the drum rotates freely without binding against the shoe. Pump the brake pedal several times and check that the wheel still rotates freely. (Fig.L.3). Replace the plug and repeat the adjusting procedure on the other three brake shoes of the front brakes. Remove the stands and lower the front end of the car.

NOTE: If disc brakes are fitted, no adjustment is necessary.

Rear brakes

Support the rear end of the car on stands and fully release the handbrake. Adjust the rear brake shoes in the same manner as described above for the front brake shoes. Check that the pedal travel is less than half the full pedal stroke. Remove the stands and road test the car to check that the brakes are not pulling or below the expected performance.

BLEEDING THE HYDRAULIC SYSTEM

If any of the brake hoses have been disconnected or replaced or if the brakes have a "spongy" feel, the brake system must be bled.

Clean the area around all brake bleeder valves and around the master cylinder reservoir to avoid entry of dirt and foreign matter in the brake system. The reservoir should be adequately filled with the recommended brake fluid during the whole of the bleeding procedure. Remove the dust cap from the bleeder valve, furthest away from the master cylinder and fit a transparent bleeder hose over the valve. Submerge the free end of the hose into a glass container, partly filled with brake fluid. Depress the brake pedal several times and with the brake pedal held in the depressed position, open the bleeder valve a third of a turn and depress the brake pedal fully. Then close the bleeder valve and allow the brake pedal to return unassisted.

Repeat this operation until no air bubbles enter the glass container. When this happens, depress the brake pedal once more, hold it in this position and close the bleeder plug, tightening it with 0.8 - 1.3 kgm (6 - 9 lb.ft.). Refit the dust cap.

Bleed the remaining wheels in the same manner, the last wheel being the one nearest to the master cylinder. Cars with drum brakes at the front are bled in the same manner as cars with disc brakes at the front.

HANDBRAKE ADJUSTMENT

The handbrake lever travel should be 5 - 9 notches. If adjustment is necessary, remove the brake cable adjuster cap and turn the adjusting nut until the correct handbrake lever travel is obtained (Fig.L.4). Check that with the handbrake released, the rear wheels rotate freely. Tighten the adjuster cap firmly after correct adjustment.

BRAKE PEDAL — Removal
(Fig.L.5)

Remove the clutch pedal (1, Fig.L.6) and the release lever (2) as described in section CLUTCH, unhook the return spring (3), withdraw the split pin and the pivot pin (4) and remove the two bolts (5) and the pedal support bearing (6) from the pedal support. Lift out the brake pedal (7) and the master cylinder push rod (8).

With the components of the brake pedal layed out as shown in Fig.L.7 clean and check all parts and replace if necessary. Check the brake pedal rubber pad (1), pedal (2), pedal damper (3), support bearing (4), bush (5) for damage, excessive wear or deformation. Check the return spring (6) for weakness or damage and the push rod clevis (7) and the clevis pin (8) for wear and damage.

BRAKE PEDAL — Installation

Grease the bushes (1) in Fig.L.8 and the pedal boss (2). Fit the bushes into the pedal support. Connect the master cylinder push rod on to the pedal support (4) by fitting the support bearing (3) to the support and attach the master cylinder push rod to the pedal with the clevis pin and the split pin.

Fit the clutch release lever shaft and the bushes on to the pedal support shaft boss and fit the clutch pedal and nut with

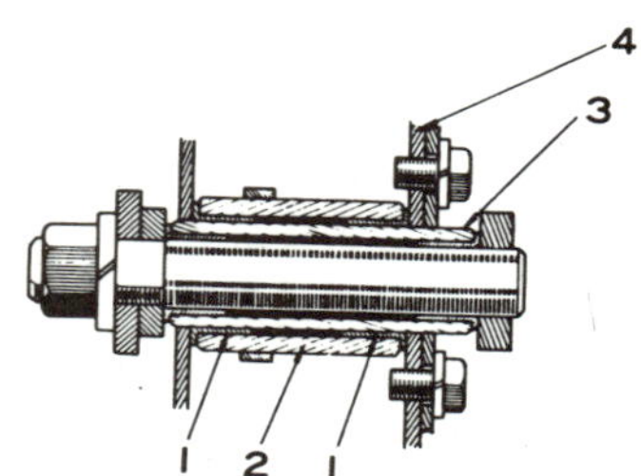

Fig.L.8. The correct assembly of the brake pedal.

1. Bushes
2. Pedal support
3. Bearing tube
4. Pedal support bracket

Fig.L.10. Removal of the master cylinder (1). Banjo bolt, (2). Securing nuts, (3), Nut.

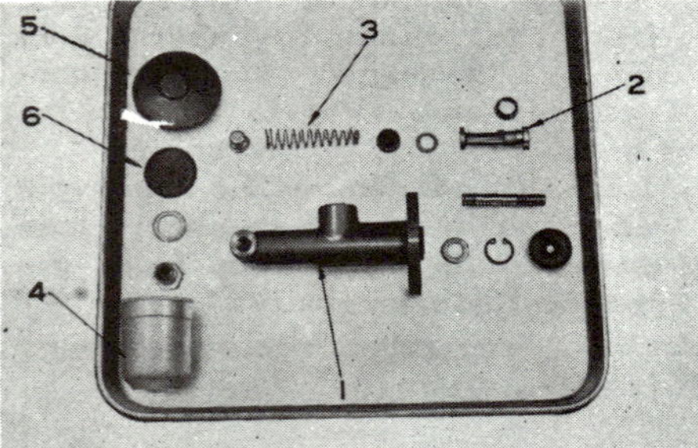

Fig.L.11. View of the dismantled master cylinder.

1. Cylinder body
2. Piston
3. Piston return spring
4. Reservoir
5. Filler cap
6. Reservoir float

Flare Nut "B"(Yellow)

Use for Wheel Brake cylinder

Flare Nut "A"(White)

Fig.L.13. The two different union nuts used on the Corolla.

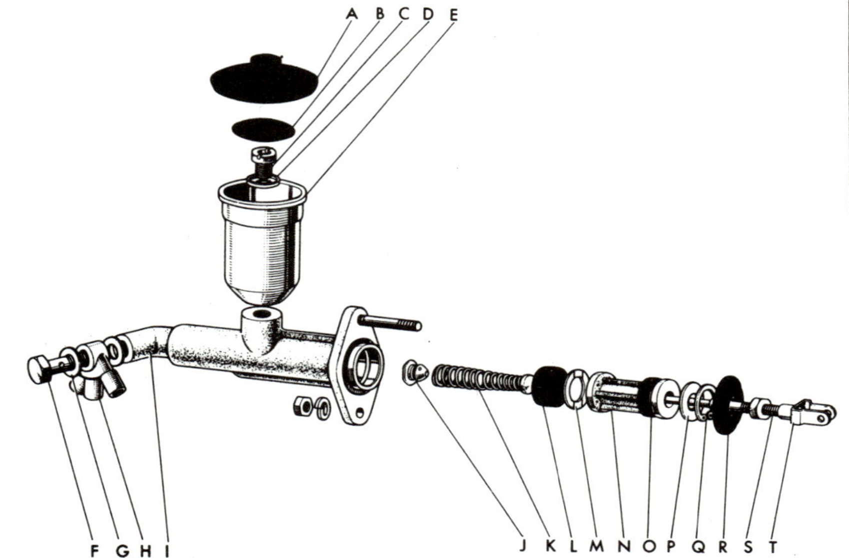

Fig.L.9. Exploded view of the single line master cylinder.

A.	Filler cap	K.	Piston return spring
B.	Reservoir float	L.	Primary cup
C.	Reservoir securing bolt	M.	Cup spacer
D.	Washer	N.	Piston
E.	Reservoir	O.	Secondary cup
F.	Banjo bolt	P.	Plain washer
G.	Gasket	Q.	Circlip
H.	Banjo connectiong	R.	Master cylinder boot
I.	Master cylinder body	S.	Push rod
J.	Outlet check valve	T.	Push rod clevis

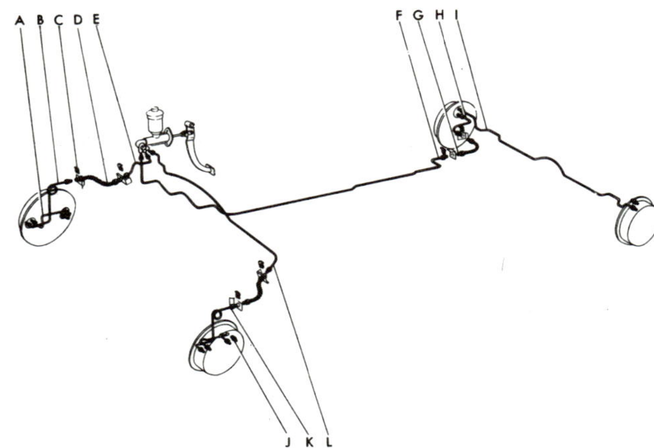

Fig.L.12. Layout of the brake lines.

A.	Cylinder bridge tube	H.	Brake hose to R.H. rear brake line
B.	R.H. front cylinder pipe	I.	R.H. rear brake assembly to L.H. assembly
C.	Clip		
D.	Brake hose	J.	Bleeder plug
E.	Master cylinder to R.H. front brake hose	K.	L.H. front cylinder pipe
F.	Master cylinder to rear brake hose	L.	Master cylinder to L.H. front brake hose
G.	Brake hose		

lockwasher on to the clutch release lever shaft, tightening the nut to 5 - 7 kgm (36 - 50 lb.ft.). Adjust the pedal height as described in this section.

MASTER CYLINDER — Removal

Referring to Fig.L.10 remove the union bolt (1) from the 3-way connector and remove the nuts (2) and (3), securing the master cylinder. Lift off the cylinder from the engine compartment.

MASTER CYLINDER — Dismantling
(Fig.L.9)

Drain the brake fluid, remove the boot from the cylinder body and remove the circlip. Grip the piston with the fingers and withdraw from the cylinder bore. Blow the primary cup from the cylinder, using compressed air. Unscrew the reservoir from the cylinder body by removing the bolt in the inside of the reservoir.

MASTER CYLINDER — Inspection
(Fig.L.11)

Thoroughly clean all parts in clean brake fluid and inspect as follows with reference to Fig.L.11: (Replace parts as necessary).

Check the cylinder bore (1) for wear using an inside micrometer (15.93 mm (0.6272 in.), scores or other damage. Check the piston (2) for wear and measure the outer diamater (15.78 mm (0.6213 in.). If the piston shows scores or grooves, replace it. The cylinder bore to piston clearance must not exceed 0.15 mm (0.006 in.). Check the piston spring for weakness. The min. free length should be 60 mm (2.4 in.). All rubber parts should be replaced every time the master cylinder is to be overhauled.

Check the master cylinder reservoir (4) and the reservoir float (6) for damage, distortion or leaks. Inspect that the vent hole in the filler cap is clear and that the thread is not damaged.

MASTER CYLINDER — Assembly

Clean all parts in clean brake fluid and follow the assembly order of Fig.L.9. Fit the reservoir on to the cylinder body and tighten the bolt to 1.4 - 1.8 kgm (10 - 13 lb.ft.). Carefully check the fitting direction of the piston secondary cup and fit the cup to the piston. Insert the check valve as shown in Fig.L.9 (J) and assemble in the order given piston return spring, primary cup and piston spacer. The groove in the piston spacer should face towards the opening of the cylinder body. Carefully insert the piston into the bore without damaging the secondary cup, place the piston washer over the piston and insert the circlip. Attach the rubber boot to the cylinder body.

Bleed the master cylinder by filling the reservoir with clean brake fluid and pushing the piston into the cylinder bore, using the push rod. Then close the outlet at the front of the cylinder and withdraw the rod slowly, releasing the piston. Repeat this operation until all air is out of the master cylinder.

MASTER CYLINDER — Installation

The installation is a reversal of the removal procedure. Before tightening the union bolt, bleed this section of the system, by depressing the brake pedal several times. Tighten the master cylinder securing nuts to 1.5 - 2.2 kgm (11 - 16 lb.ft.) and the union bolt to 2.7 - 3.5 kgm (20 - 25 lb.ft.). Fill the master cylinder reservoir completely with the recommended brake fluid and bleed the brake system as previously described.

BRAKE LINES
(Fig.L.12)

Check all metal (rigid) pipes for corrosion, leaks or damage and the flexible hoses for swelling or any other damage. Inspect connections for leaks or damaged threads. When replacing pipes check that the union nut is of type "A" in Fig.L.13 for fixing to the wheel cylinders only and of type "B" for all other connections. The difference between the two types of union nuts being the leading spigot at the front on type "B".

Replace union nut seat when any connection is removed. When replacing brake hoses, take care that the hose is not twisted after re-installation. Always bleed the brake system after replacing a brake pipe or hose. Union nuts should be tightened as follows:

Type "A" . . . . .0.8 - 1.3 kgm (6 - 9 lb.ft.)
Type "B" . . . . .1.3 - 1.8 kgm (9 - 13 lb.ft.)
Flexible hose unions . . . . .1.3 - 1.8 kgm (9 - 13 lb.ft.)

FRONT DRUM BRAKES — Removal
(For Disc Brakes see end of this section)

Support the front end of the car on stands and remove the front wheel. Remove the hub grease cap, withdraw the split pin, remove the castellated nut and pull off the hub together with the brake drum. Punch mating marks into brake back plate and brake shoes (for example two marks into the upper shoe and one in the lower with corresponding marks in the back plate).

Remove the return spring on the wheel cylinder piston side of the brake shoe (Fig.L.15) and by pushing in and turning through 90° remove the hold down spring and pin as shown in the right-hand illustration of Fig.L.15. Remove the brake shoe so released from the wheel cylinder and adjusting tappet locating slot and unhook the second return spring.

Disconnect the brake pipe from the wheel cylinder and remove the wheel cylinder by removing the securing bolts. Remove the back plate mounting bolts and lift off the back plate. An exploded view of the front brake assembly is shown in Fig.L.14.

Front Brake Cylinder - Dismantling
Remove the rubber boot and the adjuster lock spring from the cylinder body. Withdraw the adjuster from the cylinder body and unscrew the nut from the tappet. Remove the piston and the piston cup from the cylinder bore and if necessary the union seat from the body (using a left-hand tap or "Easyout").

FRONT DRUM BRAKES — Inspection and Assembly

Check the brake drum for excessive wear, eccentricity or deep scoring. If necessary skim out the brake drum, not going below an internal diameter of 202 mm (7.95 in.). If the drum is beyond wear limit or is otherwise damaged (cracks, etc.) remove the bolt, securing the drum to the hub, fit the new drum to the hub and tighten the securing bolts to 1.0 - 1.6 kgm (7 - 12 lb.ft.).

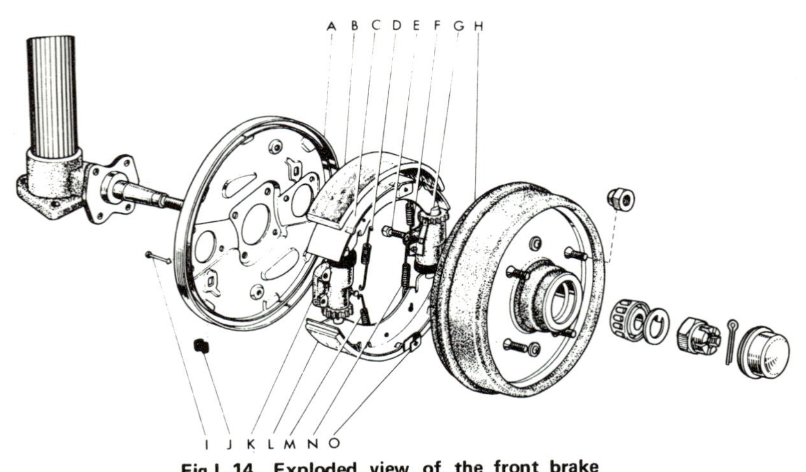

Fig.L.14. Exploded view of the front brake assembly (drum brakes).

A.	Front brake back plate	I.	Brake shoe steady pin
B.	Brake shoe lining	J.	Plug for adjusting hole
C.	Brake shoe	K.	Wheel brake cylinder
D.	Return spring	L.	Brake shoe
E.	Anchorage pin	M.	Return spring
F.	Return spring	N.	Return spring
G.	Wheel brake cylinder	O.	Brake shoe steady spring
H.	Hub and drum assembly		

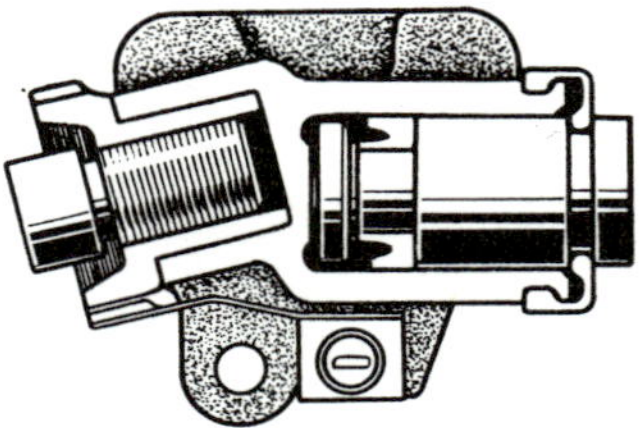

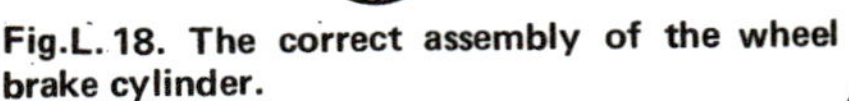

Fig.L.17. Exploded view of the front wheel cylinder.

A.	Wheel cylinder boot
B.	Wheel cylinder piston
C.	Piston cup
D.	Cylinder body
E.	Union seat
F.	Rubber dust cap
G.	Bleeder valve
H.	Spring anchorage pin
I.	Adjuster lock spring
J.	Adjusting nut
K.	Adjusting tappet

Fig.L.18. The correct assembly of the wheel brake cylinder.

Fig.L.15. Removal of the brake shoe return springs (left) and the steady pin (right).

Fig.L.16. View of the two different types of return springs.

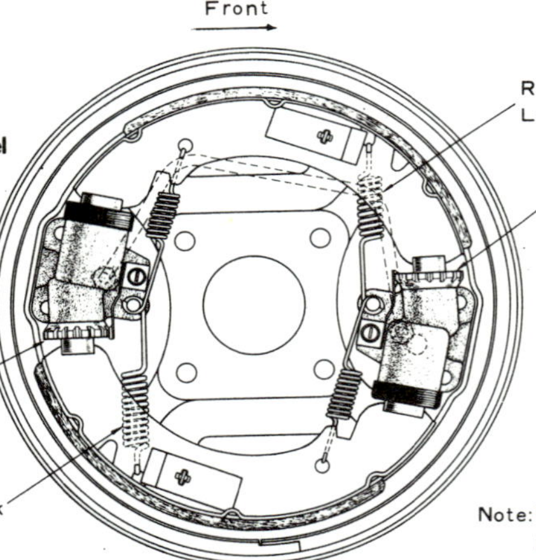

Fig.L.19. View of the assembled front brake.

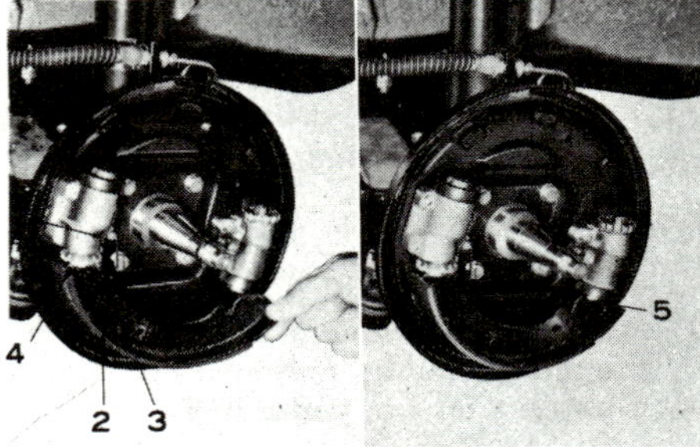

Fig.L.20. Installation of the brake shoes (for annotations see text).

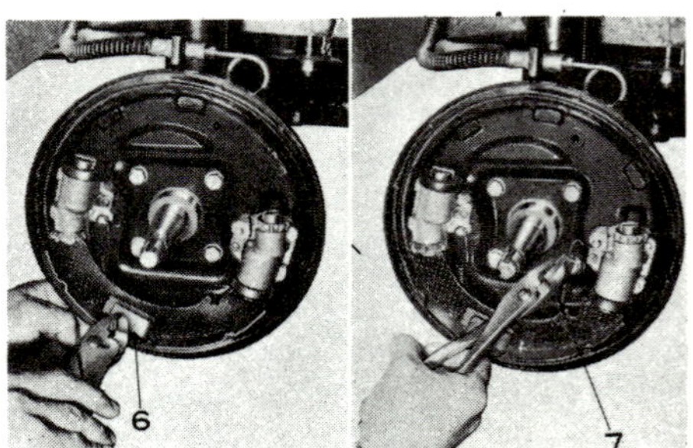

Fig.L.21. Installation of the brake shoes (for annotations see text).

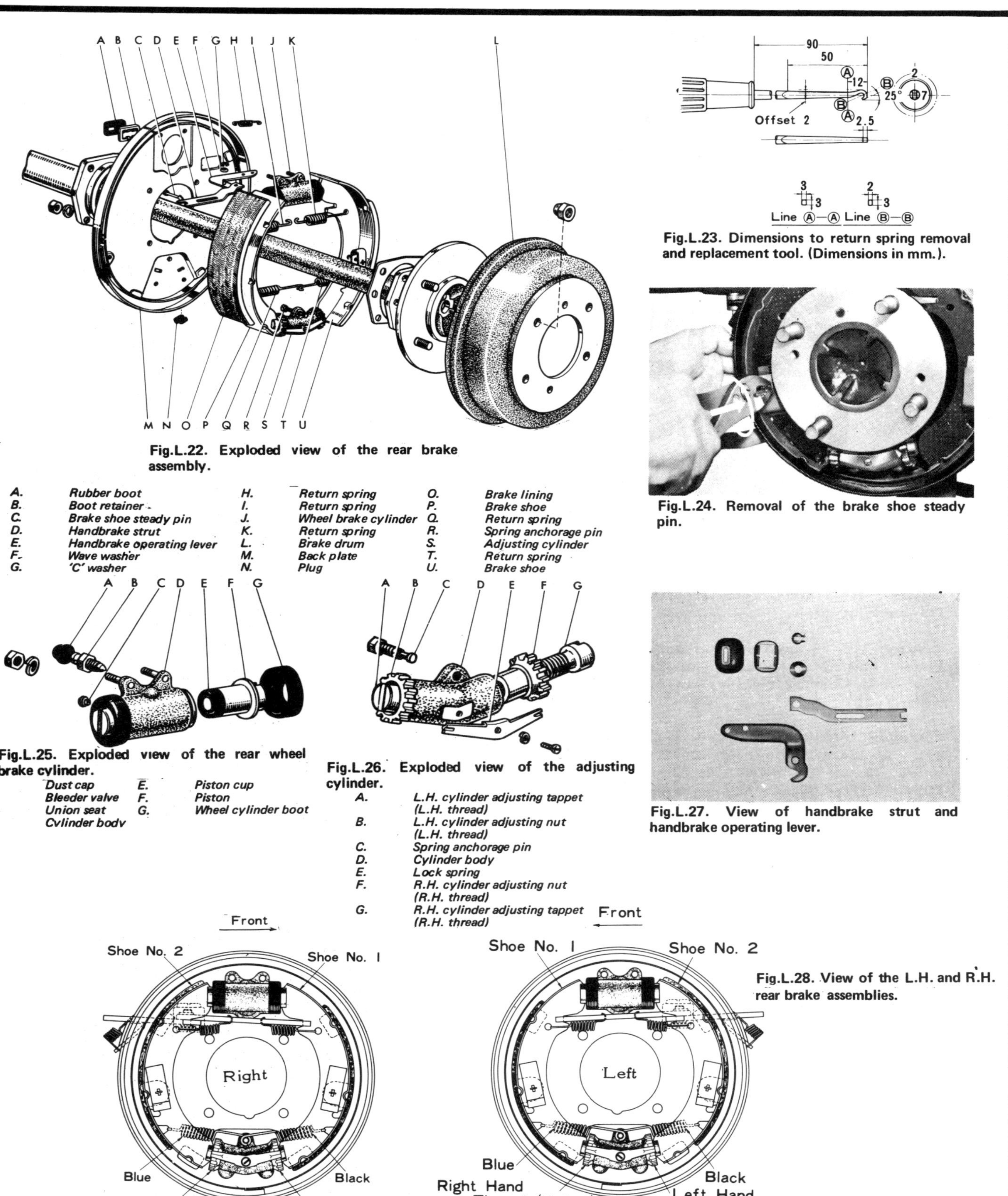

Fig.L.22. Exploded view of the rear brake assembly.

A.	Rubber boot	H.	Return spring	O.	Brake lining
B.	Boot retainer	I.	Return spring	P.	Brake shoe
C.	Brake shoe steady pin	J.	Wheel brake cylinder	Q.	Return spring
D.	Handbrake strut	K.	Return spring	R.	Spring anchorage pin
E.	Handbrake operating lever	L.	Brake drum	S.	Adjusting cylinder
F.	Wave washer	M.	Back plate	T.	Return spring
G.	'C' washer	N.	Plug	U.	Brake shoe

Fig.L.23. Dimensions to return spring removal and replacement tool. (Dimensions in mm.).

Fig.L.24. Removal of the brake shoe steady pin.

Fig.L.25. Exploded view of the rear wheel brake cylinder.

A.	Dust cap	E.	Piston cup
B.	Bleeder valve	F.	Piston
C.	Union seat	G.	Wheel cylinder boot
D.	Cylinder body		

Fig.L.26. Exploded view of the adjusting cylinder.

A.	L.H. cylinder adjusting tappet (L.H. thread)
B.	L.H. cylinder adjusting nut (L.H. thread)
C.	Spring anchorage pin
D.	Cylinder body
E.	Lock spring
F.	R.H. cylinder adjusting nut (R.H. thread)
G.	R.H. cylinder adjusting tappet (R.H. thread)

Fig.L.27. View of handbrake strut and handbrake operating lever.

Fig.L.28. View of the L.H. and R.H. rear brake assemblies.

Fig.L.29. Fitting the adjusting cylinder. (1) Securing bolts, (2) Spring anchorage pin.

Fig.L.30. Installation of the brake shoes.

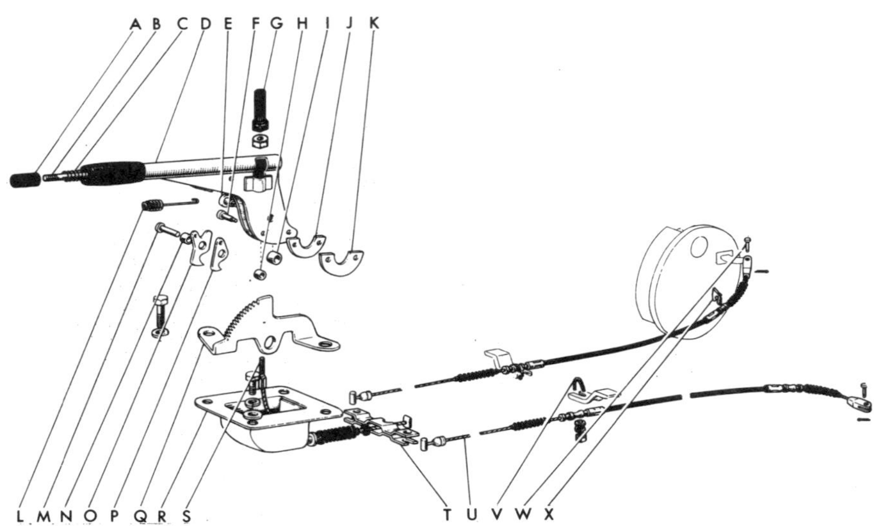

Fig.L.31. Exploded view of the handbrake assembly.

A.	Release rod knob	I.	Spacer	Q.	Toothed sector
B.	Pawl release rod	J.	Brake cable guide	R.	Dust cover
C.	Compression spring	K.	Guide support	S.	Primary handbrake cable
D.	Handbrake lever	L.	Return spring	T.	Handbrake equalizer bracket
E.	Pivot pin	M.	Pin	U.	Secondary handbrake cable (two)
F.	Pin	N.	Spacer	V.	Cable clamp
G.	Cable adjusting cap	O.	Pawl	W.	Pin
H.	Spacer	P.	Pawl	X.	Cable clip

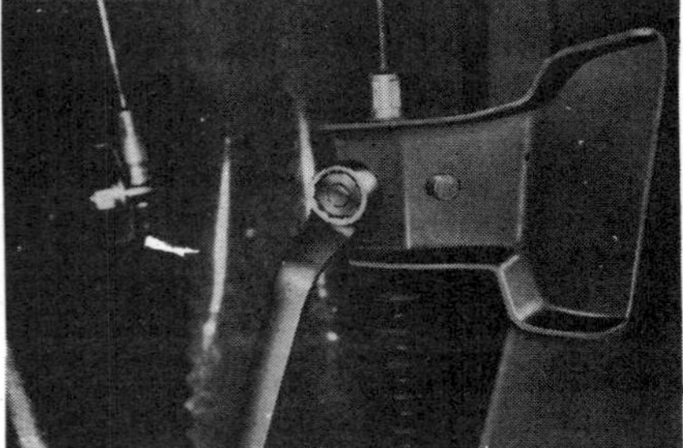

Fig.L.32. Removal of the handbrake cable clamp.

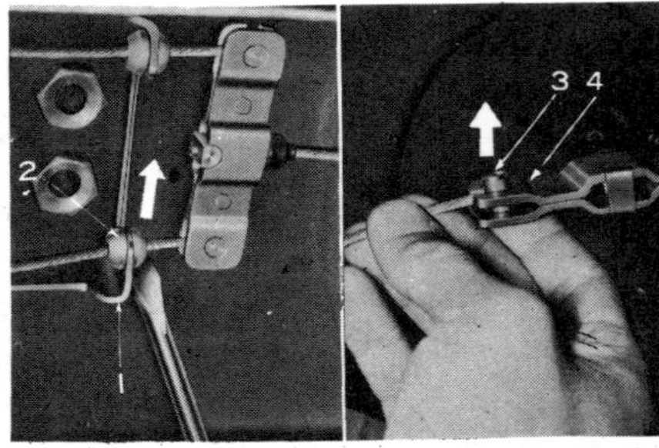

Fig.L.33. Removal of the secondary handbrake cable from the equalizer bracket.
1. Guide   3. Cable
2. Grommet   4. Equalizer

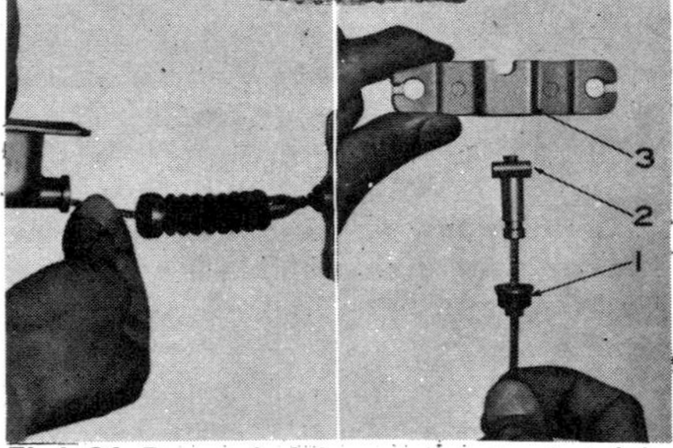

Fig.L.34. Removal of the equalizer bracket. (1). End cover (2). Cable, (3). Bracket.

Fig.L.35. Dismantling the handbrake lever.

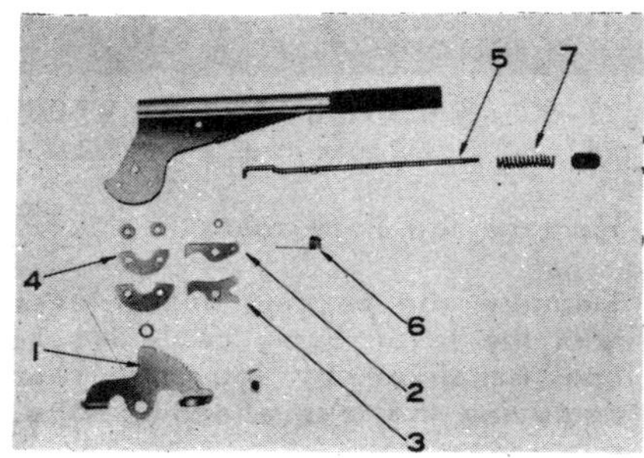

Fig.L.36. View of the dismantled handbrake lever (for annotations see text).

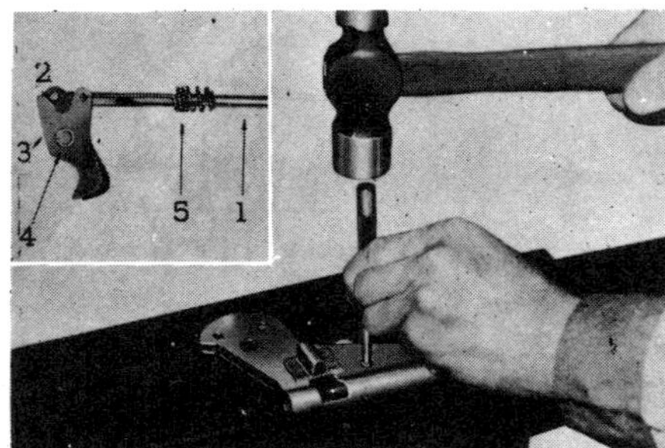

Fig.L.37. Assembling the handbrake lever. (For annotations see text).

Using a surface plate, check the back plate for deformation or other damage. Deformation can be checked by inserting feeler gauges between the surface plate and the edge of the back plate at various points on the outer diameter.

Check the return springs for weakness. The free length is 69.6 mm (2.74 in.) on the piston side and 68.1 mm (2.68 in.) on the adjuster side. The springs should be measured as shown in Fig.L.16.

Check the brake shoes for wear, damage or corrosion. The wear limit for brake linings is 1.5 mm (0.06 in.) in thickness. It is recommended to replace shoes and linings as a single item even though linings only are also available. Check the contact of the brake lining on the brake drum. If necessary dress the lining to obtain a good contact.

Check the wheel cylinder (Fig.L.17) for wear, scores or corrosion. The max. internal diameter is 19.15 mm (0.758 in.). Check the piston for the same defects. The min. outer diameter of the piston is 18.98 mm (0.747 in.). The max. permissible clearance between cylinder and piston must not exceed 0.15 mm (0.006 in.).

To assemble the brake, first clean all wheel cylinder parts in brake fluid and completely immerse the piston cup prior to assembly. Always fit a new piston cup. With the piston cup facing the correct way, fit the piston and cup into the cylinder body and fit the rubber boot. The correct assembly is shown in Fig.L.18. Lightly grease the adjuster nut and the tappet with high-melting point grease and fit into the body.

NOTE: The left-hand thread adjuster (white mark) is used for the right-hand wheel; the right-hand thread adjuster (yellow mark) is used for the left-hand wheel.

Fit the adjuster lock spring and the new union seat to the body.

Fit the brake back plate to the steering knuckle and tighten the bolts to 1.5 - 2.2 kgm (11 - 16 lb.ft.). Fit the wheel cylinder with the bleeder valve towards the rear of the car and the other wheel cylinder towards the front and tighten the bolts to 1.0 - 1.6 kgm (7 - 12 lb.ft.). Fit the brake pipes to the cylinders taking care not to damage the threads. Tighten the union nut to 0.8 - 1.3 kgm (6 - 9 lb.ft.).

Lightly grease the brake shoes with high-melting point grease where they are in contact with the brake back plate and hook the return spring (3) in Fig.L.20 on to the anchorage pin (1) and the hole (2) in the shoe in the adjuster side. Fig.L.19 shows the brake assembly in fitted position, giving the exact locations of the return springs. Fit one end of the brake shoe into the adjuster tappet slot (4) and fit the other end into the piston slot (5).

Fit the hold down spring (6) (Fig.L.21) and the pin to the back plate and the brake shoe and fit the other shoe return spring (7) to the piston end of the brake shoe. The other brake shoe is refitted in a similar manner.

Replace the front hub and the brake drum assembly as detailed under "Front Suspension" and check the bearing pre-load. Finally adjust the brakes as described earlier in this section and bleed the brake system.

REAR BRAKES — Removal

With the rear of the car resting on stands and the wheels removed, mark the brake drum and the half shaft with a centre punch, release the handbrake and remove the brake drum.

Remove the upper and the lower brake shoe return springs. A suitable tool for this purpose is shown in Fig.L.23 and can be made up in accordance with the dimensions given. Remove the brake shoe steady springs and pins by turning the pin by 90° as shown in Fig.L.24 so that the pin head will pass through the slot in the spring. Disconnect the brake cable by removing the pin and remove the return spring connected between the bell crank and the bell crank support plate. Remove the bell crank and the handbrake operating lever from the brake back plate and detach the rubber boot and the retainer from the rear of the plate. After removing the 'C' shaped clip from the bell crank pin, remove the brake shoe strut from the bell crank.

Disconnect the brake pipe from the wheel brake cylinder, remove the cylinder securing bolts and lift off the wheel cylinder. Remove the adjuster cylinder from the back plate and remove the back plate as described in section "REAR AXLE".

Wheel Brake Cylinder - Dismantling

Remove the rubber boots from both ends of the cylinder body and remove the pistons and piston cups. If necessary remove the union seat by means of a left-hand tap.

Adjusting Cylinder — Dismantling

Remove the adjuster lock spring, adjusting nuts and adjusting bolts from the cylinder and separate the nuts from the tappets.

REAR BRAKES — Inspection

Inspect all parts as follows and replace if necessary:

Clean all parts in a suitable solvent, except for the brake linings and rubber parts. Check the brake shoe return springs for weakness. The free length of the springs must be less than 41.4 mm (1.63 in.) for the piston end and 68.1 mm (2.68 in.) for the adjusting cylinder side. Check the handbrake bell crank lever and the handbrake strut (Fig.L.27) for wear, damage or deformation. Check the rubber boot for damage or swell.

Check the cylinder bore, body and piston for wear, damage, scores or corrosion. The max. internal diameter of the cylinder is 17.55 mm (0.691 in.) and the min. diameter of the pistons 17.40 mm (0.685 in.). The difference between the two diameters given indicates the running clearance for the pistons which should not exceed 0.15 mm (0.06 in.). Check the adjuster nuts and the tappets for wear and damage or corrosion and the lock springs for damage.

REAR BRAKES — Assembly and Installation

Thoroughly clean all brake cylinder parts in clean brake fluid and submerge the new piston cups in the fluid. Replace the union seat if removed from the cylinder body. Fit the piston cups to the pistons so that the sealing lips face to the inside of the cylinder bore. Fit pistons with cups into the cylinder and attach the cylinder boots.

Lightly grease the adjuster nuts and tappets with high-melting point grease and fit nuts and tappets together. Then fit the

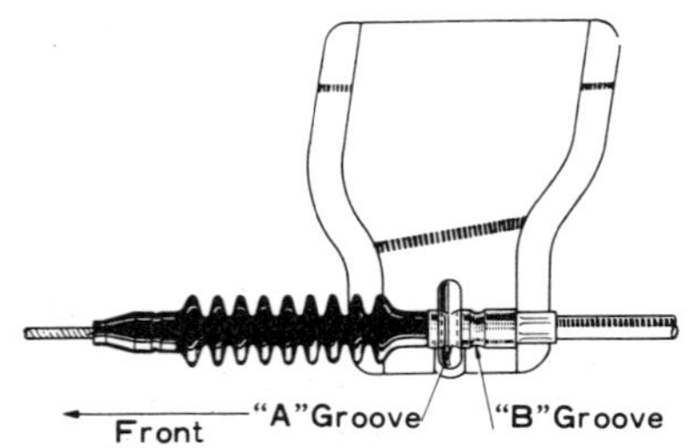

Fig.L.38. Installation of the secondary cable outer sleeve.

Fig.L.40. Removal of the disc brake guide.

Fig.L.41. Removal of the calliper mounting.

Fig.L.42. Removal of the dust shield.

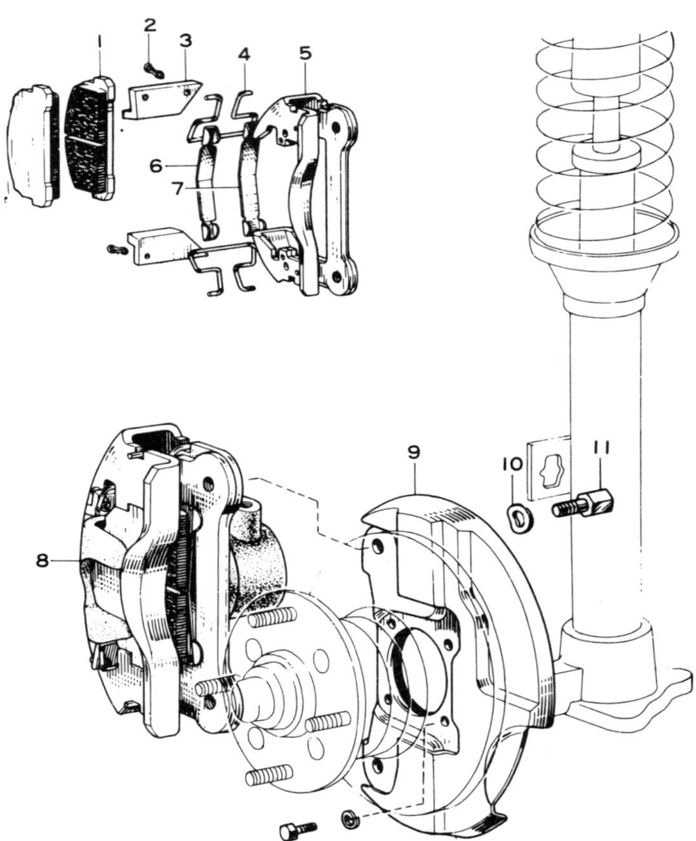

Fig.L.39. Exploded view of the front disc brake assembly.

1. Disc brake pad
2. Clip
3. Pad guide
4. Cylinder support spring
5. Cylinder mounting bracket
6. Pad support clip
7. Pad support clip
8. Brake calliper
9. Dust deflector
10. Spring washer
11. Bolt

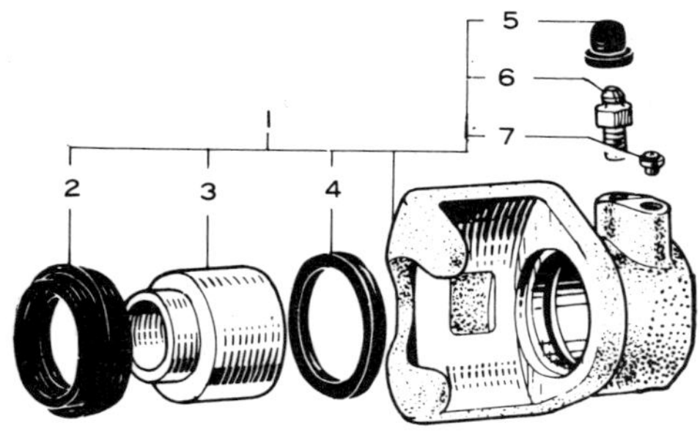

Fig.L.43. Exploded view of the brake calliper.

1. Brake cylinder
2. Cylinder boot
3. Cylinder piston
4. Piston seal ring
5. Bleeder valve cap
6. Bleeder valve
7. Union seat

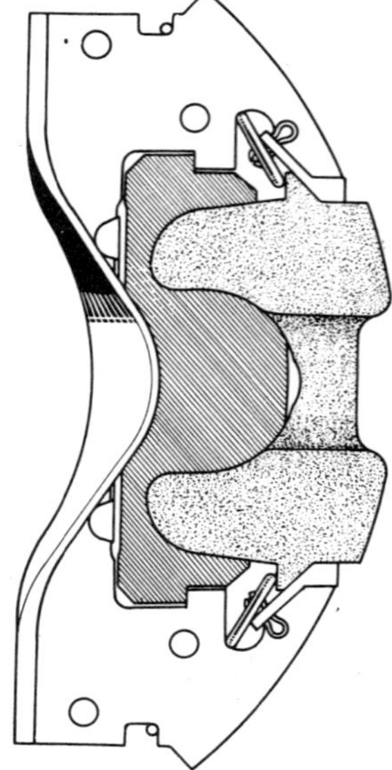

Fig.L.44. View of the assembled brake calliper.

assemblies into the bodies, checking that the correct adjuster nut and tappet is fitted to the corresponding wheel. Fig.L.28 explains the location of the various brake components. Fit the adjuster lock springs.

Lightly grease the oil seal for the rear axle tube end and the rear axle shaft bearing. Fit the rear brake back plate to the axle tube and tighten the bolts to a torque reading of 2.0 - 3.0 kgm (15 - 20 lb.ft.). Insert and fit the half shaft to the rear axle assembly.

Fit the brake adjuster assembly to the back plate (Fig.L.29) and tighten the bolts (1) and the spring anchorage bolt (2) to 1.0 - 1.6 kgm (7 - 12 lb.ft.). Fit the wheel brake cylinder on to the back plate, tightening the bolts to 0.4 - 0.7 kgm (3 - 5 lb.ft.). Taking care not to damage the threads, connect the brake pipes to the wheel cylinder and tighten the union nut to 0.8 - 1.3 kgm (6 - 9 lb.ft.). Lightly grease the bell crank where it contacts the shoe strut with high-melting point grease and fit the shoe strut wave washer and circlip on to the crank. Attach the boot retainer and the boot to the back plate and fit the bell crank lever and the shoe strut from the rear of the brake back plate. Fit the return spring to the bell crank lever and the crank support.

Connect the handbrake cable to the bell crank lever with the pivot pin and secure the assembly using a new split pin.

With reference to Fig.L.28 engage the brake shoe return springs. Fit one end of the adjuster side return spring on to the brake shoe and hook the other end over the spring post, using the tool shown in Fig.L.23. Fit brake shoe steady spring as shown in the left-hand illustration of Fig.L.30 and engage the piston side return spring as shown in the right-hand illustration. The other brake shoe is fitted in a similar manner.

Align the mating marks on brake drum and half shaft flange and fit the drum to the axle. Refit the road wheel and tighten to 9.0 - 12.0 kgm (65 - 85 lb.ft.). Bleed and adjust the brakes as previously described.

HANDBRAKE — Removal

With the rear end of the car supported on stands and the wheels removed and the handbrake released, remove the split pin, clevis pin and the brake cable from the bell crank lever at the rear of the brake back plate. Remove the cable clip securing the cable to the rear axle casing. Detach the propeller shaft and remove the cable clamp by removing the mounting bolts from the floor panel (Fig.L.32). Referring to Fig.L.33 remove the grommet (2) from the cable guide (1) and disconnect the secondary brake cable (3) from the handbrake equalizer (4). Remove the floor mat and unscrew the mounting bolts to separate handbrake lever with dust rubber boot, primary handbrake cable and equalizer bracket. From the rear of the primary cable remove the adjusting cap and the adjusting nut and remove the cable from the lever. Fig.L.34 shows how the cable is removed from the equalizer bracket.

If the handbrake lever operation is unsatisfactory dismantle the handbrake lever as follows:

With a 6 mm (0.24 in.) drill, drill out the pawl pin heads (Fig.L.35) and punch out the remaining piece of the pins. Grind off the head of the handbrake lever pivot pin and drive out the pin. Remove the release rod from the lever and dismantle the individual parts.

HANDBRAKE — Inspection and Assembly

Check the parts as follows, replacing items if necessary: Check the brake cables for wear, corrosion and freedom of movement of the inner cable in the cable sleeve. Check the brake equalizer for wear and damage or corrosion.

With reference to Fig.L.36 check the sector (1), the two pawls (2 & 3), spacer (4) and release rod (5) for wear and damage and the return spring (6) and the compression spring (7) for weakness.

When assembling the handbrake lever it is best to use the pawl repair kit, available under Part No. 04461-12010. Fit the pawls (2 & 3 in Fig.L.37), spacer (4) and return spring (5) to the release rod (1) and attach the assembly to the handbrake lever. Align the holes in the spacer, pawls and handbrake lever and insert the pivot pin. Peen over the pin head.

Fit the sector and the spacer to the rear end of the handbrake lever and fit the pivot pin. Again peen the head with a hammer to secure in position. Fit the cable guide, the guide support and the spacers to the lever with the two pins and peen over the pin heads to secure them in position.

Fit compression spring into the lever, fit and secure the release rod knob and adjust so that the knob protrudes by 9 - 10 mm (0.36 - .0.40 in.). Fit the cable to the brake equalizer bracket and grease the moving portion of the primary cable (the very short one). Fit the protective boot and the primary cable to the handbrake lever end ensuring that the cable is aligned with the cable guide. Fit the adjusting nut and the lock cap.

Install the lever and the boot into the car and tighten the mounting bolts to 1.0 - 1.6 kgm (7 - 12 lb.ft.). Connect the front ends of the secondary cables (long cables) to the ends of the equalizer bracket and fit grommets into the cable guides at the front. Fit the rear ends of the long cables to the bell crank levers, securing them with clevis pins and split pins. The outer cable sleeve must be attached to the cable bracket clip on the rear axle casing.

Fit the front end of the secondary cables to the centre bracket and tighten the clamp nuts to 1.5 - 2.2 kgm (11 - 16 lb.ft.). The outer cable groove "A" (Fig.L.38) is normally used, but groove "B" can be used if easier. Fit the propeller shaft and tighten the flange bolts to 1.5 - 2.2 kgm (11 - 16 lb.ft.). Fit the rear wheels and tighten the nuts to 9 - 11 kgm (65 - 80 lb.ft.). Adjust the handbrake lever free travel as already described under "Handbrake Adjustment".

FRONT DISC BRAKES — Removal

With the front end of the car resting on stands and the wheel removed, disconnect the brake pipe from the brake calliper and plug up the hole to prevent entry of dirt or other foreign matter. Remove the four clips and lift off the disc brake guide (Fig.L.40). Remove the cylinder assembly, take out the brake pads and remove the brake calliper mounting bolts and the mounting with the two support springs. (Fig.L.41).

Remove the brake disc together with the front hub from the end of the stub axle as described in section front suspension (grease cap, split pin, castellated nut, locating washer) and unscrew the brake disc from the hub. The dust shield can be removed as shown in Fig.L.42.

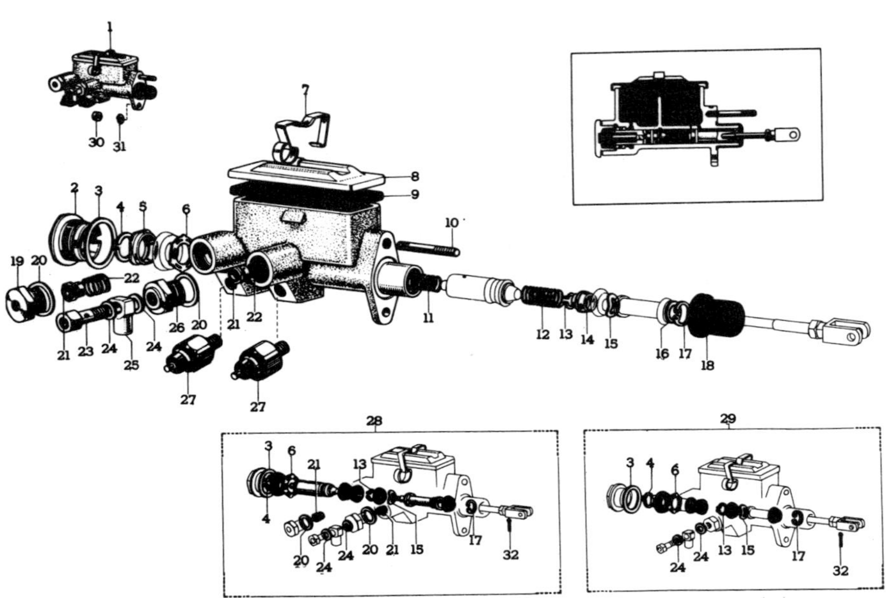

Fig.J.45. Exploded view of the tandem master cylinder for dual-line brake circuits.

1. Master cylinder
2. End plug
3. Gasket
4. Circlip
5. Piston cup retainer
6. Piston cup spacer
7. Filler cover spring clip
8. Reservoir filler cover
9. Fluid deflector
10. Stud
11. Compression spring
12. Compression spring
13. Circlip
14. Return spring retainer
15. Piston cup spacer
16. Plain washer
17. Circlip
18. Master cylinder boot
19. Outlet plug
20. Gasket
21. Outlet check valve
22. Compression spring
23. Banjo bolt
24. Gasket
25. Banjo connection
26. Outlet plug
27. Brake pressure switch
28. Brake master cylinder repair kit
29. Brake master cylinder cup repair kit
30. Nut
31. Spring washer
32. Split pin

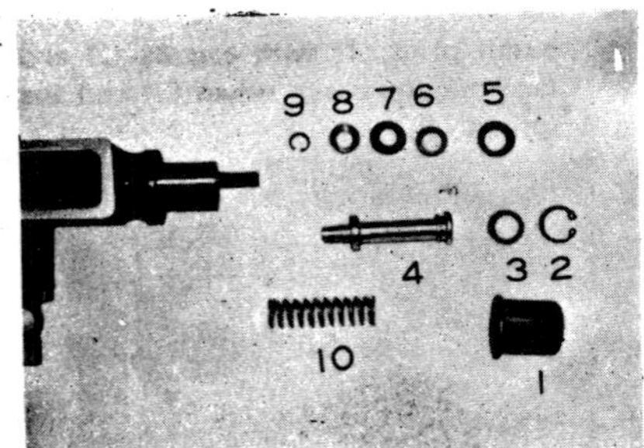

Fig.L.46. Components of the primary piston.

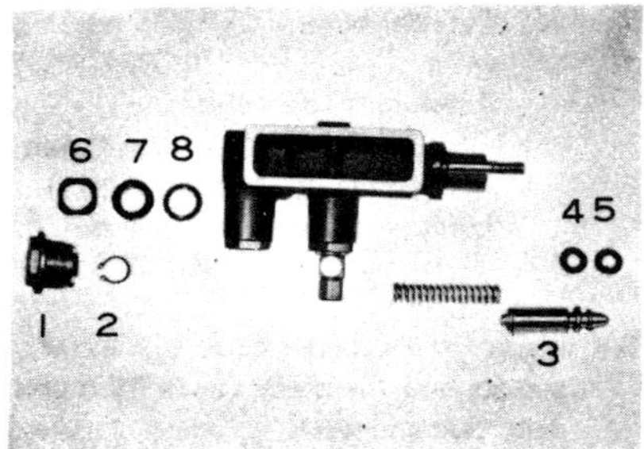

Fig.L.47. Components of the secondary piston.

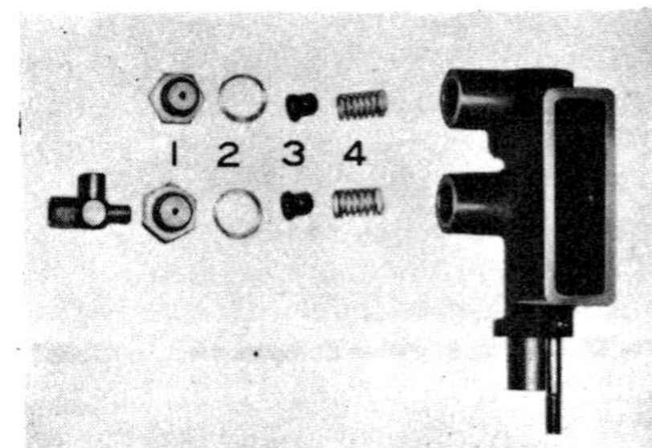

Fig.L.48. Components of the outlet check valves.

Thoroughly clean all parts, check as described below and replace parts where necessary.

Check the brake disc guides for wear or deformation, clips for weakness, cylinder mountings for cracks or wear, support springs for weakness or deformation and the pad support for damage.

Check the brake pads for wear. The min. lining thickness is 6 mm (0.236 in.). Measure the thickness of the brake disc which must not be below 9 mm (0.35 in.). The run-out of the disc must not exceed 0.15 mm (0.006 in.). The disc must be free of scores or grooves.

BRAKE CALLIPER — Dismantling

Remove the rubber boot and using an air line applied to the fluid outlet, carefully blow the piston out of the cylinder and remove the fluid seal from the groove in the inside of the cylinder bore. (See Fig.L.43 for dismantled view).

Thoroughly clean all parts in brake fluid and inspect the cylinder body for rust or damage on the piston sliding faces. Check the piston in the same manner. Replace the fluid seal and the rubber boot.

BRAKE CALLIPER — Assembly

Lubricate the cylinder bore and the piston seal with the special grease from piston seal kit, Part No. 04479-12010, fit the seal into the cylinder groove and push in the piston. Fit the cylinder boot.

BRAKE CALLIPER — Installation

Fit the dust shield on to the steering knuckle and tighten the bolts to 2.5 - 3.5 kgm (18 - 25 lb.ft.). Fit the disc and hub assembly on to the stub axle and adjust the bearing pre-load in the same manner as described for drum brakes. After the correct pre-load is obtained, check the disc run-out which should not exceed 0.15 mm (0.006 in.). Replace the disc if the run-out is excessive. Fit the brake calliper mounting and the support springs and tighten the mounting bolts to 5.0 - 6.5 kgm (36 - 47 lb.ft.). Fit the pad support plate, pads and the brake calliper noting the correct direction. Fit the guides between the cylinder and the mounting and secure the assembly with four clips. A sectional view of the assembled brake calliper is shown in Fig.L.44.

Connect the brake hose to the brake calliper and bleed the brake system in the same manner as described for models with drum brakes at the beginning of this section. Take the car on a road test and check the brakes for uneven pull. After a sudden stop, drive on for a few hundred yards and stop the car by using the handbrake only. Raise the wheels off the ground. Check the rotational torque by winding a cord around the outside of the tyre and pull with a spring balance. Take a note of the reading and multiply the spring balance reading by the radius of the tyre. The obtained value must not exceed 30 kgcm.

MASTER CYLINDER (Dual line) - Removal

Remove the brake light switch wiring, disconnect the three pipes from the master cylinder, remove the two brake light switches and unscrew the master cylinder from the engine bulkhead.

MASTER CYLINDER — Dismantling
(Fig.L.45)

Remove the filler cover clip, the cover and the fluid deflector. Referring to Fig.L.46 remove the rubber boot (1), circlip (2), stop washer (3) and the primary piston assembly (4,5,6,7,8,9) and the piston return spring (10).

From the other side of the cylinder body remove the cylinder plug (1, Fig.L.47) together with the gasket and remove the circlip (2). Push out the secondary piston assembly (3,4,5) through the rear of the master cylinder and remove the piston cup retainer (6), the piston cup (7) and the spacer (8).

Referring to Fig.L.48 remove the two outlet plugs (1) together with the gasket washers (2) and withdraw the check valves (3) and the springs (4).

Thoroughly clean all parts in clean brake fluid, inspect the parts and replace where necessary. Check the master cylinder body for cracks and corrosion or scores in the cylinder bore. Inspect the pistons for scores, damage or corrosion. Pistons and cylinder bores must be in accordance with the values given below, assuring the correct running clearance between cylinder and pistons..

Cylinder bore . . . . .17.46 mm (0.6874 in.) max.
Piston outer dia. . . .17.401 - 17.428 mm (0.6851-0.6861 in.)
Clearance . . . . .0.15 mm (0.006 in.)

Check cups, cup spacers, gaskets and check the valves for distortion, scores or other damage. Check the springs for weakness.

MASTER CYLINDER (Dual line) — Assembly

Insert the springs and check valves into the two openings shown in Fig.L.48 in the order shown in fit the plugs together with the gasket washers. Tighten the plugs to 11 - 13 kgm (80 - 94 lb.ft.).

Fit the secondary piston cup spacer, cup and retainer from the front of the cylinder. Fit the two cups to the secondary piston and insert the piston assembly from the rear of the cylinder. Secure the circlip to the end of the secondary piston. Install the spring and tighten the plug with new gasket washer to 15 - 20 kgm (110 - 145 lb.ft.). Fit the cup spacer and the spring retainer to the primary piston and secure with the circlip. Fit the other cup to the primary piston. Insert the primary piston assembly, the stop washer and the circlip. Finally fit the fluid deflector, filler cover and spring clip.

MASTER CYLINDER (Dual line) — Installation

Fit the push rod into the master cylinder, secure the master cylinder to the engine bulkhead and fit brake light switches, brake pipes, brake light switch wiring and fill the master cylinder with the recommended brake fluid. Bleed the brake system as described earlier on.

Technical Data

DRUM BRAKES

Drum diameter . . . . .200 mm (7.87 in.)

Front brake shoe liings:
   Width . . . . 35 mm (1.4 in.)
   Thickness . . . . 4 mm (0.16 in.)
   Length .192 mm (7.0 in.)

Rear brake shoe linings:
   Width . . . . 30 mm (1.2 in.)
   Thickness . . . . 4 mm (0.16 in.)
   Length .192 mm (7.0 in.)

Brake shoe lining area:
   Front . . . . 134.4 sq.cm (20.83 sq.in.) x 2
   Rear . . . . 115.2 sq.cm (1786 sq.in.) x 2

Wheel cylinder diameters:
   Front . . . . 19.05 mm (0.7500 in.)
   Rear . . . . 17.45 mm (0.6868 in.)

Master cylinder dia. . . . . 15.87 mm (0.6258 in.)

Brake pedal ratio 4.3:1
Brake pedal stroke . . . . 120 - 130 mm (4.7 - 5.1 in.)
Brake fluid pressure . . . . 108.5 kg/sq.cm (1,541 psi.)

DISC BRAKES

Front brake disc:
   Outer diameter . . . . .200 mm (7.87 in.)
   Thickness . . . . .10 mm (0.39 in.)
   Min. thickness . . . . 9 mm (0.35 in.)
   Max. run-out . . . . .0.15 mm (0.006 in.)

Brake pads:
   Braking area . . . . .30.5 sq.cm (4.73 sq.in.)
   Thickness . . . . .14 mm (0.55 in.)
   Min. thickness . . . . .6 mm (0.236 in.)

Cylinder bore . . . . .44.45 mm (1.75 in.)
Master cylinder dia. . . . . 15.87 mm (0.626 in.)
Max. fluid pressure . . . . 108.5 sq.cm (1,541 psi.)

Trouble Shooting

SYMPTOMS	PROBABLE CAUSE	ACTION TO BE TAKEN
Insufficient performance	Leak in hydraulic system Brake pads or linings excessively worn Water or oil on linings	Trace and rectify Replace pads or brake shoes Clean or replace linings
Pedal contacts floor	Pads or linings worn No brake fluid	Replace as necessary Refill and bleed system
Pedal feels spongy	Air in system Insufficient fluid in reservoir	Bleed system Top-up fluid system
Pedal can be depressed without action	Check valve in master cylinder faulty Valve seat dirty	Check and repair Clean valve seat, fit new valve
Brake effort decreases and pedal goes slowly to floor	Brake pipes or hoses leaking Damaged or defective cups in master brake or wheel cylinders	Tighten connections or fit new pipes and hoses Overhaul cylinder in question
Brakes overheat	Compensation port in master cylinder blocked Return spring weak Rubber parts swollen due to use of unsuitable brake fluid	Clean master brake cylinder Fit new springs Drain fluid, remove all rubber parts and flush system. Replace all parts in master brake cylinder
Brakes pull to one side	Loose back plate mounting bolts Oil on linings or pads Loose or damaged wheel bearings Improper operation of wheel cylinder Improper tyre inflation	Tighten Clean or replace Adjust or replace Repair or replace Correct tyre pressure

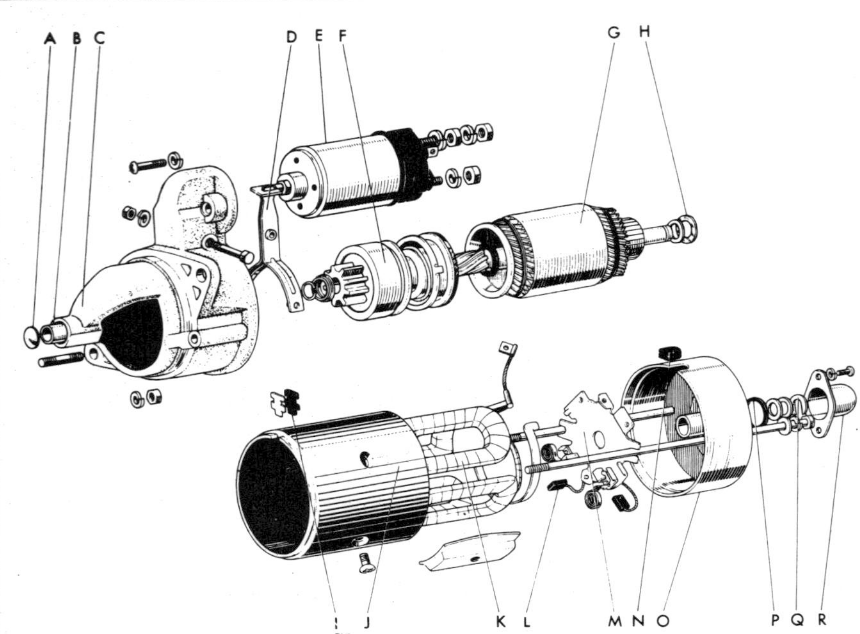

Fig.M.1. Exploded view of the starter motor.

A.	End cover	J.	Starter motor yoke
B.	Bush	K.	Field coil
C.	Drive end bearing bracket	L.	Brush
D.	Pinion engagement lever	M.	Brush holder
E.	Solenoid switch	N.	Rubber insulator
F.	Starter motor clutch	O.	Commutator end bracket
G.	Armature	P.	Rubber sealing ring
H.	Bakelite washer	Q.	Lock washer
I.	Rubber plug	R.	End cover

Fig.M.2. Removal of the solenoid switch.

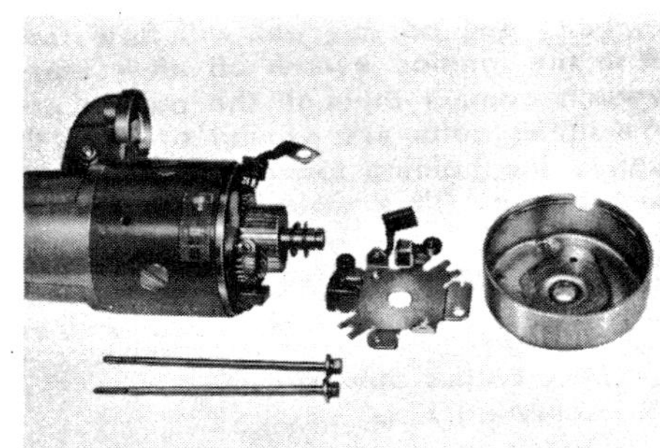

Fig.M.3. Removal of commutator end bracket and brush holder.

Fig.M.4. Removal of the starter motor clutch with the sleeve shown.

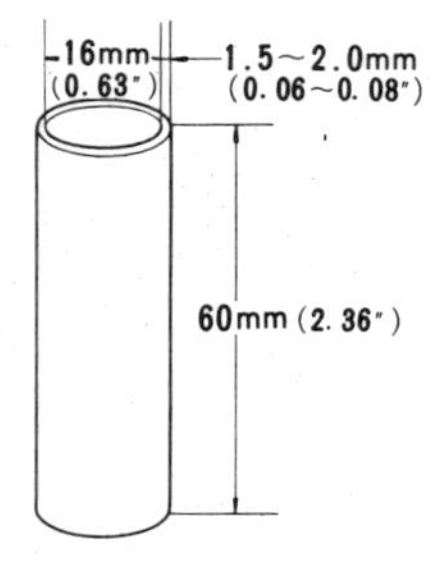

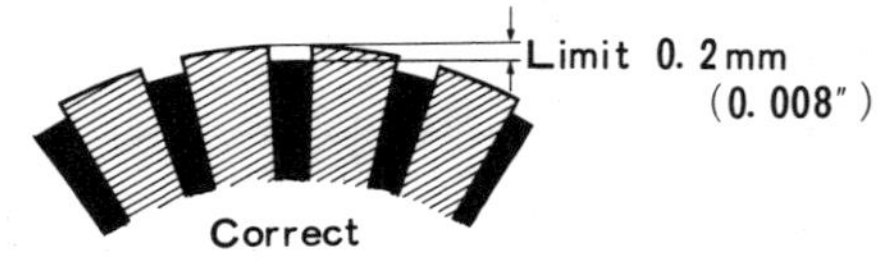

Fig.M.5. The undercutting of the mica insulation.

Fig.M.6. Testing the armature for short circuits.

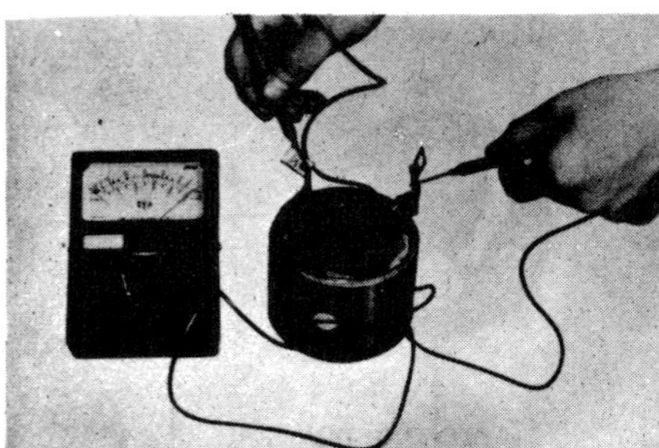

Fig.M.7. Testing the field coils for open circuits.

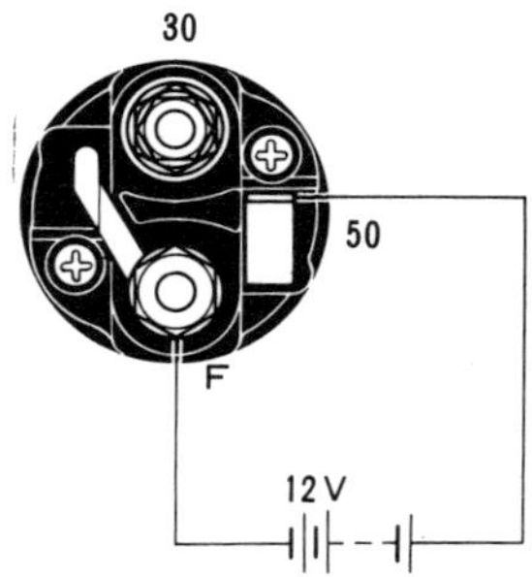

Fig.M.8. Testing the pull-in coil of the starter solenoid.

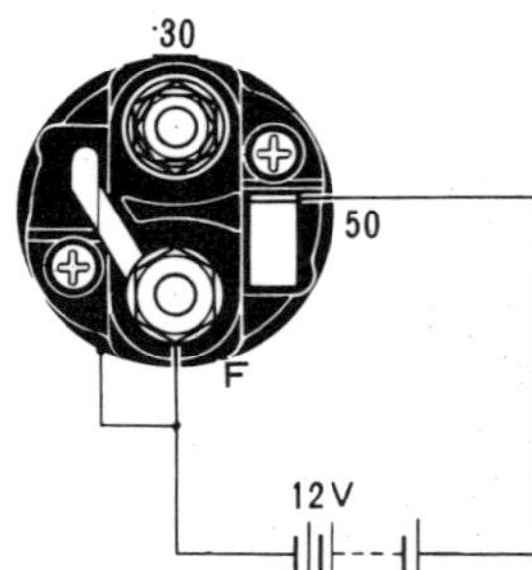

Fig.M.9. Testing the hold-on coil of the starter solenoid.

Electrical Equipment

DESCRIPTION

The electrical system operates with a supply voltage of 12 volts. A belt-driven alternator with a max. output of 300 watts supplies the current for the battery and the accessories. The alternator is attached by means of a mounting bracket to the engine block. An adjusting link provides for belt tension adjustments.

The regulator has the function to interrupt the current supply between the alternator and the battery as long as the alternator voltage is lower than the battery voltage, as this is the case when the engine is in a stationary condition and there is no supply of electrical current. When the engine is started and the alternator begins to charge, the charging control warning lamp is extinguished, indicating that the system is working properly.

The starter motor, fitted with a solenoid switch, is actuated by the ignition switch. The starter incorporates an armature brake which is applied when the starter clutch returns completely to its original position.

GENERAL REPAIR NOTE

Before starting work on any of the electrical equipment it is necessary to disconnect the battery to starter cable or the battery cable. Any repairs on the electrical system of the vehicle should be limited to the replacement of damaged or defective parts and overhauling the wiring. Repairs on starter motor, alternator and voltage regulator should be entrusted in the hands of a specialist, as comprehensive testing equipment is used to test the units before service.

STARTER MOTOR — Removal

It is necessary to remove the manifold assembly from the engine block before the starter motor can be removed. This involves removal of air cleaner, accelerator and choke cables from the carburettor and the exhaust pipe connection before the manifold is unbolted and removed.

Then disconnect the cable from the starter motor and unscrew the starter motor from the engine.

STARTER MOTOR — Dismantling
(Fig.M.1)

Disconnect the field coil lead from the solenoid switch terminal after taking out the screws and remove the solenoid switch from the drive end bracket (Fig.M.2). Remove the end frame cover and withdraw the lock plate, washer and the rubber ring.

After unscrewing the two through bolts separate the commutator end bracket from the yoke, take out the brushes and remove the brush holders from the armature shaft (Fig.M.3), and lift off the yoke.

Remove the bolt from the engagement lever from the drive end housing and withdraw the rubber, the plate, the armature, the starter motor clutch and the engagement lever. From the end of

the armature shaft remove the snap ring and the piston stop collar and slide off the starter motor clutch. The snap ring removal, and the dimensions for a suitable tool, are shown in Fig.M.4.

STARTER MOTOR — Inspection and Overhaul

Armature

Inspect the clearance between the armature shaft and the bush. The clearance should not exceed 0.008 in. (0.2 mm) and if necessary fit an undersize bush.

Check the commutator for roughness, burnt or scored surface. If necessary set up the armature in a lathe and skim off just enough material to obtain a smooth surface. The out-of-round of the commutator should not be more than 0.002 in. (0.05 mm) after turning. If the commutator cannot be skimmed to a minimum diameter of 1.46 in. (37.0 mm), replace the armature. Check the mica depth and cut down to 0.02 - 0.03 in. (0.5 - 0.8 mm) if the measured value is less than 0.008 in. (0.2 mm). (Fig.M.5).

Check the armature coil for earthing, using a continuity tester. Connect one test prod to the commutator and the other one to the armature shaft. If there is an earth connection, the armature must be replaced.

Check the armature windings for internal shorts by placing the armature on a growler and hold a hacksaw blade over the armature while rotating it. If the hacksaw blade vibrates, the windings are shorting and the armature must be replaced. (Fig.M.6).

Check the armature windings for open circuits by means of a continuity tester and connecting two commutator segments in turn to the test prods. Repeat this test for all adjacent segments. An inconsistent reading indicates an open circuit.

Field Coils

Check the field coils for open circuit, using a circuit tester. Connect one test prod to the field coil lead and the other prod to the other field coil lead. If the tester needle does not move, the field coil has an open circuit. (Fig.M.7).

Check the field coil for earth. Connect one test prod to the field coil lead and the other lead to the yoke. If the needle moves, the field coil is connected to earth and should be replaced.

Solenoid Switch

The following tests should be carried out with the starter motor assembled. When testing, disconnect the field coil from the solenoid switch.

1. Testing the pull-in motion (Fig.M.8): by connecting the test leads to the terminals "50" and "F" when the solenoid should pull-in the plunger strongly with 12 volts.

2. Testing the holding coil (Fig.M.9): by connecting the battery negative lead to the solenoid body, with the solenoid in the condition as described above, and disconnecting the test lead of the battery negative side from the terminal "F". The

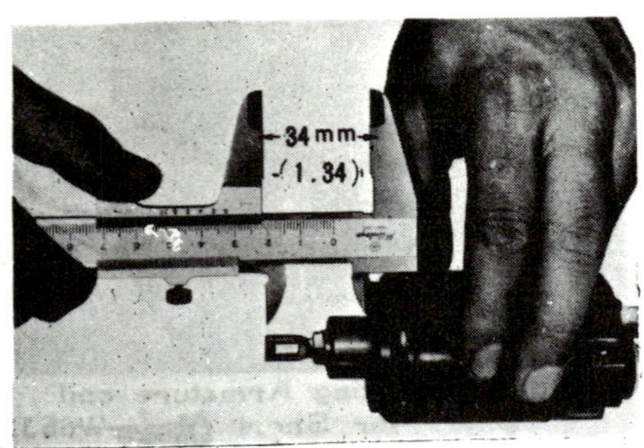

Fig.M.9A. Measuring the length of the solenoid plunger.

Fig.M.10. Locking the pinion stop nut.

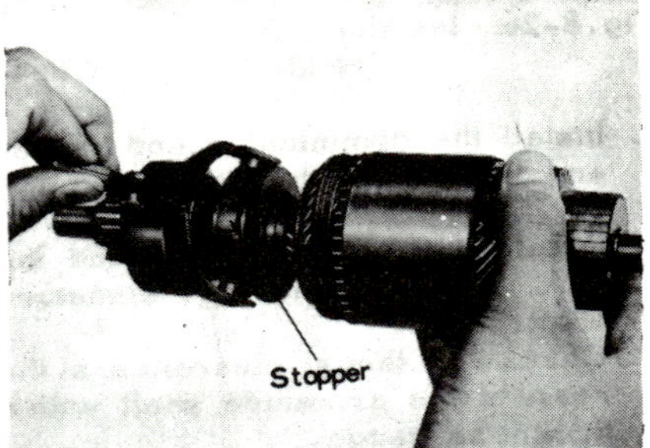

Fig.M.11. Assembling the pinion engagement lever to the armature.

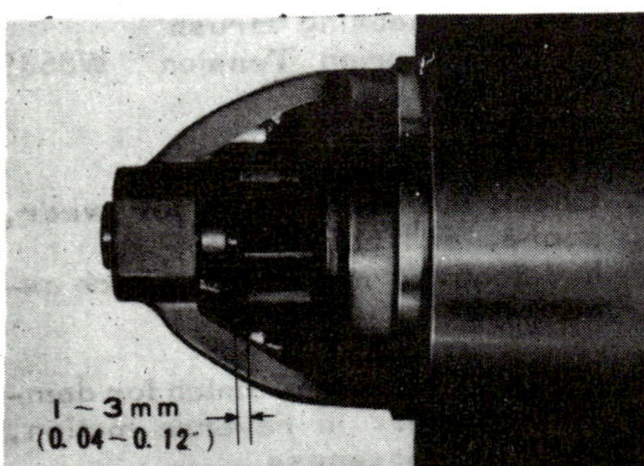

Fig.M.12. The clearance adjustment between pinion end and drive end bracket.

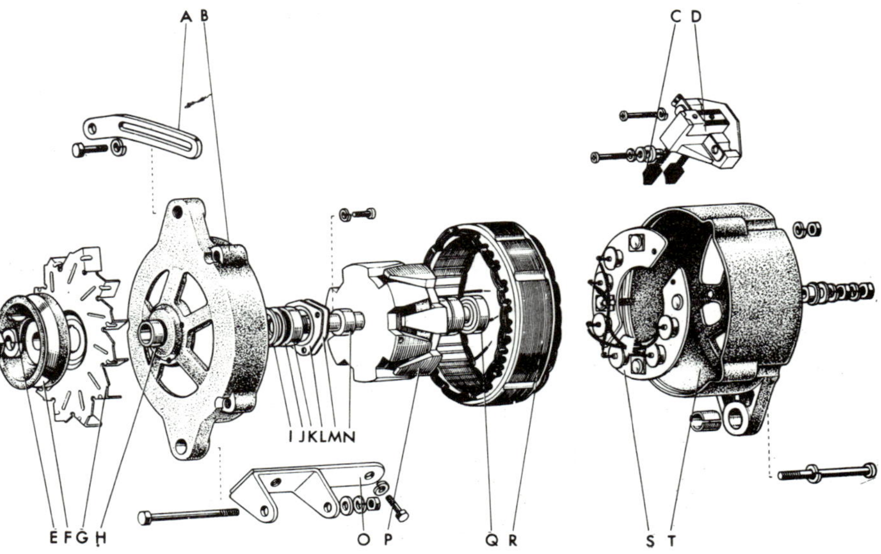

Fig.M.13. Exploded view of the alternator.

A.	Fan belt adjusting link	K.	Front bearing
B.	Drive end bracket (frame)	L.	Bearing retaining plate
C.	Brush	M.	Felt ring cover
D.	Brush holder	N.	Spacer ring
E.	Woodruff key	O.	Mounting bracket
F.	Pulley	P.	Rotor
G.	Fan	Q.	Rear bearing
H.	Spacer	R.	Stator
I.	Felt ring	S.	Diodes with holder
J.	Felt ring retainer	T.	Diode (slip ring) end bracket

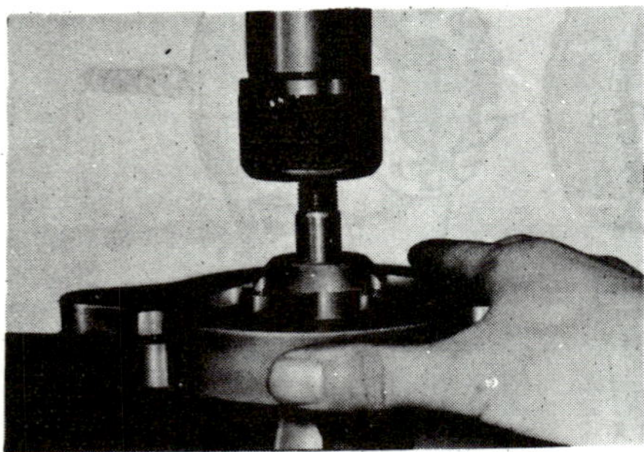

Fig.M.14. Removal of the rotor from the bearing bracket.

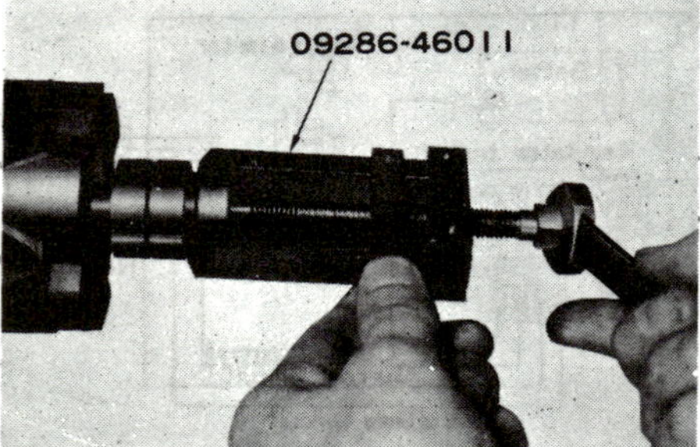

Fig.M.15. Removal of the rear rotor bearing.

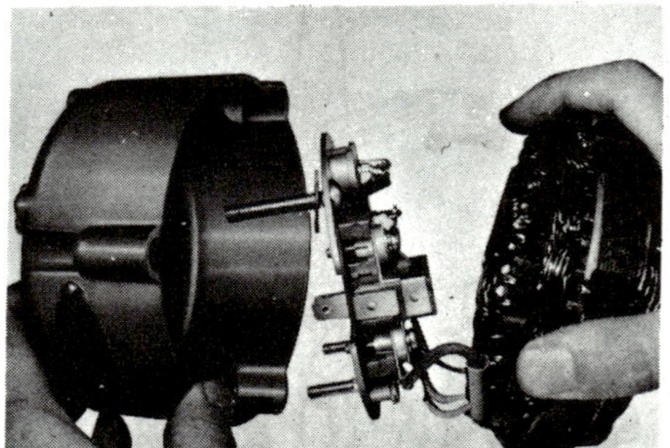

Fig.M.16. Removal of stator and diode holder.

plunger must be pulled in and held in this position with 12 volts.

3. Check the plunger return motion by connecting the battery negative lead to the terminal "F" and the positive lead to the solenoid body. Pull the pinion to the end of its travel and let it return by itself. If the plunger returns with 12 volts, the solenoid is in a satisfactory condition.

4. Check the length of the solenoid moving plunger. The length should be approx. 1.34 in. (34 mm), measured as shown in Fig.M.9a. If necessary adjust the length by slackening the locknut and turning the plunger.

Brush Holders and Brushes

Connect one of the test prods to the positive brush holder and the other to the negative side. If the tester needle moves, the brush holder insulation is faulty and should be replaced. Replace the brushes if they have worn down to 0.51 in. (13 mm).

Check the brush spring tension, using a spring scale. Take this reading when the spring lifts just off the brush. If the tension is less than 1.32 lbs. (600 grams), replace the spring(s) or brush(es).

Starter Motor Clutch

Check the pinion teeth and the over-running clutch for damage and wear and inspect the free-wheel action in one direction and the slipping action in the opposite direction. Replace if faulty.

STARTER MOTOR — Assembly

Before assembling, coat all sliding and moving surfaces of armature shaft splines, starter motor clutch, bushes, engagement lever and solenoid plunger with multi-purpose grease.

Fit the starter clutch, pinion stop collar and the snap ring to the armature shaft and lock the stop collar in place by caulking at two points. (Fig.M.10). Fit the engagement lever to the starter motor as shown in Fig.M.11. The steel washer must be installed towards the clutch side.

Install the armature and tighten the engagement lever bolt. Fit the rubber plate into the drive housing and slide the yoke over the armature and on to the drive housing. Install the brush holder and insert the brushes.

Fit the commutator end frame and secure the through bolts. Install the brake spring and the lock plate on to the armature shaft. The armature end play should be 0.002 - 0.013 in. (0.05 - 0.35 mm), but a limit of 0.030 in. (0.8 mm) is permissible. Pack the end cap with multi-purpose grease and fit to the starter motor.

Fit the solenoid and check the clearance between the starter clutch pinion and the pinion stop collar. The clearance should be 0.04 - 0.12 in. (1.0 - 3.0 mm), when the starter motor is operated under no load condition. (Fig.M.12).

STARTER MOTOR — Installation

Installation of the starter motor is carried out in reverse order to the removal procedure. A new manifold gasket should be fitted. Tighten the bolts gradually and evenly and check the manifold/cylinder block seal for leaks.

ALTERNATOR — Precautionary Service Notes

It is essential that attention is paid to the following points when working with alternators:

1. Never disconnect the voltage regulator or the battery when the alternator is running.
2. Never allow the exciter terminal (field) of the alternator or the connection lead to come into contact with earth.
3. Never confuse the two leads on the voltage regulator.
4. Never attempt to operate the voltage regulator when it is connected to earth. (Immediate damage).
5. Never remove the alternator without disconnecting the battery.
6. When installing the battery ensure that the negative terminal is connected to earth.
7. Never use a test lamp which is connected directly to the mains supply (110 or 120 volts). Only use a 0.1 amp test lamp fed by a 12 volt battery.
8. If the battery is re-charged in the fitted condition with a battery charger, it is essential that the two battery leads are disconnected. The positive terminal of the battery charger must be connected to the positive terminal of the battery and the negative terminal of the battery to the negative terminal of the charger.
9. Incorrect connection of the leads destroys the rectifier diodes and the voltage regulator.
10. Never use an ohmmeter of the type incorporating a hand-driven generator to check the diodes.

ALTERNATOR — Removal

Disconnect the battery earth cable and the wires from the alternator. Remove the bolt securing the fan belt tensioning strut, and lift away the fan belt. Remove the alternator retaining bolt and lift the alternator from the mounting bracket.

ALTERNATOR — Dismantling

Remove the three through-bolts and detach the drive end frame together with the rotor from the slip-ring end frame. Remove the pulley and the fan and press off the rotor from the drive end bracket, using a press (Fig.M.14). Withdraw the rear bearing with the special puller 09286-46011 from the rotor shaft (Fig.M.15).

Remove the bearing retainer from the drive end bracket and remove the bearing and the fan felt cover. Loosen the retaining nuts for the diode holder, 'B' terminal and insulators, and separate the stator with the diode holders from the rectifier end bracket. (Fig.M.16). Remove the brush holder assemblies by removing the brush lead wires and the terminal insulators and disconnecting the stator coil 'N' terminal lead from the holder.

ALTERNATOR — Inspection and Overhaul

Rotor

Check the rotor coil for open or short circuits, by connecting a circuit tester between the two slip rings (Fig.M.17). The coil resistance should be 4.1 - 4.3 ohms. If there is little or no resistance, this indicates the slip rings or coil may be short circuited or earthing. A high resistance indicates an open-circuit or defective connections. Replace the rotor if necessary.

Next connect the tester between the slip ring and the rotor

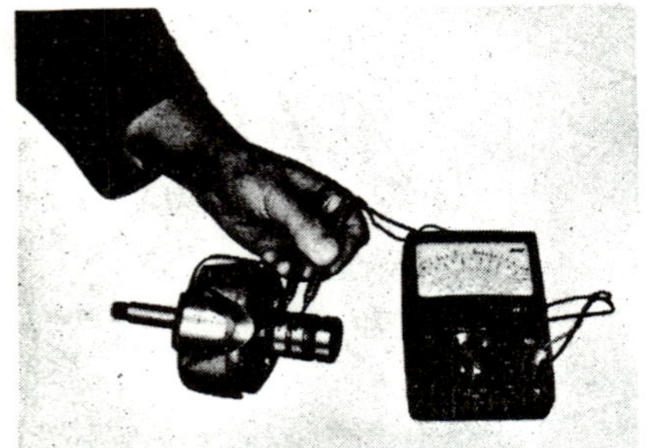

Fig.M.17. Testing the rotor for open and short circuits.

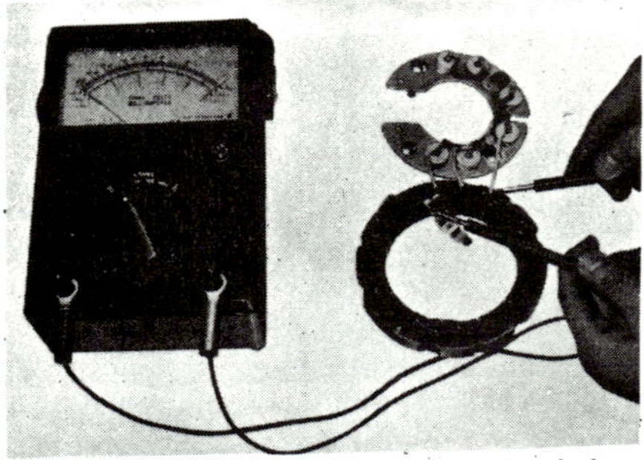

Fig.M.18. Testing the stator coil for insulation break-down.

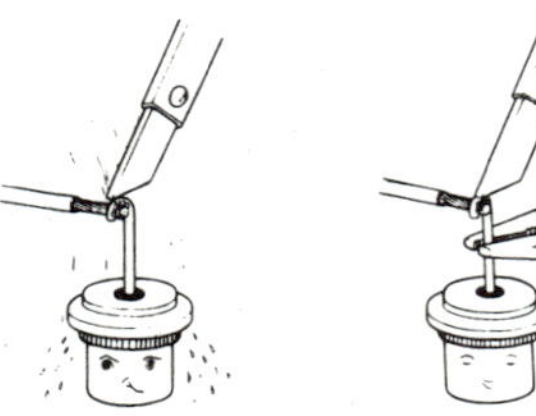

Fig.M.19. The soldering procedure for the diode pins.

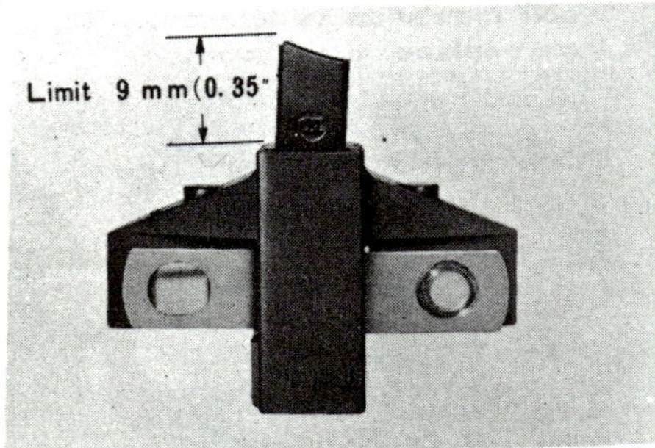

Fig.M.20. Checking the brush length.

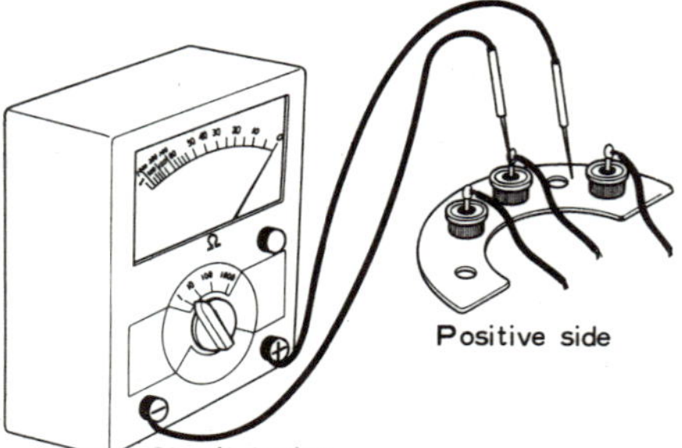

Fig.M.21. Checking the positive diodes for open circuit.

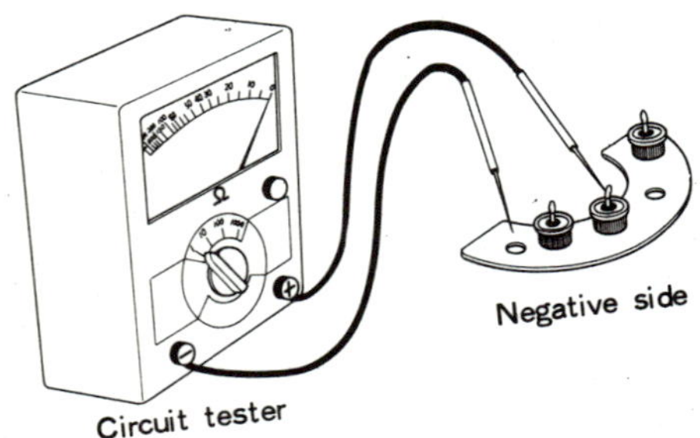

Fig.M.22. Checking the negative diodes for open circuit.

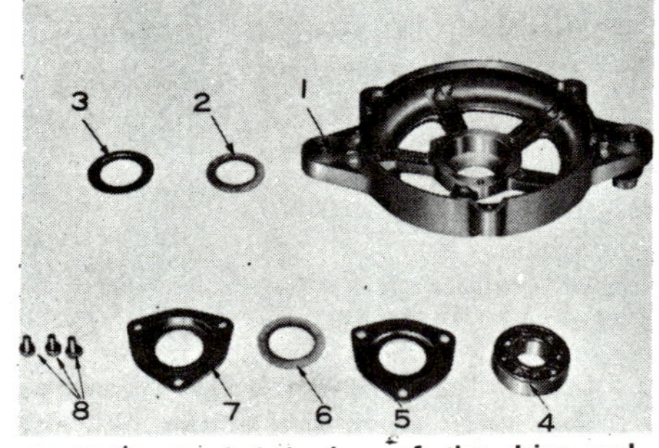

Fig.M.23. Exploded view of the drive end bracket.

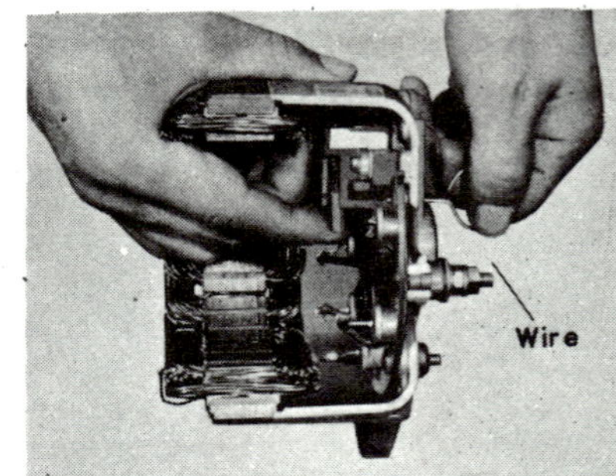

Fig.M.24. Inserting the wire to retain the brushes.

1. Drive end bracket
2. Felt ring
3. Felt ring retainer
4. Bearing
5. Bearing retaining plate
6. Felt ring
7. Felt ring cover
8. Securing screws

shaft and check the insulation between them. If the needle moves, the rotor coil or slip rings are defective, and the rotor assembly should be replaced.

Stator

Check the stator coil insulation by connecting the tester between the stator coil leads and the stator core. If the tester needle moves, replace the stator assembly. (Fig.M.18).

Check the stator coil for open circuit. This is carried out by disconnecting the stator coil leads from the diodes, using a hot soldering iron.Hold the diode pins with a pair of long-nosed pliers, to prevent the diodes from overheating, and melt the soldered connections. (Fig.M.19).

Then using the circuit tester, check the four leads of the stator coil for conductance between them. If the tester needle does not move, replace the stator coil.

Brush and Brush Holder

If the brushes are worn beyond 0.35 in. (9 mm), they should be replaced. The brush length should be measured as shown in Fig.M.21. Make sure the brushes have enough freedom of movement in their holders. When replacing the brush, fit the new brush and brush spring into the holder and then solder the brush lead wire so as to limit the brush extension to 0.51 in. (13 mm).

Diode Assembly

Good or defective diodes are classified by the resistance value between the diode holder (heat sink) and the diode leads. To perform this test, remove the diode holder from the stator.

1. Diode holder positive side.
    Connect the positive lead of the circuit tester to the diode holder and the negative holder and the negative lead to the diode pin and check the resistance. A good diode will indicate no resistance.

    Next reverse the polarity of the tester and check again. If the tester needle moves with either polarity, the diode is short circuited. If any of the diodes is defective, renew the whole assembly. (Fig.M.21).

2. Diode holder negative side.
    Check the negative side as described above, but the circuit tester leads must be reversed. (Fig.M.22).

ALTERNATOR — Assembly

Connect the stator coil "N" terminal and fit the brush holder to the diode holder.

Position the brush lead in its correct place. Position the stator together with the diode assembly on to the slip ring bracket and install the insulators on to the positive side diode assembly and on to the "B" terminal at correct positions. Tighten the securing nuts.

Install the felt ring, felt ring cover and the bearing into the drive end bracket and fit the bearing retainer with the three screws. Pack the rear bearing with multi-purpose grease and press the drive end bearing on to the rotor shaft. Fig.M.23 shows the components of the drive end bracket. Take care that the felt ring covers (3) and (7) are facing with their locking portions towards the felt rings (2) and (6).

Press in the brushes against the brush spring tension into the brush holder and insert a wire through the access hole and in the brush holder hole, to prevent the brushes from falling out. Fig.M.24).Then place the drive end bracket over the rectifier end bracket and fit the three through bolts. Remove the wire from the brush holder to release the brushes and refit the pulley to the rotor shaft. Take care that the Woodruff key is correctly located in its slot in the rotor shaft.

ALTERNATOR — Installation

The installation of the alternator is carried out in reverse order to the removal procedure. Adjust the fan belt deflection to 3/8 - 1/2 in. (9 - 13 mm).

REGULATOR — Removal

Disconnect the wiring harness connector plug from the regulator. Unscrew the regulator and lift out.

ELECTRICAL ADJUSTMENTS

Always use a fully charged battery to carry out electrical adjustments.

Voltage Relay

Connect the test circuit, operate the variable speed motor and turn on the switch "S". (See Fig.M.25). Then increase the alternator speed gradually and read off the voltage at which the lamp goes out. The operating voltage should be 4.5 - 5.8 volts. If the setting is outside the given values, adjust by bending the adjusting arm of the voltage relay. (Fig.M.26).

Voltage Regulator

Connect the test circuit as shown in Fig.M.27, operate the variable speed motor and turn on the switch "S". Check the voltage and current by varying the alternator speed gradually until the ammeter shows maximum. Increase the speed and read the voltage when the ammeter needle registers one half of the maximum amperage reading. With an alternator speed of 3000 rpm. the regulating voltage should be within 13.8 - 14.8 volts. If the setting is outside the given limits, adjust by bending the adjusting arm of the voltage regulator. (Fig.M.28).

MECHANICAL ADJUSTMENTS

The mechanical adjustments should be carried out when the specified values are not obtained during the tests. Dirty contact points can be cleaned up with a piece of suitable glass paper or fine emery cloth. After cleaning them, wash off with solvent.

Voltage Relay

Press down the armature and check the contact spring deflection with a feeler gauge. (Fig.M.29).

If the deflection is outside 0.008 - 0.018 in. (0.20 - 0.45 mm) adjust by bending the point holder "A". Then check the contact point gap (still using the feeler gauge) which should be 0.016 - 0.047 in. (0.4 - 1.2 mm), and adjust the gap if necessary by bending the contact points holder "B" (Fig.B.30).

Voltage Regulator

Check the armature gap with a feeler gauge. If the gap is outside the limits of 0.024 - 0.032 in. (0.6 - 0.8 mm), adjust the gap by bending the low speed point holder "A" as shown in Fig.M.29.

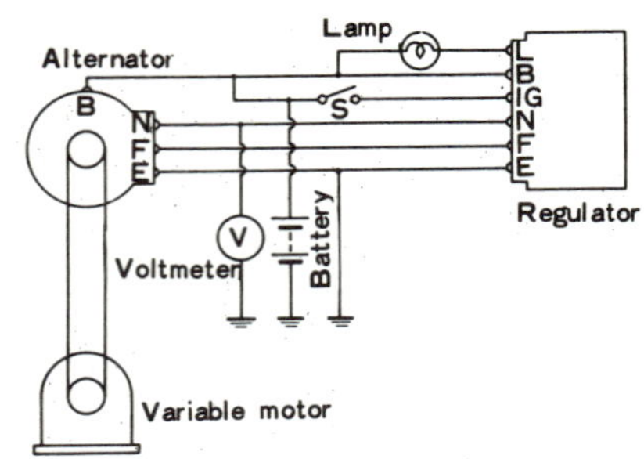

Fig.M.25. Test circuit for the voltage relay.

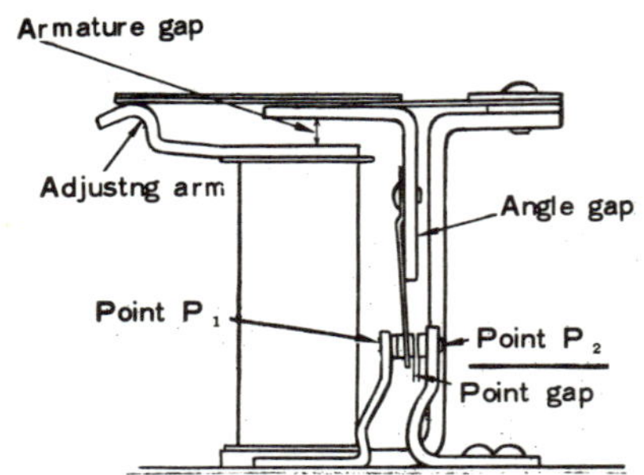

Fig.M.26. The voltage relay.

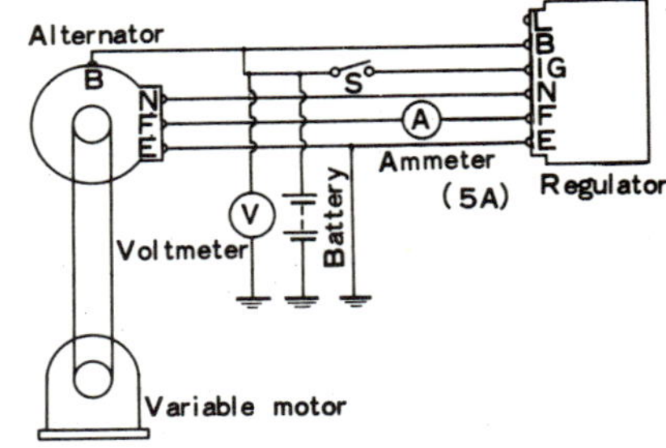

Fig.M.27. Test circuit for the voltage regulator.

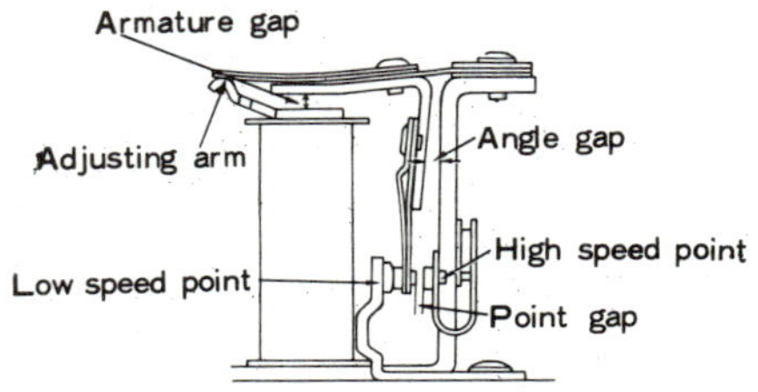

Fig.M.28. The voltage regulator.

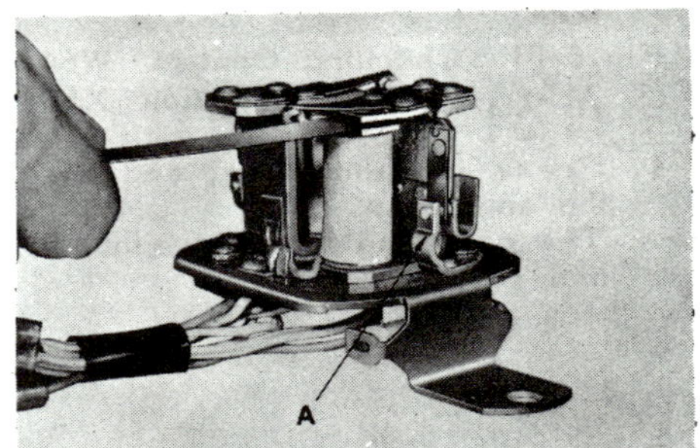

Fig.M.29. Checking the armature gap.

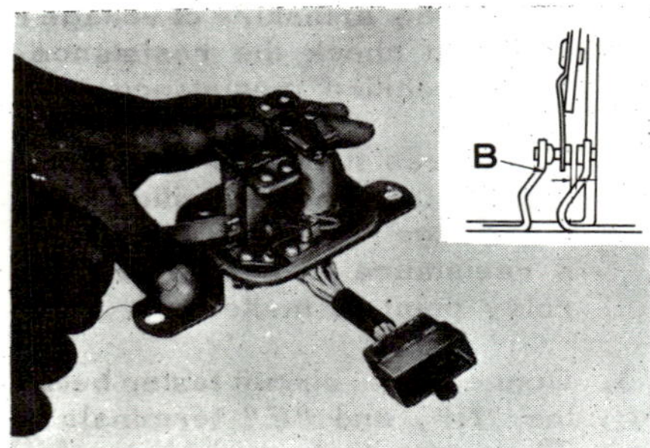

Fig.M.30. Checking the contact gap.

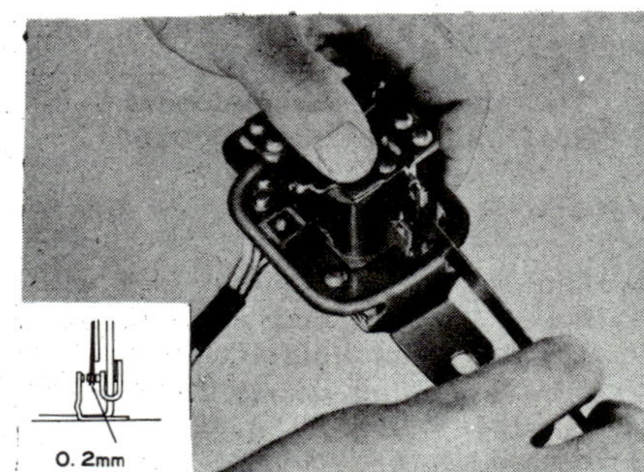

Fig.M.31. Checking the contact spring deflection.

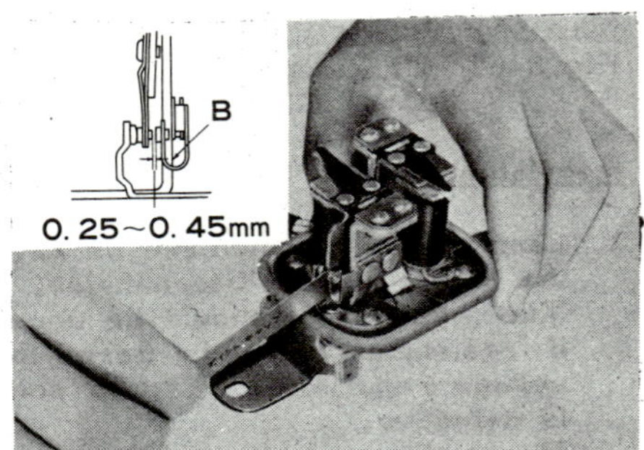

Fig.M.32. Checking the contact gap.

Check the point gap, which should be 0.010 - 0.018 in. (0.25 - 0.45 mm). If necessary adjust by bending the high speed point holder "B" as shown in Fig.M.32.

Press the armature down and check the contact spring deflection, which should be 0.008 in. (0.2 mm) and check the angle gap, with the armature pressed down. This gap should be 0.008 in. (0.2 mm). If not replace the regulator.

REGULATOR CIRCUIT TEST

Check the resistance between points "IG" and "F" terminals. If this is not zero, the low speed contact requires attention.

Press the armature of the voltage regulator and check that a resistance of 11 ohms is obtained. If this is exceeded, the control resistor is faulty.

With the continuity tester connected to terminals "L" and "E", a resistance of zero should be obtained. If this is not the case, the voltage relay contact requires attention. With the voltage relay armature pressed down, a resistance of 100 ohms should be obtained. If a high resistance is indicated, the voltage regulator coil is faulty or open circuited and should be changed. A zero reading shows that the voltage relay contact is melted.

Connect the circuit tester between the terminals "N" and "E" and measure the resistance which should be 23 ohms. A departure from this value means that the voltage relay coil is short or open circuited. (Higher - open circuit; Lower - short circuit).

REGULATOR — Installation

The installation of the voltage regulator is a reversal of the removal procedure. Refer to the notes given under "Precautionary Service Notes" to avoid damage to regulator or alternator.

BATTERY

The battery has the purpose of supplying the current consumers with power while the engine is stationary and supplying power to the starter motor. Otherwise, the battery accumulates the energy generated by the alternator and supplies the current to the consumers when required.

BATTERY — Checking and Maintenance

The battery electrolyte level is marked on the outside of the battery case and should be kept between the two lines. The specific gravity of the electrolyte should be checked regularly every two months during cold weather or more often in w. weather. The specific gravity of the electrolyte is a good indication for the charge condition of the battery. The following table can be used to determine the state of charge of the battery. If the spec. gravity is below 1.200 and the difference between each cell is more than 0.025, the battery should be re-charged or in severe cases replaced. The specific gravity of the electrolyte varies according to its temperature. Before adjusting the spec. gravity, convert to standard temperature reading, by using the following equation:

$$S20 = ST + 0.0007 \ (t-20)$$

where

S20	Specific gravity at 20°C
ST	Specific gravity at t°C
t	Temperature of electrolyte
0.0007	Temperature coefficient

Electrolyte specific gravity at 20°C (68°F)

1.260	100% fully charged
1.210	75% fully charged
1.160	50% fully charged
1.110	25% fully charged
1.060	Fully discharged

Discharged batteries must be protected against frost, as the electrolyte freezes under such conditions. Frozen batteries have a greater internal resistance which makes starting impossible. Once a year the battery connectors should be removed in order to clean the connectors and the terminals with emery cloth. After refitting the connectors coat them with petroleum jelly or other conventional battery grease. When removing the battery, the negative lead must always be disconnected first. **The battery must not be connected with the engine running.**

Charging the battery in the removed condition

Connect the battery to the D.C. source with the cell plugs removed. Positive to positive and negative to negative terminal. The specified charging rate is 1/10 of the rated capacity (e.g. 3.2 or 4.5 amps, depending on the type fitted). Charge until the cells have gassed and neither the specific gravity of the battery electrolyte nor the battery voltage of the cells have shown an increase in three consecutive hours. The electrolyte temperature should not exceed 45°C (113°F) when charging. The specific gravity of the battery must then be 1.260. The cell voltage must be approx. 2.6 - 2.7 volts. Let the battery stand for about 2 hours after charging. Slightly shake the battery so that the gas is able to escape. Recheck the spec. gravity of the electrolyte and the electrolyte level. Clean any spilled electrolyte from the battery top and grease the battery terminals lightly. Fit the cell vent plugs.

There is no objection to quick charging a battery which has been in use and is in perfect condition, if the work is carried out in accordance with the charger's operating instructions.

Charging the battery in fitted condition

If the battery is to be charged in the vehicle the two battery leads (negative and positive) must be disconnected. Do not under any circumstances disconnect the battery while the alternator is running. When charging, the positive terminal of the battery must be connected to the positive terminal of the charger and the negative terminal of the battery to the negative terminal of the charger. Incorrect connections destroy the rectifier diodes of the alternator and the voltage regulator.

Possible faults in the charging circuit

Alternator not charging:
> V-belt loose, charging or earth circuit broken, carbon brushes worn, exciter current (field) circuit broken, voltage regulator damaged, bad earth connection or defective units.

Weak or irregular charging current:
> V-belt loose, defective contacts in charging circuit. Carbon brushes worn, voltage regulator has bad earth connection or is defective. Rectifier diodes disconnected or

short-circuited. Stator disconnected, earthed or short-circuited.

Charging current too high:
Voltage regulator defective, bad connections between voltage regulator and alternator.

Alternator runs noisily:
V-belt badly worn, belt pulley loose. Alternator belt pulley out of alignment with crankshaft belt pulley. Short circuit in a diode.

Technical Data

STARTER MOTOR

Type . . . . Direct current, series wound with solenoid
Nominal voltage . . . . 12 volts
Output . . . . 0.8 or 1.1 H.P.
Direction of rotation . . . . . . Clockwise seen from pinion side
Number of poles 4
Number of pinion teeth 9
Armature shaft outer diameter . . . . . . 12.50 mm (0.492 in.)

Armature shaft bush inner diameter:
Standard . . . . . .12.535 - 12.560 mm (0.4935-0.4944 in.)
1st undersize . . . . 0.3 mm (0.012 in.)
2nd undersize . . . . 0.5 mm (0.020 in.)

Armature shaft bush running clearance:
Standard . . . . .Less than 0.1 mm (0.004 in.)
Wear limit . . . . 0.2 mm (0.008 in.)

Commutator outer diameter:
Standard . . . . .38.8 mm (1.528 in.)
Wear (or after skimming) . . . . .36.8 mm (1.449 in.)

Commutator mica depth:
Standard . . . . .0.5 - 0.8 mm (0.020 - 0.031 in.)
Limit . . . . 0.2 mm (0.008 in.)

Commutator brush length:
Standard . . . . 19 mm (0.748 in.)
Wear limit . . . . 13 mm (0.511 in.)

Brush spring tension:
Standard . . . . 1050 - 1350 grams (37 - 47.5 ozs.)
Wear limit . . . . .600 grams (21.1 ozs.)

Pinion gap . . . . 1 - 4 mm (0.039 - 0.157 in.)

No load characteristics:
Voltage . . . . 11 volts
Current . . . . Less than 55 amps
Speed . . . . 3500 rpm.

ALTERNATOR

Nominal voltage . . . . 12 volts
Nominal output . . . . .25 amps
Earth connection . . . . .Negative
Direction of rotation . . . . Clockwise, seen from pulley
Coil connection .Three-phase
Rectification . . . . .Six silicone diodes
Pulley ratio 1.69:1

Rotor coil resistance . . . . 4.3 ohms
Min. brush length . . . . 5.5 mm (0.216 in.)
Voltage - No load . . . . 14 volts
Speed - No load . . . . 800 - 1000 rpm.
Voltage - On load . . . . 14 volts
Current - On load . . . . .25 amps
Speed - On load . . . . .Less than 3000 rpm.

Rectifier characteristics in correct direction:
At normal temperature with direct current of 22 amps applied, the voltage difference between the rectifier lead and the body should be less than 1.2 volts.

Rectifier characteristics in reverse direction:
At normal temperature with direct current voltage of 100 volts applied, the reverse current should be less than 1.5 milli-amps.

ALTERNATOR REGULATOR

Type . . . . Two elements
Regulator control voltage . . . . 13.8 - 14.8 volts
Relay control voltage . . . . .4.5 - 5.8 volts

Voltage regulator adjusting values:
Armature gap . . . . More than 0.3 mm (0.012 in.)
Contact gap . . . . 0.25 - 0.45 mm (0.010 - 0.018 in.)
Angle gap (actuated) . . . . . More than 0.2 mm (0.008 in.)
Contact spring deflection . . . 0.2-0.6 mm (0.008-0.024 in.)
Contact pressure . . . . More than 180 grams (6.3 ozs.)

Voltage relay adjusting values:
Contact gap . . . . 0.4 - 1.2 mm (0.016 - 0.047 in.)
Contact spring deflection . . . 0.2-0.6 mm (0.008-0.024 in.)

BATTERY

Type . . . . Lead-acid
Capacity . . . . 32 Ah or 45 Ah.
Voltage . . . . 12 volts
Fully charged at . . . . .1.250 - 1.270
Fully discharged at 1.060

Trouble Shooting

SYMPTOMS	PROBABLE CAUSE	ACTION TO BE TAKEN
Battery in low state of charge, shown by lack of power when starting	Dynamo not charging when running at about 20 mph (30 km/h) with switched on lights:	
	Broken or loose connection in dynamo circuit or regulator not functioning correctly.	Examine charging and field circuit wiring. Tighten loose connections or replace broken lead. Particularly examine battery connections. Examine regulator.
	Commutator greasy or dirty	Clean with soft rag moistened in petrol
	Giving low or intermittent output, when car is running in top gear:	
	Dynamo belt slipping	Adjust belt tension
	Loose or broken connections in dynamo circuit.	Examine charging and field circuit wiring. Tighten loose connection or replace broken lead. Particularly inspect battery connections.
	Brushes greasy or dirty	Clean with soft rag moistened in petrol
	Brushes worn or not fitted correctly	Replace worn brushes. See that the brushes "bed" properly
	Regulator not functioning correctly	Examine regulator
Battery overcharged, shown by burnt-out bulbs and very frequent need for topping-up	Regulator not functioning correctly	Examine regulator
Starter does not operate or operates and does not turn the engine	Poor contact of starter switch contact points	Check switch and replace if necessary
	Poor brush contact	Replace brushes or springs
	Burnt commutator	Overhaul starter motor or clean commutator
	Shorted field coil	Replace coil
	Shorted armature	Replace armature
	Poor contact of battery leads	Clean and tighten leads
	Weak battery	Re-charge battery
	Open circuit between starter switch and solenoid	Check wiring and replace if necessary
	Poor earth connection	Check and rectify
Starter motor operates but does not seem to turn over engine quickly enough	Drive pinion defective	Replace drive pinion
	Flywheel ring gear worn	Replace flywheel or recondition ring gear teeth
Ignition warning lamp goes out only at high rpm.	Generator faulty	Repair generator
	Regulator faulty	Replace regulator
Ignition warning lamp does not light with ignition switched on	Discharged battery	Charge battery
	Defective battery	Replace battery
	Bulb burned out	Replace bulb
	Loose or corroded battery terminals	Tighten or replace terminals
	Loose or broken cables	Tighten or replace cables
	Defective ignition-starter switch	Replace switch
	Poor contact between generator brushes and commutator	Free or replace brushes. If necessary re-place brush springs

Ignition warning lamp does not go out or flickers when engine rpm is increased	Loose or broken fan belt Regulator defective Positive lead loose or broken Generator defective Commutator graphited	Adjust tension or replace belt Replace regulator Tighten connection or replace lead Repair generator Clean commutator
Wiper motor does not operate, turns too slowly or comes to a standstill	Brushes worn Brush spring weak or annealed Binding brush levers Dirty commutator Excessive friction in wiper linkages Low operating voltage Burnt out armature	Replace brushes Replace springs Free brush levers Clean commutator Lubricate all moving points; eliminate binding spots Check for voltage drops in connections Replace armature or complete motor
Wiper motor continues to run after switch is turned off or does not re-turn blades to parking position	Contacts in housing damaged Contact spring bent Insulating bracket broken Contacts dirty Wiper motor cannot be switched off Bad connection from wiper switch to earth	Replace contacts Replace contacts Replace contacts Clean contacts Screw switch button back slightly, bend contacts Check connection; replace switch
Motor squeaks, sometimes combined with slow operation	Wiper linkages, bushings running dry. Point of armature spindle (commutator side) against stop of brush holder Incorrect position of motor cover	Grease all moving parts of linkage. Bend stop to clear Reposition cover
Starter motor pinion does not move out of mesh	Pinion or armature shaft dirty or damaged Solenoid switch defective	Overhaul starter motor Replace solenoid switch
Engine misfires	Remove each sparking plug in turn, rest it on the cylinder head, and observe whether a spark occurs at the points when the engine is turned. Irregular sparking may be due to dirty plugs or defective high-tension cables. If sparking is regular at all plugs, the trouble is probably due to engine defects.	Clean plugs and adjust the gaps to the figure given in the Engine Tuning Data chart. Renew any lead if the insulation shows signs of deterioration or cracking. Examine the carburettor, petrol supply, etc.

If applicable, read "Dynamo" as "Alternator".

WIRING DIAGRAM FOR TOYOTA COROLLA 1200 (ALSO COVERS AUTOMATIC TRANSMISSION AND U.S.A. MODELS)

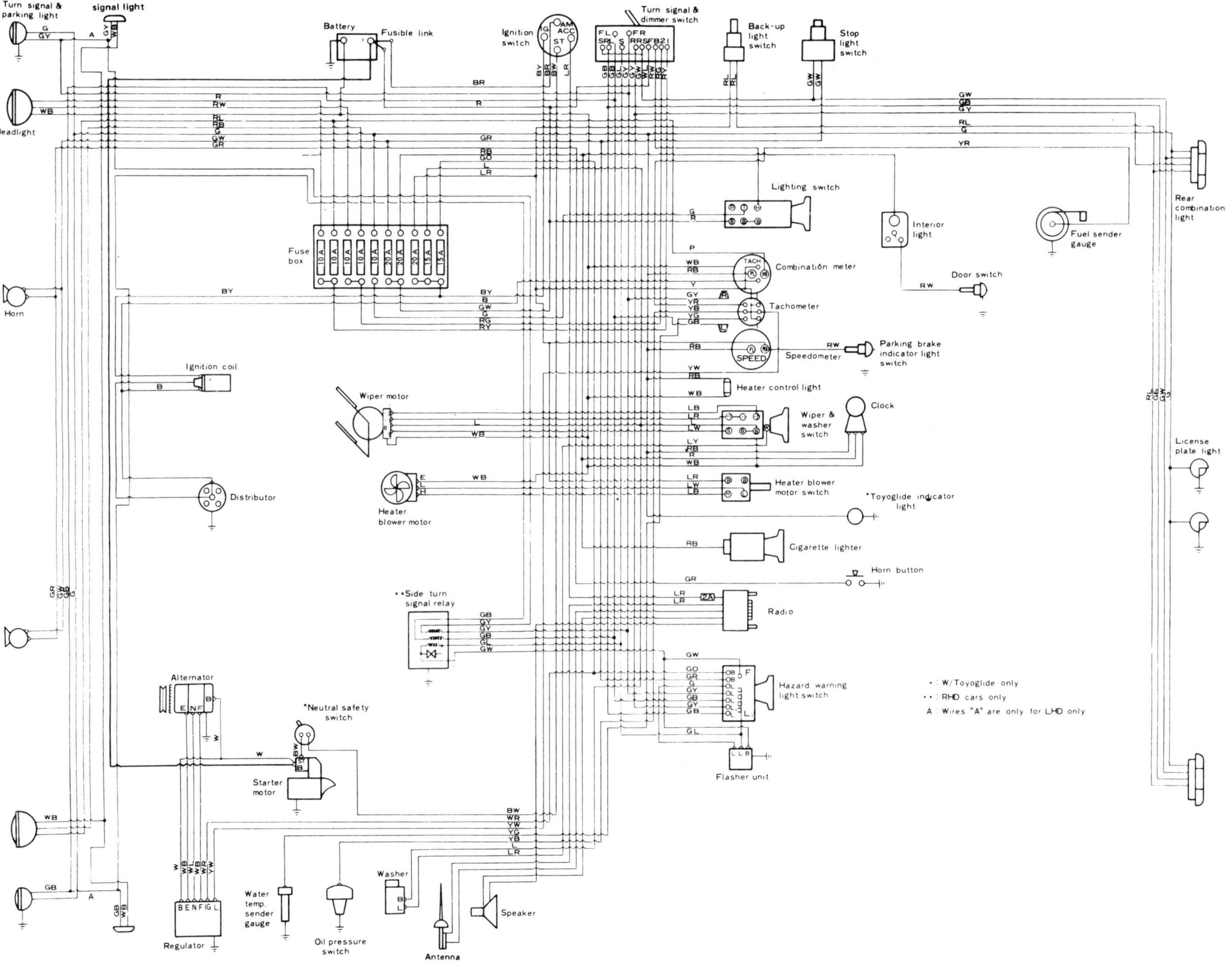

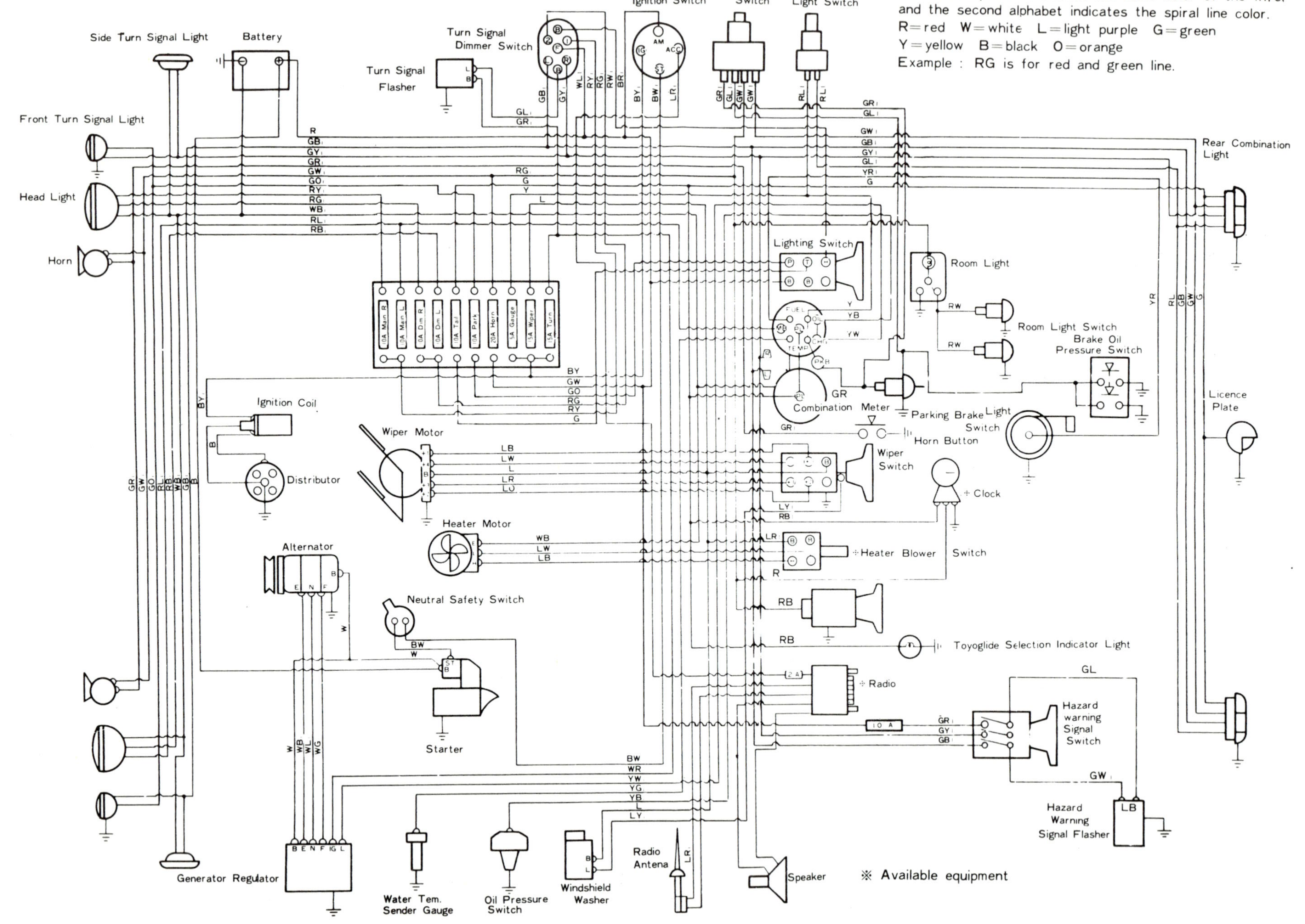

WIRING DIAGRAM FOR TOYOTA COROLLA 1100 (ALSO COVERS AUTOMATIC TRANSMISSION AND U.S.A. MODELS)

WIRING HARNESS COLR CODES
The first alphabet indicates the basic color of the wire,
and the second alphabet indicates the spiral line color.
R=red   W=white   L=light purple   G=green
Y=yellow   B=black   O=orange
Example : RG is for red and green line.

Side Turn Signal Light
Battery
Turn Signal Dimmer Switch
Ignition Switch
Stop Light Switch
Back up Light Switch
Turn Signal Flasher
Front Turn Signal Light
Head Light
Horn
Rear Combination Light
Lighting Switch
Room Light
Room Light Switch
Brake Oil Pressure Switch
Licence Plate
Ignition Coil
Distributor
Wiper Motor
Combination Meter
Parking Brake Light Switch
Horn Button
Wiper Switch
Clock
Heater Motor
Heater Blower Switch
Alternator
Neutral Safety Switch
Toyoglide Selection Indicator Light
Radio
Hazard warning Signal Switch
Starter
Generator Regulator
Water Tem. Sender Gauge
Oil Pressure Switch
Windshield Washer
Radio Antena
Speaker
Hazard Warning Signal Flasher
※ Available equipment

0A Main R
0A Main L
0A Dim R
0A Dim L
10A Tail
10A Park
20A Horn
5A Gauge
5A Wiper
15A Turn

THE NEW TOYOTA COROLLA 1200 2-DOOR DE-LUXE SALOON

Lubrication and Maintenance

THE NEW TOYOTA COROLLA 1200 COUPE SL

Lubricate and Clean

Item	Operation	Ref
CAR UP		
ENGINE	Drain oil	1
Filter	Change element	2
	Clean element	3
GEARBOX/OVERDRIVE	Check oil/top up	4
	Change oil	5
Filter	Clean element	6
AUTOMATIC TRANSM.	Drain fluid	7
Filter	Clean element	8
DIFFERENTIAL	Check oil/top up	9
	Change oil	10
De Dion Tube	Check oil level	11
	Clean rubber boots	12
Limited Slip Differential	Check oil/top up	13
	Change oil	14
PROP./DRIVE SHAFT(S)	Lubricate	15
SHOCK ABSORBERS	Check oil/top up	16
GREASE GUN POINTS	Lubricate	17
PEDAL SHAFT(S)	Lubricate	18
HANDBRAKE	Lubricate	19
GEAR LINKAGE	Lubricate	20
CAR LOWERED – WHEELS FREE		
WHEEL BEARINGS	Repack	21
WHEEL SPLINES/TAPERS	Lubricate	22
BRAKE FLUID	✳ Renew/bleed syst.	23
CAR DOWN – BONNET OPEN		
ENGINE	Refill with oil	24
	Check oil level	25
Breather Cap	Clean	26
Air Cleaner	Service element(s)	27
	Replace element(s)	28
PCV-System	Clean filter	29
	Clean valve/hose(s)	30
	Replace valve	31
Carburettor(s)	Clean jets/bowl	32
	Top up pist. damper	33
	Lubricate linkages	34
Fuel Bowl/Filter(s)	✳ Clean/replace	35
Fuel Injection Pump	Check oil level	36
Filter(s)	Clean/replace	37
AUTOMATIC TRANSM.	Refill with fluid	38
	Check fluid level	39
DISTRIBUTOR	Clean cap & ing. coil	40
Spindle/Cam	Lubricate	41
COOLING SYSTEM	Check/top up	42
	Flush system	43
Corrosion Inhibitor	Check solution	44
Anti-Freeze	Check	45
Water Pump	Lubricate	46
SCREENWASHER	Check/top up	47
BATTERY	Check/top up	48
	Check spec. gravity	49
Connections	Clean, grease	50
GENERATOR	Lubricate	51
STEERING	Check/top up	52
Power Steering	Check/top up fluid	53
	Grease ram	54
	Clean filter	55
CLUTCH/BRAKE	Check/top up fluid	56
BRAKE SERVO	Clean filter	57
	Renew filter	58
HYDR. SUSPENSION	Check/top up fluid	59
	Renew fluid	60
	Clean filter	61
CAR DOWN – EXTERNAL		
LOCKS, HINGES, ETC.	Lubricate	62
Door Drain Holes	Clean	63
WIPER SPINDLES	Lubricate	64

EVERY

MOnths · MIles (1000) · KMs (1000) — whichever comes first

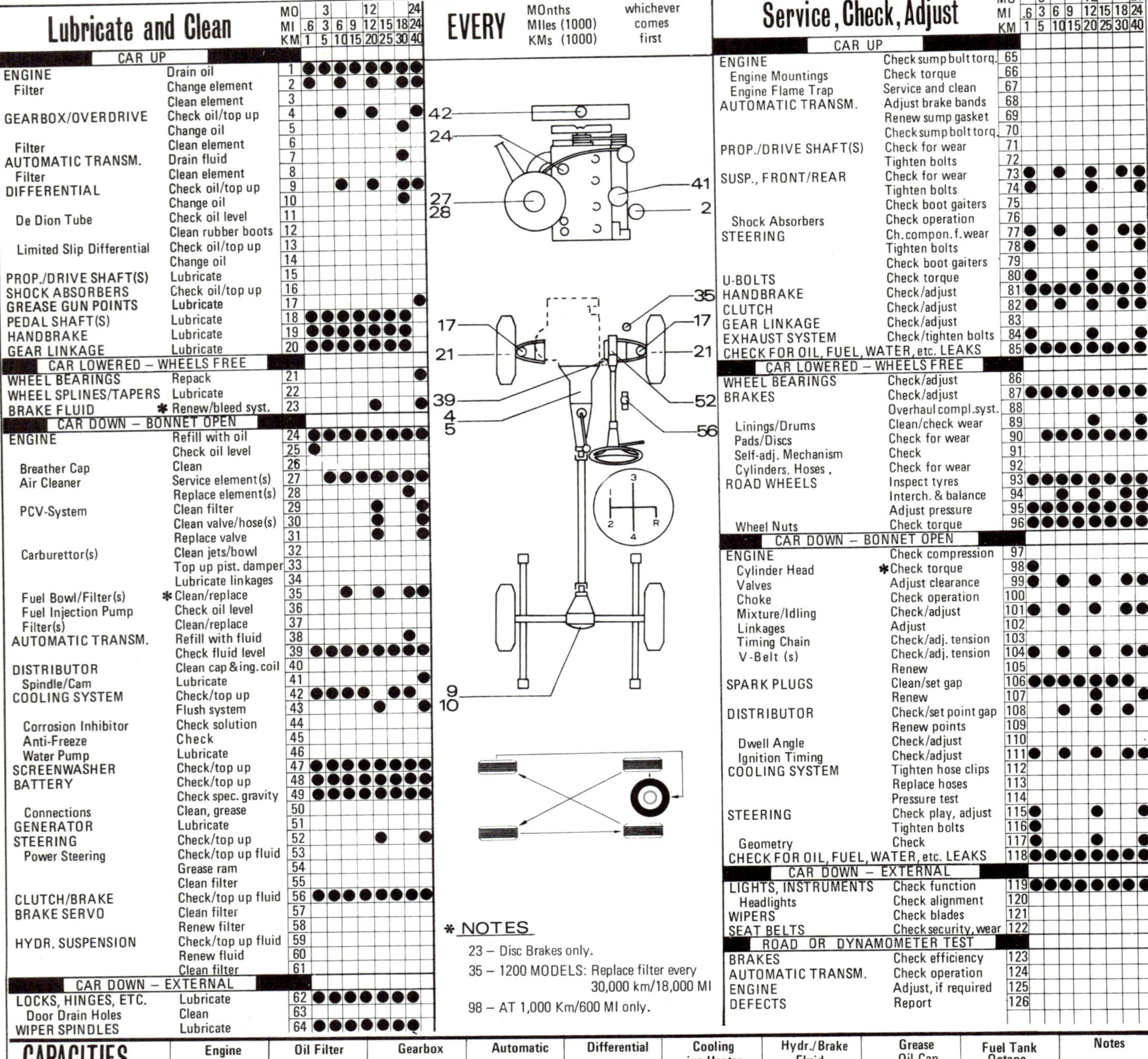

Service, Check, Adjust

Item	Operation	Ref
CAR UP		
ENGINE	Check sump bolt torq.	65
Engine Mountings	Check torque	66
Engine Flame Trap	Service and clean	67
AUTOMATIC TRANSM.	Adjust brake bands	68
	Renew sump gasket	69
	Check sump bolt torq.	70
PROP./DRIVE SHAFT(S)	Check for wear	71
	Tighten bolts	72
SUSP., FRONT/REAR	Check for wear	73
	Tighten bolts	74
	Check boot gaiters	75
Shock Absorbers	Check operation	76
STEERING	Ch. compon. f. wear	77
	Tighten bolts	78
	Check boot gaiters	79
U-BOLTS	Check torque	80
HANDBRAKE	Check/adjust	81
CLUTCH	Check/adjust	82
GEAR LINKAGE	Check/adjust	83
EXHAUST SYSTEM	Check/tighten bolts	84
CHECK FOR OIL, FUEL, WATER, etc. LEAKS		85
CAR LOWERED – WHEELS FREE		
WHEEL BEARINGS	Check/adjust	86
BRAKES	Check/adjust	87
	Overhaul compl. syst.	88
Linings/Drums	Clean/check wear	89
Pads/Discs	Check for wear	90
Self-adj. Mechanism	Check	91
Cylinders. Hoses.	Check for wear	92
ROAD WHEELS	Inspect tyres	93
	Interch. & balance	94
	Adjust pressure	95
Wheel Nuts	Check torque	96
CAR DOWN – BONNET OPEN		
ENGINE	Check compression	97
Cylinder Head	✳ Check torque	98
Valves	Adjust clearance	99
Choke	Check operation	100
Mixture/Idling	Check/adjust	101
Linkages	Adjust	102
Timing Chain	Check/adj. tension	103
V-Belt (s)	Check/adj. tension	104
	Renew	105
SPARK PLUGS	Clean/set gap	106
	Renew	107
DISTRIBUTOR	Check/set point gap	108
	Renew points	109
Dwell Angle	Check/adjust	110
Ignition Timing	Check/adjust	111
COOLING SYSTEM	Tighten hose clips	112
	Replace hoses	113
	Pressure test	114
STEERING	Check play, adjust	115
	Tighten bolts	116
Geometry	Check	117
CHECK FOR OIL, FUEL, WATER, etc. LEAKS		118
CAR DOWN – EXTERNAL		
LIGHTS, INSTRUMENTS	Check function	119
Headlights	Check alignment	120
WIPERS	Check blades	121
SEAT BELTS	Check security, wear	122
ROAD OR DYNAMOMETER TEST		
BRAKES	Check efficiency	123
AUTOMATIC TRANSM.	Check operation	124
ENGINE	Adjust, if required	125
DEFECTS	Report	126

✳ NOTES

23 – Disc Brakes only.

35 – 1200 MODELS: Replace filter every 30,000 km/18,000 MI

98 – AT 1,000 Km/600 MI only.

CAPACITIES

	Engine	Oil Filter	Gearbox	Automatic	Differential	Cooling inc. Heater	Hydr./Brake Fluid	Grease Oil Can	Fuel Tank Octane	Notes
	Ltr.Imp.Pts.USQu.	Ltr.Imp.Pts.USPts.	Ltr.Imp.Pts.USPts.	Ltr.Imp.Pts.USQu.	Ltr.Imp.Pts.USPts.	Ltr.Imp.Pts.USQu.	Ltr.Imp.Pts.USPts.	Ref.No.	Ltr.Imp.Gls.USGls	Ref.No.
	3 5,2 3,1	0,6 1 1,2	1,7 3 3,6	4,7 8 4,8	1,0 1,8 2,2	5,3 9,8 5,6		17 / 21 · 62 / 64	36 8 9,5 · COUPE: 45 10 12 · WAGON: 40 8,7 10,5	52
LUBRICANTS	MO 8, 11		ST 1	ATFF	ST 1, 2		BFL	GLM/MO		ST 1

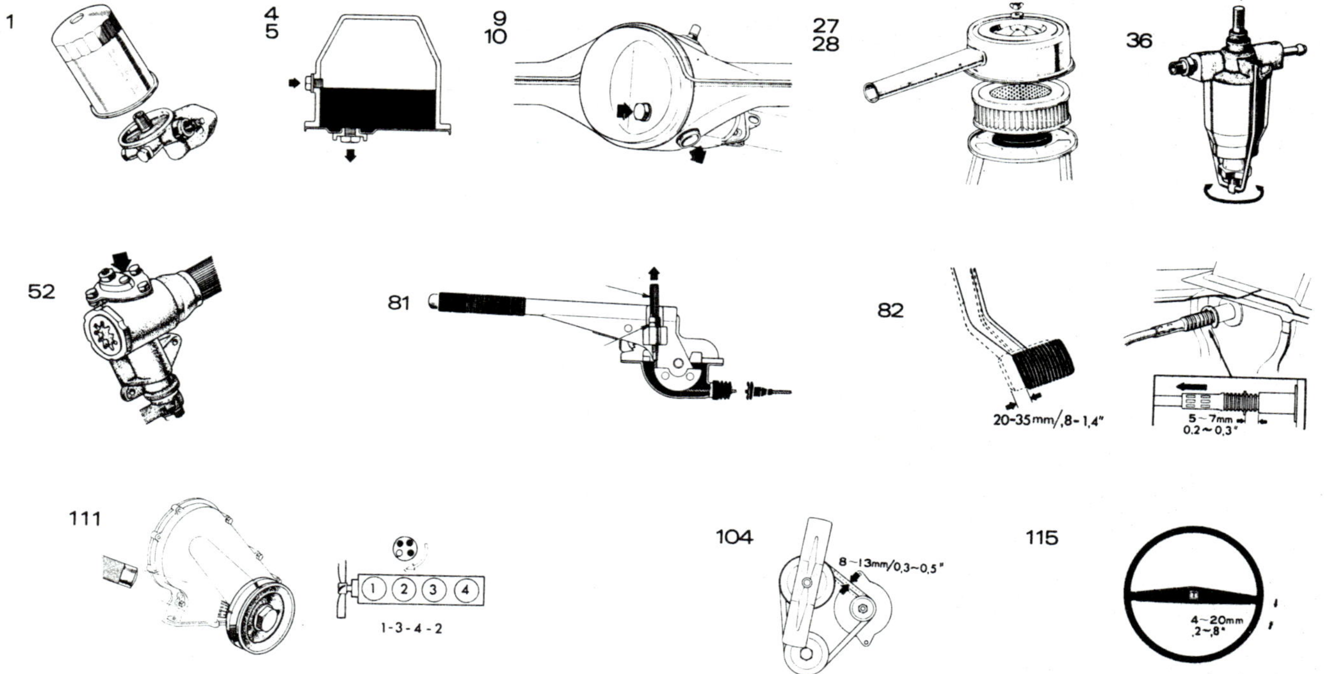

ENGINE	COMPRESSION KG/CM²/PSI	99 VALVE CLEARANCE INLET MM/IN. HOT/COLD OUTLET		101 IDLING SPEED RPM.	106 SPARK PLUG GAP MM/INCHES	108 DISTR. POINT GAP MM/INCHES	110 DWELL ANGLE DEGREES	111 IGNITION TIMING STATIC-DEGR.	STROB.-DEGR.
		0,2 / ,008	0,3 / ,012	600	0,8 / ,031				(3)K: 8/600 K-B: 10/650 K-C: ATDC 5/650

MECHANICAL	82 CLUTCH PLAY MM/INCHES	115 STEERING PLAY MM/INCHES	RAD. CAP. PRESS. KG/CM²/PSI	104 V-BELT TENSION MM/INCHES	BLEED SEQUENCE	89 MIN. LINING THICKN. MM/IN.	90 PAD THICKN. MM/IN.	81 HANDBRAKE ADJ. MM/INCHES	NOTES
	20 - 35 / ,8 - 1,4	4 - 20 / ,2 - ,8		8 - 13 / ,3 - ,5		1,5 / ,06		6 - 8 notches STROKE	

TYRES/PRESS. KG/CM²/PSI	93 STANDARD SIZE	95 FRONT PRESSURE NORMAL/FULL	REAR PRESSURE NORMAL/FULL	93 OPTIONAL SIZE	95 FRONT PRESSURE NORMAL/FULL	REAR PRESSURE NORMAL/FULL	WHEEL BEARINGS FRONT-MM/IN.	WHEEL BEARINGS REAR-MM/IN.	
	600 x 12 4 PR	1,4 / 20	1,4 / 20	155 SR 12 (SL MODEL)	1,4 / 20	1,4 / 20			
WAGON	600 x 12 6 PR								

STEERING GEOMETRY	TEST LOAD KG/LBS.	TOE-IN(i)/OUT(o) FRONT-MM/IN.	CAMBER DEGREES	117 CASTOR DEGREES	KING PIN INCLN. DEGREES	TOE-IN(i)/OUT(o) REAR-MM/IN.	CAMBER DEGREES	TOE-ON TURNS ⁰at ⁰lock	
	0	(i) 2 - 6 / ,08 - ,24	1⁰ 30' - 2⁰ 30'	- 15' — 45'	6 - 7	—	—	(i) 37 - 38 (o) 32 - 33	

TORQUES	98								MKG/FT. LBS.
	5,4 - 6,6 / 35 - 48								

TBA	93	48	107	109	2	28	105	121	114
	6,00 x 12 4 PR 6,00 x 12 6 PR 155 SR 12	12 V - 32 Ah	DENSO W17ES CHAMPION N5 BOSCH W175T2						

Engine Tuning Data

#			1967 - 70	1967 - 70	1967 - 70	1970	1970	1970
1	Year		1967 - 70	1967 - 70	1967 - 70	1970	1970	1970
2	Model		COROLLA	COROLLA	COROLLA	COROLLA	COROLLA	COROLLA
3	Engine type		K	K-B	K-C	3K	3K-D	3K-B
3A	EEC	CO %						
4	Number of cylinders		4	4	4	4	4	4
5	Firing order		1-3-4-2	1-3-4-2	1-3-4-2	1-3-4-2	1-3-4-2	1-3-4-2
6	Capacity	cu.cm	1077	1077	1077	1166	1166	1166
7	Bore/Stroke	mm	75/61	75/61	75/61	75/66	75/66	75/66
8	Compression ratio	: 1	9	10	9	9	10	10
9	Compression pressure	$psi/kg/cm^2$	170/12/250	185/13/250	170/12/250	170/12/250	192/13,5/250	192/13,5/250
10	Oil pressure	$psi/kg/cm^2$						
11	Rated output	HP/rpm	60 SAE/6000	73 SAE/6600	60 SAE/6000	68 SAE/6000	73 SAE/6600	77 SAE/6600
11A	Fuel consumption (mpg/Ltr.100 km/DIN)							
12	Valve clearance - inlet	in/mm	0,008/0,20 (h)	0,008/0,20 (h)	0,008/0,20 (h)	0,008/0,20 (h)	←	←
13	Valve clearance - outlet	in/mm	0,011/0,30 (h)	0,014/0,36 (h)	0,014/0,36 (h)	0,012/0,30 (h)	←	←
14	Inlet valve opens	^{o}BTDC	16	18	16	16	16	16
15	Outlet valve closes	^{o}ATDC	16	18	16	16	16	16
15A	Road horsepower							
15B	Km.h/rpm/gear							
16	Battery	V/Ah	12/32	12/32	12/32	12/32 (45)	12/32 (45)	12/32 (45)
17	System polarity	plus/minus	–	–	–	–	–	–
18	Carburettor make		ASIAN	ASIAN	ASIAN	ASIAN	ASIAN	ASIAN
19	Carburettor type							
20	Idling speed	rpm	600	650	600	600	600	600
21	Fuel pump pressure	$psi/kg/cm^2$						
22	Distributor make		DENSO	DENSO	DENSO	DENSO	DENSO	DENSO
23	Distributor type							
24	Contact breaker gap	in/mm	0,016-0,020/0,4-0,5	0,016-0,020/0,4-0,5	0,016-0,020/0,4-0,5	0,016-0,020/0,4-0,5	0,016-0,020/0,4-0,5	0,016-0,020/0,4-0,5
25	Dwell angle	Degrees	50 - 54	50 - 54	50 - 54	50 - 54	50 - 54	50 - 54
26	Static timing	^{o}BTDC	8	6	5			
27	Stroboscopic timing	^{o}BTDC/rpm	8/600	10/650	5/650	8/600	8/600	8/600
28	Timing mark location		P	P	P	P	P	P
28A	Ignition coil make & type		DENSO	DENSO	DENSO	DENSO	DENSO	DENSO
28B	Primary resistance	Ohms	3,6	3,6	3,6	3,6	3,6	3,6
29	Centrif. advance - starts	^{o}/rpm E	0/300 - 500	0/200	0/300 - 500	0/300 - 500	0/300 - 500	0/300 - 500
30	- intermediate	^{o}/rpm E	–	7 - 9/700	–	–	–	–
31	- intermediate	^{o}/rpm E	11 - 13/1500	–	11 - 13/1650	11 - 13/1650	11 - 13/1650	11 - 12/1650
32	- ends	^{o}/rpm E	13 - 15/3000	13 - 15/1900	13 - 15/3000	13 - 15/3000	13 - 15/3000	13 - 15/3000
33	Vacuum advance - starts	^{o}/in=min Hg	0/2,5-4,5 = 65-115	0/1,4-3,3 = 35-85	0/2,5-4,5 = 65-115	0/2,5-4,5/65-115	0/2,5-4,5/65-115	0/2,5-4,5 = 65-115
34	- ends	^{o}/in=mm Hg	6,5-9,5/10 = 270	3 - 5/4,7 = 120	6,5 - 9,5/10 = 270	6,5 - 9,5/10 = 270	6,5-9,5/10 = 270	6,5 - 9,5/10 = 270
35	Condenser capacity	Mfd	0,20 - 0,24	0,20 - 0,24	0,20 - 0,24	0,20 - 0,24	0,20 - 0,24	0,20 - 0,24
36	Sparking plug make		DENSO	DENSO	DENSO	DENSO	DENSO	DENSO
37	Sparking plug type		W17ES *	W17ES *	W17ES *	W17ES *	W17ES *	W17ES *
38	Sparking plug gap	in/mm	0,027-0,031/0,7-0,8	0,027-0,031/0,7-0,8	0,027-0,031/0,7-0,8	0,027-0,031/0,7-0,8	0,027-0,031/0,7-0,8	0,027-0,031/0,7-0,8
38A	Starter motor make & type		DENSO	DENSO	DENSO	DENSO	DENSO	DENSO
38B	Lockdraw	Amps./Volts	100/8,5	450/8,5	450/8,5	450/8,5	450/8,5	450/8,5
39	Generator make		DENSO	DENSO	DENSO	DENSO	DENSO	DENSO
40	Generator type							
41	Generator output	A/V/rpmG	19-27/13,5/1750	25/14/3000	25/14/3000	25/14/3000	25/14/3000	25/14/3000
42	Regulator make		DENSO	DENSO	DENSO	DENSO	DENSO	DENSO
43	Regulator type							
44	Cut-in closing voltage	V						
45	Drop-off voltage	V						
46	Reverse current	A						
47	Open circuit	V						
48	Closed circuit	A						
49	Current regulator	A						
50	Voltage regulator	V/A/min	13,8 - 14,8	13,8 - 14,8	13,8 - 14,8	13,8 - 14,8	13,8 - 14,8	13,8 - 14,8
51	NOTES:		* CHAMPION N5 BOSCH 175 T 2	* CHAMPION N5 BOSCH 175 T 2	* CHAMPION N5 BOSCH 175 T 2	* CHAMPION N5 BOSCH 175 T 2	*CHAMPION N5 BOSCH 175 T 2	* CHAMPION N5 BOSCH 175 T 2
52	from chassis number							
53	from engine number							

INTRODUCTION

This section is written for the thoughtful and safety-minded driver, giving recommendations to guide you safely through the hazards of driving during the winter months.

By regular maintenance you will most probably maintain your car in its top performance, however, it might be advisable to follow the instructions in this section to give you added safety insurance during the difficult months of snow, ice and hazardous road conditions.

Battery

As the battery is more called upon during the winter, it must be at all times in good condition to fulfil its function. Shorter days,with consequently more frequent use of the lights,the use of the heater blower and the increased load on the windscreen wipers during periods of snow fall all claim their share from the battery. To maintain the efficiency of the battery, check the electrolyte level and the specific gravity of the electrolyte. The battery performance will be impaired by loose or corroded connections. So in good time, make sure your terminal posts and connectors are thoroughly cleaned and that all connections at the battery, starter motor, starter solenoid switch and in particular the earth connections are absolutely tight. If your car is garaged during the winter, the battery should be re-charged every 4 - 8 weeks to be ready for the spring.

Cooling system

This might be the item every driver immediately connects with frost and winter, as the dangers of serious damage to the engine are well known, if the correct precautions are not observed. The system should be drained, flushed with clear water and then re-filled with a suitable anti-freeze solution. If your cooling system is filled already with a "all-year-round" anti-freeze solution check the specific gravity of the coolant to make sure that the cooling system is protected to the lowest temperature that might prevail in your area. As anti-freeze has a searching effect for leaks check all hoses and clips for tightness.

Brakes

There is little we can tell a driver about braking on ice and snow, but just to remember that the brakes should be in top condition and the braking power to all wheels should be in the correct relation to each other. Brake hoses and connections should be checked to make sure they are not chafed or damaged. All leaks should be rectified. Special attention should be given to the brake pedal rubber. If the rubber is worn smooth, it is easier to slip off with your foot, especially when you just stepped into the car with your shoes covered in snow. A pedal rubber with the proper profile will reduce this danger. When applying your brakes on ice or snow, it should be done firmly and an "apply/release" technique should be used to avoid locking the wheels.If you experience that your car is moving off slowly on a frosty morning, it might be advisable not to apply the handbrake the next night, as the reason for the sluggish behaviour are frozen brake linings. To free a handbrake in this condition, pull and release the lever until the ice is broken. Sudden acceleration or braking and violent movement of the steering wheel should be avoided to prevent skidding.

Tyres

The condition of the tyres is of particular importance during winter driving. Apart of the legal requirements of your country, which will require from you a minimum tread depth whatever the conditions, it will also save you embarrasing situations on ice and snow covered roads. Even if you drive with the minimum tread depth it might be that your journey becomes a nightmare, as confidence in road holding ability can be easily lost after the slightest breakaway.

Special consideration should be given to the use of snow chains or special winter tyres for extremely bad conditions. Even a set of ordinary new tyres will make already a difference when it comes to negotiating a hill or a bend when there is ice or snow on the roads. If the traction of your drive wheels is lost, engage the next highest gear, reduce the engine speed and move away slowly. If your wheels are spinning without showing any grip whatsoever, engage alternatively forward and reverse gears and bring the car to a rocking movement, controlling the accelerator pedal carefully. With patience (and luck!) it might be possible to regain grip on firmer ground. If the described method is not successful, clear away the ice and snow in front of the wheels and place grit, old sacks (or if nothing else is available your floor mats) in front of the driving wheels and try again.

Engine oil

Make sure the oil in your engine sump is suitable for the temperatures to be expected. If your engine is turned over slowly by the starter motor, depress the clutch pedal to disengage the transmission flow between engine and gearbox to remove the additional effort of turning the gears through the cold gearbox oil.

Ignition

The humid and wet conditions of winter can emphasize any weak points in the ignition system. Starting problems on a cold winter's day are not welcome. To avoid them, check all connections, spark plugs, leads and the distributor cap well in advance of the winter. In case that your engine runs normally, but will not aceelerate, check your carburettor for icing-up and don't assume immediately that it is an electrical matter. To de-ice the carburettor, stop the car and let the engine run normally for a few minutes.

Lights and lamps

Winter not only brings colder weather but longer nights and day-time fog. This means more driving in the hours of darkness and greater use of lights during daytime. Check your headlamp alignment to avoid dazzling oncoming traffic. Also make sure that all bulbs and lamps are in proper working order. It is advisable to keep a set of bulbs and fuses in your glovebox.

Body

The salt used to thaw up the roads and dissolve ice and snow has its natural usefulness, but shows also a side effect, that is to say is has a detrimental effect on the underbody of a car. It is, however, possible to avoid this disadvantage, if the underside of your car is cleaned immediately after driving over roads with road treatment salts. The investment of having underbody protection sprayed over the vulnerable areas might be well worth considering. Check the paint work of your body and repairs areas that have been scratched with a matching touch-up paint. Winter conditions accelerate the development of rust and subsequent repair of your paint work becomes more expensive than a tin or spray can of touch-up paint.

Never wash or polish your car in direct sunlight or in the open when it is freezing.

Windscreen wipers and washer

Check the condition of your wiper blades well in advance of the winter and replace your rubbers if not in absolute top Wipers have to shift snow during the winter months and they must be able to cope with it, to assure you an uninterrupted vision. Remember that your windscreen washer container will freeze if it only contains water. Yor fill find a proprietary brand of special liquid to be filled into the container, but do not use anti-freeze as used in the cooling system. Do not operate your windscreen washer if the temperatures are below freezing point, if only plain water is filled in your container. A sheet of ice will form immediately on your windscreen. In this connection it should also be remembered that the driving wind will contribute considerably to this danger.